TROUBLED TRANSITION: NORTH KOREA'S POLITICS, ECONOMY, AND EXTERNAL RELATIONS

Edited by
Choe Sang-Hun, Gi-Wook Shin,
and David Straub

SHORENSTEIN
APARC
STANFORD

THE WALTER H. SHORENSTEIN
ASIA-PACIFIC RESEARCH CENTER

THE WALTER H. SHORENSTEIN ASIA-PACIFIC RESEARCH CENTER (Shorenstein APARC) is a unique Stanford University institution focused on the interdisciplinary study of contemporary Asia. Shorenstein APARC's mission is to produce and publish outstanding interdisciplinary, Asia-Pacific–focused research; to educate students, scholars, and corporate and governmental affiliates; to promote constructive interaction to influence U.S. policy toward the Asia-Pacific; and to guide Asian nations on key issues of societal transition, development, U.S.-Asia relations, and regional cooperation.

The Walter H. Shorenstein Asia-Pacific Research Center
Freeman Spogli Institute for International Studies
Stanford University
Encina Hall
Stanford, CA 94305-6055
tel. 650-723-9741
fax 650-723-6530
http://aparc.stanford.edu

Troubled Transition: North Korea's Politics, Economy, and External Relations
may be ordered from:
The Brookings Institution
c/o DFS, P.O. Box 50370, Baltimore, MD, USA
tel. 1-800-537-5487 or 410-516-6956
fax 410-516-6998
http://www.brookings.edu/press

Library of Congress Cataloging-in-Publication Data

Troubled transition : North Korea's politics, economy, and external relations / edited by Choe
 Sang-hun, Gi-Wook Shin, and David Straub.
  pages cm
  ISBN 978-1-931368-28-5
  1. Korea (North)--Politics and government--2011-   2. Korea (North)--Economic conditions--
21st century.   3. Korea (North)--Foreign relations--21st century.   4. Kim, Chong-un, 1984-
I. Sang-hun, Choe, author, editor of compilation.   II. Shin, Gi-Wook, editor of compilation.
III.   Straub, David. IV.   Walter H. Shorenstein Asia-Pacific Research Center, issuing body.
DS935.7775.T76 2013
951.9305'1--dc23

                         2013024434

First printing, 2013.

TROUBLED TRANSITION: NORTH KOREA'S POLITICS, ECONOMY, AND EXTERNAL RELATIONS

SHORENSTEIN APARC STANFORD

THE WALTER H. SHORENSTEIN
ASIA-PACIFIC RESEARCH CENTER

Contents

Tables

Contributors

Choe Sang-Hun is the Korea correspondent for the *International Herald Tribune*. Before joining the newspaper in 2005, he worked for the *Korea Herald* and the Seoul bureau of the Associated Press. He was the 2010–2011 Fellow in Korean Studies at the Walter H. Shorenstein Asia-Pacific Research Center, Stanford University. Choe's reports on Korea and Myanmar have earned him many awards, including the Pulitzer Prize, George Polk Award, Journalists Association of Korea award, Human Rights Press Award in Asia, and two Society of Publishers in Asia awards, as well as the Asia Society's Osborn Elliott prize. He is coauthor of *The Bridge at No Gun Ri* (2001) and *How Koreans Talk* (2002), and coeditor of *Korea Witness: 135 Years of War, Crisis and News in the Land of the Morning Calm* (2006).

John Everard was a British diplomat from 1979–2008, becoming Ambassador to Belarus and later to Uruguay. His final posting was as British Ambassador to North Korea in 2006–2008. He held the Pantech visiting fellowship at Stanford University's Walter H. Shorenstein Asia-Pacific Research Center in 2010–2011, during which time he wrote the book *Only Beautiful, Please*, reflecting his experience of North Korea. He coordinated the United Nations Panel of Experts on North Korea from 2011–2012 and continues to write and to broadcast on North Korea.

Sandra Fahy is assistant professor of anthropology at Sophia University in Tokyo, Japan. Her work has been published in *Anthropology Today, Food, Culture, and Society*, and in several edited volumes. She has held postdoctoral fellowships at the Korean Studies Institute, University of Southern

California, Los Angeles, as the Sejong Society Fellow, and at the Center for Korean Studies at EHESS in Paris, France.

Thomas Fingar is the inaugural Oksenberg-Rohlen Distinguished Fellow in the Freeman Spogli Institute for International Studies at Stanford University. From May 2005 through December 2008, he served as the first deputy director of national intelligence for analysis and, concurrently, as chairman of the National Intelligence Council. He served previously as assistant secretary of the State Department's Bureau of Intelligence and Research (2004–2005), principal deputy assistant secretary (2001–2003), deputy assistant secretary for analysis (1994–2000), director of the Office of Analysis for East Asia and the Pacific (1989–1994), and chief of the China Division (1986–1989). Between 1975 and 1986 he held a number of positions at Stanford University, including director of the university's U.S.-China Relations Program and senior research associate in the Center for International Security and Arms Control. His most recent book is *Reducing Uncertainty: Intelligence Analysis and National Security*.

Rüdiger Frank is chair and professor of East Asian economy and society at the University of Vienna and head of its Department of East Asian Studies. He is also an adjunct professor at Korea University and at the University of North Korean Studies (Kyungnam University) in Seoul. He holds an MA in Korean studies, economics, and international relations and a PhD in economics. During 1991–1992 he spent one semester as a language student at Kim Il Sung University in Pyongyang and has been researching North Korea in an East Asian context ever since. Frank is deputy chief editor of the A-ranked *European Journal of East Asian Studies*, member of the editorial board for the book series "Brill's Korean Studies Library," an associate at *The Asia Pacific Journal*, and member of numerous other editorial boards. His most recent books include: (coeditor) *Korea and East Asia: The Stony Road to Collective Security* (Brill 2013); (coeditor) *Korea and East Asia in a Changing Regional and Global Environment* (KIEP 2012); and (editor) *Exploring North Korean Arts* (Verlag fuer Moderne Kunst 2011).

Donald W. Keyser retired from the U.S. Department of State in September 2004 after a thirty-two-year career. He had extensive domestic and foreign experience in senior policy positions, conflict resolution, intelligence operations and analysis, and law enforcement programs. His career focused geographically on U.S. policy toward Northeast Asia. Fluent in Chinese and conversant in Japanese, Russian, and French, he served three tours in Beijing and two tours in Tokyo. A Russian language and Soviet/Russian area studies specialist through MA work, he served 1998–99 as Special Negotiator and Ambassador for Regional Conflicts in the former USSR. He was the 2008–09 Pantech Fellow at Stanford University's Asia-Pacific Research Center (Shorenstein APARC). He is currently a nonresident senior fellow at the China Policy Institute, University of Nottingham, U.K.

Kim Hakjoon is the Kim Bo Jung Chair Professor of KAIST (Korea Advanced Institute of Science and Technology) and president of the Northeast Asian History Foundation, Seoul, Korea. He was president of the University of Incheon and of the Korean Political Science Association. He received his PhD in political science from the University of Pittsburgh in 1972. His publications in English include *The Domestic Politics of Korean Unification* (Seoul and Edison, NJ: Jimoondang, 2010).

Yu-hwan Koh is professor of North Korean Studies at Dongguk University in South Korea. He is also director of the Institute for North Korean Studies at Dongguk University. He served as president of the Korean Association of North Korean Studies in 2012. Koh's latest book is *The World of Everyday Life in North Korea: Cries and Whispers* (2010). He is also author of *North Korea and Regional Security* (2006); *Introduction to North Korean Studies* (2001); and *Understanding North Korea's Politics* (2001). Koh has published numerous scholarly articles in journals in South Korea such as *North Korean Studies Review* and the *Korean Journal of Unification Affairs*. Koh has also written opinion pieces for the Associated Press, the *New York Times*, *Yonhapnews*, *Joongang Ilbo*, *Kyunghyang Shinmun*, *Chosun Ilbo*, and *Hankyore Shinmun*. Koh's specific research has covered questions concerning North Korean politics, ideology, and military; the historical basis of contemporary Asian relations; and regional security relations in Asia. He received the BA, MA and PhD in political science from Dongguk University.

Andrei Lankov was born in 1963 in Leningrad (now Petersburg). He completed his undergraduate and graduate studies at Leningrad State University (PhD, 1989). In 1996–2004 he taught Korean history at the Australian National University, and since 2004 he has taught at Kookmin University in Seoul, where he is currently professor in the College of Social Studies. His major research interest is North Korean history and society. His major English-language publications on North Korea include *From Stalin to Kim Il Sung: The Formation of North Korea, 1945–1960* (Rutgers University Press, 2003); *Crisis in North Korea: The Failure of De-Stalinization, 1956*

(University of Hawaii Press, 2004); *North of the DMZ: Essays on Daily Life in North Korea* (McFarland and Company, 2007); and *The Real North Korea* (Oxford University Press, 2013). He has contributed to the *Wall Street Journal*, the *New York Times*, *Financial Times*, and *Newsweek*, and has published a number of academic articles.

Andrew S. Natsios is professor at the George H. W. Bush School of Government at Texas A&M University, and previously taught at Georgetown University for six years. Natsios is the cochairman of the Committee on Human Rights in North Korea, an organization that does research and publishes reports on abuses in the North Korean system. He previously served for five years as administrator of the U.S. Agency for International Development, and as the U.S. special envoy to Sudan. From 1993 to 1998, Natsios was vice president of World Vision U.S, and was a member of the U.S. Army Reserves for twenty-three years, including service in the Gulf War in 1991. He holds a BA in history from Georgetown University and an MPA from Harvard University's Kennedy School of Government. Natsios is the author of three books, including *The Great North Korean Famine* (2001) and *Sudan, South Sudan, and Darfur: What Everyone Needs to Know* (2012).

William Newcomb is a member of the Panel of Experts appointed by UN Secretary General Ban Ki Moon to monitor and report to the Security Council on the implementation of UN sanctions resolutions on the DPRK. He earlier served as senior economic advisor to the assistant secretary of the Treasury for Intelligence and Analysis, deputy coordinator of the State Department's North Korea Working Group, and as the senior economic analyst for East Asia in the State Department's Bureau of Intelligence and Research. His research interests include the economics of reform and transition and the economic challenges and opportunities of Korean unification.

Gi-Wook Shin is director of the Walter H. Shorenstein Asia-Pacific Research Center; the Tong Yang, Korea Foundation, and Korea Stanford Alumni Chair of Korean Studies; the founding director of the Korean Studies Program; a senior fellow of the Freeman Spogli Institute for International Studies; and professor of sociology, all at Stanford University. As a historical-comparative and political sociologist, his research has concentrated on social movements, nationalism, development, and international relations.

Shin is the author/editor of a dozen books and numerous articles. His recent books include *History Textbooks and the Wars in Asia: Divided Memories* (2011); *South Korean Social Movements: From Democracy to Civil Society* (2011); and *One Alliance, Two Lenses: U.S.-Korea Relations in a New Era* (2010). His articles have appeared in academic journals including the *American Journal of Sociology, Comparative Studies in Society and History, Political Science Quarterly, International Sociology, Nations and Nationalism, Pacific Affairs,* and *Asian Survey.*

Daniel C. Sneider is associate director for research at the Shorenstein Asia-Pacific Research Center at Stanford University. His research focuses on Asian regional issues, on wartime historical memory in Asia, on U.S. foreign and security policy toward East Asia, and on Korean and Japanese foreign policy. Sneider is a former foreign correspondent who served in Japan, India, and the Soviet Union.

David Straub has been associate director of the Korean Studies Program (KSP) at the Walter H. Shorenstein Asia-Pacific Research Center at Stanford University since 2008. Previously, he was the 2007–2008 Pantech Fellow at the Center. Straub retired in 2006 from the U.S. Department of State as a senior foreign service officer after a thirty-year career focused on Korean and Japanese affairs. At the Department, he served as director of Korean affairs from 2002 to 2004, and played a key role in the Six-Party Talks in Beijing on ending North Korea's nuclear weapons program. Straub has also taught at The Johns Hopkins University School of Advanced International Studies and Seoul National University's Graduate School of International Studies. He has written a number of essays and book chapters on U.S. policy and Korean and Japanese affairs, and is a frequent commentator on U.S. policy toward Northeast Asia in American, South Korean, Japanese, and other media.

Andrew G. Walder is the Denise O'Leary and Kent Thiry Professor at Stanford University, where he is on the faculty of the Department of Sociology. He is also a senior fellow in the Freeman Spogli Institute for International Studies. A political sociologist, Walder has long specialized in the sources of conflict, stability, and change in communist regimes and their successor states. His current research focuses on Mao-era China, with a focus on the mass politics of the Cultural Revolution of 1966 to 1969.

Acknowledgements

This volume is based upon thirteen essays prepared for a February 2011 conference on North Korea's "troubled transition" hosted by Stanford University's Walter H. Shorenstein Asia-Pacific Research Center (APARC). When the conferees assembled at Stanford, the Democratic People's Republic of Korea (DPRK, or North Korea) was facing a multidimensional set of complex challenges that we have addressed in this book. As this volume was being readied for publication, North Korean leader Kim Jong-il suddenly died on December 17, 2011. The planned succession to his son-and-heir Kim Jong-un began to unfold immediately, with the son leading the national mourning and rapidly assuming a series of titles in command of the military, the party, and the government. On reviewing the volume's essays in the wake of these developments, we found that, far from being overtaken by events, they had proven to be remarkably prescient and of continuing analytical value in assessing the shape, trajectory, and policy implications of North Korea's succession drama. We therefore invited essay authors to review and update their earlier drafts. Most contributors obligingly submitted slightly revised chapters, and it is these that we have included in this volume.

As always, we are indebted to the many people who made the convening of the conference and publication of this book possible. We are particularly grateful to the Koret Foundation and its chairwoman, Susan Koret, for generous support of both the conference and this publication.

The 2011 conference was special as it was held in conjunction with the 10th anniversary of the establishment of the Korean Studies Program at Stanford University. Almost twenty distinguished visitors came from

Korea to attend the conference and the ceremony, including Byongwon Bahk, Taeho Bark, Suh-Yong Chung, Dae-Chul Chyung, Jae-Hyun Hyun, Hyug-Baeg Im, Hakjoon Kim, Hyong O. Kim, Jeongsik Ko, Andrei Lankov, Choon-Geun Lee, Yong-Kyung Lee, Soo-gil Park, Jong-Chun Woo, and Young Kwan Yoon.

We would also like to thank all those who contributed to the conference as discussants: Michael H. Armacost, Byongwon Bahk, Taeho Bark, Daniel Chirot, Dae-Chul Chyung, John Everard, Thomas Fingar, Wonsoo Kim, Hyug-Baeg Im, Soo-gil Park, Young Kwan Yoon, Myung Hwan Yu, and Kathryn Stoner-Weiss.

Finally, we appreciate the dedication and hard work of all Shorenstein APARC staff members who contributed to this project, especially Heather Ahn and George Krompacky, responsible, respectively, for arrangements for an efficient and pleasant conference and for the professional editing of this publication.

Choe Sang-Hun, Gi-Wook Shin, and David Straub
Seoul, Korea, and Stanford, California, United States

Preface: About the Koret Series on Korea

This volume is the third in a series of policy-related studies on contemporary Korea. The Koret Foundation of San Francisco made the project possible by a generous grant to the Korean Studies Program at Stanford University. The Koret Foundation's gift allowed Stanford's Walter H. Shorenstein Asia-Pacific Research Center, of which the Korean Studies Program is a part, to establish a Koret Fellowship to bring leading Asian and American policymakers to Stanford to study U.S.-Korean relations. Koret Fellows conduct their own research on Korea and the bilateral relationship, with the broad aim of fostering greater understanding and closer ties between the two countries.

Gi-Wook Shin
Director, Shorenstein Asia-Pacific Research Center

TROUBLED TRANSITION:
NORTH KOREA'S POLITICS, ECONOMY, AND EXTERNAL RELATIONS

INTRODUCTION

1 Troubled Transition: North Korea's Politics, Economy, and External Relations

Gi-Wook Shin and Donald W. Keyser

In the West, North Korea (or the Democratic People's Republic of Korea, DPRK) is most frequently depicted as a rogue state, hermit kingdom, or charter member of an axis of evil. As a result, the popular perception is of a country posing a dangerous threat with nuclear weapons while allowing its people to starve. American media coverage of North Korea focuses on its weapons program—two-thirds of the coverage by three leading newspapers (the *New York Times*, the *Wall Street Journal*, and the *Washington Post*) has been on its weapons of mass destruction (WMD) program.[1] In recent years, there has been a growing number of studies on North Korea, but the focus has remained on its nuclear capabilities, proliferation activities, and military provocations.[2]

---

1 Gi-Wook Shin, *One Alliance, Two Lenses: U.S.-Korea Relations in a New Era* (Stanford: Stanford University Press, 2010). See also Donald Macintyre, Daniel Sneider, and Gi-Wook Shin, *First Drafts of Korea: The U.S. Media and Perceptions of the Last Cold War Frontier* (Stanford, CA: Shorenstein Asia-Pacific Research Center, 2009).

2 For a recent comprehensive study, see Jonathan D. Pollack, *No Exit: North Korea, Nuclear Weapons and International Security* (Abingdon, UK: Routledge/IISS, 2011). For the recent history of U.S. diplomacy to address North Korea's nuclear ambitions, see Mike Chinoy, *Meltdown: The Inside Story of the North Korean Nuclear Crisis* (New York: St. Martin's Press, 2008). A set of useful declassified U.S. government documents may be found in Robert A. Wampler, *North Korea and Nuclear Weapons: The Declassified U.S. Record* (National Security Archive Electronic Briefing Book No. 87, April 25,

North Korea does indeed represent a potential security threat to Northeast Asia and even to the United States, so the emphasis of the media, think tanks, and academia on its nuclear weapons program is understandable. However, North Korea's nuclear and other security policies reflect a multidimensional set of complex and possibly existential challenges that the regime faces. Without knowing these aspects of the North Korea problem, even our understanding of the regime's nuclear weapons policy will be partial, if not superficial, and we will not be able to anticipate how it will deal with other major issues, including its treatment of its own people and relations with its neighbors.

By the time North Korean leader Kim Jong-il died on December 17, 2011, his regime had long been facing a number of interrelated challenges: a protracted economic crisis; societal malaise, reportedly including eroding popular faith in leadership competence and legitimacy; and rising tensions with the Republic of Korea (ROK, or South Korea), Japan, the United States, and indeed almost the entire "international community." Following Kim's partial recovery from a debilitating stroke suffered in August 2008, he

2003), http://www.gwu.edu/~nsarchiv/NSAEBB/NSAEBB87/.

For earlier history of U.S. efforts vis-à-vis North Korean nuclear programs, see also William J. Perry, "Proliferation on the Peninsula: Five North Korean Nuclear Crises," in *Confronting the Specter of Nuclear Terrorism,* ed. Graham Allison (Philadelphia: The Annals of the American Academy of Political and Social Science, September 2006), 78–86; and Victor D. Cha and David C. Kang, *Nuclear North Korea: A Debate on Engagement Strategies* (New York: Columbia University Press, 2003). Stanford University Professor Siegfried Hecker and others have looked at the technical side, e.g., in Siegfried Hecker, "Extraordinary Visits: Lessons Learned from Engaging with North Korea," *Nonproliferation Review* 18, no. 2 (2011): 444–455; and Siegfried Hecker, Chaim Braun, and Robert L. Carlin, "North Korea's Light-Water Reactor Ambitions," *Journal of Nuclear Materials Management* 39, no. 3 (2011): 18–25. Another science-focused study is Olli Heinonen, "North Korea's Nuclear Enrichment: Capabilities and Consequences," *38 North,* June 22, 2011, http://38north.org/2011/06/heinonen062211/. See the following for an examination of aspects of North Korea's alleged involvement in proliferation and support for terrorism: Bruce E. Bechtol, Jr., "North Korea and Support to Terrorism: An Evolving History," *Journal of Strategic Security* 3, no. 2 (Summer 2010): 45–54; Sheena Chestnut, "Illicit Activity and Proliferation: North Korean Smuggling Networks," *International Security* 32, no. 1 (Summer 2007): 80–111; Stephen Haggard and Marcus Noland, "Sanctioning North Korea: The Political Economy of Denuclearization and Proliferation" (Working Paper 09-4, Peterson Institute for International Economics, January 2010), http://www.iie.com/publications/interstitial.cfm?ResearchID=1268; and "North Korea-Iran Nuclear Cooperation," Interview of Jeffrey Lewis, Director, East Asia Nonproliferation Program, Monterey Institute of International Studies, by Jayshree Bajoria, Senior Staff Writer, Council on Foreign Relations, December 14, 2010, http://www.cfr.org/proliferation/north-korea-iran-nuclear-cooperation/p23625.

apparently felt forced to confront his impending mortality and thus accelerated plans to anoint and empower his third son, Kim Jong-un, as inheritor of the "sacred Mt. Baekdu bloodline" and third North Korean "dynastic" leader. By early 2011 succession arrangements were well underway, though most outside observers questioned the likelihood that an untested, "Swiss-educated" man in his late twenties could assert meaningful authority, let alone consolidate power smoothly, in a regime dominated by battle-hardened revolutionaries and security apparatchiks forty to fifty years his senior.[3] Moreover, North Korea's immediate neighbors and the United States saw its nuclear and long-range missile programs as a manifest threat to regional peace and stability, all the more so given the nation's fraught political transition, its creaky economy of scarcity and recurring famine, and its abortive efforts to win international "respect" along with vital food and energy assistance.

Against this backdrop, we examine four main issues: (1) North Korean domestic politics, (2) the North Korean economy, (3) North Korea and its neighbors, and (4) scenarios for North Korean change in a comparative perspective. Chapters look closely at the likeliest plans and scenarios for

---

3 See, for example, the ten-part series in Korea's *JoongAng Iblo* [JoongAng Daily] entitled "Powers Behind the Throne," published December 26, 2011, through January 3, 2012. South Korean President Lee Myung-bak commented in his nationally televised New Year's speech on January 1, 2012, that a "big change is expected in the situation on the Korean Peninsula and northeast Asia following the death of Chairman Kim Jong-il. The situation on the Korean Peninsula is now entering a new turning point" (Choe Sang-Hun, "South Korea Predicts Changes in Peninsula," *New York Times*, January 2, 2012). Long-time Asian journalist/columnist Philip Bowring wrote in a bylined article for *Asia Sentinel* on December 22, 2011, "it seems unlikely that such a brutal and secretive dynastic regime can end in any way other than bloodshed. A popular uprising is perhaps possible but a more likely scenario is an elite revolt which sees the assassination of as many Kim relatives as necessary to kill the mythology that the family has built around itself. As often in closed regimes, rivalries are settled by assassination or execution." Even Chinese think-tank scholars and other experts, who usually adhere to cautious, officially approved language in commenting on North Korea, expressed skepticism about Kim Jong-un in initial reactions to Kim Jong-il's passing. Fudan University Professor Cai Jian commented to Australia's *The Age* on December 19, 2011, that "there are questions of whether the succession can go successfully and smoothly. . . . It is hard to say what North Korea will be like in the future." Professor Victor Cha, a Bush administration official responsible for North Korea policy, told *Financial Times* on December 19, 2011, that Kim Jong-un "may not be up to the job." A South Korean scholar at Seoul National University, Koo Gap-woo, told the same publication that "decision-making within Pyongyang will become more muddled. . . . The country will be run by a collective leadership system composed of bureaucrats and military officials, with Kim Jong-un as a figurehead."

political succession; weigh the implications of North Korea's economic entropy—severe energy and electrical power shortages, deindustrialization, widespread malnutrition and chronic famine, breakdown of the party-led food distribution system, and "remedial" measures profoundly flawed in concept and counterproductive in execution; examine North Korean foreign policy strategies to ameliorate domestic crisis and alleviate external pressure; and seek lessons in both theoretical literature and the actual reform experiences of the Soviet Union, China, Vietnam, and other once-socialist, now-market economies that seem hypothetically relevant and potentially useful for North Korea. Many of the authors also derived from these analyses their sense of the policy implications, including the optimal policy strategies, for the United States and South Korea.

However, we deliberately chose not to devote particular attention to nuclear and associated matters. These have been minutely explored in other contemporaneous studies, while the Six-Party nuclear talks process has been moribund—many believe dead and buried—since the end of the George W. Bush administration in late 2008. Such remains the case today. Nevertheless, it is inarguably the North Korean nuclear threat that rivets major power attention to the peninsula, and thus arouses particular worries about an inexperienced, unknown, and uncertain leader's finger on the proverbial nuclear trigger. Hence, many chapters in this volume implicitly and sometimes explicitly take into account North Korea's nuclear program and associated international negotiating strategy.

Character of the North Korean Regime

North Korean insularity, bellicosity, rhetorical style, "self-reliance" (*Juche*) ideology, "military-first" (*songun*) policy, and negotiating strategy have long confounded outside observers. Why does Pyongyang behave the way it does? How do North Korean leaders assess their top challenges and prioritize their goals?[4] Any effort to tease out meaningful lessons for North

---

4 Over the decades, scholars and other observers have offered various theories about the nature of the North Korean regime. Historically, many see North Korea as largely Stalinist. Even today, the *New York Times* web page on North Korea begins, "North Korea is the last Stalinist state on earth. . ." (accessed August 16, 2012, http://topics.nytimes.com/top/news/international/countriesandterritories/northkorea/index.html). Others argue that North Korea's behavior stems in large part from its Confucian traditions and nationalistic impulses. See, for example, Bruce Cumings, *North Korea: Another Country* (New York: The New Press, 2003). Hunter and many others focus on the government's Orwellian-like control of the people. See Helen-Louise Hunter, *Kim Il-sŏng's North Korea* (Westport, CT: Praeger, 1999). Buzo argues that the experiences

Korea from the experience of "other" socialist states must rest upon a confident, empirical judgment that North Korea is, for all its observed peculiarities, in fact a comparable socialist state. The chapters in this book address this question from a variety of perspectives, engaging each other but without necessarily reaching agreement.

Choe Sang-Hun describes North Korea as "a dynasty, a family state, and a gigantic cult church"; he approvingly quotes former ROK unification minister Lee Jong-seok: "While the [North Korean] system formally purports to have the outward appearance of socialism, it is actually a magnified image of the 'oriental family' in which the state is seen as an extended family." Daniel C. Sneider, on the other hand, places North Korea firmly within socialist parameters of economic structure, political-coercive apparatus, state ideology, and external behavior. He grants that early Cold War characterizations of North Korea as purely a Soviet satellite were flawed, but argues that many scholars have missed or understated the degree to which the nation adheres to classical socialist models and accordingly suffers the same inherent challenges and ultimate failures that other socialist systems faced in the 1980s and 1990s. Andrei Lankov and Rüdiger Frank, who both grew up in communist systems, agree, pointing to a substantial set of North Korean attributes and policies that mimic and mirror Soviet and East German experiences. Lankov, though conceding that "North Korea's social and political evolution is not necessarily similar to that of the USSR," nevertheless lays stress on the commonalities. For him, North Korea today manifests "Stalinism with (much pronounced) national characteristics . . . the usual late Stalinist fare of ossified Leninism and nationalism still reigns supreme in propaganda and official ideology."

Andrew G. Walder does not address this issue head-on, but implies a substantial structural commonality by contending that North Korea could—absent political impediments—successfully emulate the path taken by socialist China and socialist Vietnam in embracing a market economy. Choe, though, draws attention to a key difference between contemporary— no longer Maoist—China and North Korea: "The personality cult allows no countervailing force within the regime. Kim Jong-il sat, and now his son

of the founding leaders of North Korea in waging a guerrilla campaign against Japan's colonial rule of Korea profoundly shaped their values and methods of governance. See Adrian Buzo, *The Guerilla Dynasty: Politics And Leadership In North Korea* (London: Victoria House, 1999). Myers argues that, ironically, North Korea's leaders copied much of what they saw in Japan's ethnically based prewar fascist government. See B. R. Myers, *The Cleanest Race: How North Koreans See Themselves and Why It Matters* (New York: Melville House, 2010).

Kim Jong-un sits, like a spider at the center of a web of state, party, military, and secret police that do not necessarily communicate with each other and all ultimately report only to him." Choe also points to a fundamental difference of perception, and hence behavior, between North Korea and other nations, namely its "military-first" policy that has given rise to a "bunker state" or "guerilla state." As Choe sees it, the North Korean regime "works relentlessly" to persuade the population that "the country is under siege and surrender is not an option" while the outcome of the "coming war will determine" if Koreans remain independent or are "enslaved." If Choe's understanding of the essential mindset and attributes of the North Korean regime under the Kims is largely correct, it would tend to call into question the notion that North Korea might somehow emulate, or at least draw from, the otherwise somewhat comparable development and market reform models in former socialist states.

In their coauthored essay, Straub and Sneider usefully take issue with notions, popular with some scholars and the South Korean "progressive" camp, that North Korea's "victimization narrative" is both historically legitimate and crucial to understanding of the regime's mentality, propaganda, sway over the population, and external behavior.[5] With respect to the last, they conclude that North Korea "does not act as a victim" at all; while employing the "victimization narrative" to useful propaganda effect, Pyongyang is active in seeking to control its destiny, e.g., through its nuclear and missile program.

Straub and Sneider argue for interpreting North Korean external behavior through the lens of *Realpolitik*. They observe that Pyongyang's leaders probably know much more about the United States than American leaders and senior officials know about North Korea, but they debunk judgments ascribing to North Korea's leadership a superior strategic sense and tactical acuity. To the contrary, they suggest that because the successive Kims and their underlings have seen the United States through a prism warped by ideology and culture, they have made consistently flawed assessments of U.S. society, politics, strategic goals, and alliance requirements. They cite as Exhibit A in this regard Kim Jong-il's "quixotic quest" to enter a "strategic relationship" with the United States. North Korea has similarly overplayed its nuclear card, they believe, woefully misreading the Obama administration's political objectives and domestic constraints.

---

5 See, for example, Hongkoo Han, "Wounded Nationalism: The Minsaengdang Incident and Kim Il Sung in Eastern Manchuria" (PhD diss., University of Washington, 1999).

At the same time, Straub and Sneider caution against American ethnocentric assumptions that Washington is at the center of Pyongyang's strategic calculus. They hold that North Korea's overriding preoccupation and strategic focus has been the South Korean rival state—the ROK is manifestly already the "strong and prosperous state" (*kangsong taeguk*) that Pyongyang had formally set as its own 2012 goal. South Korea thus stands as a visible challenge to North Korean regime propaganda and legitimacy, and as an all-too-credible aspirant to absorb North Korea and rule a united peninsula. To this, Straub and Sneider add that intense intrapeninsular competition for primacy and legitimacy preordains that each side will spread misinformation and disinformation about its rival. For this reason, public statements and written works by Pyongyang's top leaders will always have a high quotient of propaganda and only limited utility for outsiders seeking to assess their true views and intentions.

Choe joins Straub and Sneider in aiming to demythologize North Korean regime pronouncements and behavior. In an implied rebuke to those who have seen subtle shifts of nuance and policy intent in North Korean public commentaries, Choe maintains that the regime has been "remarkably consistent with its core principles" over the years. It is, at base, a "gangster-like regime" that has recently utilized nuclear blackmail to pursue its goals, but North Korean leaders have also had "a far bigger chess game in mind than trading its nukes for mere economic benefits." Pyongyang, Choe concludes, seeks nothing less than winning formal international acceptance of its status as a nuclear weapons state. Playing this nuclear card, Choe believes, has simultaneously served multiple regime ends: conjuring up external threats and tension required to support its personality cult and *songun* policy; displaying to North Korea's people a visible achievement that justifies their economic sacrifices and undoubted hardship; and advancing the case, vis-à-vis South Korea, that North Korea has courageously maintained an independent identity against unremitting foreign pressure.

North Korea's Domestic Politics and the Succession

Power succession has traditionally posed a major challenge for authoritarian regimes, including each of the twentieth-century communist states. North Korea is no exception. The nation in 1994 successfully effected the first "hereditary" succession in the socialist world when Kim Jong-il took over upon his father Kim Il-sung's death. But that "dynastic" transition arguably proceeded smoothly because of the father's prestige, the son's twenty-year period of apprenticeship under his father's tutelage, the absence of any plausible individual or institutional challenger to Kim Jong-il, and the grudging acquiescence of North Korea's principal socialist ally, China. When Kim Jong-il suffered a stroke in the summer of 2008, the issue of his successor took on added urgency for North Korea. The prospect of a second father-to-son dynastic succession seemed highly problematic, as Kim Jong-il had not visibly commenced grooming a son or anyone else to follow him. He reportedly despaired of his eldest son Kim Jong-nam's indiscipline, playboy antics, and uncomfortable closeness to China; found his second son Kim Jong-chul "effeminate"—lacking the requisite toughness—and realized his youngest son Kim Jong-un, still in his mid-twenties, could not yet be credibly presented to the nation as a successor.

As Kim Jong-il remained hospitalized and out of public sight from August 2008 until April 2009, his prospects for recovery very uncertain, and a swirl of rumor issued forth from one of the world's most opaque societies, outsiders hypothesized that Kim Jong-il's death or inability to recover sufficiently to impose his will could mean a power grab by the military and secret police or even regime collapse. Outsiders were skeptical about the possibility of a dynastic succession to a son, much less a power transition heavily involving Kim Jong-il's younger sister Kim Kyong-hui and her husband Jang Sung-taek, a powerful Korean Workers' Party (KWP) official with extensive experience in both intelligence matters and economic work.[6] With an uncertain and possibly chaotic succession scenario looming, government officials in Washington, Seoul, and Tokyo, worried both about control of North Korea's fissile material and a possible Chinese military intervention in the name of stabilizing the situation, began to press Beijing to hold quiet exchanges on the various contingencies.

Defying medical odds and most foreign expectations, Kim Jong-il re-emerged in April 2009 and survived another thirty-two months. That

6 Kim Yong Hyun, a scholar based at the Institute for North Korean Studies at Seoul's Dongguk University, offered a typical view. Even before Kim Jong-il's stroke, he suggested that "It is more probable and possible that Kim will designate a successor from outside of his family circle. . . . Even the North Korean establishment would not advocate a continuation of the family dynasty at this point." See "North Korea Silent over Kim Jong Il Successor," IANS news service, Seoul, February 14, 2007. Most Chinese think-tank scholars and other well-known experts on North Korea offered similar albeit carefully phrased views through the end of 2008 and beyond. One noteworthy exception to this sort of commentary was B. R. Myers, who in *The Cleanest Race* offered the thesis that North Korea's dominant ideology boiled down to "[T]he Korean people are too pure blooded, and therefore too virtuous, to survive in this evil world without a great parental leader." Hence, Myers reasoned, a dynastic succession was again the only plausible response to a deepening regime legitimacy crisis.

afforded sufficient time for him to lay the groundwork for succession. By the time he suddenly died in December 2011, his son Kim Jong-un had already been gradually introduced to the public, given important roles and grooming assignments, made the object of a nascent cult of personality, afforded the opportunity to accompany his father on inspection trips around the country, and introduced—presumably in explicit terms as the heir—to senior Chinese visitors to Pyongyang. Thus, almost immediately after his father's death, Kim Jong-un was named the nation's new leader, in which capacity he solemnly—with the expected dignified tears of grief—led the public mourning and all related state ceremonies.

In the first weeks and months following Kim Jong-il's passing, Kim Jong-un was accorded all the most senior positions and titles atop the nation's military and party structures. He conducted an intensive round of lavishly publicized inspection tours that retraced his father's visits and presented to the public a physical appearance and personal style recalling those of his grandfather Kim Il-sung. He proceeded with plans to fire a long-range rocket (billed as a peaceful satellite launch) in April 2012, thereby scuttling an agreement reached with the United States only six weeks earlier and evidently rejecting China's private admonitions; when the launch failed, he broke precedent by quickly acknowledging it publicly. He coupled obligatory reaffirmations of his father's *songun* (military-first) policy with intriguing hints that he might reemphasize the central role of the KWP, even to the relative disadvantage of the Korean Peoples' Army (KPA), and upgrade attention to the national economy and standard of living. In a move presumably meant to sideline a possible threat, the regime in July 2012 abruptly removed Vice Marshal Ri Yong-ho "owing to illness" from his positions as Chief of the General Staff of the KPA, vice-chairman of the Central Military Commission, and member of the KWP central presidium. Despite these developments, major questions still remain: "Why Kim Jong-un?", "Can he consolidate control over the regime?", and "Can we expect any significant changes in North Korea's domestic policies and foreign relations?"

Kim Hakjoon skillfully draws out some likely answers from a detailed body of fact, plausible rumor, and informed speculation. He examines key events in Kim Jong-il's long and somewhat tortuous rise to power as a set of benchmarks for assessing Kim Jong-un's eventual success or failure in seeking to do what his father did, while lacking the same protracted period of grooming and resulting credibility. In this regard, he draws attention to an insufficiently understood aspect of the trajectory of Kim Jong-il's rise and eventual succession: in the final decade of Kim Il-sung's life, the country was in fact ruled jointly by father and son, with the father as a kind of chief executive officer and the son as chief operating officer. Kim Hakjoon makes a compelling case that Kim Jong-il—ever mindful of his father's evident greater affection for his more charismatic half-brother and Kim Il-sung lookalike Kim Pyong-il—long had a clear design, a laser focus on wresting control of the principal regime power and policy organs, the requisite ruthlessness, the mastery of internal intrigue, and superior skills in manipulating symbols and propaganda themes to his personal benefit. Kim Hakjoon's essay tells the reader that Kim Jong-il's twenty-five-year rise "overcame sibling rivalry within his family, internal opposition from Kim Il-sung's old guerrilla comrades, and Chinese criticism of a hereditary succession." Choe Sang-Hun offers much the same assessment in his essay: Kim Jong-il "fought for his inheritance as much as it was bestowed upon him by his father. He terrorized and won a grudging respect among the older elite. . . ."

Kim Hakjoon, Choe Sang-Hun, and Yu-hwan Koh all conclude, on balance, that Kim Jong-un will enjoy—for at least an initial period—the support of the regime's principal stakeholders. Kim Hakjoon examines and rejects the possibility of three hypothetical challenges to Kim Jong-un's authority: by his aunt Kim Kyong-hui and her husband Jang Sung-taek, by the senior military leadership, and by the North Korean people through mass unrest. Choe basically agrees but asks how the North Korean elite and people, having "only known deified monolithic dictators," might react if Kim Jong-un proves to be "far less than the absolute leader his father and grandfather were."

Looking at this from another angle, Yu-hwan Koh explores—presciently, as developments since the February 2011 conference have shown—whether Kim Jong-un's accession to power might shift the relationship between the military, accorded primacy under Kim Jong-il's *songun* policy, and the party, relegated to a supporting role in comparison to the stature it had once enjoyed under Kim Il-sung. Koh shows clearly that North Korea had already begun to reemphasize the KWP leadership from the moment that Kim Jong-un was internally and unofficially designated his father's successor in January 2009. He explains precisely why such a shift is mandated by the differing circumstances attending Kim Jong-il's rise to power and Kim Jong-un's sudden succession. Kim Jong-il, facing international uncertainties and domestic economic crisis spawned by the sudden implosion of the Soviet Union and other socialist states, relied upon the KPA to lead a crisis management system, ensure domestic discipline, and serve as a symbol of the requisite "revolutionary military spirit" needed to prevail over hardships. Moreover, Kim Jong-il had always mistrusted the KWP bureaucracy and placed his faith in the military hierarchy. For Kim Jong-un, on the other hand, the international and domestic challenges are different. Economic recovery had emerged as the highest priority, and the military was an unreliable pillar in supporting the policy shift. The *songun* policy had proven incapable of ameliorating the chronic economic crisis, whereas a return to "party-first" policies could potentially better support a renewed emphasis on light industry, an improved standard of living, and even cautious Chinese-style economic reform measures.

Sandra Fahy seeks in a short chapter to illuminate one of the major enduring mysteries about North Korean life: To what degree does the outward behavior of ordinary citizens reflect their genuine attitudes and expectations toward the regime? This in turn gets to the key analytical question: If there are contradictions and divergences between innermost thoughts and obligatory behavior, might one then anticipate North Korean society's gradual evolution or even a sudden challenge to the regime's legitimacy and long-standing policies? Put succinctly, her chapter focuses on what North Koreans are thinking about their leaders, their lives, and their own alternative futures.

Fahy builds upon the work of scholars Andrei Lankov, Stephen Haggard, and Marcus Noland through her own "open, unstructured interviews" with North Korean famine survivors now living as refugees in Seoul and Tokyo. She is well aware of the inherent hazards in seeking to draw confident conclusions derived from a small sample group both self-selecting—those whose destitution, despair, and/or resourcefulness led them to a new life abroad—and by definition unrepresentative of those who have remained in North Korea.

These essential caveats notwithstanding, Fahy's research sheds intriguing light on the rhythms, patterns, and underlying logic of contemporary North Korean life. She finds, for example, that while many of her subjects understood that the regime's personal classification (*songbun*) system had limited their options in life and constrained them from bettering their social and economic standing, they did not seem to equate inequality with injustice. The system had been structured so as to allocate resources rationally in a society of privation; given internal and external challenges, the nation-state understandably assigned highest priority to its own survival. Fahy's interview subjects interpreted their hardships through a uniquely North Korean prism: their lives could not be reduced to adjectives like "good" or "bad" but were "layered with complex, contradictory, and competing loyalties to the family, the self, and the land itself, not to mention the leadership." Even suicides at the height of the severe famine years, she suggests, perhaps reflected a conscious choice to die in familiar surroundings rather than to roll the dice by attempting escape to a poorly understood alternative.

When popular preoccupations so often center on ensuring economic survival for selves and family, and in the abstract for the larger community and the nation, citizens may have little time or inclination to consider the possibility of changing the fundamental system, let alone its leadership. In this sense, Fahy avers, becoming a refugee—"defecting"—is about coping with the impossible and is "only political by default." No outsider can measure, she concludes, the breadth and depth of contemporary citizen loyalty toward the regime. The country operates simultaneously on two levels: an official level, which is about *chemyon*, or saving face, and an unofficial level involving basic economic survival. She joins such scholars as Lankov in positing that this second level, which has spawned black markets and related social behavior at odds with key tenets of regime ideology, can only strengthen and spawn broader embrace of ideas at odds with regime norms.

North Korea's Economic Performance and Chronic Food Shortage

North Korea is virtually a bankrupt country that is struggling to feed its people. It has attempted to "reform" its economy, most recently in 2002 and 2009, but these efforts have largely been unavailing or deliberately reversed. Many if not most outside experts are pessimistic about the nation's ability to chart a path to a brighter economic future. However, there are lively ongoing debates about the root causes of the trouble as well as potential solutions to ameliorate the situation or even reverse the course.[7]

7 Rüdiger Frank, one of the contributors to this volume, has previously suggested that North Korea can and should seek applicable lessons in the experience of other socialist systems. See, for example, Rüdiger Frank and Sabine Burghart, eds., *Driving Forces of Socialist Transformation: North Korea and the Experience of Europe and East Asia* (Vienna: Praesens Verlag, 2009). Nicholas Eberstadt, who has studied the North Korean economy for decades, typically expresses deep pessimism that North Korea can "reform" its way out of its systemic malaise. See Nicholas Eberstadt, "What Is Wrong with the North Korean Economy," *Caijing*, July 1, 2011, and two earlier studies: Nicholas Eberstadt, "If North Korea Were Really Reforming, How Could We Tell—And What Would We Be Able to See?" *Korea and World Affairs* 26, no. 1 (Spring 2002): 20–48; and Nicholas Eberstadt, "North Korea As an Economy under Multiple Severe Stresses: Analogies and Lessons from Past and Recent Historical Experience," *Communist Economies and Economic Transformation* 9, no. 2 (1997): 233–55. Stephen Haggard and Marcus Noland have contributed many studies over the years, using both refugee interviews and number-crunching methodologies based upon admittedly partial and uncertain data. See their frequent working papers, policy briefs and lengthier studies published by the Peterson

Chapters in this book seek to assess the underlying causes of the non-performing economy and to suggest economically viable and politically sustainable options (if any) for the country to improve. These questions have recently emerged from the realm of abstract theory and gloomy hand-wringing, as the leadership under the still-untested Kim Jong-un has evinced renewed signs of interest in experimenting with the sort of economic reform long advocated by China. Moreover, Kim Jong-un's uncle Jang Sung-taek, arguably one of the most powerful and influential top leaders, has previously seemed to favor Chinese-style special economic zones, encouragement of limited foreign investment, and even material incentives for the domestic work force.

Two former U.S. government officials, State Department intelligence analyst William Newcomb and USAID administrator Andrew S. Natsios, take the reader expertly through North Korea's steady, prolonged decline during the Kim Jong-il years: deindustrialization, famine, and disruption of the national food distribution system amidst the 1990s crisis; price, enterprise, and land reforms clumsily conceived and poorly implemented in 2002; and the disastrous 2009 currency "reform" and subsequent partial retraction. They assess from different angles and career experiences the leadership's narrow range of plausible policy options. Newcomb looks broadly at the overall economy while Natsios focuses more narrowly on the food dilemma; both are deeply pessimistic that the North Korean regime can identify and adopt a meaningful reform program.

Newcomb, Lankov, and Sneider all acknowledge their debt to the work of Hungarian scholar-economist Janos Kornai, whom many consider the world's premier expert on socialist economies. Newcomb depicts North Korea as an exemplar of what Kornai calls a "shortage economy"—one in which industrial enterprise managers, confronted with "pervasive shortages," oversee production that is reliant upon makeshift inputs, sometimes inferior but cheap and sometimes superior but overly costly. The resulting products reflect those characteristics, often being simultaneously inferior

Institute for International Economics, e.g., Stephen Haggard and Marcus Noland, "The Winter of Their Discontent: Pyongyang Attacks the Market" (Peterson Institute for International Economics, Policy Brief Number PB 10-1, Washington, D.C., January 2010). Two other English-language articles published by Korean scholars are worthy of note: Kim Byung-Yeon, "Markets, Bribery, and Regime Stability in North Korea" (EAI Asia Security Initiative Working Paper No. 4, Seoul National University, April 2010); and Kim Suk-jin, "North Korea's Economic System in the Kim Jong-un Era: Prospects for Change and Implications," *Korea Focus*, May 2012, http://www.koreafocus.or.kr/design3/essays/view.asp?volume_id=122&content_id=104051&category=G.

and more expensive to manufacture than planned. Accordingly, Newcomb posits, DPRK manufacturing sectors very likely contribute negative value-added to the economy; in other words, it costs North Korea more to produce many goods than they are worth. Natsios documents the wholesale breakdown of the nation's agricultural production and food distribution system.

Newcomb, the voice of weary, frustrated experience in striving to make sense of the North Korean economy from a dearth of facts and contradictory reporting, comments wryly that "art is the inescapably necessary ingredient of an economic assessment of the DPRK." He suggests outside analysts have often been led astray by (1) false analogies with other socialist systems, (2) flawed methodologies that build models of North Korean military spending and standard of living resting upon dubious "comparability" assumptions about costs in South Korea and other advanced societies, and (3) the kind of casual extrapolation that concludes Korea will somehow "muddle through" its economic crisis. In fact, Newcomb asserts, North Korea's chances of "muddling through" are waning while its prospects of sliding into a second economic collapse akin to the 1990s are rising. Should systemic stress occur alongside severe economic hardship, a "breaking point" could be closer than many have realized.

Newcomb complains that "typical assessments" of the North's economy have rarely "incorporated even perfunctorily" developments in the military sector and what he terms "the palace economy" (that surrounds and supports the regime elite). He therefore proposes a different modeling approach for assessing the "true" North Korean economy that amounts to "an economic order of battle"—by which he means a rigorous effort to identify "who owns what" in the country. Such a model would take into account each of the four "relatively independent" (albeit to some degree necessarily interdependent) economies: the official state economy; the military economy; the palace economy; and the marketplace, including not only officially authorized but also gray and black markets. While Newcomb does not (and cannot) generate statistical measures for each of these sectors, he offers judgments regarding their relative magnitudes and vibrancy over the past decade.

North Korea's traditional food security system that Kim Il-sung implemented was, Natsios believes, politically logical and moderately effective for its era. It achieved what it aimed to do: the subordination of food security to political desiderata, in particular ensuring that the population remained wholly dependent upon the state for food and that the regime could prioritize scarce supplies so as to feed the military and reward the elite. Natsios ties that system's collapse around 1992 to familiar factors: the economically strapped Gorbachev government's cessation of food and energy assistance, Russia's and newly market capitalist China's restructuring of North Korean trade according to international pricing rather than concessional "friendship" terms, and the resulting sharp decline in North Korean oil imports and fertilizer production (given insufficient electricity to run the factories). Consequently, in Kim Il-sung's final years and the first years of Kim Jong-il's rule, North Korean agriculture slipped back into traditional practices, harvests dropped precipitously, hoarding intensified, and "the volume of food being pumped into the PDS [public distribution system] from the collective farms collapsed the entire . . . food security system." To ensure that sufficient food still reached the military and other regime-favored populations, Pyongyang reduced or even eliminated rations to the disfavored and even deliberately cut internal rail and road ties to the northeast to guard against potentially socially disruptive movements of hungry citizens.

Such measures turned "a manageable crisis into a catastrophe" with acute malnutrition and famine. Natsios concludes bleakly that the 1990s famine "traumatized North Korean society," altered political expectations and rules of the game, and produced a class of farmers and small merchants forced to survive the famine through personal initiative, energy, and semilegal coping mechanisms, all independent of state control. Natsios points to the irony that Pyongyang's response—deliberate subterfuge and diversion—to the well-intentioned international humanitarian food assistance effort had the unintended by-product of accelerating the "reach and volume" of private-sector farmers' markets. Natsios shares the view of most experts that the regime's 2002 and 2009 reforms were ill-conceived and wholly counterproductive. The 2002 move to address the famine by tolerating greater market-based activity had the consequence of strengthening farmers' markets, which in turn produced sharp increases in grain prices, runaway inflation, elevated mortality rates, and creation of "a new chronically food-insecure class of permanently destitute urban workers and miners." The 2009 currency reform measures wiped out savings for many North Koreans, devastating the finances and hopes of all those who had been living just above basic survival level.

Newcomb, Natsios, and other volume contributors see few available options for North Korea—and no palatable ones for a regime that assigns paramount weight to the maintenance of unchallengeable political control. Newcomb summarizes bleakly: "Whatever the regime's true agenda, chances of success are slight." Natsios allows that prospects for improved food security in the future are "dismal at best." Choe Sang-Hun sees the regime's options as extremely circumscribed, the strongest likelihood being that the Kim Jong-un succession leadership will pursue familiar policies and strategies, i.e., trying to win aid and recognition from "sworn enemies" while cultivating ties with China as its principal ally and guarantor.

Newcomb draws attention, in this regard, to the "oddity" that during a period that saw the rapid rise of the Asian tigers, and then of China, North Korea's leadership "made no effort to adapt its policies so the North's economy could draft in the slipstream of booming neighbors." He recalls, with a palpable sense of déjà vu, the assessment that Dr. Hong-Tack Chun offered fifteen years earlier at another Stanford conference: "North Korea's economic problems are structural . . . full-scale economic recovery is, thus, unlikely without fundamental reform . . . . But if [the] current policy of limited opening without reform continues, the possibility of crash will grow." In sum, the regime recognizes the problems, but lacks both the ability to retreat to its former system and the will to proceed toward genuine reform.

Natsios states succinctly the options—and countervailing pressures—regarding food security: (1) maximizing food assistance by opening up to the international humanitarian aid system—thus exposing regime weakness both to the world and the domestic population; (2) stimulating growth through the adoption of Chinese-style reforms—thus permitting a level of private investment and economic freedom that would chip away at the foundation of the regime's control and ideological legitimacy; and (3) reducing expenditures for the military and the nuclear program—thus weakening the military and risking a backlash from that quarter against the regime. Natsios therefore predicts unchanged North Korean policies and familiar challenges to the international community. When North Korea's food system is under greatest stress, he posits, Pyongyang uses "its reputation for provocative behavior to command more food aid from donors."

North Korea and Its Neighbors:
Major Power Policies and Options

In light of the foregoing assessment of North Korea's uncertain political succession and abiding economic challenges, essay contributors took on the question of how the United States, South Korea, and other nations might optimally craft their policies toward the Kim Jong-un regime. The United States, China, Japan, and South Korea all form new administrations in 2013, a development that might offer a good opportunity to seek improved relationships with the North, as well as challenges.

Choe Sang-Hun pronounces a clear failure of the U.S.-ROK policy of "strategic patience" pursued by presidents Obama and Lee Myung-bak. Choe points to one principal stumbling block: China, an ambiguous party at best, and one possibly interested in thwarting and scuttling American, South Korean, and Japanese efforts to wean Pyongyang away from its nuclear program. Choe offers that Washington and Seoul should acknowledge China's paramount policy goal of averting regional instability and seek to "convince" Beijing that North Korean regime change or collapse need not threaten China's security nor erode its regional influence. Choe concedes that for Beijing, bolstering an anti-American North Korea on its borders might be preferable to pushing an ally, albeit a prickly and recalcitrant one, into reforms both too sudden and too far-reaching.

Straub and Sneider argue, in any case, that for the foreseeable future any U.S. administration, given strategic and domestic political realities, cannot but adhere to a policy of "strategic patience" that is, in effect, a containment policy masked in more benign rhetorical trappings. In his separate essay that closes out the volume, Sneider reiterates that there is, for the United States and the international community, little alternative to a consistent strategy of deterrence and containment. He recommends—as does Andrew Lankov in his comparison of the Soviet Union and North Korea—that the U.S. policy goal should not obsessively focus on denuclearization per se, but should rather aim patiently for a long-term transformation of North Korea to a reformed socialist economy. At the same time, Sneider emphasizes the need for unambiguously tough-minded assurances to allies and warnings to Pyongyang. Washington should accordingly make clear to Japan and South Korea that it will defend them against any North Korean attack; take care to avoid the perception by allies and others that it might tacitly acquiesce in North Korea's desire to be treated as an acknowledged nuclear weapons state; and warn Pyongyang that any resort to nuclear weapons against U.S. allies, bases, or interests will call down massive military retaliation.

Natsios, similarly decrying what he regards as past U.S. food aid policies of illusions, false starts, and abrupt reversals, proposes ten "general guidelines" informed by his personal experience as a senior Bush administration policy official. He argues that scrupulous adherence to his guidelines will ensure that "reactionary elements within the regime seeking to turn the clock back and crush the emerging new market economy" cannot prevail. He insists upon a tough-minded, uncompromising approach that no doubt betrays enduring scars from past Bush administration battles: no explicit or implicit linkage of food assistance to broader policy goals, intrusive verification measures for all food aid tendered, and deliberate supply of those grains that the North Korean elite consider inferior (e.g., maize vs. rice) but which a hungry population has proven willing to consume.[8]

Thomas Fingar's chapter tackles the origins, objectives, and implications of China's significantly—albeit quietly—accelerating pace of bilateral commercial arrangements in North Korea, including mineral exploitation concessions, joint ventures, and construction of infrastructure and facilities. Fingar importantly notes that China's new economic penetration began in 2009, under Kim Jong-il, despite Kim's prior resistance to Beijing's blandishments. In this, he implies strongly that one ought not credit some recent media and other speculation that Kim Jong-un has already embraced a set of reformist policy correctives in tacit repudiation of his father's vision. Fingar assesses, to the contrary, that the ailing Kim personally launched the policy shift, aiming to bolster prospects for a smooth succession by improving the nation's living standards, ensuring China's goodwill at a sensitive moment, and having no viable alternative to this "least bad option" in light of the regime's failed strategies and frozen ties vis-à-vis Washington, Seoul, and Tokyo. Any North Korean ideological or practical qualms about China's increased potential influence are offset by promised material benefits, bolstered regime and national security, and the new policy's identity as a political legacy passed down by Kim Jong-il to his son. Fingar consequently foresees small likelihood of any near-term policy reversal by Pyongyang.

Fingar turns next to China's apparent strategic calculus and to South Korean, Japanese, and U.S. perspectives and policy concerns with respect to the thickening of Sino–North Korean economic ties. For China, he reasons, the new relationship, especially in mineral extraction and processing facilities, has the "triple advantage of Chinese control, more secure access, and lower costs." This in turn serves to nudge North Korea toward experimentation with Chinese-style economic reforms, to support an abiding Chinese strategic interest in ensuring stability on its borders, and potentially to reduce the future financial drain on China from indefinitely propping up the North's moribund economy. In these respects, Fingar's analysis buttresses the logic of other essays in this volume that envisage a path forward for the North Korean economy in culling lessons from the reforming experience of other socialist systems.

---

8 For another approach to the question of North Korean food security and food assistance, see Randall Ireson, "Food Security in North Korea: Designing Realistic Possibilities" (working paper, Walter H. Shorenstein Asia-Pacific Research Center, Stanford, California, February 2006).

Fingar suggests that it is too early to judge how the new Sino–North Korean economic ties will play out or how Seoul, Tokyo, and Washington might assess the impact for their national interests. Instead, he identifies some of the relevant factors and considerations: whether China's new economic presence in North Korea will benefit ordinary North Koreans; whether it will promote reformist impulses including a less repressive domestic regime and more pragmatic foreign policies; whether it will encourage or rather act to deny access to North Korea's economy by other nations; and, crucially for the United States and its allies, whether it might prompt any rethinking by Pyongyang of its nuclear program and policies. Fingar observes that domestic politics in each of the nations will impact, though to an unknown degree, on relevant policy analysis and decision-making.

Former British ambassador to North Korea John Everard's essay summarizes the history of European dealings with the DPRK, paying particular attention to the sharp differences between the experience of East Europeans, whose Warsaw Pact governments established "fraternal socialist" missions in Pyongyang during the 1950s, and the West European nations, most of which developed relationships and in some cases established Pyongyang embassies only relatively recently. Everard highlights the important role played by the Neutral Nations Supervisory Commission, established by the 1953 Korean War Armistice Agreement, in developing North Korea expertise among its member states Sweden, Switzerland, Poland, and Czechoslovakia. He also touches on work done within and with regard to North Korea by a variety of European nongovernmental organizations, educational institutions, foundations, assistance missions, and trade offices. Everard briefly surveys some of the central items on the European official, semi-official, and unofficial agendas: immigration; North Korean workers in European Union countries; human rights issues and humanitarian assistance programs; and, increasingly, the pros and cons of continuing to maintain resident missions in North Korea.

Everard also speculates usefully on what the DPRK regime has sought to achieve in its dealings with Europeans. He suggests motives including: (1) visibly demonstrating that the regime is not isolated and indeed commands international importance and stature; (2) satisfying the self-image and self-importance of regime leaders; (3) counterbalancing, at least potentially, its relationships with China, the United States, and South Korea, especially in crucial areas of need such as humanitarian aid; and (4) leveraging to regime advantage Europe's presumed political influence in Washington.

Viewing all this, Ambassador Everard bleakly acknowledges, with admirable understatement, that "it has been hard to demonstrate that a decade of expenditure of senior European time, treasure, and heartache has had any effect either on the DPRK regime's appalling human rights record or on its habit of threatening its neighbors with a growing arsenal of weapons." There is little daylight, then, between his core judgment from the European perspective and those from Washington and Asian capitals that past assumptions about North Korea have been shattered while past policies have palpably failed to achieve even modest goals. Everard nevertheless concludes, taking the long view, by pointing to certain plausible, albeit modest, benefits of European engagement: (1) exposing North Korean officials to Western thinking and culture, which might pay long-term dividends when (or if) the regime evolves toward openness and reform; (2) providing ground-level truth, or at least credible observations, to counter the wealth of rumor and disinformation that attends much reporting on North Korea; and (3) preventing North Korea's even greater isolation, thereby serving as an "investment against the day when the DPRK finally decides to engage seriously with the international community."

North Korean Scenarios for Change in Comparative Perspective

The concluding essays in the volume aim to draw lessons from the reform (or collapse) experiences of other socialist systems and to suggest a menu of policy actions should the North Korean regime choose—contrary to regime political requirements and therefore to the authors' own skeptical expectations—a reformist approach. Andrei Lankov examines the relevant Soviet societal attitudes and economic experience; Rüdiger Frank focuses on German unification building blocks and outcomes; Andrew G. Walder proposes that a China-style formula of de facto capitalist reforms coexisting with continued authoritarian political control is feasible—in the abstract—for North Korea; and Daniel C. Sneider agrees with Lankov on the strong parallels between Soviet and North Korean political cultures and their respective systemic crises, but stresses that North Korea has even greater disincentives to reform owing to the regime's contest for legitimacy and leadership with rival South Korea. Sneider observes also that North Korea lacks a key asset enjoyed by both China and Vietnam as they embarked on reform: a productive agricultural sector and a large, energetic rural population that could supply a ready workforce to special economic zones and newly emerging urban industrial centers.

Lankov, acknowledging the inexact points of comparison and indeed the profound dissimilarities between Soviet/Russian and North Korean societies and external circumstances, nevertheless points to aspects of the Soviet experience that help to illuminate North Korean leadership perspectives and policy choices. In his essay Lankov aims to produce, based primarily upon personal experiences in the former Soviet Union and in studying North Korea over many years, what he terms an admittedly "impressionistic . . . quick snapshot of Soviet society in the last decades of its history . . . [and to compare this] with present-day North Korean society." Some of Lankov's anecdotal judgments are as striking as they are contrary to received wisdom from other outside observers: "few if any people [in North Korea] take the state's official line at face value, even though many seem to buy at least some elements of the official ideology . . . . Most North Koreans seem to suspect that something is wrong with the entire system or at least some important parts of it . . . . Many North Korean bureaucrats seem to understand that in the long run the current economic and social model is unsustainable." Lankov also holds that North Korean bureaucrats, no fools, are risk-averse precisely because they understand the inherently hazardous consequences of any system change for their own positions.

Lankov asserts that the single crucial factor in accelerating the demise of the former Soviet Union was the "spread of . . . subversive information . . . about the economic success of the developed West . . . [which] slowly undermined and eventually wiped out the popular belief in the superiority or, at least, potential, of the Leninist state socialism." The same logic, he contends, applies to the analogous set of attitudes and economic realities pertaining in contemporary North Korea. Such logic induces Lankov to advocate, if only implicitly, a U.S.–South Korean–Western policy of engagement with North Korea aiming to hasten erosion of faith in the system and concomitant adoption of outward-oriented reform policies that can only precipitate the regime's eventual collapse. Lankov does add two cautionary notes, however, on major Soviet–North Korean dissimilarities: (1) the Soviet leadership and Russian people measured their aspirations and quality of life against the "civilized West"—the United States and Western Europe, whereas for North Korea the "other" has been South Korea, while the model for possible reform has been China; and (2) Soviet bureaucrats saw little threat posed by radical reform to their personal power and privileges, whereas North Korea's elite equates regime collapse with absorption by South Korea and hence loss of everything, including possibly their own lives à la the Ceausescus.

Rüdiger Frank takes a somewhat different tack in looking for parallels and lessons in the East German experience. He shines a spotlight on issues, rather than on solutions and outcomes, which he hopes will help to ensure dispassionate analysis and a "less imminent expiration date." Observing that Seoul policymakers have learned "surprisingly little" about Germany's unification and its corresponding lessons—both positive and negative—for Korea, and that ROK officials and South Korean academics commonly voice doubts that such a comparison is even relevant and worthy of attention, Frank seeks to fill the gap by drawing upon recently published analyses of German reunification. He applies a "politico-economic perspective . . . hoping to duly consider not only the economic logic but also the options and limitations posed by the specifics of time and place." He devotes principal attention in his analytical framework to the financial costs of the German unification process, advancing hypotheses—"weighted and filtered" according to "current knowledge about both Koreas"—about the financial requirements and political ramifications of a future Korean unification.

Frank acknowledges at the outset that German unification and future Korean unification manifest both significant similarities and marked differences. But he argues that while North Korea is undeniably a "very special" case, it has undergone a certain "normalization" since the 2002 reforms (which Frank sees in far more positive terms than Newcomb and Natsios) such that "it increasingly develops features that make it more similar than ever to classical socialist systems." Such being the case, Frank posits that "formal steps" taken in the course of German unification are indeed relevant to Korea's future challenge, and he proceeds to generate a working list of key issues for detailed analysis. He proposes: currency union, domestic production, wages and workforce mobility, privatization, property and capital, foreign trade, business promotion, welfare and social policies, pensions, and political campaigns and promises.

Frank flags the issue of monetary transfers (eastward) as "the core of the still-negative perception of unification by West Germans." He suggests that North Korean initial expectations of material improvement in their lives and security are probably lower than in East Germany, owing both to cultural factors and to the dearth of information available in the closed North Korean society. Nevertheless, he predicts that the issue of the magnitude of financial transfers will be a thorny one for the future unified Korean government (located in Seoul) and for the citizens of the former North Korea. He anticipates that in North Korea, as in the former East Germany, there will likely emerge before long a pronounced nostalgia for the past relative security afforded by the Pyongyang regime. North Korean laborers will initially lack both the requisite skills to be competitive and the existing resources and social safety set to feel secure amidst sweeping political, economic, and social change; thus, the magnitude of pension appropriations and other financial transfers will loom large and be politically sensitive. Given Seoul's lack of financial resources and popular pro-unification support as compared with Bonn's situation two decades ago, international financing will need to play a substantially more prominent role in Korea's unification.

In his concluding and rather provocative analysis of North Korea's "current status and development trends"—i.e., its potential readiness for unification along German lines—Frank paints a canvas notably more optimistic than one is apt to discover in studies by most South Korean and Western specialists. He finds that North Korea has already "become very similar to East Germany" in significant dimensions of policy and social attitudes. In this regard, he identifies North Korea's embrace of alternative currencies (foreign exchange certificates), toleration of the semi-legal circulation of hard currencies, and acceptance of inflation as a way station toward establishing a stable currency reflecting the true value of goods and services. He also sees perverse promise in North Korea's increased economic interaction with China—born of sheer necessity, to be sure, but a trend that will eventually promote economic reform in North Korea while serving to buffer the nation post-unification against the otherwise predictably negative impact of the globalized economy. For all this, Frank also notes the two opposing trends in North Korea: on one hand, the society is becoming less centralized, with individual economic activities looming larger and more visible, but on the other the regime has sought since 2009 to rein in the nascent private sector and to reimpose tight political and economic controls over society. Without minimizing any of the myriad challenges that lie ahead, Frank writes that South Korea has much to learn from Germany's experience and enjoys the "great advantage [of] time" in which to identify ways and means of addressing them before unification.

Andrew G. Walder, a political sociologist and specialist on the Chinese economy, asks in his essay (1) whether North Korea might find a viable solution to its moribund economy in the experience of Chinese- and Vietnamese-style reforms, (2) if Pyongyang's adoption of such policies could stabilize and prolong the regime, and (3) whether economic progress might negate the arguments for North Korea's nuclear program and cyclical use of military provocations and threats to extract food and other economic assistance from South Korea and the United States.

To answer these interlinked questions, Walder concisely identifies the principal elements of "Chinese-style market reform," assesses the purely economic calculus favoring North Korea's embrace of such a program, makes plain the political risks and disincentives for the North Korean regime, notes the "fundamentally different" geopolitical circumstances of North Korea and China (or even Vietnam), and from this offers his measured judgment that North Korean market reform would be "risky business."

Walder posits that Chinese (or Vietnamese) reforms would not only "work" in economic terms but that Pyongyang's best and perhaps only way to avoid permanent stagnation and/or regime collapse is to undertake economic restructuring and integration with the global economy. The Soviet and Eastern European failure to adopt far-reaching reforms, Walder argues, led inexorably to their economic stagnation, political crisis, and implosion during 1989–91. Walder believes that North Korea's readiness to embrace reform would bring a substantial Chinese subsidization and invite a generous international response (especially if reform measures were accompanied by concessions on nuclear and security matters of paramount concern to the West). He also holds that the West, for its part, must not hesitate in response to pledge increased aid, investment, and technical assistance, and must also offer credible guarantees that it will respect North Korea's sovereignty.

Despite the lessons of recent history and plausible suppositions about the economic and political advantages of reform, Walder joins other contributors to the volume in expressing strong doubt that Pyongyang's leadership—at least so long as the Kim dynasty reigns—can or will change direction. Reforms themselves would represent an implied admission of past errors; a challenge to regime legitimacy and authority; an invitation to North Korea's population to look southward for inspiration and goals; and, as in China's case, an opening up not only to rapid development but to runaway inflation, spreading corruption, corrosive disillusionment, and rejection of party membership and state jobs in favor of more remunerative positions outside the "system." As Walder observes, the regime elite would surely see the handwriting on the wall in terms of its loss of political control, ideological authority, and monopoly of the routes to personal security and relative material success.

Sneider agrees with other contributors' bottom-line analysis about North Korea's fundamental systemic similarity to other, failed socialist systems; the theoretical efficacy of reform according to the Chinese/Vietnamese model; the complexities posed by the proximity of South Korea; and the daunting challenges that a reform program would present to regime authority and control. He joins other analysts, notably Lankov, in assessing that the North Korean regime, for all its woes and apparent brittleness, can endure—or, in Newcomb's parlance, "muddle through"—for some time. But Sneider avers that the North Korean state, for reasons illuminated by Kornai's work, cannot find solutions to the underlying pathologies producing socialist systemic failure. He envisages, though, that the regime can "prolong its slow death"—if permitted to do so—by familiar patterns of ruthless repression at home combined with success in extracting foreign assistance through strategies of military provocations and tacit nuclear blackmail. Hence, as noted earlier in this chapter, Sneider insists upon U.S., South Korean, and international policies that explicitly encourage reform while laying down clear markers that North Korea's past approach will not be rewarded but will be countered.

Prospects and the Problems of Extrapolation

Despite the sober mood and outlook conveyed by all these concerns and reservations, we still hope that the year 2013 and those following could yet offer an opportunity for North Korea to embrace economic changes and to pursue a more pragmatic, mutually beneficial relationship with South Korea, Japan, the United States, and the international community. Recent history warns us against the perils of comfortable straight-line projections. Contrary to mainstream views overwhelmingly advanced by academics, think-tank scholars, journalists, and government officials, Gorbachev adopted *glasnost* and *perestroika*, the Berlin Wall fell, the Warsaw Pact and Soviet Union imploded and reemerged as market economies, China rose rapidly to the status of the world's second economy and nascent superpower, Vietnam pulled out of Cambodia and opened to the region and the West, de Klerk and Nelson Mandela reached a peaceful accord on South Africa's transition to majority rule, and long-isolated Myanmar (Burma) freed Aung San Suu Kyi and embarked on careful political and economic reforms.

There were some early indications that North Korea's new leader Kim Jong-un—and the elite coalition around him—might seek to adjust the nation's domestic and foreign policies in an effort to address perennial economic woes, popular restiveness, and estrangement from the international community. The new South Korean government has vowed to pursue a "trust diplomacy" aimed at improving inter-Korean relations, in some departure from the previous administration's policy requiring the North to move first toward abandoning nuclear weapons. The United States and China also have reelected and newly elevated leaders in place who may yet explore new initiatives toward North Korea despite frustrations over the years. China's new leaders have shown markedly greater readiness both to join the international community in sanctioning North Korea and to offer stern counsel to Pyongyang's leaders that they must rejoin the Six-Party Talks. All these developments will certainly create many new uncertainties and challenges but it is too early to make confident predictions about the meaning and ultimate direction of these straws in the wind. Still, the United States, South Korea, and China can help—individually and working in concert—to turn North Korea's "troubled transition" into a valuable opportunity to pursue enduring peace and prosperity on the Korean Peninsula.

I   NORTH KOREAN DOMESTIC POLITICS

2 The Hereditary Succession from Kim Jong-il to Kim Jong-un: Its Background, Present Situation, and Future

Kim Hakjoon

On September 27, 2010, Kim Jong-il, the one-man dictator of the Democratic People's Republic of Korea (DPRK or North Korea), in his multiple capacities as general secretary of the Korean Workers' Party (KWP), chairman of the Central Military Committee of the KWP (KWPCMC), and chairman of the National Defense Commission (NDC), appointed his third son, Kim Jong-un, to the rank of four-star general under the order of the supreme commander of the Korean People's Army (KPA)—Kim Jong-il's other official title. The next day, for the first time since 1966, the Third KWP Delegates' Conference convened in Pyongyang and elected new members for its Central Committee (CC), with Kim Jong-un among those chosen. The plenary session of the KWPCC immediately created the position of vice-chairmanship within the KWPCMC, and Kim Jong-il subsequently appointed Kim Jong-un to that post in his own capacity as its chairman. On October 10, during a celebration of the sixty-fifth anniversary of the founding of the KWP, Kim Jong-un made his public debut at a military parade as the successor-designate. About fourteen months later, Kim Jong-il died. During the subsequent national mourning period, the KWP and the North's state-run media repeatedly emphasized that Kim Jong-un was the new leader of the country.

As this series of appointments and events carried the Kim dynasty over Stalinist North Korea into a third generation of rule, the outside world focused its attention on the new political situation evolving in the reclusive and repressive DPRK. The first question was raised about the man per se: Who was Kim Jong-un? Second, how was he groomed as the successor? Finally, what does the succession mean in the larger scheme of North Korea's internal politics? This chapter attempts to answer these interrelated questions.

Rivalry and Intrigue inside the Royal Family

As monarchic history has shown, love and hate—even betrayal and intrigue—among members of the royal family are more important than existing institutions or principles for succession. North Korea is not an exception. The succession from Kim Il-sung, the key leader in the founding of both the KWP and the DPRK, to his first son Kim Jong-il was replete with conspiracies, purges, power alignments, and manipulations among family members. The second succession from Kim Jong-il to Kim Jong-un shows a similar pattern.

Kim Il-sung's Two Marriages

The origins of the feud in the Kim family may be traced to Kim Il-sung's second marriage. Kim Il-sung (April 15, 1912–July 8, 1994) joined the Chinese Communist Party (CCP)-organized Northeastern Anti-Japanese United Army and soon was promoted to commander of its Korean unit. Before he fled to the Soviet Far East in 1940, he married Kim Jong-suk (b. 1917 or 1919), one of his female comrades. She gave birth to their first child and son Jong-il in 1942 in the outskirts of Khabarovsk. With the defeat of Japan in August 1945, they returned to Pyongyang and had their first daughter Kyong-hui (Kim Kyŏnghŭi) in 1946. After Kim Jong-suk died during a miscarriage in 1949, Kim Il-sung began to live with his telephone operator, Kim Song-ae (b. 1924). She gave birth to daughter Kyong-jin (1952), and sons Pyong-il (1954) and Young-il (1955). Kim Il-sung supposedly had great affection for son Pyong-il, who looked just like him, and he would say that Pyong-il would become a superior general after him—to Jong-il's chagrin. In 1963, Kim Il-sung and Kim Song-ae's marriage was officially announced. Under this new family dynamic, Jong-il and Kyong-hui had lonely childhoods lacking in maternal affection. While their biological mother was an anti-Japanese guerrilla fighter, their stepmother was merely the household telephone operator, and furthermore only seventeen years older than Jong-il himself. Jong-il and Kyong-hui grew to despise their stepmother and her offspring; they referred to Kim Song-ae not as mother but *ajumi*, a Korean euphemism for "housemaid."

Kim Jong-il's Multiple Relationships

The feud among the royal family members later intensified due to Kim Jong-il's complicated private life, as he was "married" five times and father of six or seven children. His first relationship was with Hong Il-chon (b. 1942), a classmate at Kim Il-sung University; he was said to have married her in 1965 and she gave birth to their daughter, Kim Hye-kyong, in 1968. After a divorce that probably took place the same year, Hong Il-chon and Kim Hye-kyong were completely forgotten, not only within the Kim family but also in the sphere of North Korean politics. [1]

The second woman was Song Hye-rim (Sǒng Hye-rim, 1937–2002). Song had gone to the North from Seoul with elder sister Song Hye-rang (Sǒng Hye-rang, b. 1935) during the Korean War (probably in August 1950) following their communist parents, who came from wealthy and intellectual backgrounds. In 1956, she married Ri Pyong (Yi P'yǒng), the first son of Ri Ki-young (Yi Ki-yǒng, referred to as "Korea's Maxim Gorki" and president of the [North] Korea–Soviet Union Friendship Association). She gave birth to a daughter, Ok-dol. Three years later, while attending the Pyongyang University of Drama and Film, she played the main role in the DPRK film *Punkaesǒnǔi Maǔl* (In a village near the demarcation line), and was acclaimed by Kim Il-sung for her performance. She also came to the attention of Kim Jong-il, who, it was later said, was attracted not only to her beauty but because at five years his senior she filled his need for the maternal affection he lacked since childhood. Beginning in 1969, they secretly lived together without being married. According to Song Hye-rang's post-defection autobiography, anyone who dared talk about the secret life of the two lovers was executed. On May 10, 1971, their son Kim Jong-nam (Kim Chǒng-nam)

---

1 At least three books have been written by Kim Jong-il family relatives who have defected to the West. The first one was *Taedonkang Royal Family Seoul chamhaeng sipsanyon* [Taedong River royal family: fourteen years in Seoul after my secret defection], by Yi Han-young (Yi Han-yǒng, birth name Ri Il-nam) and published in 1996. Yi was the nephew of Kim Jong-il's mistress Song Hye-rim. The second book was published in 2000; written by Yi Han-young's mother Song Hye-rang (Sǒng Hye-rang), it was titled *Tungnamujip; Song Hye-rang jasojon* [The wisteria house: the autobiography of Song Hye-rang]. See also Chung Chang-hyun, *Kyoteso bon Kim Jong-il* [Kim Jong-il as seen by the side]. The third book, based on recollections by Sin Kyong-wan, defected KWP cadre, was published in 2000.

was born. He was reared in secret by his maternal grandmother in Kim Jong-il's home.

Kim Il-sung, unaware of his son's hidden life with Song Hye-rim, urged Kim Jong-il to find himself a wife. Consequently, in October 1973 Kim Jong-il reluctantly married Kim Yong Suk (Kim Yŏngsuk, b. 1947), one month after he was elected the KWPCC secretary in charge of organizational affairs and ideology and thus entered the core of the KWP. Kim Yong Suk was the daughter of a vice-dean of a local college and was herself a clerk of the KWPCC. She gave birth to a daughter, Kim Sul-song (Kim Sŏlsong), in 1974. While Kim Il-sung fully embraced daughter-in-law Kim Yong Suk and granddaughter Sul-song, he never recognized Song Hye-rim as his daughter-in-law and was not even aware of grandson Kim Jong-nam's existence. Even Kim Jong-il's own sister Kim Kyong-hui demanded that Song Hye-rim part from her brother. Song Hye-rim was furious and, according to Ri Il-nam (aka Yi Hanyoung [Yi Hanyŏng]), who as Song Hye-rang's son and Kim Jong-nam's cousin frequently visited Jong-nam's home, Song Hye-rim demanded that Jong-il reveal the truth to his father, threatening to appear with Kim Jong-nam in person before Kim Il-sung. While—according to Ri Il-nam—Kim Jong-il apparently told his father the truth around 1975 and Kim Il-sung accepted the fait accompli, Song Hye-rang claimed that Kim Il-sung died unaware of Kim Jong-nam's existence, and that only a very few members of the Kim family knew of him. According to her, Jong-il, fearing that the knowledge of his illicit affair with Song Hye-rim and his illegitimate son might infuriate his father and cost him his place as successor, decided to forever conceal the truth.[2] Because of this, Kim Jong-nam could not attend a regular school and was instead tutored by Song Hye-rang at home.

The Complicated School Years of an Illegitimate Son

Around 1974 Song Hye-rim fell ill, suffering from insomnia, a nervous breakdown, and finally heart disease, and in 1975 Kim Jong-il sent her to a Moscow hospital. Three years later, Kim Jong-il sent Kim Jong-nam away to study at an elementary school in Moscow. Song Hye-rang, son Ri Il-nam, and daughter Ri Nam-ok were likewise sent to Moscow, so that Song Hye-rang could supervise Kim Jong-nam's studies. But the boy, having grown up in a luxurious residence in Pyongyang, could not adapt to the low-level facilities—the bathroom, in particular—of his Soviet neighborhood's ordinary

2 Yi, *Taedonkang Royal Family*, 27, 84.

elementary school. In March 1980, Kim Jong-il allowed Kim Jong-nam to study instead at an international school in Geneva. Song Hye-rang became his guardian there, and her children Ri Nam-ok and Ri Il-nam his companions. Two years later, supposedly fearing that nearby South Korean agents were planning to "kidnap" them, they returned to Moscow.[3] Kim Jong-nam, Ri Nam-ok, and Ri Il-nam were all enrolled in a French school in Moscow. In September 1982, Kim Jong-il allowed them to return to study in Geneva with Song Hye-rang as their supervisor. A week later, Ri Il-nam materialized in Seoul as a political refugee, but Song Hye-rang claimed that her son had actually been kidnapped by South Korean agents.[4]

As a consequence, Kim Jong-nam and his entourage again had to return to Moscow. But Mikhail Gorbachev's advancement of *perestroika* in 1986 led Kim Jong-il to say that the USSR was "not our ally but a dirty country bought by U.S. dollars," and he thus allowed Kim Jong-nam to leave the country and study in Switzerland, "a neutral country maintaining high morality."[5] Kim Jong-nam studied fine arts in Geneva and showed some talent in portraiture. But when the young man began to frequent bars at night, developing relations with Western girls, Kim Jong-il became enraged and recalled him—along with Song Hye-rang and Ri Nam-ok—to Pyongyang, sending him to live in a local village. Although he was allowed to return visits to Pyongyang, during those visits he was only given a two-month supply of daily necessities to take back with him. Song Hye-rang recalled in her autobiography, "At that time, Kim Jong-il never visited our home. We were completely forgotten. Our home was a high-level prison, and we were lifers."[6] Before long Kim Jong-il allowed Song Hye-rang and daughter Ri Nam-ok to join Song Hye-rim in Moscow. In May 1992 Ri Nam-ok sought political refuge in the West via Geneva, leaving behind a letter to Kim Jong-il asking for his forgiveness.

The Decline of Kim Jong-nam

Kim Jong-nam's political standing was hurt when his mother Song Hye-rim and aunt Song Hye-rang attempted to take refuge in the West.

---

3 By this time in Geneva, North and South Korea had each opened diplomatic missions and there were a number of intelligence agents in the area; in contrast, there was no diplomatic relationship between Moscow and Seoul until 1990, so presumably Moscow was free of South Korean agents in the 1980s.

4 Sung, *The Wisteria House*, 436–43.

5 Ibid., 464.

6 Ibid., 484–85.

In February 1996 Song Hye-rang succeeded in defecting to Paris (and ulti-mately to the United States) from Moscow via Geneva, but at the last mo-ment Song Hye-rim returned to Moscow in fear of her son's safety. A year later, Song Hye-rang's son Ri Il-nam, who had on more than one occasion exposed the private lives of the "holy family" after his defection to South Korea, was assassinated in Seoul. South Korean intelligence speculated that Kim Jong-nam had sent his agents to kill his cousin to win back his father's confidence. However, a futile attempt to visit Tokyo Disneyland a few years later had a more serious impact on Kim Jong-nam's reputation. On May 1, 2001, he was caught with two women and one boy—believed to be his wife, maid, and son—when he arrived at Narita International Airport from Singapore. Japanese authorities leaked that they carried forged Dominican passports (travellers holding these are waived from the visa requirement) and deported them to Beijing, in full view of about a hundred reporters and photographers. Pictures showing him disheveled and unshaved, ca-sually dressed, and the two women with fashionable sunglasses, designer handbags, and other luxury goods, were enough to damage the North's international image. Enraged, Kim Jong-il reportedly ordered him to live outside the country.[7] One year later (May 2002), Song Hye-rim died of a chronic disease in a Moscow hospital. With Kim Jong-nam in attendance, a simple funeral service was held for her in secrecy. She was buried not in Pyongyang but in Moscow, and without any formal announcement by the North Korean government. Since then, Kim Jong-nam has lived in Macao, sometimes visiting Hong Kong and Beijing and giving the occasional (paid) interview to Japanese television.

Ko Young-hee: A Trusted Liaison

Returning back to the 1970s, Kim Jong-il's 1973 marriage to Kim Yong Suk did not last very long, although he never legally divorced from her. Sometime in the mid-1970s he fell in love with Ko Young-hee (Ko Yŏnghŭi, 1950–2004). She was born in Japan, the daughter of Ko Kyong-taek, a man of uncertain background. She moved with her family to Pyongyang, was trained as a dancer, and joined the national ballet troupe (Pyongyang Mansudae Art Troupe). Fujimoto Kenji (pseudonym), Kim Jong-il's Japanese chef who defected to Japan in 2001, noted that she was "indeed beautiful," reminiscent of Hara Setsuko or Yoshinaga Sayuri, famous Japanese movie actresses. Kim Jong-il started living with Ko Young-hee in

---

7 Yi Chong-hwan, "Beijingso Sarajin Kim Jong-nam [Kim Jong-nam who disap-pears in Beijing]," *Dong-A Ilbo*, May 7, 2001, A 3.

1976, despite not being legally married to her. Two sons, Kim Jong-chul (Kim Chŏngch'ŏl) and Kim Jong-un (Kim Chŏngŭn), were born in 1980 and 1983, respectively, and a daughter, Kim Yo-jong, was born in 1987.[8]

In the late 1980s there was an incident that drew Kim Jong-il even closer to Ko Young-hee. One night, after having dinner in his villa in Hamhung, Kim Jong-il was taking some air when a drunken bodyguard attempted to kill him. According to Fujimoto, Ko Young-hee threw down the drunken bodyguard, while the other guard killed his coworker. Confessing that "I thought it was my last," Jong-il was said to have expressed his deep appreciation to her. On another occasion, immediately after the death of Kim Il-sung, she happened upon Kim Jong-il in his room and saw that he was staring at a pistol, apparently in great emotional turmoil. Fujimoto recalled that she took away the pistol, shouting "What are you thinking about?" He added, "This made Kim Jong-il trust her more strongly."[9] In 1998, Ko Young-hee's younger sister Ko Young-suk, her husband Pak Kun (the North's diplomat active in Geneva), together with their sons, defected to the United States from Geneva with a huge amount of U.S. dollars that had been deposited in a Swiss bank for Kim Jong-il. Nevertheless, Kim Jong-il did not punish Ko Young-hee, recalling that "a couple of times, Young-hee saved my life."

Ko Young-hee died in a Paris hospital in May 2004, due either to breast cancer or a cerebral embolism. In contrast with Song Hye-rim, a funeral service for Ko was held in Pyongyang and she was buried there, although the two events were carried out in secrecy. Kim Ok (b. 1964), a close friend of Ko Young-hee, was entrusted by Kim Jong-il with the secret task of escorting the body from Paris to Pyongyang aboard his private jet. Two years after Ko's death, the same Kim Ok became Kim Jong-il's common-law wife. A graduate of Pyongyang University of Music and Dance, she worked as Kim Jong-il's secretary, in charge of his schedule. Kim Ok assisted Jo Myong-rok (Cho Myŏngrok), vice-marshal of the KPA and first vice-chairman of the NDC, on his official visit to the White House in October 2000; she also accompanied Kim Jong-il on his unofficial visit to China in January 2006. On both occasions, she was referred to as "division director of the NDC of the DPRK."

8 Fujimoto Kenji, *Pukhanui Hukaeja, Oe Kim Jong-un inka* [Why was Kim Jong-un chosen as North Korea's successor?], translated by Han Yu-hee (Seoul: Maxmedia, 2010), 59.

9 Ibid., 69.

Who Are Kim Jong-chul and Kim Jong-un?

Having traced through the confusing history of Kim Jong-il's wives, mistresses, and common-law wives, we should now turn to the question of what is known about Kim Jong-chul and Kim Jong-un. It should be stressed at the start that information about both sons is extremely limited, and what does exist relies heavily on somewhat anecdotal statements from Fujimoto. It was only after 2007 that Jong-chul and Jong-un made regular public appearances, but still without being identified in the media. Fujimoto might be the only person outside the family who was able to closely observe them in the North. In January 1990, at his special villa in Sinchun County, South Hwanghe Province, Kim Jong-il had a meeting with the cardinal secretaries of the KWP Central Committee. After the lunch, Kim Jong-il, accompanied by Ko Young-hee, ordered everyone to gather at the center of the villa. When they arrived, Jong-chul and Jong-un were already there, in military uniforms and standing at attention, despite being only ten and seven years old. Fujimoto, who was attending Kim Jong-il, saw the two boys for the first time. Kim Jong-il allowed all attendants to introduce themselves to his sons. It seemed that except for Jang Sung-taek (Chang Sŏngt'aek), who was in charge of KWP organizational affairs, and their uncle (Kim Kyong-hui's husband), all the other secretaries were likewise seeing the boys in person for the first time. They referred to the two boys as "princes" (Fujimoto later came to know that daughter Kim Yo-jong was called "princess"). They also called Jong-chul "Big General" and Jong-un "Little General," but when Jong-un expressed his dislike of the latter, they instead referred to him as "Comrade General," and Jong-chul as "Comrade Big General."[10]

According to Fujimoto, when he offered his hand first to Jong-chul, the boy shook his hand warmly. However, Jong-un reportedly "glared fiercely" at him, as if he were thinking "an abhorrent Japanese!" When Kim Jong-il introduced him as Fujimoto, Jong-un barely shook his hand. A week later, as the two "princes" tried to fly kites in the villa's garden, Fujimoto lent them a hand. Seeing they became happy to get his help, Kim Jong-il instructed Fujimoto to become their play companion. As Fujimoto recalled,

> Jong-chul and Jong-un always played together. They especially loved playing basketball. Jong-un loved watching American basketball games on television. The eldest son of Ko Young-hee's younger sister, who seemed to have been Jong-un's age,

---

10 O Tong-ryong, "Fujimoto Kenji Interview: Neka mannan Kim Jong-un"[An interview with Fujimoto Kenji: Kim Jong-un whom I met," *Wolgan Chosun* 368 (November 2010): 66–7.

frequently joined them. In addition, two pretty girls of similar age [to the boys] were assigned to Jong-chul and Jong-un.[11]

Fujimoto further recalled, "Jong-un really loved basketball and played every waking chance he got. Kim Jong-il instructed him that he had to rest for forty-five minutes after eating, but he could not wait five minutes and would say, 'Let's go play.'"[12]

Neither Jong-chul nor Jong-un were ever enrolled in elementary schools or junior-high schools in the North. They were instead tutored by specially selected teachers at Kim Jong-il's Pyongyang residence. They loved Japanese comics and movies, and occasionally Fujimoto would teach them some Japanese. According to him, while Jong-chul had a gentle character and showed interest in music in general and popular guitar in particular, Jong-un tended to be competitive. Jong-un was assigned top-notch instructors to teach him marksmanship and how to drive a car. Jang Sung-taek was solely responsible for the boys' home-schooling. Since they lacked classmates, whenever they wanted companions to play with, students their age were called in. Fujimoto recalled that Jong-un showed a disposition to be a leader. He elaborated that "Jong-un had always been at the center of groups and he truly received Kim Jong-il's DNA."[13] With Jong-chul and Jong-un being raised in such "royal" and completely secluded environments, we can wonder how well Kim Il-sung knew these two grandsons; yet, a former KWP cadre once recalled the story, well known to every senior secretary, of the time Kim Il-sung praised Jong-chul by saying "If Jong-il is a genius, Jong-chul is a super genius."[14]

In the 1990s, Kim Jong-il sent his two sons to Berne, Switzerland. First, Jong-chul, under the pseudonym Pak Chol, studied at the International School of Berne from September 1993 to August 1998. According to the school's principal, Jong-chul was "an ordinary boy with a good sense of humor who liked sports and worked hard." He continued, "By the time he left school, Jong-chul could speak English fluently. It must have been difficult for him to catch up with his classwork because lessons were given in English, but Jong-chul always completed his assignments."[15] Surprisingly, Jong-chul kept company with students from the United States, North Korea's sworn

11 Ibid., 68.

12 Lee Young-jong and Jeong Yong-soo, "Kim's Sushi Chef Shares Memories of Jong-un," *Korea JoongAng Daily*, October 26, 2010, 3.

13 Ibid.

14 Cheong Seong-chang, "Kim Jong-il's Illness and Prospects for Post-Kim Leadership," *East Asian Review* 20, no. 4 (Winter 2008): 22.

15 Ibid.

enemy, as well as with students from South Korea, at a time when hostility prevailed in inter-Korean relations. Friends recall that Jong-chul liked playing basketball and admired Dennis Rodman, the NBA player. Whenever he played basketball, he wore a Chicago Bulls shirt with Rodman's uniform number on the back. His American friends added that "Jong-chul is not the type of guy who would do something to harm others. He is a nice guy who could never be a villain."[16] Later, Jong-chul would idolize Hollywood action star Jean-Claude Van Damme's physique. After returning to the North, Jong-chul was enrolled in a special class at Kim Il-sung Comprehensive Military University from 2001 to 2006.

Kim Jong-un followed his elder brother's steps. In 1996, under the alias Pak Un, he was also admitted to the International School of Berne. As a classmate recounted, "His English was bad at first. He had a strong accent and was given extra lessons. He also studied German. His English got better but not his German. He was good in math."[17] As Jong-un was unable to earn even the equivalent of a General Certificate of Secondary Education, despite an extravagant outlay of money, Kim Jong-il allowed him to study at a public school, Liebefeld School, beginning August 1998. Wearing Nike trainers, a Chicago Bulls sweatshirt, and jeans, he was introduced to class 6A as a son of a North Korean diplomat. His classmate Joao Micaelo, son of a Portuguese diplomat, recalled, "We weren't the dimmest kids in class but neither were we the cleverest. We were always in the second tier. He tried hard to express himself but he was not very good at German and became flustered when asked to give the answers to a problem. The teachers would see him struggling ashamedly and then move on. They left him in peace." Micaelo continued, "He left without getting any exam results at all. He was much more interested in football and basketball than lessons. He was a big fan of Michael Jordan, an NBA player." Joao spoke about Kim Jong-un's private life: "He didn't live at the embassy but in a flat in a nice residential area near the school. He had a private chef who cooked whatever he wanted. He was surrounded by the best gadgets that the rest of us kids couldn't afford—TVs, video recorder, a Sony PlayStation."[18] Other students recalled that he was skilled in skiing and snowboarding. His former homeroom teacher added that he was "quiet, and appeared as if he were hidden in a veil of mystery."[19] In January 2001 Kim Jong-un returned to the North.

16 Ibid., 18–21.
17 "Features: Dim Jong-un," *The Sun* (London), November 24, 2010, 24–26.
18 Ibid.
19 Quoted in Cheong Seong-chang, "Kim Jong-un's Early Life and Personality," *Vantage Point*, July 2009, 11.

The picture above of a teenaged Kim Jong-un gives the superficial impression of a boy interested in sports and luxury living. However, there is some evidence that he was maturing and thinking about more serious subjects. During an August 2000 summer vacation spent in North Korea, Kim Jong-un had hours-long talks with Fujimoto, during which he raised a number of serious questions on his country's situation. For example, he asked Fujimoto, "Why are goods so insufficient and rare in the DPRK's department stores and ordinary stores in contrast to those in Western countries?" He observed, "North Korea lacks natural resources, except uranium; it also suffers from a lack of electricity. Even in the our family villas, we sometimes experience power failures." Lamenting the underdevelopment of industrial technologies in the North, he asked Fujimoto, "Under such conditions, how are our people managing their lives?" Jong-un also mentioned the "economic success" of the People's Republic of China. He said, "I heard from my father that China is doing very well in many fields, including industry, commerce, hotels, and agriculture. In particular, I praise China's success in agriculture. While feeding its own 1.3 billion people, China is also exporting grains to foreign countries." He concluded, "After exhaustively examining our problems and China's methods, the DPRK should emulate China as its model." Kim Jong-un also revealed that he had secretly visited Japan with his mother: "Japan was defeated in the Second World War by the United States. But they have succeeded in rehabilitating their country and are living in material prosperity. What should the DPRK do?" Fujimoto felt that he found the new and matured Kim Jong-un completely changed from before. But he was still strong-willed and overbearing.[20]

Between 2002 and December 2006, as his elder brother had done, Kim Jong-un studied in a special class at the Kim Il-sung Comprehensive Military University. North Korean publications claimed that he graduated summa cum laude from the three-year course for artillery commanders and its two-year graduate course. He was said to have submitted the dissertation, "A Simulation for the Improvement of Accuracy in the Operational Map by the Global Positioning System (GPS)," in fulfillment of the final requirement for the graduation. Major General Kim Young-chul allegedly helped him with the dissertation. More important to Kim Jong-un's career was that at this school he was able to make friends with the future elites of the North Korean military.[21]

20 O, "An Interview," 78–79.

21 Cheong Seong-chang, "Kim Jong-un, Nukuinka?" [Who is Kim Jong-un?], *Wolgan JoongAng* 420 (November 2010): 38.

Kim Jong-il's Vacillation between Kim Jong-chul and Kim Jong-un

With three sons—the eldest Kim Jong-nam, whose mother was Song Hye-rim, and Kim Jong-chul and Kim Jong-un, children of Ko Young-hee—why then did Kim Jong-il choose the third son as successor? It may be illuminating to review the process by which Kim Jong-il himself became Kim Il-sung's successor and the theories he developed for that purpose. Kim Jong-il did not simply smoothly transition into becoming Kim Il-sung's successor. His preparation for that role went through four stages even before the death of Kim Il-sung.

The Stages of Kim Jong-il's Own Path to Successor

The first (late 1960s–1974) was a preparatory stage to become the de facto successor. In this period, he led a nationwide mass movement, the Three Revolution Team Movement, and succeeded first in entering the KWPCC Secretariat (1973) and then its Politburo (1974). The second stage was one in which he consolidated his status as the de facto successor and became the official successor (1974–1980). At the sixth KWP congress (October 10–14, 1980), Kim Jong-il succeeded in entering both the Politburo's Standing Committee and the KWPCC's Military Commission. Thus he became the only one—apart from Kim Il-sung—holding concurrent membership of three cardinal organizations of the KWPCC, i.e., the Secretariat, the Politburo Standing Committee, and the Military Commission. In the third stage (1980–1990) he consolidated his status as the official successor. In 1983 Kim Jong-il became the second ranking member of the Secretariat. In 1984 he became the second ranking member of both the Politburo's Standing Committee and the Military Commission. In addition, in 1984, the People's Armed Forces Ministry (PAFM) and the Public Security Ministry were taken out of the Administration Council, i.e., Cabinet, and were placed under his direct control. The fourth stage (1990–1994) was Kim Jong-il's full-scale assumption of power. In this period, he finally took control of the military by becoming vice-chairman of the NDC (1990), supreme commander of the KPA (1991), marshal of the DPRK (1992), and chairman of the NDC (1993).

Kim Jong-il's elevation from first stage to fourth showed two characteristics. First, he took a prolonged and step-by-step approach, one that in all consumed about twenty-five years. Second, he first captured the party leadership, then control of public security organs, and finally the military leadership. At every stage except the last he struggled hard to win his own aims, although his father's assistance was decisive, particularly in the first two stages. He overcame sibling rivalry within his family, internal opposition from Kim Il-sung's old guerrilla comrades, and the Chinese criticism of a hereditary succession.

Creating a Theoretical Basis for Inherited Succession

Apart from going through these four steps to secure his place, Kim Jong-il went a step further, devising and disseminating theories that rationalized his assumption as successor. First, suggesting that a socialist revolution in the North should continue without interruption, he stressed that only the correct choice of a successor would guarantee the correct continuation, i.e., the correct succession of the revolutionary spirit and tradition over generations. Because of Stalin's failure in correctly choosing a successor, he argued, Khrushchev ended up "degenerating" socialism and "ruining" the Soviet Union. He also pointed out the failed coup d'état by Lin Biao, who had been designated as successor by Mao Zedong. Since Mao did not correctly choose his successor, he argued, the continuation of the socialist revolution in China was, for the time being, in jeopardy.[22]

If the correct choice of a successor was so critical, then on what basis should the North make the choice? Kim Jong-il proposed the primacy of "purity in blood," a pedigree that originated in those who participated in the anti-Japanese independence movement during Korea's colonial period. Kim Il-sung and first wife Kim Jong-suk fought against the Japanese while based at the Sino-Korean border at Mount Baekdu, Korea's highest mountain. Thus, the theory goes, Kim Il-sung's successor should be someone who has inherited his "purity of blood imbued with the holy spirit of Mount Baekdu." Based on this sort of logic, Kim Jong-il—as early as March 1967—helped Kim Il-sung devise "ten principles for establishing the KWP's monolithic ideology system based on Kim Il-sung's thoughts," a system under which any thoughts apart from the thoughts of Kim Il-sung were to be eradicated. Kim Jong-il went even further, pushing for the demotion of Kim Il-sung's then-wife Kim Song-ae's political status. She had no connection with the anti-Japanese guerilla movement ,while Kim Il-sung's deceased first wife, Kim Jong-suk, was sanctified for her participation in it. In order to back up this demotion, Kim Jong-il—with leading military leaders who held anti-Japanese guerrilla qualifications—investigated the "wrongdoings" committed by Kim Sung-kap, Kim Song-ae's brother and chief secretary of

---

22 Summarized in Paik Hak-soon, *Pukhan Kwonryokui Yoksa: Sasang, Chongche-song, Yoksa* [The history of power in North Korea: ideas, identities, and structures] (Seoul: Hanul Academy, 2011), 653–54.

the KWP Pyongyang City Chapter; he reported to Kim Il-sung that Kim Sung-kap's statements and activities, carried out under the aegis of Kim Song-ae's influence, violated the "ten principles."[23]

About this time, Kim Kyong-hui—Kim Jong-il's sister and the sole daughter from Kim Il-sung and Kim Jong-suk's union—likewise took part in attacking Kim Song-ae by openly humiliating her. After his defection to Seoul in the early 1980s, a former KWP cadre close to Kim Jong-il recounted, "At the banquet celebrating Kim Il-sung's sixtieth birthday in 1972, Kyong-hui wept aloud before Kim Il-sung, Kim Song-ae, and Kim Il-sung's top-level lieutenants, complaining that the sacred position of the first lady was occupied by an woman who had no career in the anti-Japanese guerrilla movement. . . . [Upon hearing this] many of the participants wailed, even cried out Kim Jong-suk's name."[24] Kim Il-sung later purged Kim Sung-kap, imprisoned his followers, and forced his wife to retire from all official activities. It was not until June 17, 1994, when Kim Song-ae would reappear in a public event, when Kim Il-sung accompanied her during his Pyongyang reception of former U.S. president Jimmy Carter and his wife when Carter held talks with Kim Il-sung to diffuse nuclear tensions on the Korean Peninsula. Just three weeks later, Kim Il-sung died at the age of 82; Kim Song-ae's name appeared 104th on the state funeral service committee's list, and her sons were entirely omitted. While her name resurfaced for Kim Il-sung's third memorial service in 1997, she never again appeared in the North Korean media.

As he eradicated the influence of Kim Song-ae, Kim Jong-il also invented the "side-branch" concept for the Kim Il-sung family tree. This theory posits that only Kim Il-sung and Kim Jong-suk's offspring inherited Kim Il-sung's "pure blood imbued with the holy spirit of Mount Baekdu." All other members of the Kim Il-sung family were mere "side-branches" of the family tree.[25] Kim Yong-ju, the only living biological brother of Kim Il-sung, was no exception. As the powerful director of the KWP Organization and Guidance Department (KWPOGD) as well as a member both in the KWP Politburo and Secretariat, he was once regarded as Kim Il-sung's successor. However, in 1974 Kim Jong-il succeeded in demoting his uncle to the level of deputy prime minister, without membership in the Politburo or Secretariat. Not long after, Kim Yong-ju was sent to a local rehabilitation center on the pretext of "curing his failing health."[26] Just a year before the

23 Yi, *Fourteen Years*, 72–74.

24 Chung, *Kim Jong-il*, 80–81.

25 Yi, *Fourteen Years*, 73.

26 Hwang Jang yop, *Naui Hoekorok: Nanun Yoksaui Chinrirul PoAta* [My memoirs: I saw the truth in history] (Seoul: Hanul Publishing Co., 1999), 173.

death of Kim Il-sung, he was allowed to hold KWP Politburo membership and the position of vice-chairman of the DPRK. In 1999, at the age of 77, he was transferred to the position of honorary vice-chairman of the Supreme People's Assembly (SPA) Presidium.

Kim Jong-il's half-brothers and half-sister were also treated as "side-branches." After becoming the official successor at the sixth KWP congress, Kim Jong-il forced them to live silently in foreign countries. To date Kim Pyong-il has roamed abroad as North Korea's military attaché at its embassy in Yugoslavia, and as ambassador to Hungary, Bulgaria, Finland, and finally Poland. Kim Kyong-jin has lived as a housewife with a North Korean diplomat first assigned to Czechoslovakia and then to Austria. Kim Young-il, counselor at the DPRK Representative Mission in Berlin, died in a German hospital in 2000.

In the 1980s and 1990s, North Korean ideologues intensified their creation of succession theories. These theories were replete with abstract terminologies that sound ridiculous to those from Western democracies.[27] Still, two of these theories merit comment. The first is the theory that successors should be chosen not from the present leader's peers (Kim Il-sung's generation), but instead from the coming generation (Kim Jong-il's). There was, of course, only one person in that generation who also inherited the "purity of blood imbued with the holy spirit of Mount Baekdu": Kim Jong-il. The second theory stated that the successor should be chosen within the party by the party, thereby reconfirming the principle of the party's primacy over the military.

Kim Jong-il's Other Strategies to Hold Power

While using those theories to legitimize his succession—in addition to conventional totalitarian dictatorship methods of control such as the personality cult, systematic surveillance, informing and denunciation, and torture—Kim Jong-il resorted to at least three other strategies. First, he constantly found ways to publicize the veneration of Kim Il-sung. To gratify Kim Il-sung's ego, he built many monuments commemorating his father's achievements in the independence movement and in nation-building. However, at the same time Kim Jong-il gradually weakened Kim Il-sung's real power. Consequently, from 1984 the North Korean regime became the "joint regime of Kim Il-sung and Kim Jong-il." In the ten years before the death of Kim Il-sung, the formula was subtly altered as the DPRK became

---

27 Summarized from the North Korean publications in Paik, *History of Power in North Korea*, 656–57.

the "joint regime of Kim Jong-il and Kim Il-sung," with Kim Il-sung reigning and Kim Jong-il ruling or governing.[28]

A second strategy Kim Jong-il used was to consistently align himself with select military and public security leaders favorable to his succession. With their support, he occasionally purged party and military cadres who were suspected of being disloyal to him. Among those were many former anti-Japanese guerrilla fighters and even Kim Il-sung's own lieutenants, who had argued that a father-to-son succession was against communist principles. Kim Jong-il showed great ruthlessness and cruelty in these purges. Most of the purged were sent to concentration camps along with their families—the so-called living hells; others faced summary execution before firing squads. Cruelty was perhaps Kim Jong-il's most distinctive leadership attribute. According to Hwang Jang-yop, the former KWPCC secretary in charge of international affairs and SPA chairman who defected to Seoul in 1997, Kim Il-sung once said that "Jong-il's strong point is his brutality, while Yong-ju's weak point is his lack of brutality." Hwang added, "Kim Jong-il would tell his lieutenants, as well as party and military leaders, that were any of them to lose his confidence, he or she would become a mere lump of meat."[29] Defected chef Fujimoto also attested to many examples of his cruelty. For example, on the early morning of December 30, 1995, Kim Jong-il asked seven generals who gathered before him, "Did you shoot them?" The generals were said to have replied that "they" had been shot yesterday. Fujimoto recollected that the number of those shot at this mass execution was between twenty-four and twenty-five. While brutally crushing opposition, Kim Jong-il rewarded loyal retainers and those in strategic posts with expensive cars, television sets, refrigerators, liquor, watches, clothes, and necessities of life that were rare in the North.[30]

Third, Kim Jong-il was an effective manipulator of symbols. As a number of close observers noted, he was skilled at arts in general and at drama, movies, and music in particular.[31] He applied these talents to symbol manipulation. For example, in the preparatory stage for the de facto succession, he made the official media call him not by his name but by the euphemism "party center," lending him an air of mystery. Another example—some

28 Hwang, *My Memoirs*, 244–47.

29 Ibid., 284.

30 Fujimoto Kenji, *Kim Jong-il no Ryorinin* (Tokyo: Fuso Publishing Inc., 2003), translated by Sin Hyun-ho as *Kim Jong-ilui Yorisa* [Kim Jong-il's chef] (Seoul: Wolgan-chosunsa, 2003), 154–55. See also Fujimoto, *Why Was Kim Jong-un Chosen?*, 204.

31 For example, see Ch'oe Un-hee and Sin Sang-ok, *Kim Jong-il Wangkuk* [The Kim Jong-il kingdom] (Seoul: Dong-A Ilbo Company, 1988), vol. 2, 125.

North Korea specialists in Seoul argue that he even changed his birth year from 1941 to 1942 to make it precisely thirty years after his father's. Doing so allowed father and son to simultaneously celebrate five- and ten-year birthday anniversaries together, further cementing Kim Jong-il's image with Kim Il-sung's.[32] Kim Jong-il's birthdate, February 16, was also raised to special significance. Cars whose license plate numbers began with 216 were reserved to those vehicles allocated to a select number of his loyal retainers. Likewise, a school or military unit whose name began with 216 was highly valued by North Koreans.

Beginning on Kim Jong-il's fortieth birthday on February 16, 1982, North Korean publications began to spread a new legend that Kim had been born in one of the secret guerrilla camps at Mount Baekdu, "the sacred mountain of the Korean nation where the first ancestor of the whole Korean nation founded the original Korean state in ancient times."[33] In addition, Kim invented a new catchphrase, "Three Great Generals of Mount Baekdu" (i.e., Kim Il-sung, Kim Jong-suk, and Kim Jong-il), and ordered the nation to pay homage to this "trinity." At the same time, North Korean publications began calling him the "lodestar guiding the Korean nation to its bright future."[34]

Applying His Strategies to His Own Succession

Kim Jong-il applied his theories and methods in the selection and grooming of his own successor. To begin with, his successor should be only be chosen from his sons, for only as sons of Kim Jong-il did they inherit the "pure blood of Kim Il-sung imbued with the holy spirit of Mount Baekdu"; similarly, the successor needed to belong to the generation following that of the present leader, Kim Jong-il. His first son, Kim Jong-nam, could be considered the first possible candidate for successor. But he was an illegitimate child, and his mother, Song Hye-rim, already had a daughter from her first marriage. Worse, Kim Jong-nam's mother belonged to a family who had come to the North from the South, and who had wealthy and intellectual backgrounds—triple jeopardy in the North. Moreover, his maternal family members—Song Hye-rang, Ri Il-nam, and Ri Nam-ok—had defected to the West.

32 Chin Sung-kae, *Kim Jong-il* (Seoul: Tonghwayunkuso, 1990), 33.
33 Ibid.
34 A broadcast by Chosun JungAng T'ongsin ([North] Korean Central News Agency) on May 8, 1982, monitored by Reuters in Tokyo, May 9, 1982, and subsequently printed in *Dong-A Ilbo*, May 10, 1982, 2.

Admittedly, much of the criticism of Kim Jong-nam's worthiness was applicable to Kim Jong-il's other sons. Second and third sons Kim Jong-chul and Kim Jong-un were also illegitimate children; their mother, Ko Young-hee, was a "Japo," an offensive term applied to those who had returned to the North from Japan in the 1950s and the 1960s; and their mother's sister defected to the United States with her husband and sons. However, there are considerable differences between Kim Jong-nam and Kim Jong-il's other two sons. First, Ko Young-hee had no previous record of marriage. More important is that Kim Jong-il turned away from Song Hye-rim to Ko Young-hee and maintained their de facto marriage for more than twenty-eight years, until her death. Recall, too, that Ko Young-hee was buried in Pyongyang, while Song Hye-rim was buried in Moscow.

In the choice between Kim Jong-chul and Kim Jong-un, it could be argued that in some respects Kim Jong-il seemed to have blessed the latter as successor from childhood. In 2003 Fujimoto had already predicted that not Kim Jong-chul but Kim Jong-un would become the successor. Fujimoto recalled that as a child Kim Jong-chul never got angry and had little ambition. Kim Jong-il on more than one occasion noted that "Jong-chul cannot be the successor, since he is effeminate."[35] Of the sons, Kim Jong-chul physically favors his mother, while Kim Jong-un more resembles his father. From childhood, Kim Jong-un showed leadership and a strong desire to win—in short, while Kim Jong-un evinced a ruthlessness that Kim Il-sung and Kim Jong-il regarded as an important leadership attribute, Kim Jong-chul lacked that very quality.

Fujimoto recalled a celebratory banquet for Kim Jong-un's ninth birthday held on January 8, 1992, at a villa in Wonsan. At Kim Jong-il's instructions, the band began playing a new song, "Footsteps." Its lyrics, in essence, are:

Following our General Kim's footsteps,
Spreading the spirit of February,
We, the people, march forward to a bright future.[36]

"The spirit of February" was a reference to Kim Jong-il, who was born in February. Thus, "our General Kim" was the person who would lead the country in the future, spreading the spirit of Kim Jong-il. In light of the fact that the song was dedicated to Kim Jong-un, Fujimoto immediately sensed it signaled Kim Jong-il's tacit designation of Kim Jong-un as the successor.

35 Fujimoto, *Kim Jong-il's Chef*, 130.
36 Quoted in Fujimoto, *Why Was Kim Jong-un Chosen?* 125–26.

Initial Movements Toward Finding a Successor

Although these events suggest that for some time Kim Jong-il had already decided upon Jong-un as his successor, for a number of years the successor was unnamed and there was no grooming process in place. In hindsight, it may be in 2002 that Kim Jong-il decided to start the campaign to prepare the succession; that was the year of his sixtieth birthday, or *hwankap*, a period that is regarded in Korea as a turning point in one's life. Moreover, three months after his *hwankap*, his de facto wife and Kim Jong-nam's mother (Song Hye-rim) died. With her death, Kim Jong-il may have decided to omit her son from the line of succession. Ko Young-hee had pushed Kim Jong-il to designate their first son, Kim Jong-chul, as successor. Ko, who had been treated for a breast infection in 1993 and for paralysis in her right hand in 2000, might have anticipated her premature death and wanted to see her eldest son designated as successor as early as possible. But in actuality, Kim Jong-il had started the campaign to prepare for succession in August 2002 without even mentioning Jong-chul's name. It was then that the KPA published a sixteen-page pamphlet, *Chonkyonghanun Omonimun Kyongaehanun Ch'ungjikhan ch'ungsinjungui Chungsinisida* (Our respected mother who is loyal to our beloved supreme commander is the loyalist among the loyalists). Although the pamphlet did not reveal the mother's name, most cadres of the KWP and the KPA could identify her with Ko Yong-hee. It is notable that she was elevated to the status of Kim Jong-suk, Kim Jong-il's natural mother, who had herself been sanctified as one of "Three Great Generals of Mount Baekdu."[37]

The Rise, Fall, and Rise of Jang Sung-taek

The North Korean succession issue inevitably triggered a series of debates in South Korea. In early July 2003, speaking at a public seminar held in Seoul, the high-ranking defector Hwang Jang-yop said, "In the event the Kim Jong-il regime collapses, there are many people who can succeed him. At this point, Jang Sung-taek is the most likely to succeed. For, as Kim Kyong-hui's husband and first vice-director of the KWPOGD, he has placed his supporters everywhere."[38] Not long after, an influential daily and monthly in Seoul both reported that the Bush administration was preparing

37 Cheong Seong-chang, "Kim Jong-il Sidae Pukhanui Hukaemunjae" [North Korea's succession issue in the times of Kim Jong-il], *Korean Political Science Review* 39, no. 2 (Summer 2005): 350–53.

38 Pak Min-hyok, "Hwang Jang-yop kukhoejungon" [Hwang Jang-yop's testimony at the National Assembly], *Dong-A Ilbo*, July 5, 2003, A4.

a contingency plan to form an interim government led by Jang, in case of serious turmoil and drastic change in the North.[39] After these reports, which attracted much attention in the foreign media, Jang disappeared from all public events in the North. A North Korea watcher in Seoul observed, "Ko Young-hee, who wanted to promote Jong-chul as her husband's successor, must have taken Hwang's statements and those reports seriously. Subsequently, Jang was forced to stop all public activities starting in July 2003 and his official duties were suspended in 2004. Apparently, Ko and her aides. . . incapacitated Jang."[40]

Jang underwent intensive interrogation by a team led by Ri Je-gang (Ri Che-kang) (first vice-director for organizational life of central party staff members) and Ri Yong-chul (first vice-director for military affairs), both key cadres of the powerful KWPOGD. As top lieutenants loyal to Kim Jong-il and Ko Young-hee, and supporters of the succession to Kim Jong-chul, they played a critical role in relieving Jang from his duties. They also dismissed or demoted Jang's close allies in the KWP and the KPA. Among those were Jang's elder brother, Vice-Marshal Jang Song-wu, commander of the KPA Third Corps, a post responsible for the defense of Pyongyang, and Choe Ryong-su, People's Security Minister. With Jang's disappearance in July 2003, Kim Jong-chul became vice-director of the KWPOGD, a powerful organization with authority over human resource management and thus control over elites in the party, the military, and the government. Five months later, at the joint meeting among cadres working at the KWPCC and DPRKNDC, Kim Jong-il stressed the necessity of grooming Kim Jong-chul as his successor.[41]

Then came the incident of the mysterious train explosion. On April 22, 2004, two trains loaded with chemicals exploded at Ryongchon Station on the Sino-North Korean border, destroying many nearby buildings. The North Korean government announced that 154 people had died and 1,300 more were injured. Since the incident occurred a few hours after Kim Jong-il's train had passed through, returning from his trip to China, Western media speculated that the incident might have been an assassination attempt by his opponents. Some even alleged that certain leaders familiar with Chinese reform policies agreed to prevent a hereditary succession by

39 Hwang Il-do, "Mikukui Puklidersip Change Scenario" [America's scenario for the collapse of the Kim Jong-il regime], *SindongA* 528 (September 2003): 212–19.

40 Cheong, "Kim Jong-il's Illness," 23–30.

41 Cheong Seong-chang, "Pukhan Kim Jong-un Hukyejongkwanui Kongsikchulpom" [The official inauguration of the Kim Jong-un succession regime in North Korea], *Wolgan Chosun* 368 (November 2010): 89–90.

assassinating the dictator. They were said to have been executed within a few days after the incident.[42]

It was not until late January 2006 when Jang Sung-taek reappeared in public. He was among a group of officials who accompanied Kim Jong-il at a lunar new year ceremony. Jang was designated the first vice-director of the KWP department for workers organizations and construction of the capital. Jang's reappearance coincided with Kim Jong-il's return from China. On January 17, 2006, Kim held talks in Beijing with Chinese president Hu Jintao, who on the one hand endorsed Kim's leadership, yet also advised Kim to adopt reform policies. Kim reportedly responded that the North would pay more attention to business and trade. Accordingly, some South Korean observers argued that Kim needed someone like Jang to support his new policy, one that would emulate China's economic policy. Others argued that Jang was necessary as the only person experienced and able to manage another hereditary power transition.[43] Kim Jong-il might have allowed Jang to appear in public once again with the August 2004 death of Ko Young-hee, who had kept him under strict guard. Following the reappearance, however, Jang Sung-taek experienced a series of misfortunes in his personal life. His elder brother, Jang Song-kil, political commissar of a KPA corps with the rank of lieutenant general, died in July 2006; his only child and daughter Jang Kum-song, who was studying in Paris and disobeyed a summons to return to the North, died after taking an overdose of sleeping pills in August 2006; and Jang himself had a September 2006 car accident in Pyongyang in broad daylight. Given the relative paucity of cars on Pyongyang streets, some interpreted the accident as an assassination attempt.[44]

While allowing Jang to return to the political stage, Kim Jong-il forbade talking about prospective successors, saying, "Our enemies are backbiting us by speculating about our country's future leadership and a father-to-son succession. I ask party and military leaders to strictly crack down on any public discussion."[45] His remarks might have reflected dissatisfaction with Kim Jong-chul's performance at the KWPOGD—in early 2006, Chinese intelligence sources provided information to South Korean intelligence officials that showed Kim Jong-chul had failed to prove his ability

42 Hwang Il-do, "Ryongchun Pokpal" [The Ryongchun explosion], *SindongA* 541 (October 2004): 120–27.

43 Lee Young-jong, "North Korea Seen as Ready to Focus on Business," *JoongAng Daily*, February 10, 2006, 1.

44 Cheong, "Kim Jong-il's Illness," 30.

45 "North seen as wary over next dear leader," *JoongAng Daily*, December 12, 2005, A2.

as a leader. His exposure on Japanese Fuji TV in early June 2006 worsened his image among the North Korean leadership: accompanied by a young woman, he attended an Eric Clapton concert in Frankfurt. Moreover, when asked whether he came from North Korea, he answered the reporters that he "came from Hong Kong."[46] By North Korean standards, such a statement might be regarded as a betrayal of the nation.

The Final Selection of Jong-un

Kim Jong-il began to groom Jong-un as his successor among the ruling circle in December 2006. One important document that supports this is *Chonkyonghanun Kim Jong-un Changkun Dongjiui Widaesong Kyoyang Charyo* (The material in teaching the greatness of respected comrade general Kim Jong-un), which was distributed by the KPA to every military unit during May and June, 2009. The pamphlet noted Kim Jong-un's December 24, 2006, graduation from Kim Il-sung Comprehensive Military University and highlighted his pledge at the graduation ceremony to be successful, based on Juche, in revolutionary achievements. On that graduation day, Kim Jong-il praised Kim Jong-un's graduation dissertation and commented that it reflected "the great theories of military strategy" developed by Kim Il-sung and Kim Jong-il.

About ten months after Kim Jong-un's graduation, North Korean authorities designated the house in which he had been born in Ch'angsung County, North Pyongan, as a historical site. Around the same time (October 2007), Kim Jong-il promoted Jang Sung-taek to director of the KWP administration department and allowed him to take over the responsibilities he had before his duties were suspended in 2004. Upon Jang's appointment as its head, the administration department became responsible for providing administrative guidance to the State Security Safeguard Ministry (SSSM, in charge of secret and political police), People's Security Ministry (in charge of regular police), the Central Prosecutors' Office, and the Central Court.[47]

Then there was a significant development that hastened the succession process—in August 2008 Kim Jong-il had a stroke and underwent an operation. His unusual absence from the September 2008 events celebrating the sixtieth anniversary of the founding of the DPRK fanned suspicion about his health. This turn of events, and the possibility of his sudden death or incapacitation, perhaps prompted Kim Jong-il to accelerate the original plan

46 Ch'on Kwang-am, "Puk Kim Jong-chul" [North Korea's Kim Jong-chul], *Dong-A Ilbo*, June 16, 2006, A2.

47 Cheong, "The Official Inauguration," 90–91.

to officially make Kim Jong-un his successor. As the first step in this process, on January 8, 2009 (Jong-un's twenty-sixth birthday), Kim Jong-il officially notified the KWPOGD and the KPA General Political Bureau (GPB) of his decision that Kim Jong-un would be his successor. As a symbol of this first step, the reconstruction of the house where Kim Jong-un was born as an "historical site" was simultaneously completed with this notification. Soon a special task force consisting of top experts in the fields of politics, economics, culture, and military affairs, most in their forties and fifties, was formed to assist the grooming of the successor-designated.[48]

The most significant institutional measure taken in the North after the notification took place on April 9, 2009, when the DPRK constitution was revised at the first session of the 12th SPA. Last revised in 1998, the new constitution put primary emphasis on the importance of the armed forces in North Korea. To elaborate, the newly revised constitution made it the obligation of the DPRK's armed forces to safeguard the "core of the revolution," i.e., Kim Jong-il and Kim Jong-un, by accomplishing "the policy of military-first revolution" suggested by Kim Jong-il back in January 1, 1995. The new constitution also extensively strengthened the rights of the DPRKNDC chairmanship. Declaring that DPRKNDC chairman is "the highest leader of the DPRK" and "the highest commander of the DPRK armed forces," the new constitution granted the chair more authority in "leading the country as a whole." On the same day, the SPA proclaimed Kim Jong-il as chairman of the NDC. Next, the SPA expanded the NDC membership from four to eight, and elected Jang Sung-taek its new member. The implication of these changes was that Kim Jong-il could resort to the armed forces and the NDC to prevent and suppress any organized resistance to the consolidation of the succession regime, and that Jang would play a crucial role in the whole process of consolidation.

After becoming the de facto successor, Kim Jong-un moved quickly to tighten his grip over both the KWP and the KPA, assisted by Jang Sung-taek, director of the KWP administration department and NDC member, and particularly on the military side by Kim Jong-gak (Kim Chŏng-kak), first vice-director of the powerful KPAGPB, and Ri Yong-ho (Ri Yŏngho), KPA chief of staff. In March, Kim Jong-il appointed Kim Jong-un as minister of the SSSM, an appointment with important political significance. Kim Jong-il himself started his career as the KWPCC secretary for organizational affairs and ideology before assuming full-scale power of the KWP. In contrast, Kim Jong-il had Kim Jong-un start his career by assuming power of the SSSM,

---

48 Ibid., 92–93.

the DPRK's core instrument for intelligence, coercion, and terror. To assist him, Kim Jong-il appointed U Tong-chuk (b. 1942), who had grown up in this apparatus, as the SSSM's first vice-director.[49] The "150-day battle" that began in April and the subsequent "100-day battle," mass movements that both aimed at mobilizing all available North Korean human resources to increase productivity, as well as the DPRK's second nuclear test on May 25, might have been aimed at tightening national unity through the creation of national tension. Symbol manipulation followed. Notifying its foreign embassies that Kim Jong-un was to be the successor, the regime began to popularize the song "Footsteps" and to disseminate leaflets and posters in an effort to sanctify Kim Jong-un.

From early 2010 Kim Jong-un began expanding his activities in general and in particular his creation of economic policy. The regime's joint party, government, and military New Year's editorial of 2010 was commonly seen to have paid primary attention to the improvement of the peoples' economic conditions. North Korea watchers in Seoul regarded the message as Kim Jong-un's idea. During Kim Jong-il's visit to China in early May (accompanied by Jang Sung-taek), some Western media reported that Kim Jong-un was acting as leader in place of Kim Jong-il. The sinking of the South Korean corvette *Cheonan* by a North Korean torpedo in March and the bombardment of South Korea's Yeonpyeong Island by North Korean artillery in November were also seen in the South as the North's show of strength under Kim Jong-un's direction. In late August, Kim Jong-un accompanied Kim Jong-il on his unexpected visit to China and his talks there with Chinese president Hu Jintao.

As Kim Jong-un played major roles in initiating and executing important national tasks, Jang Sung-taek's role also rapidly expanded. On June 7, 2010, the third session of the 12th SPA elected him vice-chairman of the NDC, "at the recommendation of" Kim Jong-il. On the contrary, Ri Yong-chul and Ri Je-gang, the two core first vice-directors of the KWPOGD who had investigated the "wrongdoings" of Jang Sung-taek in 2003 and contributed to his being relieved of responsibilities in 2004, died in April and June, respectively. The official announcement that Ri Je-gang died in a car accident on a Pyongyang street three days before Jang's elevation to NDC vice-chairman in particular stirred up speculation in the West that he might have been assassinated. In addition to Jang, Choe Ryong-hae, (b. 1950, first son of late Choe Hyon, a close partisan comrade of Kim Il-sung) helped

---

49 At the third KWP Delegates' Conference, he was elected candidate member of the politburo and member of the KWPCMC with the rank of four-star general.

Jong-un develop his relations with social organizations, ones that Choe had led for years. At the third KWP Representatives Conference, Choe secured concurrent membership in the Politburo, Secretariat, and central military committees, with the rank of four-star general.

The Death of Kim Jong-il and the Rise of Kim Jong-un

In a special broadcast at noon on December 19, 2011, the North's Korean Central Television announced that Kim Jong-il had died of heart failure while aboard a train. A joint statement announcing Kim's death was made by the KWPCC, the KWPCMC, the DPRKNDC, the SPA Presidium, and the cabinet. The North said the national mourning period would take place December 19–29. During the eleven-day national funeral period, a newly formed hierarchical order emerged among North Korean power elites. First and foremost, Kim Jong-un was clearly identified as the top leader. At the funeral held in Pyongyang's Kim Il-sung Plaza on December 28, Kim Yong-nam, the titular head of state as chairman of the Presidium, announced that Kim Jong-un was supreme leader of the party, military, and people.

The state funeral additionally provided early glimpses of who would be serving as Kim Jong-un's guardians. As noted by journalist Choe Sang-Hun:

> Leading the funeral alongside and behind Mr. Kim was a familiar mix of military generals and party secretaries. The group included elderly stalwarts from the days of Kim Jong-il and his father, the North's founding president, Kim Il-sung. But younger officials who expanded their influence while playing crucial roles in grooming the son as Kim Jong-il's successor were also represented. [50]

On the right side of the hearse were KWP secretaries Jang Sung-taek, Kim Ki-nam, and Choe Tae-pok; on the left side, KPA generals Ri Yong-ho, Kim Yong-chun, Kim Jong-gak, and U Tong-chuk. The funeral itself gave clues to the important question of who was rising and who was fading as a new leadership emerged in the world's most secretive regime. There was little change in the ruling structure formed in late September 2010—in other words, the ruling structure formed by Kim Jong-il, who had perhaps anticipated his impending death and had prepared for his successor, remained as before.

---

50 Choe Sang-Hun, "At Kim Jong-il's Funeral, Pyongyang Elite Offer Hints at Heir's Inner Circle," *International Herald Tribune*, December 29, 2011, 1.

The "Group of Seven"—Kim Jong-un's Fellow Mourners

On the premise that the men who accompanied Kim Jong-il's hearse did so as a result of their status under the new leadership, let us start with the examination of that "group of seven" who walked with Kim Jong-un. Most prominent of the group were Jang Sung-taek and Ri Yong-ho.

Jang, husband of Kim Jong-il's biological younger sister Kim Kyong-hui and vice-chairman of the DPRKNDC with the rank of general, walked behind Kim Jong-un. Jang built up his career in connection with the Socialist Labor Youth League, the youth organization of the KWP. Its membership is assumed to be five million, about two million more than the KWP membership. Since 1982, when Jang was appointed to vice-director of the KWP's youth and boys department, he has maintained a close relationship with cadres of the Socialist Labor Youth League. In particular, Jang has succeeded in securing the full support of Choe Ryong-hae, who led this massive organization.

Many regarded the military leader Ri Yong-ho, vice-marshal, chief of the KPA general staff, and co-vice-chairman of the KWPCMC with Kim Jong-un, as someone who would take the role of a guardian protecting the new, young leader. However, on July 16, 2012, the North's official media announced that he had been relieved from all party, military, and administrative posts. It was speculated that he was purged by Jang in order to weaken the power that the military had over the party.

Kim Ki-nam, the man just behind Jang Sung-taek in the procession, worked in the fields of propaganda and agitation in the KWP. From 1985–2010, he was either director of the KWP propaganda-agitation department or KWPCC secretary for propaganda-agitation. Choe Tae-pok, the last man on the right of the hearse, was an unremarkable scholar. After serving as researcher and professor at various institutions, he was elected to the KWPCC in 1986. Since then, he occupied a number of important posts, including the KWPCC secretary for education or international affairs and SPA chairman. He is regarded to have little desire for power.

Kim Yong-chun, the general just behind Ri Yong-ho, was educated at Mankyŏngdae Revolutionary School, Kim Il-sung University, and the Soviet Military Academy in Frunze (now part of the Republic of Kyrgyzstan). In the 1970s and 1980s, he fervently supported Kim Jong-il's successorship, and was rewarded with a promotion to full general in 1992 and to sixth corps commander in 1994. From 2005 to 2009 he was promoted to vice-chairman of the NDC and appointed PAFM minister. Kim Jong-gak was just behind

Kim Yong-chun in the funeral procession; however, before long Kim Jong-gak replaced Kim Yong-chun as PAFM minister.

U Tong-chuk, the fourth general on the left side of the hearse, was first vice-director of the SSSM, the national security affairs agency, i.e., the powerful and dreaded secret police. He was born in 1942, the same as Kim Jong-il's official year of birth, and the two men attended Kim Il-sung University together. In 2009, he became the first vice-director of the national security affairs agency, and was named a vice-chairman of the NDC with Kim Jong-un. It was the first time a national security affairs agency official had been named to the NDC. After the January 2011 execution of Ryu Kyong, head of the SSSM, U Tong-chuk took full charge of the SSSM through the support of Kim Jong-un and Jang Sung-taek.[51]

Kim Jong-un's Future

How should we see the future of Kim Jong-un? Celebrating Kim Il-sung's birth centennial on April 15, 2012, the North solidified Kim Jong-un's status by promoting him to first secretary of the KWP and first chairman of the DPRKNDC. Will Kim Jong-nam challenge his half-brother? One day before Kim Jong-un's public debut as the successor, Kim Jong-nam told Tokyo's TV Asahi, "I am against a third-generation succession." However, in the same interview, he backpedaled, saying, "I believe there must have been some reasons, and if those reasons exist, I think they should be followed." He added, "I hope my brother will do his best for the people and their material lives. I am willing to help my brother even if I am abroad. I will help him whenever."[52] About a hundred days after his initial reaction, Kim Jong-nam more clearly elaborated his stance. In an interview with *Tokyo Shimbun* (published on January 28, 2011), he asserted, "I have no intention to challenge or criticize my younger brother."[53]

Will Kim Jong-chul challenge his younger brother? Most observers speculated that in light of his gentle character, he would never oppose his younger brother's succession. Fujimoto claimed that "Jong-chul is kind and he will support Jong-un, not attack him."[54] In February 2011 Kim Jong-chul

51 Ko Soo-suk and Kim Hee-jin, "Pyongyang's Pain Powerful Wingmen," *Korea JoongAng Daily*, January 2, 2012, 2.

52 Christine Kim, "Kim's Eldest Son Breaks Silence on Brother's Climb," *JoongAng Daily*, October 13, 2010, 1.

53 Yun Jong-ku, "Kim Jong-il Changnam Kim Jong-nam Interview" [An interview with Kim Jong-nam, the first son of Kim Jong-il], *Dong-A Ilbo*, January 29, 2011, A 2.

54 Quoted in Lee Young-jong and Jeong Yong-soo, "Kim's Sushi Chef Shares Memories of Jong Un," *Korea JoongAng Daily*, October 26, 2010, 3.

was seen in an aquarium in Singapore watching a dolphin show surrounded by young North Korean women, giving the impression that he had no interest in politics and power.[55]

Will Jong Un's aunt (Kim Kyong-hui) and uncle (Jang Sung-taek), together considered the DPRK's most powerful couple, challenge their nephew? Among the two, Kim Kyong-hui seems to be the real power holder. At the 4th Conference of KWP Delegates, held April 11, 2012, she gained a double promotion. In the release of the list of the Politburo members, her name was first on the list; then, she entered the secretariat for the first time in her career, and this time, too, her name was first on the list.

What will the relations between Jang Sung-taek and Kim Jong-un be in the future? Liu Ming, a Chinese scholar with the Shanghai Academy of Social Sciences, has observed, "Generally speaking, Jang Sung-taek is seemingly a reform-minded politician, and he will try to shape Kim Jong-un's mind to certain degree. They will have more policy consensus in the first several years in the post-Kim Jong-il era. But it will not be long before he is removed from the high position. Kim Jong-un will not allow this ambitious and powerful old man to look after him for long."[56]

Which courses will the North's neighbors take? In short, neither China, Japan, Russia, nor South Korea want a North Korean collapse that would flood those countries with starving refugees. Contending that the North's "greatest deterrent lies not in its power but in its weakness," Professor Jennifer Lind elaborates that "the grim specter of the potential chaos associated with the collapse of the Kim regime in the event of war has led neighboring countries to treat it with kid gloves." She continues:

> Outside countries fear that the government's collapse could unleash a civil war; send refugees streaming into China, South Korea, and across the sea to Japan; and let "loose nukes" from North Korea's arsenal find their way onto the global black market. . . . As a result of these fears . . . countries have chosen to keep their swords sheathed.[57]

What is the North's internal situation? Russian scholar Andrei Lankov observes:

55 Kim Young-sik, "Sokp'yonhan Dekun" [A happy prince], *Dong-A Ilbo*, February 17, 2011, A6.

56 Liu Ming, "Elite Cohesion: Probability of a Power Struggle among the Elite" (paper delivered at the conference on "The Viability of the North Korean Regime," Asian Institute for Policy Studies, Seoul, September 8–9, 2011), 4–5.

57 Jennifer Lind, "The Once and Future Kim: Succession and Stasis in North Korea," *Foreign Affairs*, October 25, 2010, 4.

The survival strategy of the North Korean political system has been based on the combination of three important strategies: intense police surveillance, harsh oppression of even the slightest dissent, and maintaining a strict information blockade. . . . Recently these measures have been relaxed somewhat, not least because maintaining such an exhaustive self-isolation is expensive and the government no longer has the money to support it.[58]

As a result, in the long run, the North Korean political system appears doomed. Professor Lankov writes, "Sooner or later the gradual disintegration of the police and security apparatus, and increasing access to unauthorized information, along with manifold social changes, will bring it down, probably, in a chain of dramatic, even cataclysmic events."[59]

Will Kim Jong-un pursue a reform policy, albeit limited? It is almost impossible to answer. Dr. Liu argues that it would depend on a number of factors:

. . . the worsening degree of its economic situation; . . . U.S. and South Korea policy—reconciliatory or coercive; the influence of conservative group[s] in the North Korea[n] military—falling into disgrace or maintaining robust; the position and role of the young and relatively liberal elites; the effects of Chinese advice and policy influence on Kim Jong-un.[60]

Liu warns against holding excessively optimistic hope for Kim Jong-un and concludes:

Though the personality cult will die out in the short [term] . . . they will re-constitute it and enforce the people to embrace it. In addition, the system inertia, the embedded autocracy will automatically prevent this country from self-reforming. Without any [normal] political life in the party or [the manifestation of] a life-and-death struggle among different political forces in . . . North Korea, a top-down reform change is less likely to happen.[61]

Events in North Korea over the first year of Kim Jong-un's rule have made the future of his regime still more unpredictable.

Kim himself is contributing to North Korea's instability with an unpredictable personnel management style that disregards principles and hierarchy. High-ranking officers of the KPA have continuously been shuffled. For example, the PAFM minister was changed in April 2012 from Kim Yong-chun to Kim Jong-gak (Kim Chŏng-kak), who himself was replaced by Kim Kyok-sik in October of that year; then Jang Jong-nam assumed the position in May 2013. In case of the KPA chief of general staff, which is another critical position, Ri Yong-ho was replaced by Han Myong-cheol in

58 Lankov, "Soft Landing," 15–16.
59 Ibid., 22.
60 Ibid.
61 Ibid.

July 2012, and in May 2013 Kim Kyok-sik was sworn in as the new KPA chief of general staff. Furthermore, in April 2012 Choi Bu-il replaced Kim Myong-guk—who had been in Kim Jong-il's close confidence—with Choi serving as the KPA director of operations until Ri Yong-gil took his place in February 2013.

Unlike under Kim Jong-un, many commanding officers during Kim Jong-il's rule held their positions for nearly a decade, which contributed to the internal stability and the relative predictability of the North Korean regime. However, Kim Jong-un's approach to personnel management poses significant risks to the North Korean regime in the long run, because these new commanders, lacking experience and only sharing a strong sense of loyalty to the new leader, are unpredictable.

Another event that emphasized the unpredictability of Kim Jong-un's regime was the North's third nuclear test on February 12, 2013, conducted despite China's strong opposition. The decision to hold the test instantly poisoned the North's relationship with China, which for a long time could be reliably counted as a supporter of North Korea. Likewise, the North's provocative actions of a long-range missile launch in December 2012 and the firing of short-range missiles off the Korean Peninsula's east coast in May 18–19, 2013, rubbed China the wrong way. These provocations came as South Korean and U.S. forces remained on high alert amid high tensions that were triggered by the nuclear test.

In fact, China has never been eager to implement the United Nations Security Council resolutions that include sanctions on North Korea; now, however, that attitude may be changing. Shortly after UN Security Council resolution 2094—condemning the North's most recent nuclear test—was adopted on March 7, 2013, Li Baodong, Chinese ambassador to the United Nations, asserted that the goal itself was not the adoption of sanctions, but rather the thorough enforcement of sanctions.

At a summit in early May 2013, presidents Park Geun-hye and Barack Obama agreed to coordinate closely on their North Korea policies. Against this background, Choe Ryong-hae, vice-marshal of the KPA, was sent to China on May 24 as the special envoy of North Korean leader Kim Jong-un. One of the aims of this visit seemed to be to alleviate the country's international isolation.

Unlike previous visits, this time China treated the special envoy rather poorly. Chinese President Xi Jinping didn't meet with Choe until the day of his return to North Korea. At the meeting, Choe did not make a single mention of nuclear weapons, despite China's strong request for the denuclearization of the Korean Peninsula.

Taking these recent developments into account, the future of Kim Jong-un's regime has become even more of a puzzling enigma. Piecing together these and other events, we can assert with some caution that, although Kim Jong-un acceded to the throne with meager authority, the young leader will not be challenged by other leading figures in North Korea. It also seems that the regime still has adequate power to nip any potential civil uprisings in the bud. However, should the tight and perfect oppression of North Korea falter, and if the gradual erosion of the government's control is in fact un-stoppable, it is quite doubtful that the regime is sustainable. North Korea's internal situation, plus the nation's place in the international environment, will be the determining factors in its survival.

3 North Korea's Leadership Succession: The Logic and the Process of Succession to Kim Jong-un

Yu-hwan Koh

When Kim Jong-il suffered a stroke in August 2008, the Democratic People's Republic of Korea (DPRK, or North Korea) initiated a succession process according to an internal logic based on the concepts of continuous revolution and lineage succession, concepts embedded in the DPRK slogan "the revolution based on the *Juche* idea created at Mount Baekdu must continue until the end." This logic was borne out when Kim Jong-un, Kim Jong-il's third son, was officially announced as successor at a meeting of party representatives of the Korean Workers' Party (KWP) in September 2010 .

As North Korean leadership actualized the succession of Kim Jong-un, it also began to reemphasize the leading role of the party. The North Korean regime under Kim Jong-il was characterized by *songun* (military-first) politics, and military-first politics was described by the government as the main mode of socialist politics. Although the strategy of *songun* politics might place North Korea at an advantage in crisis management, the nation's overdeveloped military power often infringes on the regime's autonomy and creates external conflict when it interferes and imposes its hard-line military positions on political affairs.

With an overgrown, powerful military posing a potential threat to the succession process, the North Korean leadership attempted to reclaim the KWP's political power. But even while emphasizing the leading role of the party, the North Korean regime based the legitimacy of Kim Jong-un's succession in his virtue as a peerless great commander, committing to the logic of a "great leader" from the "Baekdu bloodline" as North Korea's avenue to greatness.

This chapter aims to examine Kim Jong-un's succession against the backdrop of the DPRK power struggle between restoration of the party-state system and the established military-first regime based on *songun* politics.

An Overview of *Suryong* Succession Propaganda in North Korea

The North Korean regime ascribes its legitimacy and traces the origin of its political leadership to the 1930s–40s anti-Japanese guerrilla activity based around Mount Baekdu, near Manchuria, and led by Kim Il-sung. North Korea stipulated the tradition of the guerrilla lifestyle as its guiding philosophy, promoting slogans like "Let us produce, study, and live like the anti-Japanese guerrillas" since 1974.[1]

Standing above this political system rooted in anti-Japanese guerrilla warfare stands the *Suryong*—the military "Great Leader"—and a *Suryong*-centered military regime has come to be regarded as the core characteristic of North Korea. Unifying symbols used by the regime to support and legitimize the *Suryong* concept include the enshrined birthplace of Kim Il-sung, *Mangyongdae*; Mount Baekdu, a location long sacred to Koreans throughout history and now imbued with the added significance of the struggle against Japanese imperialism; and the sun, as Kim Il-sung's given name literally means "the sun of the world."

With origins rooted in anti-imperialism and anti-Japanese warfare, and with the concept of *Juche* (self-reliance), the titles of the North Korean leadership reflect the regime's inherent military characteristics. Within the three generations of Kim hereditary power succession, top North Korean leaders held both political and military titles: Generalissimo Kim Il-sung was *Suryong*, general secretary of the KWP and president of North Korea; General Kim Jong-il was general secretary of the KWP, supreme commander of the Korean People's Army (KPA), and chairman of the National Defense Commission (NDC); and (prior to taking his place as supreme leader in

---

1 This slogan was put forward by Kim Jong-il in March 1974; he explained that doing so meant "following the path on the revolutionary ethics of production, education, and lifestyle created during the anti-Japanese revolution." Party History Institute of the Central Committee of the Korean Workers' Party, *Chosun Rodongdang Ryuksa* [History of the Workers' Party of Korea] (Pyongyang: Korean Workers' Party, 2004), 418.

December 2011) four-star General Kim Jong-un was named vice-chairman of the Central Military Commission of the KWP.

Calling Kim Il-sung the "Mount Baekdu tiger General Kim" and Kim Jong-il the "invincible *songun* commander," North Korea has asserted that "the bloodline of Baekdu is *Chosun's* (Korea's) existence and the lifeline of generations to come." In its attempt to justify Kim Jong-un's succession, the regime emphasized notions of a "continuous revolution" and hereditary power succession, thereby underscoring the succession of a *songun* Great Leader who had inherited the "bloodline of Baekdu." Following the September 2010 official announcement of Kim Jong-un's succession, the North Korean regime firmly espoused the idea that the country could become stronger only with a military Great Leader, thus emphasizing the legitimacy of Kim Jong-un's succession.[2]

Perhaps in anticipation of possible party, military, and leadership conflicts amidst the succession, during the DPRK's quest to achieve regime solidarity the idea of "single-minded unity" became its most frequently used phrase. Single-minded unity, the regime argued, was the "lifeline of the Baekdu bloodline" and "the best weapon and the greatest foundation for its revolution." And North Korea further argued for the total support of "General [Kim Jong-il], who established the single unified ideological, as well as political, system in the party and North Korean society, in carrying out the tradition of loyalty."[3] The idea of unity has been based on collectivism and the "theory of the sociopolitical life" in North Korea.[4]

In late 2009, before Kim Jong-un was officially named successor to Kim Jong-il, the propaganda ("Young General Kim Jong-un's Greatness Material") targeted toward the KWP leadership and members referred to Kim Jong-un as "Young Leader" or "*Daejang* (Four-star General) Kim," depicting him as the "General of Baekdu." The propaganda, highlighting Kim Jong-un as "militarily gifted" and "loyally supporting and carrying out the *songun* revolution," stated that Kim was a peerless great general. The propaganda machine created a song called "Footsteps" that symbolized Kim

2 "The Uplifted Banner of Winning Every Battle and All Powerful Swords," *Rodong Sinmun*, February 2, 2011, 2.

3 "Always Win with the Power of Idea and Weapons," *Rodong Sinmun*, November 1, 2010, 3.

4 The theory of sociopolitical life was proposed in the July 1986 discourse by Kim Jong-il titled "Juche sasangui myukagi munje e daehahyu" [Problems posed to the *Juche* ideology], which stated "the leader, party, and people collectively form the *Juche* revolution." North Korea proposed this new idea of social unity and collectivism in fear of the potential impact of the North Korean community's socialist reform and transformation.

Jong-un's place in the succession. Fujimoto Kenji, the defector who was Kim Jong-il's chef from 1989 to 2001, said that he argued that he had to sing "Footsteps" in praise of Kim Jong-un for his ninth birthday to demonstrate loyalty. Prior to the official succession announcement, North Korean leadership suggestively referred to Kim Jong-un as "Young General and the leadership of the party."

The regime has variously characterized Kim Jong-il's rule as "*songun* politics," "Kim Jong-il's politics of love, trust, and benevolence," "the all-embracing politics," and even as the "politics of music," and not surprisingly it has used music as a propagandistic method. In the late 1960s the regime promulgated a song written by Kim Hyung-jik, Kim Il-sung's father. The popularization of "The Green Pine Tree at Mt. Nam" was an attempt to further the establishment of a monolithic ideological and political power system centered on Kim Il-sung.[5] In the lyrics, the green pine tree stood for the revolutionary's principles and fidelity, and was a symbol similar to the "red flag idea" (*Pulgŭn'gi sasang*) that stressed the revolutionary's unwavering commitment to the cause. The "spring season" sowed seeds of hope and optimism in the minds of North Koreans that a bright future would come following the "Arduous March"; and the phrase "generation after generation" emphasized the idea of continuous revolution and Kim family hereditary succession.

Since the late 1960s, during which period the Kim Il-sung–centered revolutionary tradition became the only legitimate form of revolution, North Korea's propaganda focused on honoring Kim Il-sung's father—Kim Hyung-jik—as an "anti-Japanese revolutionary fighter." They began calling his educational ideology "Kim Hyung-jik's idea of *Jiwon* ['aiming high']."[6] The idea of *Jiwon* became the origin of the *Juche* concept and "the red flag idea." And the trio of Kim Hyung-jik, Kim Il-sung, and Kim Jong-il were together named "the three heroes of *Mangyungdae*." Kim Hyung-jik became the origin of the "idolization of the revolutionary family," which means that the Kim family members are *all* revolutionary fighters, and North Korea

5 The complete lyrics to the song can be found in Seung-chil Song, *Chosun inminui uidaehan suryongui hyukmyunggeok gajeong* [The revolutionary family of the great Leader Kim Il-sung] (Pyongyang: People's Publishing House, 1969), 146.

6 Kim Hyung-jik regarded education for future generations as an important aspect of the revolution, and dubbed his philosophy on education as *Jiwon*, meaning "future-oriented value." From sources in 1960 on North Korea, *Jiwon* had a broad definition, which included developing a strong patriotic spirit and fighting for a better future, and to overcome any obstacles by looking forward to a grand vision and hope for the future. Song, *Chosun inminui uidaehan*, 49–50.

takes their bloodline as the stamp of legitimacy. This idea is deeply related to Kim Jong-un and the authority he has assumed.

Throughout Kim Jong-un's unofficial succession process, the North Korean regime promoted the use of the song "Footsteps" and after the official announcement of the succession another song, "The Road to Success," was also used. Written in the mid-1990s, the period of North Korea's famine—the so-called Arduous March—"The Road to Success" was highlighted when the KWP official daily newspaper *Rodong Sinmun* published the song on its front page in its January 1, 2011, issue in connection with the succession of Kim Jong-un.[7]

The Official Nomination of Kim Jong-un as Successor: North Korea's Third *Suryong*

At a meeting of party representatives in September 2010, shortly after being made a four-star general, Kim Jong-un was appointed vice-chairman of the Central Military Commission and a member of the Central Committee of the KWP, thereby essentially becoming the third *Suryong* following Kim Il-sung and Kim Jong-il. While observers outside North Korea for the most part find these three generations of hereditary succession hard to swallow and even laughable, all citizens of North Korea—which in just over a half-century transitioned from the rule of the Chosun Dynasty to Japanese colonialism to the leader-centered *Suryong* system—seem to accept it as though part of an unwritten constitution, and to approve of Kim Jong-un as the next *Suryong*.

The well-known saying in socialist states—"power comes from the muzzle of a gun"—rightly suggests that Kim Jong-un's succession process began in the military division. In consideration of his young age (late twenties), he was not appointed a member or a high-ranking official in the Politburo or as a secretary of the Central Committee; nonetheless, his appointment as vice-chairman in the Central Military Commission of the KWP, the number two position in that organization, officially confirmed his succession.

The case of Deng Xiaoping—who for a relatively short period was chairman of the Central Military Commission of the Chinese Communist Party (CCP)—shows that the individual who holds military power is ultimately the de facto leader in a socialist country. Similarly, Xi Jinping's October

7 July 2012 saw the popularization of "Onward Towards the Final Victory," yet another paean to Kim Jong-un; see "North Korea's Kim Jong-un gets new official theme song," *The Guardian*, July 6, 2012, http://www.guardian.co.uk/world/2012/jul/06/north-korea-kim-jong-un-song.

2010 appointment as vice-chairman of the Central Military Commission of the CCP revealed him to be the emerging leader of the party's fifth generation of leadership. This shows that it is essential for the succeeding leader to seize military power.

Kim Jong-un's appointment as vice-chairman of the Central Military Commission of the KWP can be interpreted as an act of institutional provision, one that enabled Kim Jong-un to immediately seize and exercise military power upon Kim Jong-il's death. A similar step was taken for Kim Jong-il before his succession, when he was named supreme commander of the KPA in December 1991 and chairman of the NDC. The revised party constitution states that the general secretary of the party also holds the position of chairman of the Central Military Commission. This meant that upon succeeding to the position of general secretary, Kim Jong-un also assumed total power over the party and the military.[8]

The reshuffling of military personnel by the KWP leadership resulted in the replacement of the veteran officials who had led *songun* politics after 1995 (Jo Myong-rok, Kim Yong-chun, and O Kuk-ryol) with officials of Kim Jong-il's generation. In particular, the rapid rise of Ri Yong-ho, chief of the general staff of the KPA in February 2009, and Choi Ryong-hae, a KPA general without military experience, were notable. Ri Yong-ho was appointed as a member of the Politburo standing committee of the KWP and the Central Committee and was promoted from general to vice-marshal in the Central Military Commission. Just as O Chin-u was a military custodian for Kim Jong-il's succession, Ri Yong-ho seemed to have played the same role for Kim Jong-un and his succession process.[9] However, he was suddenly purged of all his positions in July 2012; the precise reason for the purge is unknown.

Choi Ryong-hae, the sixty-year-old civilian-turned-general, was appointed as a secretary of the Central Committee, a member of the Central Military Commission of the KWP, and an alternative member of the political bureau of the KWP in 2010. He was promoted to vice-marshal of the KPA, director of the General Political Department of the KPA, vice-chairman of the Central Military Commission of the KWP, and a member of the NDC. Interestingly, his father is Choi Hyun, one of the anti-Japanese guerillas and minister of the KPA. Choi Ryong-hae played a decisive role

8 In fact, at the meeting of party representatives of the KWP, Kim Jong-il was named an "eternal general secretary," and in deference the title given to Kim Jong-un became first secretary of the KWP.

9 Ri's role changed dramatically in July 2012; in an unexpected development he was relieved of all his duties, a move attributed to illness, but in fact the true cause remains open to speculation.

in helping and stabilizing Kim Jong-il's succession process in the 1970s as director of the Kim Il Sung Socialist Youth League. He is one of Kim Jong-un's most trusted aides, with close family ties to the KWP.

It is important to note that unlike other minor elites who were purged from the party and military after the death of Kim Jong-il, Choi continuously promoted Kim Jong-un and helped him to effectively dominate the party and military. It was obvious that appointing officials from Kim Jong-il's generation to key positions within the Politburo and the Central Committee, rather than those of Kim Jong-un's generation, seems to have been aimed at appeasing possible opposition and dissent from the North Korean population as well as at preventing a rapid shifting of power. This explains why it is essential to have the political and ideological support of the KPA and to make the KPA compliant in order to become a top leader in the DPRK—it is because politics are much more important than the military in the DPRK.

Transfer of Power from the Military to the Party

In socialist countries, the system of party dominance (i.e., the party-state system) allows the party to fulfill a leadership role across society. Even with the collapse of the socialist bloc and the rise in importance of the role of the state, the party still constitutes the core leadership of North Korea.

In December 1972, by adopting a president-centered constitution, North Korea strengthened the authority of the state. Kim Jong-il was appointed as Kim Il-sung's successor from within the party in February 1974. Even though Kim Il-sung maintained symbolic power as the "leader" and president, a considerable amount of governing power was transferred to Kim Jong-il when he took over the party. Hwang Jang-yop, ex-secretary of the KWP, president of Kim Il-sung University, and the DPRK's highest-ranked defector, argued that a "Kim Il-sung–Kim Jong-il joint governance" started in February 1974. In order to become a tested and seasoned leader, Kim Jong-il was in essence required to rely on Kim Il-sung's legitimacy to strengthen the role and authority of the KWP.

Kim Jong-il's "Military-First" Policy

While Kim Il-sung was alive, even as the state became more powerful, the leadership role of the party was maintained. Although the Sixth Congress of the KWP in October 1980 was the last of its kind, the Central Committee of the KWP continued to meet every six months until the end of 1993. However, as the Kim Jong-il era opened, governance through the party was bypassed, and "Kim Jong-il's direct rule" according to the "military-first rule" began, supposedly empowered by instructions left by Kim Il-sung.

In July 1994, following the collapse of socialism in most of the world and the death of charismatic leader Kim Il-sung, and amidst economic crisis, the bona fide "Kim Jong-il era" began. For his first three years, Kim Jong-il governed according to the "instructions" of Kim Il-sung. By installing Kim Il-sung as an "eternal leader" and an "eternal president," Kim Jong-il attempted to rely on his father's authority to survive crises. In addition to this rule by Kim Il-sung's deathbed instructions, Kim Jong-il emphasized the establishment of a crisis management system based on the role of the military. While Kim Il-sung was alive, Kim Jong-il had already held positions such as the supreme commander of the KPA in 1991 and chairman of the NDC in 1993. Upon his father's death, he immediately pushed the military further to the forefront by supporting the *songun* policy.

There is some difference of opinion in the DPRK concerning the origin of *songun*. According to Chun Duk-sung, military-first politics was created on January 1, 1995, when Kim Jong-il visited the Dabaksol military post and gave his first direct instructions to the KPA.[10] However, *The* Songun *Politics of Our Party*, published in 2006, argued that the creation of Kim Il-sung's *songun* idea occurred at the Karyun conference held from June 30 to July 2, 1930, and that Kim Jong-il's guidance to politics and military activities had already begun in the 1960s.[11] The *songun* revolutionary principle started when Kim Jong-il visited the Seoul Ryu Kyung Su 105 Guard Tank Division of the KPA on August 25, 1960. Therefore, according to this theory, the history of military-first politics goes back more than forty years.

Kim Jong-il's concept of military-first politics was based on the "revolutionary philosophy" that "the party-military-state and the people are one and the same."[12] Under military-first politics, while the party's role in leading the military is unchanged, the party apparatus is relatively reduced. Kim Jong-il was witness to the Communist Party's relinquishment of its leadership role and its loss of control in the former Soviet Union. In response to this crisis, he emphasized the leadership of the party and its role

10 Chun Duk-sung. *Understanding* Songun *Politics* (Pyongyang: Pyongyang Publishing House, 2004), 15–18.

11 Party History Institute of the Central Committee of the Korean Workers' Party, *The* Songun *Politics of our Party* (Pyongyang: Korean Workers' Party, 2006), 41.

12 North Korea placed *songun* politics as the foundation for governance for the Kim Jong-il era in "Our party's *songun* politics is victorious and invincible," *Rodong Sinmun*, June 16, 1999, 1.

in the early 1990s through his papers and speeches.[13] Kim Jong-il saw the Communist Party's abdication of its leadership role in a socialist country as tantamount to bringing about the end of socialism. Nonetheless, after the death of cult figure-like Kim Il-sung, instead of strengthening party leadership, Kim Jong-il started to establish a crisis management system through the "military-led revolution."

There are several reasons why Kim Jong-il pushed the military forward as he gained power. First, in the face of a national crisis precipitated by such unprecedented events as the collapse of socialism and the passing of Kim Il-sung, he wanted to stabilize the regime via a military-led crisis management system, similar to South Korea's emergency use of martial law. Second, it can be said that Kim attempted to solve the economic crisis by systemically employing the military. In order to deal with chronic economic difficulties, the North Korean authorities emphasized the "revolutionary military spirit," arguing that the military should set good examples in North Korean society and the military example should be followed in combating economic woes. However, the attempt to deploy the military into the trenches of economic development did not see much success. Third, Kim Jong-il's dependence on the military stemmed also from his mistrust of the party and its inefficiency. The KWP Congress convened in October 1980 for the sixth and last time, although the KWP was supposed to convene every five years according to its charter. This resulted in a lack of fresh talent entering the party. In his address on December 7, 1996, in commemoration of the fiftieth anniversary of the foundation of Kim Il-sung University, Kim criticized the KWP, calling it the "party of the elderly" and the "party of the dead," and urged the party to follow and learn the example of the military.[14]

Kim Jong-il anointed the late Kim Il-sung as an "eternal leader" and an "eternal president," while appointing himself as the KWP general secretary and chairman of the NDC. Kim and the leadership of the party carried out the military-first principle. As Kim Jong-il took over, the governing

13 Kim Jong-il, *Saheoijuui gunseolui ryuksajeok kyuhungoa uridangui chongrosun* [Historical lessons from socialist thought and our party's way forward] (Tokyo: The Central Standing Committee of the General Association of Korean Residents in Japan, 1992); *Hyugmyungjeog danggunseole daehayu* [With regards to the fundamental problems in constructing a revolutionary party] (Tokyo: Guwolseobang, 1992); and *Saheoijuuie dahan hueibangun heoyongdoilsuuqda* [Slander against socialism cannot be permitted] (Tokyo: The Central Standing Committee of the General Association of Korean Residents in Japan, 1993).

14 "Kim Jong-il States 'We are Experiencing Anarchy Due to Food Shortages'," *Monthly Chosun*, April 1997, 309.

core shifted from the Central Committee of the KWP to the NDC. In the constitutional revision of September 5, 1998, North Korea abolished the presidency and the Central People's Committee, and instead installed the chairman of the NDC as the head of the state, thus formally establishing a military state. Even though it was a state-level organization, the Central People's Committee by composition was a mix of the party, armed forces organs, ministries, national institutions, and working people's organizations. With the presidency abolished and meetings of the KWP's Central Committee meetings not being held, the principle of party-state governance in a socialist state lost ground.

In the Kim Jong-il era, governance through the party was bypassed, and the military state was installed with the chairman of the NDC—namely, General Kim Jong-il—as head of the revolution. This was likely because with the overall concern about a state-level crisis, preservation of the regime and the system was a priority. Military-first politics as a crisis management system led to a weakening of the party's influence and led to certain problems, including decreasing government independence due to excessive military growth and increasing dissatisfaction of the populace with military rule. The DPRK regime's emphasis on military-first, while strengthening the military's position with the development of weapons of mass destruction (WMDs) such as nuclear weapons and long-range missiles, resulted in a failed state unable even to feed its own people. Governance by the military through the chairman of the NDC might have been a useful short-term solution in addressing a crisis in a transition period, but it presented an unavoidable long-term problem of excessive military growth.

However, the DPRK began to reemphasize the role of the party once the formation of the succession plan for Kim Jong-un intensified in 2009. This was closely related to the hereditary power transfer. In addition to that, Kim Jong-il felt keenly the necessity of providing institutional strategies for Kim Jong-un due mainly to the shortened period of the third-generation power succession. Kim Jong-il proclaimed that "the leadership of the party is a critical factor in strengthening the driving force behind the socialist cause and elevating its role." While the North Korean regime maintained that "the driving force behind the revolution in the military-first era is the unity of the leader, party, military, and people," it also argued that "the party's leadership is the very source that allowed the strengthening of the driving force behind the military-first revolution."[15]

---

15 "Continuously Strengthen *Songun* Revolution Under the Leadership of the Party," *Rodong Sinmun*, November 16, 2010, 2.

Therefore, in North Korea, the relationship between the party and the military can be described as follows: the success of the party of the revolution is secured when the party is protected by the guns of the military, and the revolutionary army can exert its mighty power when the leadership of the party guides the army and directs the people.[16] In other words, without leadership roles, the KPA is powerless politically and is not able to perform its role.

Naming of Kim Jong-un as Successor and Emphasis on the Leadership Role of the Party

The stroke Kim Jong-il suffered in August 2008 made the naming of his successor an urgent matter. It was on January 9, 2009—Kim Jong-un's birthday—when Kim Jong-il was said to have given "succession instructions."[17]

In 2009, designated by the DPRK as a "year of major change," North Korea seemed to try to portray the heir-apparent in a leadership light. Kim Jong-un was said to have presided over two economic productivity drives—the so-called 150-day and 100-day campaigns—as well as the 2009 currency reform, efforts that turned out to be either ineffective, or in the case of currency reform, downright disastrous. North Korea's attempt to overcome its economic crisis by mobilizing internal resources met with little success. In an effort to bolster Kim's thin resume, the North Korean government counted among Kim Jong-un's accomplishments the organization of evening festivities to celebrate Kim Il-sung's birthday on the shores of the Daedong River on April 15, and the promotion of the use of "computer numerical control (CNC)" for all industries. The regime also announced that Kim Jong-un had accompanied Kim Jong-il at the launch of the long-range rocket, Daepodong II,[18] and used the occasion as propaganda for Kim Jung-un's "military-first" accomplishments.

With Kim Jong-un unofficially named as the successor to Kim Jong-il in January 2009, the DPRK started to reemphasize the party's leadership role. The phrase the "leadership of the party" (hyangdoui dang) has a double meaning: it refers to the role of the party as providing leadership

16 "Act Like Descendants of Kim Jong-il," *Rodong Sinmun*, October 14, 2010, 1.

17 Kim Jong-un's birthday was originally rumored to be January 8, 1983, but it has been confirmed to be January 8, 1984. Practically the only information known about him during the succession process was that after graduating from Bern International School in Switzerland in the 1990s, he returned to Pyongyang and attended a five-year program at Kim Il-sung Military Academy from 2002 to December 2006.

18 North Korea asserted that this was a communications satellite, the Kwangmyŏngsŏng-2.

and guidance, but it also points to Kim Jong-un as the successor. Just as Kim Jong-il was euphemistically referred to as the "center of the party" (*dang jung-ang*) after he was appointed as successor in February 1974, Kim Jong-un was referred to as the leadership of the party before the succession plan was finalized.[19]

The succession procedure for Kim Jong-un was similar to that of Kim Jong-il. The successor receives education from the party and starts gaining influence over both the party and the military, while the predecessor retains control of the country as ex-president (Kim Il-sung) or as chairman of the NDC (Kim Jong-il). When the successor takes an important position in the military in preparation for the death of the predecessor, both figures rule the party in a dual administration.

As Kim Jong-un's succession materialized in North Korea, references to *songun* politics decreased dramatically and the leadership role of the party was increasingly emphasized. The 2011 Joint New Year's editorial was a reflection of the flow of events after the September 2010 succession announcement, stating that the party would heighten its control over the army to fulfill its role in the construction of a "great, powerful and prosperous nation." The decrease in references in the annual editorial to the military and military-first politics and its emphasis on the leadership role of the party were most likely meant to center Kim Jong-un's succession on the party and prevent an overgrown military from posing a threat to the succession process. By referring to the party's leadership strategy as an "offensive strategy" in the 2011 editorial, the party demonstrated that it was intent on standing in the forefront of state administration and aggressively leading the construction of a "Great Prosperous Powerful Nation."

North Korean efforts to create party momentum included holding the first KWP convention in thirty years, announcing the succession, and revising the charter of the KWP. The regime proclaimed it had achieved its goal of becoming a strong political and military power, but what remained to be done—becoming a strong economic power—was crucial to carrying out Kim Il-sung's instructions to build a "great nation that is powerful and prosperous."[20]

The DPRK regime argued that the fundamental mentality of the KWP convention must be to follow Kim Il-sung's instructions, and in order to

19 Yu-hwan Koh, "The Succession Process of Kim Jong-un," *Tongil munje yeongu* [The Korean journal of unification affairs] 22, no. 1 (Seoul: Institute for Peace Affairs, 2010): 93–122.

20 As reported in *Yonhap News*, November 1, 2010.

do so, the party's leadership capacity and the role of the party should be increased. Furthermore, it emphasized that "unifying and solidifying the pursuit of revolutionary ranks" and "exerting ourselves once more to the march for the great upsurge" were also important mentalities for the KWP convention.

The revised charter of the KWP commanded the military, which had grown considerably under military-first politics, to "obey the party in all political activities" and dictated that "the politicians dispatched to each military unit, as representatives of the party, are responsible for and in control of the military unit," so that the party would maintain tight control over the military.[21]

A phrase frequency comparison of the 2009 and 2011 Joint New Year's editorials shows dramatic shifts that highlight the regime's new approach (see table 3.1).

TABLE 3.1

Frequency of select phrases in the Joint New Year's editorial, 2009 vs. 2011

Phrase	2009 editorial	2011 editorial
Socialism	35	12
Light industry	1	21
Life of the citizens	1	19
War	1	10
Kim Il-sung	2	10
Party	40	63

Source: Yonhap News, January 3, 2011.

The DPRK revealed through its language its view that a successful transfer of power depended on the party being strengthened by reliance on Kim Il-sung's authority, and that the life of its citizens would improve by the promotion of light industry. The increase in references to light industry and the life of the citizens reflected the fact that economic recovery was (and still is) the most urgent issue for the party to address.

It seems that the purpose of Kim Il-sung's reappearance as a symbol of both unity and identity was to legitimatize the power succession. The "Military-Party-Labor" hierarchy from the previous year changed to "Party-Military-Labor," and calls to "safeguard the headquarters of the revolution" changed to "we will defend the leadership of the revolution at the cost of our lives." This demonstrates that along with the succession of Kim

21 As reported in *Yonhap News*, January 1, 2011.

Jong-un, the regime was determined to strengthen the leadership role of the party.

The 2011 editorial repeatedly exhorted the military with slogans such as "Let us defend with our very lives the Party Central Committee headed by the great Comrade Kim Jong-il," and called for a continuation of the tradition of absolute submission to the orders of the party and the leader. In fact, this was to done to formulate a phase of dual administration by Kim Jong-il and Kim Jong-un and maximize Kim Jong-un's influence over the party and military. The representative example was that Kim Kyong-hui, Kim Jong-il's younger sister, was named a four-star general, Politburo member, and Minister of Light Industry, and Jang Sung-taek, her husband, was selected to be a member of the Central Military Commission, a vice-chairman of the NDC, and an alternative member of the Politburo.

Through internal machinations, Kim Kyong-hui and Jang Sung-taek could be deeply involved in the work of the party and military, and properly check rising elites' power. This was done because the relatively short period of the succession was a constant source of concern and anxiety for the regime. More importantly, due to his long period of study abroad in Switzerland, Kim Jong-un was not part of the party and military's bedrock formation. Therefore, these internal machinations made it impossible for the new elites to challenge Kim Jong-un, and played a key role in stabilizing Kim Jong-un's authoritarian muscle.

Reemphasis on Kim Il-sung: Reproduction of Kim Il-sung's *Chosun* (the Kim Regime)

The North Korean regime locates its legitimacy in its history of anti-imperialism and its autonomy as a *Juche* nation. North Korea, a country formulated on such internal logic, is a leader-centered centralized regime. Therefore, a power succession is equivalent to a succession in the leadership.

North Koreans consider Kim Il-sung to be the founder (*sijo*) of the DPRK; he is revered as the "founder of socialist Korea" and the "eternal sun of *Juche*." The regime has its citizens idolize the former DPRK leader and urges them, with Kim Il-sung as a role model, to "pursue all affairs as the great leader has taught and continue to revolutionize and construct in the great leader's ways."[22]

With the nation considering itself the "*Chosun* of Kim Il-sung," its citizens consequently are all "descendants of comrade Kim Il-sung." The

---

22 "Always Be with the President," *Rodong Sinmun*, January 24, 2011, 2.

KWP is more than the party *of* Kim Il-sung and Kim Jong-il—in essence the two former leaders, father and son, have *become* the KWP. Furthermore, the party of the two has naturally also become the party of Kim Jong-un. Because of the nation's dependence on the deity-like qualities of its leaders and on power transferring through them rather than in accord with the law, calling the DPRK a "religious state" is not far off the mark.

The point of interest in Kim Jong-un's succession process was the emphasis on the party and on Kim Il-sung's achievements. Since Kim Jong-il's only accomplishments were military-related, Kim Jong-un's succession was promoted by resurrecting and equating Kim Il-sung to the KWP. At the September 2010 KWP conference, the introduction of the KWP's charter was revised to claim the "KWP is the Great Leader comrade Kim Il-sung's Party," to revere Kim Il-sung as the "eternal leader," to call North Korea "Kim Il-sung's *Chosun*," and to claim that the "KWP seeks to employ the methods of the anti-Japanese guerrilla movement and of the *Juche* ideology." The revision of the KWP's charter can be viewed as the foundation on which Kim Jong-un's succession was legitimized and the Kim's regime would be reestablished.

As the 2011 Joint New Year's editorial stated that "the great father and leader's lifetime instructions should never be disregarded," so the charter of the KWP has idolized the past achievements of Kim Il-sung and used them to support the succession process. The concept of eternal leader was used to persuade the citizens of North Korea of the inevitability of Kim Jong-un's succession of power.

Conclusion

After the death of Kim Il-sung, Kim Jong-il pursued military-first politics, a strategy that was sustained through constant reference to threats to the DPRK, but one that he could not use to solve the economic issues of North Korea. Military-first politics moreover caused an overgrowth of the military that prevented the party from freely exercising its power. The DPRK's strategy in supporting the succession of Kim Jong-un was one that referred to the theories of "continuous revolution" and "hereditary succession," and that joined Kim Il-sung's charismatic leadership to Kim Jong-un by equating Kim Il-sung to the KWP.

The North Korean regime seems to have, at least initially, overcome the many challenges facing its third hereditary succession—including the questionable capability of whether the young Kim Jong-un would be able to lead the DPRK amid the problems and challenges that the nation faces. Even after his successful succession, it still remains to be seen if Kim Jong-un will demonstrate that he can overcome these difficulties in order to establish a stable leadership.

The DPRK attempted to preemptively address some of these concerns. First, one strategy to legitimize the succession was to portray Kim Jong-un as a member of the "Baekdu bloodline." By his August 2010 visit to the memorials of Kim Il-sung's anti-Japanese guerrilla days in Manchuria, Kim Jong-il sought to awaken a longing for Kim Il-sung in the people of North Korea, and to suggest that Kim Jong-un was a legitimate hereditary leader who will one day be another great general of Mount Baekdu. Second, by emphasizing that Kim Il-sung had fought as an anti-Japanese revolutionary fighter at an early age and that Kim Jong-il was involved in the military affairs of North Korea from his early twenties, the regime attempted to settle the uncertainties that the North Korean people may have held about Kim Jong-un being named as successor and assuming power at such a young age.

Third, if Kim Jong-un is to be successful in the power transition and evolve into a successful North Korean leader, he must address the current economic crisis, especially the food crisis, in North Korea. In this respect, the DPRK's recent March 2013 announcement that it would simultaneously develop nuclear armaments and its economy is neither productive nor reasonable, since the military has always been the highest priority in maintaining the safety of the regime, and the economy will by default suffer.

I believe that the DPRK knows that the only method to solve this economic crisis, with its limited resources, is to seek external aid. Therefore, the DPRK needs to set a new political and diplomatic route to solve tensions on the Korean Peninsula and reestablish constructive relationships with neighboring countries. In this sense, the meeting of the DPRK special envoy with PRC president Xi Jinping in May 2013 to deliver word of North Korea's willingness and commitment to rejoin the Six-Party Talks and take active measures to ensure political and military stability on the Korean Peninsula was a crucially important one. The pursuit of the Six-Party Talks by North Korea can be regarded as another means by which North Korea can seek to ease tensions with the international community, especially South Korea. Such steps to ease tensions can play a decisive role not only in stabilizing the Korean Peninsula, but also in maintaining stable external conditions for North Korea's economic growth, which will improve the quality of life for the North Korean people.

4 Making Sense of Daily Life in North Korea

Sandra Fahy

Little is known about what North Koreans think of their government
and the sense they make of the country's internal changes since the collapse
of the Soviet Bloc and the famine of the 1990s. To those with minimal or
no contact with them, North Koreans might seem both profoundly indoc-
trinated, and thus supportive of a system that oppresses them, and powerless victims biding their time for escape from the prison house of North
Korea. These two portrayals, though conflicting, are the typical mentalities
attributed to North Koreans. Such perspectives assume that North Korean
thought-life is at root pathological and devoid of common sense. In this
chapter I draw on my research with defectors, as well as on existing literature on the North, to establish a picture of the social milieu in which North
Koreans live. In the course of my analysis I identify the meanings ascribed
to behavior, objects, and time periods as explained to me by North Koreans
during our interviews in Seoul, Tokyo, and other locations. The conclusion I
draw from these reflections is simple: North Koreans are aware of social and
national incongruities, but it is in how social and national incongruities are
understood that makes all the difference. Such awareness does not translate
into a radical political opposition, but instead manifests as a desire to make
daily life better and make do with what is.

When Kim Jong-il died in late 2011, popular presses across the globe
asked the same question they did when his father Kim Il-sung passed away

in 1994: were North Koreans genuinely upset? Were their tears for real or could it be that the keening masses demonstrated loyalty because it was required of them? As Suk-Young Kim has observed, such acts may be genuine, they may be performative, or they may be both.[1] Such gestures—North Koreans pounding the pavement and wailing despairingly—are reminiscent of the greengrocer Václav Havel wrote about in his 1978 essay "The Power of the Powerless." The greengrocer puts out his fruits and vegetables each day along with a sign that reads "Workers of the World Unite" because "it has been done that way for years, because everyone does it, and because that is the way it has to be. If he were to refuse, there could be trouble," reproach, or accusations of disloyalty. So he puts out the sign because "if one is to get along in life" this is the way it is done.[2] After the official development of *songun* ("military-first") policy in 1994, small picture frames with the slogan "military-first" could be seen above the doors of Pyongyang apartments. To borrow insights from Suk-Young Kim and Vaclav Havel, such communication styles convey the message that the subject is beyond reproach. Through conveying the message of being beyond reproach, *vital interests are preserved.*

Cultural cosmologies—or local ways of knowing—shape how individuals behave and interpret their environment. The context of daily social life in North Korea shapes individual behaviors and ideas. To view North Koreans as an undistinguished mass is not realistic, and yet to describe the people as diverse, heterogeneous, and varied—in the way these terms are usually understood—is not quite accurate either. Understanding how North Koreans behave and what meanings they attribute to behavior, objects, and time periods is crucial to sociopolitical development in the North and on the Korean Peninsula. I begin by outlining the basic classifications within North Korean society.

Social Organization

Access to a comfortable life in North Korea is largely determined by one's political classification, which in turn is largely determined by one's past and lineage. In recent years this has changed somewhat since money—in particular foreign currency—can be used to bribe one's way to a quasi-liberalized

[1] Suk-Young Kim, *Illusive Utopia: Theater, Film, and Everyday Performance in North Korea* (Ann Arbor: University of Michigan Press, 2010).

[2] Václav Havel, "The Power of the Powerless," in *Open Letters: Selected Writings 1965-1990*, ed. Paul Wilson (Vintage Books, Random House, Inc., New York, NY., 1992), 132.

entitlement in social and political affairs, though not entirely and is always a risky undertaking. Political classifications have ultimate bearing on how the vast majority of North Koreans live and whether they can access, or alter their access, to a good life.

Since the 1950s, North Korea has examined individuals' backgrounds to determine political loyalty. The population of North Korea was officially divided into three political categories during the Fifth Korean Workers Party (KWP) Conference in 1970. At that conference, Kim Il-sung designated three political categories: core (loyal) groups, wavering (suspect) groups, and hostile (unreliable) groups.[3] These three groups were further divided and classified into fifty-one subcategories. For example, the wavering class includes subcategories such as people who held land prior to the formation of North Korea, or people who resided in the southern half of the peninsula prior to 1945. There are likewise privileged subcategories, such as those for children of revolutionaries, or of those who died in the Korean War, categories that grant favored access to opportunities for education and advancement. Scrutiny of political lineage is crucial to the classification process since the ramifications of national crimes—or valorous acts—are passed down through generations. Based on this process, approximately 25 percent of the population is classified as "core," another 50 percent is "wavering," and the remaining 25 percent is considered "hostile."[4]

Each time individuals come to the attention of the authorities—for employment, housing, or travel, for example—their political loyalty is re-examined.[5] It is not clear whether people, in general, know their own classifications, but my research with North Koreans reveals that many do know roughly where they stand and accordingly perceive the limitations of their lives in the North.[6] However, when I asked interviewees whether they viewed classification as political discrimination when they lived in the North, I was

3 Ministry of Unification, *An Overview of North Korea* (Seoul: Ministry of Unification, 2000), 420.

4 Ibid.

5 A personal tale of this can be found in Yong Kim and Suk-Young Kim, *The Long Road Home: Testimony of a North Korean Camp Survivor* (New York: Columbia University Press, 2009). When Kim Yong is promoted to a higher position, he comes up for reexamination. It is discovered that his father supposedly worked as a spy for the American army during the Korean War. He is promptly sent to a political prison camp.

6 Sandra Fahy, "Famine Talk: Communication Styles and Socio-Political Awareness in 1990s North Korea," in *Food, Culture and Society* 15, no. 4 (December 2012): 535–55; Sandra Fahy, "Tales from the Bottom of the Well: Famine Survivor Testimonies from North Korea" (PhD diss., University of London, School of Oriental and African Studies, 2009).

told that that was just the way of distributing resources. During interviews these social divisions were not identified as part of a systemic abuse of power, but rather they were described as something indelible to the country. Even though for example those who fall into the "hostile" class are discriminated against in terms of types of work, allotment of food, housing, medical care, and even their geographic location in the country (the majority of less desirable groups live in the northernmost regions, for instance), and despite recognition of these inequalities in the North, such inequalities are not of personal concern because they derive from the survival of the nation-state. Unequal, perhaps, but not unjust according to North Korean rationale, the triage of resources is not without sense. As Charles Armstrong identified, Kim Il-sung emphasized the suffering nation and also himself as suffering when he was in exile.[7] Throughout the extreme shortages of the 1990s, the "famine" was never a famine, but a march of suffering.[8] Unlike South Korea, the North elicits a "positive action as the necessary response to suffering."[9] If you were suffering it was because you were part of a process of nation building.

Another significant and omnipresent aspect of social life in the North Korea is known as *chochik saenghwal* (organizational life). This network of organization has been identified by Andrei Lankov and his coauthors as a primary means of surveillance and indoctrination.[10] Five organizations arrange regular and frequent meetings that include mutual and self-criticism sessions, along with other activities, and every adult in North Korea belongs to one of these organizations.[11] Far from arguing that this system brainwashes North Koreans, Lankov and his coauthors explain that the "all-encompassing nature of this OL [organizational life] implies that virtually every North Korean has a good understanding of how the OL grassroots activities are *supposed* to be performed—and also how they are *actually* performed."[12] According to their sources, the mutual criticism

7 Charles K. Armstrong, "Familism, Socialism and Political Religion in North Korea," *Totalitarian Movements and Political Religions* 6, no. 3 (December 2005): 383–94.

8 Fahy, "Famine Talk."

9 Armstrong, "Familism," 388.

10 Andrei Nikolaevich Lankov, In-ok Kwak, and Choong-Bin Cho, "The Organizational Life: Daily Surveillance and Daily Resistance in North Korea," *Journal of East Asian Studies* 12, no. 2 (May–August 2012): 194.

11 The five centralized nationwide networks are the Korean Workers' Party (KWP), the Youth Union, the Trade Union, the Farmers' Union, and the Women's Union. Lankov, Kwak, and Cho also identify the Children's Union, though it is not considered an organization in its own right (195).

12 Lankov, Kwak, and Cho, "Organizational Life," 195. Emphasis added.

sessions—where one member openly criticizes another member of the organization—sometimes had an air of make-believe about them. Rather than reveal something too risky such as market trade (which violates official norms) more benign occurrences such as the failure to be punctual or tidy were shared as a means to avoid social conflict by denouncing peers openly.[13]

While Article 67 of the DPRK constitution states that citizens have freedom of association and assembly, the only assemblies and associations permitted are those of the KWP. Unauthorized assemblies and associations are regarded as collective disturbances that cause social disorder. North Korea's 2005 Penal Code stipulates that "those individuals or groups unresponsive to or resisting against the instructions of government agencies shall be given up to five years of correctional labor penalty"(Article 219).

North Korean authorities implement what are called "harmonious life" sessions for citizens from the top official to the lowest ordinary person. During these sessions, self and mutual criticisms occur. They are held once a week on average, but it is unclear to what extent individuals engage in earnest self-criticism or criticism of others. Personal privacy is also violated in North Korea, where inspections are sometimes conducted between midnight and three o'clock in the morning to ensure that people are where they should be. The *inminban* (neighborhood unit) leaders are charged with minding the keys of households and inspecting sanitary conditions, as well as the state of Kim Il-sung, Kim Jong-il, and more recently Kim Jong-un paraphernalia in the houses. Effectively there are double and triple circles of surveillance around the population at any given time. Since the economic hardships and the death of Kim Jong-il, surveillance security in North Korea is reportedly on the rise. Thus while there may be increased access to foreign broadcasts and foreign items, and increased selling in the black market, surveillance of these activities, punishment, and the collection of bribes are also on the rise.

Although life in North Korea is highly political and politicized, even under these conditions most people "attempt to live normal lives and generally succeed at it."[14] Most North Koreans may be more interested in ensuring economic survival for themselves, their family, and the country at large, above and beyond any interest to overhaul or change the country's political system.

13 Lankov, Kwak, and Cho, "Organizational Life," 208.

14 Andrei Lankov, *North of the DMZ: Essays on Daily Life in North Korea* (Jefferson, NC: McFarland & Co, 2007), 1.

Migration

In a 1998 revision of its constitution, North Korea decided to introduce a new provision with Article 75: "Citizens shall have the freedom of residence and travel." However, there is a gap between this provision and reality. Under the rationale that people need to register their current residence to benefit from the nationwide ration system, North Korea has always enforced control over residence and movement. One consequence of residential registration is severe restriction of the potential for assembly, protest, and engagement with external contacts. Movement is regulated through travel permits, which are required for all citizens, regardless of age. Regionally, provincially, and nationally, North Koreans are restricted in their movements. Money can, however, make access to travel permits easier and quicker.[15] With the deteriorating economic situation and food shortages, controls over travel have weakened. Defectors report that clerks request gifts when processing travel permits. Bribes of money, cigarettes, and other items have increased as more and more people need to travel to peddle their wares. One result of economic changes in North Korea—what has been called a "marketization from below"—has increased internal migration through illegal channels.[16]

From the end of the Korean War (1950–53) until the 1980s, there were only 420 North Koreans who defected to South Korea.[17] With the famine of the 1990s, the number of out-migrations from the North significantly increased. Since the 1990s economic standards in North Korea have continued to dwindle; out-migration continues at a steady pace of about 1,500 arrivals in South Korea each year. Today the total number of resettled North Koreans to the South is approximately 25,000. The first small numbers of North Korean migrants were largely driven by political factors. Since the 1990s, the majority of North Koreans identify economic, medical, and familial reasons for defection—and though trouble in the area of economic, medical, and social resources is inherently political, North Koreans I interviewed tend to separate these causes from political forces.[18] Interviewees explained that it

15 Park Young-ho, Kim Su-am, Lee Keum-soon, and Hong Woo-taek, *2010 White Paper on Human Rights in North Korea* (Seoul: Korea Institute for National Unification, 2010), 268.

16 Stephan Haggard and Marcus Noland, *Witness to Transformation: Refugee Insights into North Korea* (Washington, DC: Peterson Institute for International Economics, 2011), 7.

17 Y. C. Kim, "Talbookja jeongchak eul wihan beopryoolan maryeon euimi" [The significance of legislation helping North Korean defectors resettled in South Korea], *Tongil Hankook* [Reunified Korea] (1996): 154, 82–83.

18 Fahy, "Tales from the Bottom of the Well." The precipitating factors of outward

was difficult for them to connect the appearance of communicable diseases with shortages in medicine that related to larger decision-making processes by government officials and of course Kim Jong-il. Economic shortages were politicized to the precise extent that they could be attributed to the evils of imperialist forces.

Thus outward migration, although typically termed "defection," is politicized insofar as anyone who leaves North Korea is criminalized for leaving without permission. Although leaving the country is largely motivated by a lack of basic life-sustaining necessities, and while some of the individuals I interviewed said they would never have left "if only the North had been able to give us a living," their act of border crossing is made political by the North Korean government.[19] North Koreans who cite political reasons for leaving are disproportionately college educated and from Pyongyang, or the rare few who survived and escaped prison camps.[20] Generally, positive assessments of the regime and Kim Jong-il's rule were on the decline since the mid-1990s, though Kim Il-sung's perceived paternal care of the country and society was recalled with nostalgia for his benevolence and seemed to echo state-sanctioned textbooks.[21] The media have already likened the physical appearance and demeanor of the new leader of North Korea, Kim Jong-un, to his grandfather Kim Il-sung. This may shore up hope within society that it is possible to finally realize *Juche*-socialism and resume the progress toward attainment of a strong nation. Those who left during the famine had a more positive view of the regime, in particular towards Kim Il-sung, than those who left after the famine.[22] According to Haggard and Noland the poor performance of the state, rather than any outside source, caused many recent defectors to disbelieve state propaganda.[23] Such observations are highly regional, as Brian Myers observed that "the propaganda apparatus in Pyongyang has generally been careful not to make claims that run directly

migration as driven by economic forces are also identified in Stephan Haggard and Marcus Noland, *Political Attitudes Under Repression: Evidence from North Korean Refugees* (Honolulu, HI: East-West Center, 2010).

19 Fahy, "Tales from the Bottom of the Well."

20 But not always, as Shin Dong-Hyŏk's autobiography testifies he escaped the camp because he longed to taste meat, something he learned about via his cellmate during his interrogation in Camp 14 (Shin 2007). Shin Dong-Hyŏk, *Chŏngchi'pŏp Suyongso Wanchŏn T'ongje Kuyŏk Sesange Pakŭlo Naoda* [Complete control political prison camp: out into the world] (Seoul: Pukhan Inkwŏnchongbŏ Sentŏ, 2007).

21 Fahy, "Tales from the Bottom of the Well."

22 Haggard and Noland, *Political Attitudes Under Repression*, 10, 14.

23 Ibid., 24.

counter to its citizens' experience or common sense."[24] However, in 2010 increased numbers of elite and middle-class North Koreans left the country, as described in the *Chosun Ilbo*.[25] Among these were the first secretary of the Youth League, the chief of an overseas mission in Northeast Asia, a former head of a North Korean corporation, and an interpreter for the North Korean military. Defections such as these might have been precipitated by increased difficulties in day-to-day life resulting from the botched currency reform of 2009. Since the reform was sprung on the public without warning and included limits on the conversion of currency holdings for citizens, many were left with no opportunity to salvage their savings.[26] This suggests that daily life for the elite was not satisfactorily provided for despite the privileges of their social classification and that, ultimately, loyalty to the regime is not a barrier to bribery.

Markets

Making money in North Korea is often linked with illegal forms of association.[27] Even members of the KWP are not immune to economic benefits where they arise—many cadres' wives benefited from resources of spare time and connections to facilitate market trade.[28] Similar incongruities between ideology and practice have contributed to stability more generally through the activities of "Bureau 39" and other operations under the government.[29]

24 Brian Myers, *The Cleanest Race: How North Koreans See themselves and Why it Matters* (New York: Melville House Publishing, 2010), 13.

25 See, for example, these articles in the *Chosun Ilbo*: "More Middle-Class N. Koreans Defect," August 7, 2010, http://english.chosun.com/site/data/html_dir/2010/08/07/2010080700207.html; "Top-Level Defectors from N. Korea Identified," December 3, 2010, http://english.chosun.com/site/data/html_dir/2010/12/03/2010120300898.html; and "Former N. Korean 'Military Interpreter' Held in Russia," December 15, 2010, http://english.chosun.com/site/data/html_dir/2010/12/15/2010121501127.html.

26 Haggard and Noland, *Political Attitudes Under Repression*, 2.

27 Myers, *Cleanest Race*, 60.

28 Andrei Lankov and Kim Seok-Hyang "North Korean Market Vendors: The Rise of Grassroots Capitalists in a Post-Stalinist Society" in *Pacific Affairs* 81, no. 1 (Spring 2008).

29 John Park, "North Korea, Inc.: Gaining Insights into Regime Stability in North Korea from Recent Commercial Activities" (working paper, United States Institute of Peace, Washington, DC, 2009); and Paul Rexton Kan, Bruce E. Bechtol, Jr. and Robert M. Collins, "Criminal Sovereignty: Understanding North Korea's Illicit International Activities" Strategic Studies Institute, March 2010.

Market activities are heavily restricted, though a vast majority of North Koreans depend on the markets as a means to make money and acquire food.[30] The government response to "marketization from below" has been slow and ambivalent.[31] In 2008 markets were converted back to a more restrictive farmers' market format, where they could only open on the first, eleventh, and twenty-first days of the month. They were limited to retail sales of individually cultivated food, and other foodstuffs and manufactures were to be sold through the public distribution system (PDS) and state-run stores.[32] In addition to these restrictions, there were renewed efforts to limit other market activities. Women under forty were banned from markets and there were efforts to redeploy them to workplaces. There were bans on the market sale of certain items, such as shoes. Back-alley markets and "sell and run" sales were punished, and public education campaigns against market activities were increased.

Haggard and Noland found that among the 300 North Koreans they surveyed, over 70 percent perceived market activities to be the best way to make money, particularly as it related to the 2002–05 period of reforms and retrenchment.[33] Becoming a party official, on the other hand, was seen by 70 percent as the best way to get ahead, but less than 10 percent selected "joining the army" as a means to get ahead.[34] In this study neither political classification, mentioned above, nor occupation had any "effect on their propensity to engage in market activity."[35] The economic privilege that resulted from marketization in North Korea did improve the livelihoods of people. Although making money in the markets may ensure survival and even physical mobility, it remains to be seen if it allows for social mobility through the political stratum. It has encouraged out-migration, for instance, as described by Haggard and Noland.

While these refugees do not appear unrepresentative in terms of identifiable demographic markers, they may be distinctly disaffected and, because of their disaffection, they may have relied more on the market than typical North Koreans. Moreover, these individuals might have sought additional

30 See Stephen Haggard and Marcus Noland, *Reform from Below: Behavioral and Institutional Change in North Korea* (Washington, DC: Peterson Institute for International Economics, 2009), figure 3.

31 Haggard and Noland, *Witness to Transformation*, 8.

32 Haggard and Noland, *Political Attitudes Under Repression*, 5.

33 See Haggard and Noland, *Reform from Below*, 31, figure 8.

34 Ibid., 31, figure 7.

35 Ibid., 8.

sources of earnings to finance their exit from the country; income-earning strategies may be endogenous to subsequent exit.[36]

Access to Foreign Media

The presence of black markets, along with their liberalization, has led to increased access to food and other resources for portions of the population. Likewise, access to foreign media and foreign goods has increased in recent years. Listening to foreign media may indicate a decreased inhibition to consume foreign media—consumption of foreign news, for instance, is on the increase[37]—but this does not necessarily mean such consumers wish to defy the government; it could merely indicate curiosity or boredom with existing media resources. Therefore, just as leaving North Korea may not be politically motivated, but becomes political by default, so too the consumption of foreign media is political by default. Consuming foreign media and engaging in somewhat illicit economic activities may be associated with a greater propensity to communicate unsanctioned information. Haggard and Noland suggest that as the repressive apparatus is expanded in response to socioeconomic changes, this may contribute to politicizing the populace. They conclude that many in North Korea are engaging in a "kind of quiet exit from the system" through market activity and consuming alternative media that challenges the regime's narrative.[38] A similar vein of analysis can be found in a recent report that discusses how this media exposure has resulted in increased outward migration and in the greater movement of media resources inside North Korea.[39] What is less clear is the extent to which these exposures will result in internal political change. The North Korean authorities tightly control the circulation of information. In order to catch citizens violating penal codes against corruptive culture (Art. 193, 2004 Penal Code), local authorities may inspect houses during blackouts, or even cause electrical blackouts prior to their investigation, a strategy that aims to trap illicit videos in unpowered VHS players.[40] While such crimes can result in lengthy prison terms, bribes often procure lenient sentences for those who have the money, so there may be a cash-flow incentive for local government officials

---

36 Ibid., 8.

37 Haggard and Noland, *Political Attitudes*, 20.

38 Ibid., 20, 5, 25

39 Nat Kretchun and Jane Kim, *A Quiet Opening: North Koreans in a Changing Media Environment* (Washington, DC: InterMedia, May 2012), http://audiencescapes. org/sites/default/files/A_Quiet_Opening_FINAL_InterMedia.pdf.

40 Park et al., *2010 White Paper on Human Rights*, 302.

to continue to snare violators of these codes. Like the watching of foreign videos, the reading of foreign books is also strictly punished. Nonetheless, some defectors have reported seeing unofficial translations of foreign books sold secretly at markets. Mostly Japanese and American books were mentioned, on topics ranging from American business ventures to fairy-tale stories.[41]

Privileges are accorded to those in higher social classifications, but freedom of speech is not something that can be achieved through monetary or any other resources. No one in North Korea reaches a level of privilege where thoughts and opinions can be discussed without impunity. While there may be the presence of "everyday forms of resistance"[42] seen in market trade, border crossing, and consumption of foreign media, adverse feelings toward the government are rarely if ever articulated. There is no sure way to verify the opinions or inner thoughts of others.[43] Likewise, we on the outside cannot accurately assess how loyal the majority of the population is, how dissatisfied, or even how pleased. Recent research has demonstrated the existence of joking and complaining in the North, with scholars clarifying that the "crucial question for the future of the regime is the extent to which such views are communicated and become the basis for collective action."[44] My research identified nuanced communication between individuals, particularly during the famine years, when they used humor and sarcasm to criticize social inequalities of gender and occupation, but none of these inequalities were identified as political or resulting from the government.[45] This echoes Armstrong's observation that suffering is about positive action, such as getting on with things, rather than about wallowing in self-pity.[46]

Human Rights in North Korea

In 1981 North Korea signed both the United Nations International Covenant on Civil and Political Rights and the United Nations International Covenant on Economic, Social and Cultural Rights. In 2000 and 2001 North Korea signed the Convention on the Rights of the Child and the Convention on the Elimination of All Forms of Discrimination Against

41 Ibid., 308.
42 James C. Scott, *Weapons of the Weak: Everyday Forms of Peasant Resistance* (New Haven: Yale University Press, 1985).
43 Ibid., 4.
44 Ibid., 17.
45 Fahy, "Famine Talk."
46 Armstrong, "Familism."

Women, respectively. On March 22, 2013, the president of the UN Human Rights Council, Ambassador Remigiusz A. Henczel (Poland), established a commission of inquiry that will, over the period of one year, investigate the alleged widespread and grave violations of human rights in North Korea, with the aim of establishing accountability, particularly for violations that may amount to crimes against humanity.[47] However, North Korea has still not granted entry to the UN special rapporteur on North Korean human rights and it has denied access to international human rights organizations and nongovernmental organizations. A truly accurate picture of the extent of violations is thus unknowable at this point. Although North Korea is a signatory to several international human rights treaties, information from defectors repeatedly demonstrates that North Koreans do not have the right to life, individual liberty, the right to due process of the law, the right to equality, civil liberties, freedom of religion, or the right of political partici-pation. Among economic, social, and cultural rights, North Koreans do not have the right to food, social security rights, the right to work, or the free-dom to choose a job. Where minority rights are concerned, the rights of women, children, and the disabled are not honored. With the exception of disabled Korean War veterans, physically handicapped people are subject to special discrimination. North Koreans I worked with in Seoul often re-marked on the number of disabled people in South Korea, as they were un-accustomed to seeing these individuals in the North. The *2010 White Paper on Human Rights in North Korea* details the sterilization and segregation of disabled people.[48] Where other groups and noncitizens are concerned, the rights of abducted South Koreans, Korean POWs, and defectors are not honored. In North Korea there are no national mechanisms for the redress of human rights abuses.

Although freedoms of speech and expression are granted in the North Korean constitution, the penal code stipulates in Article 103 that anyone disrupting social order will be punished up to five years in a correctional labor prison, and leaders or instigators will be punished up to ten years. Specific proscribed acts are listed in the code, such as listening to South Korean broadcasts, collecting, possessing, and circulating South Korean

47 United Nations General Assembly, Human Rights Council, "The Situation of Human Rights in the Democratic People's Republic of Korea," A/HRC/22/L.19, March 18, 2013, http://ap.ohchr.org/documents/dpage_e.aspx?si=A/HRC/22/L.19.

48 Park et al., *2010 White Paper on Human Rights in North Korea* (Seoul: Korea Institute for National Unification, 2010), 249–52. However, see also page 259 where the Lighthouse Foundation's efforts to improve the rights of the disabled inside North Korea are outlined.

printed matter, and spreading unfounded rumors. Individuals engaging in such acts can be punished with up to five years of correctional labor (Article 195 of the 2005 Penal Code). Up to three months of unpaid labor or labor education and a stern warning or penalty would be applied to those circulating or bringing into North Korea pornographic or corruptive audio and video tapes, or copying and circulating these tapes, and to those who use tape recorders, video tapes, computers, CD-ROMs, or cellular radios without proper registration. Despite these numerous laws and regulations, on a practical level enforcement can be difficult. For example, despite the regime's efforts to control access, foreign broadcasts have been accessed through tampering with dials on televisions and radios, leaving many free to watch and listen to what is available.[49]

Human rights violations in North Korea not only occur from the top down; violence between family and community members has been revealed through research with former North Koreans.[50] Like state violence, this also lacks an avenue for redress. For example, in research with 248 former North Koreans, the National Human Rights Research Center found that 44 percent of informants experienced domestic violence related to economic difficulties.[51] Of women who experienced violence from their husbands, only 9 percent sought recourse through neighbors or the law. "Receive and endure" was selected by 58 percent of women as a response to domestic violence. Meanwhile, nearly 70 percent of informants risked violence as a result of economic hardship, citing that they left the North for economic reasons. Gendered violence during times of war or economic hardship is not a social anomaly, but rather a more intense and distilled version of the violence that typically exists in a society. Increased socioeconomic difficulties contribute to increased numbers of people abusing alcohol or other drugs, along with a rise in domestic violence and family breakups or dispersals, and to increased accidents and injuries due to hazardous work, risk-taking, and self-neglect.

49 Park et al., 2010 *White Paper on Human Rights*, 293.
50 Bae Ewha, Sin Nanhee, Kim Minho, Kim Insil, Kim Joeun, and Lee Eunsil, *Journey for Survival: A Report on Female North Korean Refugees and Human Trafficking* (Seoul: The Coalition for N. K. Women's Rights, 2011).
51 Kukka Inkwŏn Wiwŏnhoe [National Human Rights Research Council], *2009 kukka inkwŏn wiwŏnhoe pukhan inkwŏn siltae chosa yongyŏk kwache: talpuk yosongui talbuk mit chŏngchak kwajŏngaesŏŭi inkwŏn ch'imhae siltae chosa* [2009 National Human Rights Research Council report on violations of human rights in the process of North Korean women defectors' escape and settlement] (Seoul: Kukka Inkwŏn Wiwŏnhoe, 2010), 10.

On the domestic front, North Korea has had an official discourse on human rights since the division of Korea in 1945, and while many of the official statements have come from Kim Il-sung and Kim Jong-il, there are human rights specialists who write in state-controlled journals.[52] Within this discourse, rights are the property of the virtuous leader, who grants them to people who are deemed worthy, but before this the individual "relies upon society for the realization of his rights to the extent that the rights of society must logically come first."[53] While the reader may recall that North Korea is a supporter of civil and social rights, the internal discourse on rights has provided for this incongruity by stipulating that in order for the individual right to food, clothing, accommodation, and employment to be fulfilled, the "national right of survival within an international environment of hostile powers" is asserted over the individual because without the right to national survival, society itself will not survive.[54]

Findings from North Korean Famine Survivors

My research with survivors of the 1990s famine, one of the most difficult periods in the nation's contemporary history, reveals insights into the social mood of people during that time. By using open, unstructured interviews—rather than survey methods—my research methodology permitted informants to speak at length about life during the famine years. What resulted was a deep description of the competing loyalties of nation and self-preservation. Up until the very end of their time in North Korea—by which I mean the point of crossing the border into China—many interviewees reported a reluctance to leave and a strong desire to return after crossing into China to get what they needed, whether that was medicine, food, money, or other resources. Exceptions to this group were in the minority of individuals, people who felt betrayed by the country because of the death of a child from starvation, or because of their own incarceration in a political prison camp. My experience of working with North Koreans shows that their lives in the North were not singularly interpreted as either good or bad, but were instead layered with complex, contradictory, and competing loyalties to the family, the self, and the land itself, not to mention the leadership. While the focus of my research was on the famine, many of my findings are relevant to

52 See Robert Weatherly and Jiyoung Song, "The Evolution of Human Rights Thinking in North Korea," *Journal of Communist Studies and Transition Politics* 24, no. 2 (2008): 272–96.

53 Ibid., 281, 274.

54 Weatherly and Song, "Evolution," 289.

present-day North Korean lives. These personal histories shed light on the context that shaped the different types of response to the famine: from market activities, to border crossing, to the selling of blood, and the abandoning of family—the decisions North Koreans made were largely influenced by the range of possibilities available to them, and these possibilities were contingent on the flexibility or rigidity of local government officials. Solutions to problems and struggles will be highly culturally influenced. Just as the famine and subsequent problems were incorporated into preexisting models of interpretation, solutions were likewise interpreted along the same lines. Reactions and coping strategies were connected to preexisting and acceptable modes of behavior that were circumscribed by the local authorities. This pattern is not unique to North Korea. The tendency to adherence to authority, rather than resist in times of increased stress, such as during times of famine, has been observed elsewhere.[55] When there are increased difficulties in securing enough food, or a basic livelihood, there is an increased tendency to maintain former ways of life. Preserving ways of life such as social and political norms are prioritized over preserving life itself. Anecdotal evidence of family suicides in North Korea during the famine years suggest prioritizing staying with what is familiar—staying in North Korea—rather than opting for lesser-known alternatives, such as crossing into China.

The overlapping chronology of the famine, along with the loss of Kim Il-sung, convinced many whom I interviewed that the "food shortage"—as they called it—was related to the Kim Jong-il leadership. Witnessing contradictions to socialist ideology, engaging with the contradictions themselves, participating in the deception of the international community, and facing life-threatening personal situations led those North Koreans I interviewed to

55 Cawte's psychiatric field research among the Kaiadilt, an Australian aboriginal community, demonstrated that long-term deprivation resulted in "increased attraction to social authority as a source of stability and control" (cited in Robert Dirks, "Social Responses during Severe Food Shortages and Famine [and Comments and Reply]," *Current Anthropology* 21, no. 1 [February 1980]: 21–44). The desire to be controlled, as opposed to the desire to control others, has been observed by other researchers as well. Social relations among hungry groups were said to be strongly shaped by authority attributes; see Richard Seaton, "Hunger in Groups: An Arctic Experiment," Quartermaster Food and Container Institute, United States Army, 1962, http://oai.dtic.mil/oai/oai?verb=ge tRecord&metadataPrefix=html&identifier=AD0284922. In Seaton's study of starving soldiers on forced march in the Arctic, he found mutual respect and congeniality despite mounting difficulties with food resources, suggesting that a higher ordering of power and shared ideology found in military settings may strengthen the expectation of mutual respect and honor otherwise dissolved in famine stress situations. For more information see Fahy, "Tales from the Bottom of the Well," 81–83.

make the ultimate coping strategy of defection. These events were not experienced by all defectors and some events played a larger role than others. As I noted earlier, defecting was essentially only political by default. First and foremost, it was about getting through an impossible situation. There was a great deal of reluctance to defect, and the familiarity of home—though riddled with difficulties—held powerful sway in delaying decision-making. The decision was never made lightly, and all informants spoke of people for whom the decision to defect was never made (for reasons of loyalty to the country, to their family, to their home town, and so on). Interviewees frequently reported that deaths among those most loyal to the government were common. Those individuals, I was told, were unwilling to try moonlighting—activities the government did not condone—to make ends meet. People also trusted that the government would eventually provide—this response could be called "the delusion of reprieve" stage.[56] Postponement or "states of deferral" were also a prominent feature for those facing difficult times in the People's Republic of China in the period 1949–1979.[57] North Koreans were under a similarly powerful persuasion that tomorrow would find a better day. North Koreans were repeatedly told that although things were currently difficult, if they did not give up, a better time would come. Meanwhile, as this promise continued unfulfilled, many grew ill and less capable of taking matters into their own hands. Others, who earlier doubted the government could help, had already engaged in market activities and other means of survival. Among those who survived the latter stages of the famine, some achieved increased comfort of living through their market activities and bribes, while others made the ultimate decision to defect.

Conclusion

Changes have occurred in North Korea, in particular since the 1990s: markets, migration, defection, exchange of material across the border, information flows, small enterprise, not to mention the changes in leadership. North Korea is not stagnant. Specialists confirm that changes in behavior are taking place. However, we need to know how much of these behavioral

---

56 After Victor E. Frankl, *Man's Search for Meaning* (New York: Simon & Schuster Inc., 1946).

57 Klaus Mühlhahn, "Hunger, Starvation and State Violence in the PRC, 1949–1979" (paper presented at the "Hunger, Nutrition and Systems of Rationing under State Socialism [1917-2006]" workshop, Institute for East Asian Studies/Sinology, University of Vienna, February 23, 2008).

changes result in changed ideas.[58] For instance, scholars have highlighted changes observed in the country's literary traditions.[59] According to an article in *Time* magazine, "to the surprise of foreign observers, new topics are appearing in North Korean fiction: poverty, starvation, even the hint that not all officials are paragons of virtue."[60] Do these literary changes reflect wider changes in the country's socio-political fabric? Tatiana Gabroussenko's in-depth analysis of the literature has demonstrated that this is not the case and that North Korea's literary canon in no way resembles the liberalization of literature seen in the Soviet Union under Khrushchev or during *perestroika* in the late 1980s.[61]

Culture is socially mediated; it is not necessarily what you find when you study Cho Ki-chon, or read from North Korea's official Korean Central News Agency (KCNA). The culture of North Korea is shaped by socially mediated learning. This learning takes places throughout the weekly self-criticism sessions, delivered in earnest or otherwise, through the local control of the *inminban*, through witnessing punishments dealt to others, exchanging bribes, buying and selling in the markets, and so on. In times of economic struggle, do ordinary people's survival choices tell something about what they are thinking? Does changed behavior result in changed thinking?

It is my assessment that life in North Korea operates on many levels and some invariably contradict one another, for instance, illegal market selling and anti-capitalist ideology. There is an official level that is about *chaemyun* (saving face), and an unofficial level that is about basic economic survival. Many activities centered on economic survival result in collective survival and national endurance. North Koreans I interviewed spoke about their lives in the North and their future aspirations, they expressed the belief that Kim Jong-il's leadership failures contributed to the country's miserable conditions, and they hoped to return to the North when "the country can

58 After Marvin Harris, *Theories of Culture in Postmodern Times* (Walnut Creek, CA: AltaMira Press, 1999), 19.

59 See, for example, Stephen Epstein, "North Korean Short Stories on the Cusp of the New Millennium," *Acta Koreana* 5, no. 1 (2002): 33–50; Kim Chae-yong, *Pukhan munhak ŭi yŭksajŏk ihae* [Understanding the Historicity of North Korean Literature] (Seoul: Munhakkwajisŏngsa, 1994); Kim Chae-yong, *Pukhan munhak ŭi yŭksajŏk ihae* (Seoul: Munhakkwajisŏngsa, 1994); and Donald Macintyre and Kim Yooseung, "A Literary Thaw in Korea," *Time*, June 21, 2004, http://www.time.com/time/magazine/article/0,9171,655483,00.html.

60 Macintyre and Kim, "Literary Thaw."

61 Tatiana Gabroussenko, "North Korean 'Rural Fiction' from the Late 1990s to the Mid-2000s: Permanence and Change," *Korean Studies* 33 (2009): 69–100.

provide" for them and they are under no threat for defecting. Many North Koreans migrate out of and back into their country, "*voluntarily* return[ing] to their homeland."[62] Research by Haggard and Noland indicates dissatisfaction with the leadership and way of life in the North, but I suspect this will translate into a "wait it out" mentality, rather than rebellion.[63] This sort of *chamulsong* (endurance) approach to the famine was prevalent during the 1990s and may be the same today.

There is the question of whether there is the formation of alternative thought systems or dissident groups inside North Korea. Haggard and Noland surveyed 300 defectors, asking about joking, complaining, and speaking openly about dissatisfaction with the government. Their findings show that individuals who took part in joking and complaining never exceeded more than 40–45 percent of their sample, respectively. "Even among an unusually disaffected subgroup of the population—refugees—and despite their overwhelmingly negative assessment of the regime, less than half of the sample report that their peers joked or complained about the government."[64] In short, there is less talk and more action where dissatisfaction with life is concerned. While many might interpret the defection of North Koreans as "voting with their feet," or market selling as "everyday forms of resistance" in my analysis such activities are about compromise, and they are viewed as short-term solutions to temporary problems, though they have seemingly become the "new norm."

North Koreans have lived with famine, severe food shortage, terrible infrastructure, and grave economic difficulties for well into three decades. This is enough time for the practice of making ends meet to become habituated and ordinary. Along with this practice, North Koreans have continued to fulfill citizenly obligations by participating in rituals that demonstrate the quality of their loyalty to the government. Under the current system, that loyalty may well be impossible to measure. This leads to many puzzling situations where large sectors of the society act in ways that diminish their practical well-being, instead of enhancing it.[65] The end result is that those who benefit least can in fact be the most ardent supporters of the system.

When we look at the behavior of North Koreans, we are trying to get from an objective world of materiality to that other world that exists in

62 Myers, *Cleanest Race*, 17 (italics in original).
63 Haggard and Noland, *Political Attitudes Under Repression*.
64 Ibid., 17–18.
65 Marvin Harris, *Cultural Materialism: The Struggle for a Science of Culture* (Walnut Creek, CA: Altamira Press, 2001), 61–62.

the minds of our fellow man.[66] Culture is an indicator of how people solve problems, but it is only one of the guiding forces that influence the nature and form of behavior.[67] The geographic and political environment of North Korea restricts full articulation of desire and yet, some social behavior is autonomous and in direct contradiction to the government. The black market emerged out of necessity in North Korea. In the short term, ideas did guide behavior—people were hesitant to participate in the markets, but now they are more familiar—in the long term behavior guides and shapes ideas. The more behaviors diverge from the norm in North Korea, the greater the likelihood that ideas divergent from the norm will emerge too.

66 After Ward Hunt Goodenough and George Peter Murdock, *Explorations in Cultural Anthropology; Essays in Honor of George Peter Murdock* (New York: McGraw-Hill Book Co, 1964), 39.

67 William H. Durham, *Coevolution: Genes, Culture, and Human Diversity* (Stanford, Calif: Stanford University Press, 1991), 4.

II THE NORTH KOREAN ECONOMY

5 Continuity and Change: Assessing North Korea's Economic Performance and Prospects

William Newcomb

Capital formation can be permanently successful only in a capital-conscious community, and this condition, which is just as important for the continued maintenance as for the initial creation of capital, is promoted by a wide diffusion of investment activity among individuals. Nothing matters so much as the quality of the people. The personal habits and traits associated with the use of capital— among them initiative, prudence, ingenuity and foresightedness—give a deeper and surer base to a nation's economic advance than the blueprints of a planning commission. Therefore it is well for the state to leave scope for the exercise of these qualities and to reduce barriers to their development. . . .

A nation cannot be strongly capital-conscious unless the individuals that compose it do some saving of their own and can see from their own experience the point of roundabout methods of production. If this requisite is not fulfilled foreign business capital is apt to remain a mere projection of the creditor economy. Direct foreign investment in these circumstances is not always a happy form of cultural contact, and this aspect of it may lie at the root of some of the trouble in which it has often resulted.[1]

The title of this chapter is a play on the title of a previous conference at Stanford, "North Korea after Kim Il Sung: Continuity or Change?", that was hosted by the Hoover Institution and took place nearly fifteen years to

---

[1] Ragnar Nurkse, *Problems of Capital Formation in Underdeveloped Countries* (New York: Oxford University Press, 1964), 155–56.

the day before the one for which this chapter was written.[2] Besides both conferences being convened to focus on North Korea's (or Democratic People's Republic of Korea, DPRK) future, somewhat eerily there are several other similarities:

- Participants at the prior conference also had to contend with policy and decision-making uncertainties of a regime in leadership transition, albeit at a much more advanced stage, and in serious economic trouble.
- The North's economy in 1996 was failing; industry was operating at about a third of capacity, and energy and food shortages were worsening rapidly. Widespread malnutrition was apparent to foreign aid workers who had been allowed unprecedented access following the DPRK's international appeal for help to recover from devastating floods the prior fall; starvation conditions would emerge before the year was out.
- North-South relations were poor—the Blue House was debating supplying another round of food aid versus a hard landing, eventually tilting in favor of the latter course. Seoul later that year would forbid large South Korean (or Republic of Korea, ROK) companies from participating in the development of the DPRK's Rason Special Economic Zone (or Rajin-Sonbong free trade zone), a decision in retrospect that seems to have doomed this initiative. The North, for its part, provided ample cause for the South to turn a cold shoulder towards economic cooperation by infiltrating the South by submarine with an armed reconnaissance team. Seoul launched a widespread manhunt, and several deadly firefights erupted.

Dr. Hong-Tack Chun, an eminent and insightful ROK analyst of North Korea's economy, provided a conference paper that took stock of the DPRK's difficulties and assessed the prospects for reform.[3] He noted that while the economy was ripe for reform, political change had been insufficient, unlike in China and Eastern Europe. A number of his concluding observations about the DPRK leadership's reform dilemma proved prescient and are worth repeating because of continued relevance to assessing the DPRK's strategic calculus:

- "The more unstable [the] Kim Jong Il regime, the greater the possibility for sustaining hitherto limited opening without reform. . . . If North Korea can induce foreign capital by enhancing its relationship with the U.S. and Japan,

---

2 For the proceedings of this earlier conference, see Thomas H. Henriksen and Jongryn Mo, eds., *North Korea and Kim Il Sung: Continuity or Change?* (Stanford, CA: Hoover Institution Press, 1997).

3 Hong-Tack Chun, "Economic Conditions in North Korea and Prospects for Reform" (paper presented at "North Korea after Kim Il Sung: Continuity or Change?" conference, Stanford, California, February 27–28, 1996).

economic condition may improve to a certain extent without fundamental reform."

- "North Korea's economic problems are structural. . . full-scale economic recovery is, thus, unlikely without fundamental reform. . . . But, if current policy of limited opening without reform continues, the possibility of crash will grow. . ."

Fifteen Years Later

Time has proved Dr. Chun correct. Most observers contend that Kim's concerns about regime stability were the critical factor in postponement of far-reaching measures to reform the economy. A unique opportunity was thus foregone. The deindustrialization of North Korea in the late 1990s broke up established intra-industry relations and thereby wrecked the planning apparatus. The regime lost the ability to formulate appropriate planning targets and the administrative control measures needed to attain objectives. Cascading shortages led officials to shorten their decision horizons. The regime in 2002 clumsily implemented limited price, enterprise, and land reforms but shied away from changes to finance and banking.[4]

In the decade since this stealth reform, the economy has strayed from trodden paths of transition in search of its own way forward, and it entered a no-man's land between plan and market. Attempts to roll back some of the changes brought on by reform, such as consumers' reliance on markets rather than state distribution channels to meet daily needs, have failed. On the reform front, the regime evidently lacks the ability to retreat and the will to proceed.

North Korea remains impoverished, a nation isolated and saddled with debt. Fuels are scarce, and the supply of electric power uncertain. The trade deficit is large, and the direction and content of trade are overly concentrated. The military burden is extraordinarily high, and the rate of consumption is abnormally low. Food is in critically short supply, and international food donors once again are considering providing aid. An economic snapshot provided in the World Food Programme's (WFP) recent appeal cribs from the Economist Intelligence Unit's 2010 North Korea Country Report to make a few quick but telling points:[5]

---

4 For further discussion on the 2002 reforms, see William J. Newcomb, "Reflections on North Korea's Economic Reform," *Korea's Economy* 19 (2003), 57–60.

5 WFP/FAO/UNICEF, *Special Report: Rapid Food Security Assessment Mission to the Democratic People's Republic of Korea* (March 24, 2011), 10. The Economist Intelligence Unit's figures for GDP traditionally are taken from Bank of Korea calculations. (Perhaps secondary sourcing was used to avoid offending DPRK sensitivities.)

- Per capita gross domestic product (GDP) growth has been stagnant,
- Agricultural output has been volatile,
- Commercial import capacity has declined, and
- The trade deficit hit an estimated record high of $1.53 billion in 2008, in large part because of high fuel prices.

Caution is required in the use of trade data. Because the DPRK does not report any partner country data, figures on exports and imports must be cobbled together from several sources. Some important trade partners also do not publish figures. Even when available, data reported by a number of partners seem suspect. Customs confusion over North and South Korean–origin goods seems to be a recurring problem. Odd and highly variable figures in UN-compiled statistics both for exports and imports during 2006–2011 for such countries as India, Brazil, Mexico, Peru, Congo, and South Africa call into question the accuracy of totals and deficit calculations that are routinely published.[6] Figures available for some key partners appear a bit more reliable, although they too have quirks and omissions:

- Trade with China in 2010 was up sharply but at the expense of partner diversification. According to Chinese figures, People's Republic of China (PRC) trade with North Korea reached $3.5 billion, a whopping 53 percent over 2009; China probably accounts for about one-third of North Korea's turnover.
- North Korea's trade with the ROK amounted to a record $1.9 billion, up 14 percent, but only because Kaesŏng turnover rose more than 53 percent to $1.4 billion. After concluding its investigation of the March 2010 sinking of the ROKS *Cheonan*, Seoul in May banned general trade with the North. General trade for the year amounted to only $118 million, down 54 percent compared with 2009. Processing-on-commission trade similarly fell to $318 million, down 23 percent from the prior year.
- Tokyo has continued the trade ban on the DPRK it imposed in October 2006 in response to the North's nuclear test. Trade flows remain a trickle of former amounts.

The economic condition of the DPRK populace is even bleaker than described in assessments of UN organizations. On November 30, 2009, the regime surprised the nation by ordering a one-to-one-hundred currency redenomination of the DPRK won. It set a funds exchange cap per household of 100,000 old won for ready cash and a cap of 500,000 old won if the 5,000 new won received were placed on deposit in the Central Bank. Adding to

6 See, for example, the adjustment of India's reported trade with the DPRK in Dick Nanto and Emma Chanlett-Avery, *The North Korean Economy: Leverage and Policy Analysis* (Congressional Research Service, January 22, 2010).

turmoil, the regime on January 1, 2010, banned the domestic use of foreign currency, and on January 14 it ordered general markets closed and restricted sales at farmer's markets to foodstuffs.

This confiscatory action, officially justified as an anti-inflation measure but more likely taken to weaken markets and help restore state control over distribution, impoverished citizens, sparked widespread protests, and led to chaotic responses in markets, prices, and wages.[7] Within a month, popular anger forced the government to backtrack, and the prime minister made an unprecedented public apology. To further appease the people and divert responsibility for the blunder, the regime identified and possibly executed scapegoats.

Looking for a "Quick" Fix

Dr. Chun's other major point about the regime's inclination to substitute foreign assistance for policy reform also seems on the mark. Efforts to create a broad-based foreign investment push a decade ago floundered. But ROK trade and aid in prior administrations provided badly needed support that helped the ease economic pressure. Even though business conditions today are even less favorable because of increased diplomatic and financial isolation and heightened tension with the ROK and Japan, North Korea again is in the hunt for foreign investment. In one telling episode, in 2010 it was announced the well-connected Korea Taepung International Investment Group would be the agency responsible for implementing an ambitious ten-year infrastructure development project.[8] The Taepung Group also would take the lead in establishing both a State Development Bank and an Import-Export Bank. Subsequently, the group was shuttered, reportedly for poor performance, and the "Development Bank" was said to have been dismantled. News accounts speculated that the closure also was aimed at reducing the military's influence in economic development.

In January 2011, North Korea's press revealed that the cabinet had adopted a "Ten-Year State Strategy Plan for Economic Development" and put a newly established high-level office, the State General Bureau for Economic

---

7 For an examination of the implications of the currency redenomination on food security, see chapter five, Andrew S. Natsios, "North Korea's Chronic Food Problem."

8 The Taepung IIG was established in 2006 for the express purpose of attracting foreign investment. According to the Korean Central News Agency (KCNA), the group's board of directors has representatives of the National Defense Commission, the Cabinet, and the Ministry of Finance among others. It reached an agreement with a Chinese steel company in 2007, but otherwise had a lackluster record.

Development, in charge of attaining the plan's major targets. This reassignment of responsibility conveys a sense of frustration and rising impatience with an apparent lack of progress in obtaining foreign financial support, which is understandable in view of the plan's ambitious targets and the relatively short time frame provided for accomplishing them.

Details of the new long-term plan are sketchy. According to the South Korean press, the DPRK's development objectives list $100 billion worth of new investment projects, including new and upgraded roads, rails, air and sea ports, significant boosts in energy and basic industrial capacity, and programs to further develop urban and agricultural sectors. To kick-start the plan, North Korea reportedly inked a deal in December 2010 with a Chinese company that stated its intentions to invest $2 billion in the Rason Special Economic Zone (SEZ).[9] Development of this SEZ recently has taken on a higher profile, with presentation of ambitious construction plans. Similarly, the DPRK is pursuing joint regional development projects with China and Russia, and counting on the latter to help improve its northbound rail connectivity.

A look at North Korea's economy today may give long-term watchers a sense of déjà vu. The list of notional projects sounds faintly familiar, as if planners dusted off some of the old economic assistance requests made of the USSR. Industry, transportation, and public utilities nonetheless are in dire need of this promised makeover.

The new leadership has associated itself with a few projects and initiatives, but no development course is yet apparent. Should it make efforts to implement a new economic plan after operating so many years without one, it would send a signal that a policy change is in the works.[10] The regime time and again over the past fifty years postponed implementation of policies that would have promoted intensive growth and bettered the lot of its citizens in favor of further investment in heavy industry and military sectors. By

---

9 The prospective size of this deal doubtlessly was inflated to grease the way to an agreement and grab headlines, but should even half this amount be realized it would chart a sharp rise in cross-border investment.

10 The most recent ten-year economic plan was the first long-term plan announced by North Korea since it launched the Third Seven-Year Economic Plan in 1987. The regime formally revealed the failure of the 1987–1993 plan in December 1993 and designated following years as a buffer period, much like it termed the two years that followed the 1978–1984 Second Seven-Year Plan as a period of adjustment. A high-ranking North Korean official in late 2002 revealed that a long-term economic plan was being prepared and that it would be announced in early 2003, according to the South Korean press. No new long-term plan surfaced, however, until January 2011.

embracing *Juche* so tightly throughout this period, the DPRK failed to take advantage of the overall growth in world trade that in recent decades helped so many nations increase per capita incomes; evidently, a rising tide does not lift all boats. Even more oddly during these years, the regime made no effort to adapt its policies so the North's economy could draft in the slipstream of booming neighbors.[11]

With much of the planned investment in infrastructure evidently focused on transportation, is the North unconsciously signaling it realizes the importance of trade? Is the DPRK preparing to reverse course, curb its heavy spending on the military, turn away from self-reliance, and begin to integrate its economy in the global marketplace? If so, North Korea is launching its efforts at a distinctly inauspicious time, and its chances of getting the new development plan off to a good start seem quite poor. The multitude of UN, U.S., EU, ROK, and Japanese financial and trade sanctions currently imposed on North Korea for its involvement in weapons of mass destruction (WMD) proliferation and illicit activities elevate risks and otherwise strongly discourage many potential foreign investors.

Alternatively, heavy investment in infrastructure could equally signal the regime's intention to rebuild the socialist economy that collapsed in the 1990s. The regime thus may be figuring on China and eventually the West taking up the role that was played by the USSR and Eastern Europe during earlier decades.

The ambiguity of the evidence about where the regime is headed is why the title of this chapter looks at continuity *and* change. Whatever the regime's true agenda, chances of success are slight. If the North decides to proceed with its new plan despite substantial initial obstacles to obtaining sufficient foreign investment, it would be the DPRK's fourth attempt at opening. Each of the preceding efforts faltered, spectacularly so in the case of the opening attempted in the late 1960s and early 1970s, mostly due to poorly executed policies.

Even should the DPRK attract some foreign investment, its absorptive capacity appears quite limited. Nor are internal conditions in the North ripe for a foreign-investment–led development push. Harsh social controls remain in force and would inhibit the diffusion of new technology and likely snuff out sparks of innovation that accompany robust foreign investment initiatives. Hence, my inclusion of the rather long, leading quote from

11 Kim Il-sung visited China twice in the early 1980s and there was fleeting talk of reform, but, in the end, the DPRK studiously ignored China and cast its lot with the USSR.

Ragnar Nurkse taken from a book based on lectures he delivered sixty years ago when competing economic systems of East and West began to engage in bitter contest to win over Third World countries.

The DPRK's Longer-term Outlook

Economic assessments of the DPRK during the past decade have a distinct narrative flavor compared with the drier, statistically laced accounts of the 1960s, '70s, and '80s. In general, trade data still play a leading role on the factual side of the story; partner country trade data, from one or another source, are combined with reports about domestic policies and happenings. The modern recipe, however, has two new ingredients that play an increasingly important role in helping judge both the depth of DPRK economic troubles and how well it deals with them. The most widely used new source is official and informal reporting by those sent to the DPRK by international and private aid agencies that the North invited to help it deal with widespread famine and health emergencies. Through this opening, much was learned about land use, grain production, food availability, population, nutrition, rural conditions, and public services. The second is the systematic evaluation of personal experiences of refugees who fled the North. Refugee accounts provide valuable insights into the structure and functioning of the DPRK's system and indicate ways in which it is changing.[12]

---

12 Until recently, analysis based on defector reports was received as though it were somehow tainted. In earlier years when their numbers were few, defectors stories were valued for specifics on topics of key interest, such as military doctrine or weapons developments, but otherwise their accounts were treated as though not quite reliable, at best, and perhaps deliberately misleading to make themselves look more valuable or their reasons for defecting more honorable. Moreover, defectors in general are viewed as a self-selected population, and, therefore, many assert, their individual experiences cannot be reliably generalized to draw inferences about the DPRK as a whole.

An early exception to that mistrustful view that demonstrates just how valuable defectors can be as a source of information is Helen-Louise Hunter, *Kim Il-song's North Korea* (Westport, CT: Praeger, 1999). Mrs. Hunter's groundbreaking sociological study of the DPRK was first written in the early 1980s as a classified intelligence report and relied nearly exclusively on defector reporting to describe and examine life in the North.

Over the past few years, there has been a noticeable uptick in analytic work with defectors. Kudos earned by Barbara Demick, *Nothing to Envy: Ordinary Lives in North Korea* (New York: Spiegel & Grau, 2009), and strongly positive reviews earned by Stephan Haggard and Marcus Noland, *Witness to Transformation: Refugee Insights into North Korea* (Washington, DC: Peterson Institute, January 2011), suggest that the general disregard of this source of information has been replaced with appreciation of its potential contribution.

In formulating a narrative economic assessment, just as in a more quantitatively based review, rigor is sought in the technique of assembling the bits and pieces of economic information. This is most evident in selection of partner countries and evaluation of customs data for the mirror statistics used to construct estimates of DPRK exports and imports. Even so, art is the inescapably necessary ingredient of an economic assessment of the DPRK.

Analogous to an economic forecast, art is used to fill in the blanks or connect the dots.[13] Art, for example, comes into play as a critical ingredient in making subjective probability decisions, such as about which trade data to include and exclude. Art is indispensable in designing an abstract construct of the DPRK economy, a framework for the facts. Differences among various analyses of the DPRK's economy more likely spring from competing frameworks than from the assembled "facts." These differences become especially pronounced as analyses proceed from describing performance to evaluating prospects.

Commonly accepted facts too can be sources of disagreement. A statistical feature in many assessments of the current economic situation and trends in performance is a table showing Bank of Korea (BOK) estimates of the size of the DPRK economy and its rate of growth. Basing conclusions on trends shown by these figures would quickly put an assessment off track.[14] The problem is the BOK's decision to use South Korean prices and value-added weights to aggregate North Korean output. This may be of some utility for the South, but, as several analysts have pointed out in recent years, this weighting scheme is totally inappropriate for measuring the DPRK's economic performance since it calculates what the North would have achieved if it were organized like the South and had similar technology and productivity.[15]

The North's economy perhaps is best characterized as what the Hungarian economist Janos Kornai labeled the shortage economy. Because

13 In this context, *art* is the term used to reflect the value judgments that underpin analysis.

14 The BOK originally estimated GDP but later began to add in aid received from abroad to calculate gross national income as well; this change resulted in a significant increase in announced growth rates, which may have been a consideration in making the revision.

15 For a detailed explanation of current approaches to estimating North Korea's GDP see Mika Marumoto, *Democratic People's Republic of Korea Economic Statistics Project* (US-Korea Institute, School of Advanced International Studies, Johns Hopkins University, March 31, 2009).

of pervasive shortages, enterprise managers are under enormous pressure to meet production goals and routinely practice forced substitution—using either inferior or superior inputs in production because they cannot obtain sufficient inputs with optimal characteristics. The resulting product is either of poorer quality or more costly than it should be to manufacture. Moreover, factory production runs are frequently interrupted by power outages or equipment failure. Marketing is fretfully difficult except to established suppliers, and transport of inputs and outputs is not timely because of equipment and fuel shortages and the poor condition of rails and roads. All these inefficiencies drive up costs of manufacture. Because of soft budget restraints, chronic cost overruns are not penalized as they would be in a market economy, where firms would face bankruptcy and exit. Firms and workers run the risk of being significantly penalized only when production falls short. In this environment, odds are that many DPRK manufacturing sectors contribute negative value-added.[16] If so, even a longer-term growth trend derived from the BOK's estimates of economic aggregates is an artifact.

This problem with the BOK's methodology is old news. Many assessments currently look to constructs based on purchasing power parity (PPP). Others note the existence of measurement problems inherent in constructing aggregates and avoid them in favor of using "raw" output data. Alternative approaches, however conceived, seem to share a basic hidden assumption that introduces the possibility of serious error. Official reports of increases in output of a product, even if judged to be roughly correct, cannot unambiguously be assumed to be a positive economic outcome and evidence of the DPRK's progress in overcoming its difficulties. Before such a conclusion can be drawn, the likelihood of negative value-added in that industrial sector must first be considered and dismissed.

Overlooked Approaches for Economic Assessments

With few trustworthy clues available for evaluating the DPRK's economic performance and its prospects, it is puzzling why the economic organization of North Korea is not routinely incorporated into analyses. One

---

16 It is likely that antiquated plant and equipment and widespread shortages in the North result in even greater manufacturing inefficiencies than were uncovered during postmortem examinations of East European economies, which found numerous cases of negative value-added. In this regard, see Jan Prybla's comments in "Quotation of the Month," *Beyond Transition: The Newsletter About Reforming Economies* 7, no. 5–6 (May–June 1996).

useful way of breaking down the economy is by *de facto* property rights—sort of an economic "order of battle" or a listing of who "owns" what. This organizational division is implicit in discussions of what is often termed the economies of North Korea. Aside from the traditional ministerial, or official, economy, other principal economic spheres include a military economy, a palace economy, and a marketplace economy. While these economic spheres share interdependencies to one degree or another, they are distinguished by their relative independence.

The initial division of the economy was the separation of civil and military sectors with the establishment of the Second Economic Committee. In less militarized command economies, the public portion of the defense budget funded troop pay and allowances, hidden parts of the budget covered weapons development and procurement, and differential pricing was used to obtain quartermaster items from civilian factories (compensated in turn via subsidies from state banks).[17] In North Korea, the military portion of the economy simply grew too large to follow this model. Because the civil manufacturing sector has proven to be unreliable, over the years the Second Economic Committee has built up a largely independent, vertically organized military economy that operates its own mines, workshops, factories, research institutes, stores, trading companies, and banks.

Perhaps the most intriguing of the economies is the palace economy that supports the Kim family.[18] It appears to have its roots in the establishment in the mid-1970s of the off-budget Daesong Economic Group and similar trade and banking conglomerates that were granted nearly exclusive rights to export hard-currency earning resources, such as gold.[19] The palace economy includes the operations of Office 38 (procurement) and the notorious Office 39, which, among other dealings, engages in illicit activities. The palace economy also manages (and profits from) the operation of special stores that serve the elite. Once thought to be relatively small, its span of control over economic resources appears to have expanded significantly.

17 Personal conversations with the late Eugen Loebl, former First Deputy Minister of Commerce for Czechoslovakia, one of three survivors of the Slánský Show Trial, political prisoner, director of the Czechoslovak State Bank in Bratislava, refugee, and author.

18 What I label the palace economy is similar to what is termed the court economy in Kong Dan Oh and Ralph Hassig, *North Korea: Through the Looking Glass* (Washington, DC: Brookings Institution Press, 2000). I have long used and prefer the term palace economy because obtaining special building materials and furnishings for Kim family palaces was one of the reasons this system of off-budget organizations was established.

19 Off-budget is another way of saying excluded from the plan.

Economic crisis and reform brought about the rise of an economy of the marketplace. Farmers' markets have transformed into formal and informal general markets and have taken up the task of keeping consumers supplied with food, clothing, medicines, and even a few durable goods.[20] Markets operate independently of the administered sector, and vendors engage in extensive cross-border trade with China. While markets have become numerous, they are shallow. Inventories are small, and all transactions are cash based. Nonetheless, the expansion of market-type activities, relatively freely fluctuating prices, and the lack of any state subsidy intuitively suggests that the share of GDP accounted for by this sector likely has risen substantially over the past decade.

The second economy may make up as much as half of the total economy, according to ROK researchers.[21] Yet neither review of developments in the military sector nor in the palace economy are incorporated even perfunctorily into typical assessments of the North's economic performance, except perhaps for the ritual noting of the military burden and a brief review of the DPRK's involvement in illicit activities. Only a few economists have taken pains to base their assessments on the DPRK's unique economic organization. In 2004 Lee and Yoon published a monograph that parsed North Korea's economic organization to assess how its economy was changing following the 2002 reforms.[22] They reviewed development trends in what they term the official (falling), military (holding its own), and private (growing) economies. They also acknowledged a workers' party economy but asserted it was too small to matter.[23]

While this methodology provides a useful model for others to follow in assessing DPRK economic developments, it seemingly has not attracted a following among economists who watch the North. A compelling case for analyses to integrate more fully the side-by-side operations of these various economies, however, has been made by two non-economists. In discussing

20 For a firsthand description of the markets in 2006–2008, see John Everard, "The Markets of Pyongyang," KEI Academic Paper Series, January 2011.

21 See *North Korea Development Report 2003/04* (Korea Institute for International Economic Policy, 2004).

22 Young-Sun Lee and Deok Ryong Yoon, *The Structure of North Korea's Political Economy: Changes and Effects* (KIEP Discussion Paper No. 04–03, Korea Institute for Economic Policy, 2004). Lee and Yoon also discuss problems with BOK GDP data and note that the use of ROK prices means that the data reflect scarcity relations of the South and "do not necessarily reflect the correct picture of the North's economy."

23 Lee and Yoon do not discuss the organization or activities of a palace or court economy and may view it as part of the workers' party span of control.

the complexities of economic reform in North Korea, Robert Carlin and Joel Wit observe:

> For reform measures to have an impact, they must eventually deal with inequities not only within the circles [i.e., parallel economies] but, more importantly, between them. Although the specific reform measures under discussion appear to many outside observers to be minor or insufficient—mere tinkering with resource allocation within each circle—the crux of the debate in the North lies in the larger question of the apportionment of resources between the circles.[24]

Despite receiving relatively little attention over the years in various analyses of the North Korean economy, the peculiar economic organization of the DPRK has figured significantly in the calculus of policymakers who have crafted and implemented strategies to deal with the regime's involvement in proliferation and illicit activities, especially in the design of "smart sanctions." For example,

- The U.S. Treasury in 2005 targeted the financial activities of Tanchon Commercial Bank and Korea Mining Development Trading Corporation (KOMID), respectively the principal banking and trading arms of the military economy.
- Executive Order 13551 issued August 30, 2010, contained an annex that added to the sanctions list (1) Green Pine Associated Corporation—a trading company for the Second Economic Committee; (2) Reconnaissance General Bureau—the newly created (2009), premier intelligence organization; and (3) Office 39—principal manager of the palace economy.
- On the same day, the U.S. Treasury and State Department jointly designated five North Korean entities and three individuals under the authority of E.O. 13382, including the Second Economic Committee itself and two trading companies that were used by KOMID.
- On November 18, 2010, the Treasury Department added to its list of Specially Designated Nationals Korea Daesong Bank and Korea Daesong General Trading Company, which provide the same services in the palace economy that Tanchon and KOMID provide in the military economy.

24 Robert L. Carlin and Joel S. Wit, *North Korean Reform: Politics, Economics and Security* (Abington [England]: Routledge for the International Institute for Strategic Studies, 2006), 11–12.

Prospects

"If something cannot go on forever, it will stop."

Herbert Stein

Too little is known about the new Ten-Year Plan to speculate about its parts, about sequencing and timing, about how projects may complement each other or compete for priority in the implementation phase, and about project costs and benefits. Nor, other than a push to obtain sizable amounts of foreign direct investment, has the regime made public its strategy or identified economic policy measures it plans to use to attain plan targets. Do they even exist? The Swedish economist Bent Hanson, in an introductory lecture on policy and planning, said, "Plans without measures are merely building castles in the air; on the other hand measures without plans are simply idiotic. This is true for all kinds of policy in all types of economies, be they feudal, capitalist, socialist, communist, cooperative, corporative, or what you will."[25]

Viewing the DPRK's economic prospects over the coming decade invites speculation on what may happen in the struggle between plan and market: will the regime gradually undertake a general market opening and globalization or continue to wall off from the rest of the country areas where it permits some reforms to take root?

There are almost an infinite number of ways interactions among variables could lead events to play out, but the range of possible outcomes reduces to the usual three:

- The regime gets its footing right for once, and the DPRK begins the long steep climb out of poverty.
- The regime stumbles, possibly due to early and recurring crises in food and/or energy, but the innate resilience of the system, passivity of the populace, and timely foreign financial and political support enable it to "muddle through."
- Unanticipated systemic shock puts the economy in a vicious, rapid downward spiral and events unseat the regime before outside rescue could be arranged.

If required to place a bet on the outcome at even odds, most analysts—particularly those who are risk-averse—probably would choose the second outcome on the list. Turning points are notoriously difficult to predict. Almost all assessments of North Korea's economic prospects similarly rest on extrapolation. Just as in most conferences, many of the papers, monographs, and books that peer into one or another facet of North Korea

25 Bent Hanson, *Lectures in Economic Theory: Part II The Theory of Economic Policy and Planning* (Lund: Studentlitteratur, 1967), 2.

contain a section or chapter describing its economic plight to provide context for discussion of other topics. It probably is only a slight exaggeration to say that this has produced a received view of North Korea as a nation able to "muddle through" despite its dire economic straits. Moreover, certain "strengths" often are noted in support of continued regime stability, including a ruthless internal security apparatus that guards against the rise of organized opposition.[26] Should conditions become truly desperate, many presume a Chinese or South Korean safety net would catch a falling DPRK economy before it lands so hard it shatters.

If "muddling through" is the favorite horse in the race, what odds would need to be assigned to other outcomes to even out the betting? Would success be more likely than collapse? In figuring these odds, a bookmaker would take stock of the regime's strengths and weaknesses but would give much greater weight to how these attributes were changing, especially the consequences of changes for managing shocks. The bookmaker's task should sound familiar to many who live around the seismologically active West Coast. Seismologists are unable to predict the location, timing, and magnitude of earthquakes, but can map seismic hazards and assess probabilities of a major quake over the longer term. In the case of North Korea, internal pressures and strains likely are building.

For those living in a fault zone, it is only prudent to be prepared. Preparing for the possible collapse of the North Korean regime similarly would seem to be a sensible precaution but has proven to be a topic a bit too hot for its neighbors to touch, at least in any coordinated fashion. Even so, many in South Korea and elsewhere periodically give serious thought to the complexities and costs of stabilizing and rebuilding economic activity in the northern part of Korea should the DPRK collapse.[27] These, however, are examinations of alternative futures, not probabilistic projections.

With "muddling through" being such a dominant view, it is rare today to hear anyone informed about North Korea express serious doubts about its staying power. In fall 2011 Ambassador Mitchell Reiss delivered the keynote speech to launch a conference on "Tomorrow's Northeast Asia" organized by American University and the Korea Economic Institute. In answering questions afterward, he took pains to express clearly his personal conviction

26 For an excellent review of the regime's core strengths and examination of its ability to use authoritarian controls see Daniel Byman and Jennifer Lind, "Pyongyang's Survival Strategy," *International Security* 35, no. 1 (Summer 2010): 44–74.

27 For a discussion of these issues, including the dynamics of economic system change, see Bradley O. Babson and William J. Newcomb, "Economic Perspectives on Demise Scenarios for DPRK" (unpublished paper, February 2004).

that North Korea was "on the wrong side of history" and the regime's collapse was not a question of if, but when. The when, he added, potentially could come quite soon.[28]

The reflexive rejoinder to this provocative view is "in the 1990s everyone predicted the North's collapse, yet it survived." Many who point this out hold a view of North Korean exceptionalism, and generally contend that those who had predicted collapse did not really "understand" North Korea; thus, those who now believe the regime will not survive are wrong too. The rejoinder is wrong: in the 1990s not everyone assumed the DPRK would collapse; at that time, views on North Korea's prospects were polarized.[29] Many of those who thought collapse likely fully "understood" North Korea but did not foresee the international rescue mission that helped restore stability. Similarly, those who hold the view that North Korean exceptionalism accounts for its staying power may not fully appreciate the crucial role of foreign support.

Looking strictly at the economy, chances for muddling through appear to be declining and risks of a second economic collapse rising. In metallurgical terms, North Korea's economy could be considered brittle. The stress on the system in the 1990s led to its permanent deformation—the system's inability to recover its previous form shows plasticity, not elasticity. While North Korea's "hardness" remains intact, little ductility remains, suggesting that should stress rise, a breaking point may be "nearer" than most would assess.

Assume the hypothesis is correct that many industrial sectors in North Korea are producing negative value-added; then the economic system would be far more inefficient than currently imagined.[30] The growth trend in per capita GDP over the past decade is less likely to be flat and is more likely to be declining, despite the rise of a private sector. As GDP falls, the share of trade and aid would loom ever larger in importance. The shock of an abrupt drop in either could be as devastating today or tomorrow as it was when DPRK-USSR trade and aid arrangements ended.

28 An audio transcript of the speech and follow-up remarks is available at http://www.keia.org.

29 William Newcomb and John Merrill, "North Korea's Economic Opening," in Young Back Choi, Yesook Merrill, Yung Y. Yang, and Semoon Chang, eds., *Perspectives on Korean Unification and Economic Integration* (Northhampton, MA: Edward Elgar, 2001).

30 For example, a ton of coal in a rail car may be worth more than a ton of coal yet to be mined; but, a ton of crude steel likely embodies greater resource and production costs than its own price would command.

In many ways and reluctantly, China has replaced the USSR as the DPRK's principal trade partner and economic booster.[31] It is seen by many as the regime's lifeline and guarantor of its stability. China's roughly one-third share of DPRK imports is only half as large as the level reached by the USSR and Eastern Europe at the end of the 1980s. Nonetheless,

- China is the DPRK's major source for petroleum and coke and largest supplier of concessional assistance.
- Excluding ROK investment in Kaesŏng, Chinese firms are the largest foreign investors in the North.
- The markets in the DPRK are heavily stocked with Chinese consumer goods obtained in cross-border trade.
- The military and palace economies operate numerous trading firms in the PRC, in large part to evade sanctions, such as those imposed in UN Security Council Resolution 1874, and procure directly or use Chinese ports to transship restricted technologies and luxury products.
- Some Chinese banks continue to help DPRK firms and banks access the global financial system, maintain accounts for DPRK firms, and are a channel for repatriating earnings from arms sales.

Like the USSR in the 1980s, China has become not only a savior of the regime but an additional vulnerability, alongside fuel, food, and finance. There is little risk that China will take steps to exert its growing economic leverage for one objective or another, miscalculate the pressure, and destabilize the regime. But North Korea is dangerously exposed to any economic shock that might shake China and disrupt the flows of fuel and food and cause Chinese investors to suspend projects. The North Korean regime seems to have placed its bet—not on its own ability to muddle through—but on China's ability to stay free from economic crises and extend its already long growth spurt. What are the odds for that continuing over the next ten years?

---

31 See Dick K. Nanto, Mark E. Manyin, and Kerry Dumbaugh, *China-North Korea Relations* (Congressional Research Service, January 22, 2010); also, see Drew Thomson, *Silent Partners: Chinese Joint Ventures in North Korea* (U.S.-Korea Institute, School of Advanced International Studies, Johns Hopkins University, February 2011).

6 North Korea's Chronic Food Problem

Andrew S. Natsios

This chapter examines the three economic shocks the North Korean people suffered between 1994 and 2010—the roots and consequences of the North Korean famine that devastated the country between 1994 and 1999, the market reforms of 2002, and the disastrous currency manipulation scheme of 2009—and how these three events affected the food security of the population. I conclude with recommendations on how future food aid programs should be designed for North Korea given this analysis.

The North Korean Food Security System

Japan colonized Korea in 1905 and introduced modern scientific agriculture to the country between 1919 and 1939; however, little of the increased food production remained in Korea. Most was sent to Japan to address the growing food deficit facing its burgeoning population and as a result the Korean population during this period faced severe food insecurity, and at times near-famine conditions. Japan itself faced chronic hunger in its rural areas in the 1930s and even sporadic localized famine conditions, which fueled Japanese expansionism.[1] The North Korean state (the Democratic People's Republic of Korea, DPRK) that emerged in the aftermath of World

---

1 Paul Johnson, *Modern Times: From the Twenties to the Nineties* (New York: Harper Perennial, 1992), 158.

War II and the Korean civil war (1950–1952) was born as a satellite of the Soviet Union and China and thus integrated into the Eastern Bloc economic system from the start. The DPRK seized control of the farming system that the Japanese abandoned as they withdrew from Korea after their defeat in World War II, and in the 1950s the North Koreans established a system of collectivized agriculture. Farmers became rural proletariat who worked for the state, but did not own the land they tilled or food they produced, and thus had few incentives to increase production. Early on Kim Il-sung, the founder and leader of the DPRK, embraced the Leninist formula for modern scientific socialist agriculture—mechanization, chemicalization, irrigation, and electrification—but implemented it without regard to market economics or good agricultural practices.[2]

The socialist planning system in Pyongyang established food production quotas for each farm, but allowed each farmer a small plot to grow household vegetables for personal consumption and distributed to each farming household a food ration from the harvest each year. The command and control agricultural system instructed farmers exactly what to plant, when, and where in minute detail. Like the Soviet system after which it was modeled, the North Korean agricultural system sold its surplus to the central government after each harvest at very low prices, in exchange for which the state provided inputs of seed, fertilizer, insecticides, and farm equipment such as tractors (and consumer goods for farm families, such as clothing). The surplus bought by the central government was then transferred into the public distribution system (PDS), from which non-farm workers received a ration twice a month—again at a very low, subsidized price.

This ration, however, was not equal for all North Koreans. Rations were differentially distributed based on the political rank of the recipient. The population was divided into sixty-four categories with the Kim family and Politburo members at the top, and below them Communist Party cadres, internal security, military officers, and at the bottom descendants of families who had been members of the old Korean nobility, business people and large land owners, and finally inmates in the North Korean prison system, who received a ration less than that needed for survival.[3] Many inmates died of starvation within two years of incarceration. During the famine of the 1990s these sixty-four categories were collapsed into three. Access to the food

2 Andrew Natsios, *The Great North Korean Famine: Famine, Politics, and Foreign Policy* (Washington D.C.: United States Institute of Peace Press, 2001), 13.

3 Richard Kagan, Matthew Oh, and David Westbrook, *Human Rights in the Democratic People's Republic of Korea* (Minneapolis: Minnesota Lawyers International Human Rights Committee; Washington D.C.: Asia Watch, 1988), 192–93.

ration system was not a mobile benefit: because families could only obtain their bimonthly food ration at local food warehouses, movement outside of home villages was severely limited. Thus the food system was an aggressive and very effective mechanism for social and political control: it subordinated food security to political objectives, which reinforced the system of control limiting population movement, making the people completely dependent on the state for their food, and rewarding those categories of people most important to the survival of the regime.[4] This was the food system that fed the North Korean population from the 1950s through the mid-1990s, when it collapsed for reasons described below.

The Collapse of the System

This system worked as long as China and the Soviet Union provided subsidies to the North Korean government in the form of reduced "friendship" prices for energy, particularly oil, and food, resources North Korea bartered for with the export of its industrial goods to both countries. Food production appears to have precipitously declined in the 1980s and was made up by Chinese food shipments. In 1990 the Soviet Union informed the shocked North Korean government that it intended on establishing formal diplomatic relations with South Korea, the North's mortal enemy. In 1992 China did the same. It was about this time that both China and Russia (the Soviet Union had collapsed) began to transition their friendship subsidies to North Korea into regular commercial transactions at international prices. This caused a precipitous drop in oil imports and, since it was dependent on electricity that North Korean generating plants could no longer produce, fertilizer production. The reduction in electricity production also meant that water pumps could no longer be used to irrigate the rice paddies. Lacking diesel fuel, farmers were forced to abandon tractors and to resort to ox plowing to till the fields. The North Korean socialist scientific agriculture slid back into traditional practices as inputs stopped, and harvests continued their downward spiral, which became life threatening by 1993. The quality of seed stock used to plant the crops each year also deteriorated, so that by the mid-1990s farmers reverted to the use of traditional varieties of rice and corn instead of the improved, higher-yielding seed varieties used earlier.

North Korean geography does not lend itself to agriculture: the growing seasons are short, the population density very high, and the arable land limited. Only about 15–20 percent of the land is suited for agriculture—the rest

---

4 Cited in Natsios, *Great North Korean Famine*, 74.

is mountainous. The arable land per person is one of the lowest in the world: only ten countries have ratios lower than those of North Korea.[5] Countries with industrial bases—like the Persian Gulf states and European democracies such as the Netherlands and Switzerland—can export production and with foreign exchange earnings import more than enough food to feed their populations. But North Korea had stopped producing industrial goods, and such goods as it would have been able to produce were in any event likely unmarketable in a competitive international trading system.

The social compact that tied the collective farms with the central government was thus broken as inputs disappeared and production declined. As harvests suffered, the central government began reducing the food ration farming families would get from the annual harvest before the surplus was moved into the PDS. According to the World Food Programme/Food and Agricultural Organization (WFP/FAO) crop assessments in 1996 and 1997, farmers began questioning why they should produce food for urban areas—where factory workers and the miners lived—when they received nothing in return.[6] By 1996 the steep decline in the volume of food being pumped into the PDS from the collective farms collapsed the entire North Korean food security system.

The Great North Korean Famine: The First Shock

While the North Korean famine peaked between late 1996 and the first six months of 1997, mortality rose beginning in 1994 and returned to pre-famine levels by 1999. While we do not have definitive data on the mortality rates during this first shock and there continues to be a wide range of mortality estimates from 600,000 deaths to 3.5 million, we do have one authoritative source who had access to information for the period 1994 through January 1997—when he defected to South Korea.[7] And that was Hwang

5 World Resources Institute, United Nations Environment Programme, United Nations Development Programme, and World Bank, *World Resources: A Guide to the Global Environment, 1996–1997* (Oxford: Oxford University Press, 1996), 240–41.

6 FAO/WFP, *Crop and Food Supply Assessment Mission to DPRK: Special Report* (World Food Programme, November 1997), 13.

7 It is important to note that there has been a significant amount of disagreement regarding the famine's severity and subsequent death toll. Steven Haggard and Marcus Noland have taken exception to the higher estimates of deaths resulting from the famine and estimate excess mortality to be between 600,000–1,000,000. See Steven Haggard and Marcus Noland, *Famine in North Korea: Markets, Aid, and Reform* (New York: Columbia University Press, 2007), 73–76.

Jang-yop—member of the Politburo, tutor to Kim Jong-il, president of Kim Il-sung University, and party theoretician who developed the *Juche* ideology.

In his 1998 book *North Korea: Truth or Lies?* Hwang relates a conversation he had with the director of the North Korean Office of Statistics:

> In November 1996, I was very concerned about the economy and asked a top official in charge of agricultural statistics and food how many people starved to death. He replied: "In 1995, about five hundred thousand people starved to death including fifty thousand party cadres. In 1996, about one million people are estimated to have starved to death." He continued, "In 1997, about two million people would starve to death if no international aid were provided."[8]

Now it is possible, given that his book was published while the famine was ongoing, that he invented or exaggerated the numbers to encourage more aid to the North. But just before his death in 2010 he was asked at a Washington briefing how many people died in the famine; his reply—3.5 million—is consistent with his earlier claim.[9] Given Hwang's very high rank, he would have had access to statistical data of this sort prior to his defection, data that would have showed deaths at 1.5 million by the end of 1996, before the famine had peaked. The North Korean famine was thus one of the deadliest in the world in the last quarter of the twentieth century. The first shock traumatized North Korean society and its political system, and permanently altered the mindset and worldview of the public, who blamed the North Korean government for their predicament—this from interviews conducted by both Good Friends, a South Korean nongovernmental organization (NGO); and by Cortland Robinson, a researcher from the Johns Hopkins School of Public Health. The people no longer trusted the state to provide for their needs or feed them; those people who did, died. It was farmers and traders, now independent of the state, who survived the famine by their own initiative, cleverness, and energy—and did so using coping mechanisms that were illegal (such as buy and selling grain in the farmers' markets, escaping to China, and stealing the harvest on the collective farms).[10]

The famine had profound political implications as well. According to the South Korea Buddhist Sharing Movement (later renamed Good Friends) interviews conducted in China of North Korean food refugees from 1996

8 Hwang Jang-yop. *North Korea: Truth or Lies?* (Seoul: Institute for Reunification Policy Studies, 1998), 15.

9 Center for Strategic and International Studies, "Korea Platform Special Session with Mr. Hwang Jang-yop," March 31, 2010, http://csis.org/event/korea-platform-special-session-mr-hwang-jang-yop.

10 Cited in Natsios, *Great North Korean Famine*, 113.

to 1998, public support for the DPRK government—which as a matter of political ideology taught that it was the state's responsibility to ensure everyone was fed, housed, and clothed—suffered a precipitous decline as the famine spread across the country.[11]

This eroding popular support for the Kim regime even found its way into the North Korean military. In late 1995, Don Oberdorfer reported in *The Two Koreas* that the People's Army Sixth Corps assigned to the Northeast region headquarters in Chongjin was "disbanded, its leadership purged, and its units submerged into others, under circumstances suggesting disarray in the ranks."[12] A defector I interviewed in November 1998 told me that a corps-level army unit had been planning a coup in Hamhung City where it was headquartered and that the secret police discovered the plot before it was carried out, arrested the mutineers, and promptly executed them. Food refugees I interviewed in China from the city said as much as 40 percent of the population had died in the famine, which if they were correct was one of the highest death rates in the country and the likely cause of the coup plot. Food refugees reported that between late 1995 and early 1997, at the height of the famine a truck would travel around Hamhung City every morning and workers would pick up the bodies of people who had died on the streets the night before.

The Farmers' Markets

At the heart of it, the North Korean famine was caused by the collapse of the public distribution system—the principal means through which the non-farm population was fed—over the period 1994–1997.

By the summer of 1996 many farmers—particularly in the maize-growing areas of the northeast—took matters into their own hands and secretly pre-harvested crops before they could be officially taken by the central government, as the percentage from the harvest being taken had been steadily rising. The WFP reported that 1.3 million metric tons of corn was missing from the 1996 harvest.[13] This massive hoarding of the maize crop by farmers allowed them to feed their families—at a time when the government rations

---

11 Korea Buddhist Sharing Movement (KBSM), *The Food Crisis in North Korea Witnessed by 1,019 Food Refugees: The Fifth Phase of Research*, 30 September 1997–19 May 1998 (Seoul: KBSM, June 1998), 23.

12 Don Oberdorfer, *The Two Koreas: A Contemporary History* (Reading, Mass.: Addison-Wesley, 1997), 375.

13 FAO/WFP, *Crop and Food Supply Assessment Mission to the DPRK: Special Report* (December 1996), 5.

were being cut—by the income generated through selling grain they had pre-harvested at the rapidly expanding farmers' markets springing up across the country—grain that would normally have gone to provision the PDS.

From the inception of the communist state, the central government had allowed farmer's markets to function, but only as a supplement to the PDS, never as the principal means for feeding the population. As a result of the chaos of the famine and breakdown of the system of social, economic, and political control, people were now feeding themselves from markets outside the control of the state, based on their ability to barter or make enough money to access the markets. In December 1996 Kim Jong-il, in a speech at the fiftieth anniversary celebration of the founding of his alma mater, Kim Il-sung University, warned "the party and the government have full responsibility for the care and well-being of the lives of the people" and "if the party lets the people solve the food problem themselves, then only the farmers and merchants will prosper, giving rise to egotism and collapsing the social order of a classless society. The party will lose its popular base and will experience meltdown as in Poland and Czechoslovakia."[14] Kim Jong-il and his father Kim Il-sung were friendly with the presidents of Romania (Nicolae Ceauşescu) and East Germany (Erich Honecker) and were obsessed with their fates as the Soviet Empire collapsed: Ceauşescu and his wife were executed by firing squad in December 1989 by the Romanian military, and Honecker ended up in prison.[15]

The farmers' markets received an unexpected boost that accelerated their growth from a very unlikely source: the international food aid program for North Korea. In response to the famine, Western donor governments, a consortium of NGOs, and the UN's World Food Programme initiated a large-scale food aid program by mid-1997 to address the famine. The DPRK regime resisted all of the international monitoring and accountability systems required by the humanitarian aid delivery system everywhere else in the world, so they could use the food for their own purposes. An unintended, but salutary, consequence of this compromised food aid delivery system was widespread diversion of food aid to the farmers' markets, a regular supply source that only expanded their reach and volume.[16]

14 "Kim Jong Il Berates Cadres for Food Anarchy," translated in Foreign Broadcast Information Service as "Kim Jong Il, Speech at Kim Il Sung University." Don Oberdorfer, author of *The Two Koreas*, discovered that Hwang Jang-yop was the source of the text of this speech of Kim's published in *Wolgan Chosun*.

15 Cited in Andrew Natsios, *Great North Korean Famine*, 10.

16 See Andrew S. Natsios, *The Politics of Famine in North Korea* (Washington, DC: US Institute for Peace Special Report, August 2, 1999), http://www.usip.org/publications/

In the decade following the famine—from 1999 to 2009—expanded farmers markets replaced the collapsed PDS as the principal means of access to food for the North Korean population and fueled the growth of a nascent class of merchants and traders. Good Friends—a South Korean NGO with good internal access to North Korea—reports that some of the merchants in the farmer's markets were the wives and parents of party officials and the security apparatus. Thus even the party and police—pillars of the state system—were now no longer completely dependent on the state for their survival.

During this first food shock, the North Korean government subordinated the food security of their people to one overriding and ultimate objective: survival of the regime. They believed if they took the measures necessary—economic and agricultural reforms—to save the population, they would endanger their control of the country and make them more vulnerable to intimidation or potential attack from their enemies—the United States, South Korea, and Japan. Pyongyang had three options: maximize humanitarian food aid by opening the country to the international aid system (which would have shown the world the severity of the famine), adopt Chinese-style economic reforms to stimulate growth (which would have allowed a measure of private investment and economic freedom the regime was unprepared to risk), or reduce military expenditures on weapons systems (which would have weakened the military and even risked a military backlash against the Kim family). Kim Jong-il was focused on keeping the old order in place and hiding the famine because he feared the military and political consequences if the world knew the severity of the crisis. He explained what those consequences would be in his anniversary speech at Kim Il-sung University:

"The People's Army is not being properly supplied with food. Seeing that we face temporary difficulties, the enemies rave that our socialism will fall as well, and they are looking for every possible chance to invade us. If they knew we did not have military provisions, the U.S. imperialists might immediately raid us." [17]

The July 2002 Economic Reforms: The Second Shock

The famine ended in 1998, as measured by the number of deaths. Four years later, in July 2002, the central government announced economic reforms—major by North Korean standards, but modest compared to Deng Xiaoping's Chinese reforms—in the agricultural, food, and industrial

politics-famine-north-korea.
17 Cited in Natsios, *Great North Korean Famine*, 40.

sectors that affirmed and to a limited degree built upon the farmer's markets, which had so dramatically expanded in the previous decade. The 2002 reforms raised the price of grain paid to farmers by the state and the price recipients paid to the PDS to purchase grain; in theory this eliminated the incentive for farmers to divert the harvest each year to sell on the farmers' markets. (In practice, however, the reforms were ineffective because of high rates of inflation.) In addition the central government now allowed the collective farms to make their own decisions on what crops to plant, where, and when. Finally, the reforms expanded private farmer's plots by 1,200 percent—from 100 square meters to 1,320 square meters—but at a price, since farmers had to pay the state rent for the use of the expanded land.[18] During the 1990s famine the government tolerated the markets, but did not sanction them and in fact harassed merchants and traders in them from time to time. These reforms sanctioned them for a while, presumably hoping the market reforms would help the country deal with its chronic food security problems and might stimulate economic growth.

What the reforms did do was to cause high rates of inflation—Noland and Haggard in their fine book on the North Korean famine estimate that in the year following the reforms, the price of grain increased 300 percent. This massive increase in prices likely caused elevated levels of excess mortality from acute malnutrition among some populations. The reforms also led to a general annual inflation rate of 100 percent for years following the reforms, only stabilizing briefing in 2007. The inflationary pressures meant that the attempt to eliminate the incentive for diversion failed because the price of food in the PDS and the price paid to farmers by the state for their harvest did not rise to the same level as the price farmers could get on the private markets. While some workers' wages were also increased to soften the blow to their purchasing power, the increases had a differential impact on families depending on where they lived, their profession, and the party and military status (which affected their access to food). The reaction of the central government to the price increases was to impose price controls on items in the market, particularly food, controls that were largely ignored by merchants and traders.

Thus the inflationary pressures after the 2002 reforms caused a major economic and food security shock to a population that had come to rely on the markets for its survival. In particular, workers and miners—whose mines and factories produced limited or no output—were most vulnerable to this shock, as they had been to the 1990s famine itself. They had become

18 Noland and Haggard, *Famine in North Korea*, 179.

the poorest and most economically vulnerable population in the country. This second shock was likely as destabilizing to some people's food security as was the first shock caused by the famine, precisely because this second shock came upon the population precipitously and thus did not give families time to adjust to the higher prices. The hesitant efforts at reform unintentionally created a new chronically food-insecure class of permanently destitute urban workers and miners (the same class of people who experienced disproportionately high mortality rates during the famine, compared with those of farm families). Many were permanently unemployed and stopped receiving wages when their industries collapsed as the Soviet economic system unraveled, or were underemployed at substantially reduced wages. The 2002 reforms significantly increased inequities in North Korean society, but did not offset this by increasing jobs or the level of wealth through rapid and sustained economic growth.

During the period between the reforms of 2002 and 2005 a nascent North Korean market economy began to evolve, however fitful, however inequitable, and however limited it was. By 2005 Pyongyang began to crack down on the markets, probably because of the high inflation rates and increasing opposition from opponents of reform in the senior ranks of the party, opposition likely attributable to the failure of the reforms to stimulate higher levels of economic growth or agricultural production.

The November 2009 Currency Reforms and Food Security: The Third Shock

On November 30, 2009, and later on December 28, 2009, Pyongyang announced three new economic "reforms" that had a profound effect on the North Korean currency, household savings, and new emerging businesses. The first was to redenominate the won (the North Korean currency) at a rate of 100 old won to 1 new won, with the stipulation that the population was given a week (November 30–December 6) to exchange the old currency for new, while limiting the amount an individual could exchange to 100,000 won (which at black market exchange rates amounted to $40 at the time).[19] The second reform was to ban the use of foreign currency (Japanese, U.S., and Chinese currency were commonly used in economic transactions) and criminalize its possession. Finally, authorities shut down general commercial markets across the country, restricting their activities to food production,

19 Scott Snyder, "North Korea Currency Reform: What Happened and What Will Happen to Its Economy," March 31, 2010, http://asiafoundation.org/resources/pdfs/SnyderDPRKCurrency.pdf.

theoretically for a limited list of food items only. North Korean officials claimed that the purpose of the reforms was to restrain inflation that was complicating government efforts to achieve prosperity by 2012, the year that would mark the hundredth anniversary of Kim Il-sung's birth—an event that would be accompanied by major celebrations requiring money the government may not have had.[20]

In fact, the reforms caused the third major economic shock to the North Korean people since the collapse of the Soviet system, sparking rage among the population. There were some reports of people burning banknotes over the government's decision.[21] The reforms wiped out savings for many North Koreans; those living just above survival were financially devastated. Reports circulated of people killing themselves, swearing publicly against the government, and others organizing public protests.[22] Food prices soared as uncertainty led to hoarding and there were reports that by mid-January starvation deaths were occurring. According to the *New York Times*, a group of military veterans from the 1950–53 Korean War staged a protest in January 2010 in front of a party office in Danchon, a town on North Korea's eastern coast.[23] This show of public discontent took place after some people in Danchon had died of hunger.

The reaction of the government was unprecedented: it quickly released emergency food in late January to quell the unrest. It then also raised the limit an individual could exchange to 150,000 won (originally 100,000) in cash and 300,000 won in bank savings.[24] This did not placate the population and as a result the regime actually apologized for the botched reforms, a historic event in North Korean history.[25] Pak Nam-gi, the 77-year-old senior Finance Ministry official who was ostensibly responsible for the reforms, was blamed for the financial debacle and in mid-March 2010 he was

20 James Lister, "Currency Reform in North Korea," *The Korea Times*, January 8, 2010, http://www.koreatimes.co.kr/www/news/nation/2011/01/120_58710.html.

21 "North Korea Currency Reform Sparks Anger," BBC News, December 4, 2009, http://news.bbc.co.uk/2/hi/8395268.stm.

22 "North Korea Admits Drastic Currency Reform, is Silent on Protests," *The Christian Science Monitor*, December 4, 2009, http://www.csmonitor.com/World/Asia-Pacific/2009/1204/p06s07-woap.html.

23 "Economic Measures by North Korea Prompt New Hardships and Unrest," *New York Times*, February 3, 2010, http://www.nytimes.com/2010/02/04/world/asia/04korea.html.

24 Jun Kwanwoo, "North Korea's Shock Currency Revaluation Sparks Anger," Agence France Press, December 2, 2009.

25 "North Korea Is Said to Apologize for Currency Changes," *The New York Times*, February 12, 2010, http://www.nytimes.com/2010/02/12/world/asia/12korea.html.

executed by firing squad.[26] By late January 2011 some of the reforms were rescinded, but in many cases it was too late to repair the damage that had been done to people's savings and to merchant's businesses.

The net effect of these reforms was to strike a devastating blow to the nascent middle class of merchants and traders not dependent on the state for their income and standard of living, pauperize them, and destroy their tenuous food security. The government in effect destroyed the money supply and with it people's savings, and allowed the central bank to print new money and use it for Pyongyang's own purposes. Some North Korea watchers argued this was done deliberately in a futile attempt to reestablish state control over the economic system and abolish the new middle class. Other believe the regime's objectives were narrower—confiscating people's savings for use by the state—but whatever the motivation may have been, the economic consequences were devastating.

The Consequences of the Three Shocks to Food Security

What do these three shocks have to do with food insecurity, acute malnutrition, and famine deaths? In 1982 the Nobel-Prize–winning economist, Amartya Sen, published his now celebrated work called *Poverty and Famines: An Essay on Entitlement and Deprivation*, in which he changed our understanding of famines and their relationship to poverty. Prior to Sen, the food availability decline theory (of Thomas Malthus) dominated famine analysis, which explained famines as a reduction in aggregate food supply, when in fact it is much more related to poverty. Sen writes: "Starvation is the characteristic of some people not having enough food to eat. It is not the characteristic of there being not enough food to eat."[27] I have managed humanitarian relief efforts in famines over a twenty-three-year period and food was almost always available; it was simply the case that the poorest people without money were shut out of the market, particularly during rapid price increases, because they did lacked both a tradable commodity and enough political clout to command food in a socialist economy through the PDS. Sen tells us that some famines are sometimes caused by a decline in the aggregate food supply—which was certainly the case in North Korea in the 1990s—but the questions of who gets to eat what food when has a great deal

26 "N. Korean Technocrat Executed for Bungled Currency Reform: Sources," *Yonhap*, March 18, 2010, http://english.yonhapnews.co.kr/northkorea/2010/03/18/72/040100 0000AEN20100318004400315F.HTML.

27 Amartya Sen, *Poverty and Famines: An Essay on Entitlement and Deprivation* (New York, NY: Oxford University Press, 1981), 1.

to do with people's ownership of food and access to markets, and—in the case of North Korea—who has political power to command food.

A food crisis usually occurs, in my own experience, when the pricing system and people's assets (or means of producing food) are skewed in their relationship to each other over a relatively short period of time because of a very steep and very rapid rise in prices.[28] This likely took place in the year following the 2002 reforms, when food prices increased by 300 percent. People are remarkably resilient when suffering under acute food distress, but at some point their coping mechanisms collapse and they begin the downward spiral to an early death.

The three shocks to the North Korean population I described above caused acute food insecurity, hunger, and even widespread deaths among certain populations, in the case of the first shock in the mid-1990s. How did the government respond to these shocks? And what in their response can provide any hint of what they might do to address chronic and severe food insecurity in the future? As food availability declined in the DPRK during the first 1994–99 shock, the central authorities responded with a series of measures that exacerbated the crisis. Officials panicked in the fall of 1996 because of the abysmal harvest and they withheld food from the PDS just when people needed food, fearing they would not have enough to feed the party, security apparatus, and military over the next year (1996–97). Since many people had not received rations since late in 1995 and many were acutely malnourished (and some had died), this action made a manageable crisis into a catastrophe.

The second action they appeared to have taken was to shut off food aid shipments to the northeast through the international aid system and perhaps even internal trade, particularly to North and South Hamhung and Ryangang provinces.[29] I documented this triage by reviewing the shipping manifests of the WFP in 1995–97, which showed that only 18 percent of food aid went to eastern ports, where 33 percent of the population lived.[30] The east was chronically much more food insecure and should have received the bulk of the shipments. Hwang Jang-yop told a Japanese scholar of a proposal (which was never approved) discussed at a 1996 senior leadership meeting to destroy several of the major bridges through the mountains that connected the northeast to the western region of the country, in order to

28 For a further explanation of this phenomenon, see Andrew Natsios and Kelly Doley, "The Coming Food Coups," *Washington Quarterly* 32, no. 1 (January 2009): 7–25.

29 Cited in Natsios, *Great North Korean Famine*, 106–09.

30 Personal copies of WFP shipping manifests and shipping records of bilateral imports.

limit or stop internal food trade from the surplus west to the deficit east. Given the most food insecure region of the country was the northeast, this amounted to regional triage—deliberately shutting off the northeast from the country's food supply to allow the rest of the country to survive.

The North Korean government addressed the famine-crisis with appeals for more intense political education of the people, more repression, counterproductive command and control measures, and nearly continuous confrontation with the very groups—the donors, the UN humanitarian agencies, and NGOs—that were trying to feed their own people when they refused to take the measures to necessary to feed them. The first shock suggests the North Korean government's central, overriding imperative had become survival—no matter what the human cost.

The magnitude and breadth of the famine was an epoch-changing event in North Korean history—the chaos it unleashed, the deaths of as many as 3.5 million people, the uncovering of a coup plot in the revered North Korean People's Army, the trauma suffered by the population, the searing memories of the horrors of the famine for the common people, the mass movement of people to China in search of food and back, and finally the decline of popular support for the Kim dynasty—changing the country in ways the outside world and dry data and analysis can only dimly understand. These changes provided the foundation for a new North Korean economic order to unfold. It was the reforms of 2002 that began the process.

We do not have to go very far to consider the long-term consequences of a famine for a totalitarian regime. Dali Yang argues in his book on Mao Zedong's Great Leap Forward famine (1958–62)—which some scholars estimate now claim killed nearly 40 million people—that the memory of the famine led to economic reform in those provinces most severely affected, even before Deng Xiaoping began the economic reform process on the national level.[31]

The Reforms of 2002

The reforms of 2002 did accelerate the movement of North Korea to a more market-based economic system. *The Economist* in May 2010 documented some consequences of the evolving new economic order:

> According to Park In-ho, an editor at *Daily NK*, a web-based news agency based in Seoul but with informants inside North Korea, the markets not only supplied food

31 Dali L. Yang, *Calamity and Reform in China: State, Rural Society, and Institutional Change Since the Great Leap Famine* (Stanford, CA: Stanford University Press, 1996), chapter 3, particularly p. 96.

but also functioned as labor exchanges, gave birth to a private transport industry and led to the emergence of financial services, such as street-corner currency exchanges. There was even, he says, a type of "mutual fund" in which villagers would pool their savings to buy goods from China. When they were sold in North Korea, the profits were distributed.[32]

Even more important was that the markets served as a location for information exchange. Mobile phones could be bought there, which were tapped into signals from across the Chinese border, leading to the dissemination of financial information that led markets to become more efficient and reduced rice prices in different parts of the country.[33] Nothing like this kind of economic activity existed in prefamine North Korea. Despite this evolving economic system and perhaps because of it, the chronic food problems grew more acute for the destitute population of the country.

While the reforms of 2002 were meant by the leadership to address some of the country's chronic food problems, they did not succeed in doing that. In fact the reforms set off a period of prolonged and severe inflation beginning in 2002 that abated in 2007, only to increase again in 2008–09. Since these reforms took place three years after the end of the famine, when the country had just begun to recover its equilibrium, these appear to be the one attempt by Kim Jong-il and the party elites at any incentive-based-reforms. The fact that they came at a heavy price—increased food insecurity—may undercut any future attempts by reformers in the government to try again.

The 2009 Currency and Market Policy Changes

The third shock—and the most severe since the 1990s famine—was entirely a consequence of the disastrous currency and market policies announced in November and December 2009. We do not have to go too far to determine just how disastrous the policies were because the regime itself provides us the evidence: they apologized, tried to modify the reforms, executed a senior official by firing squad, and then abolished the reforms altogether, though too late to undo the damage.

The WFP/FAO 2009/2010 crop assessment noted, using sanitized prose:

A large number of low income non-farming households faced a significant food consumption gap as the cereals received from the public distribution system provided only about half the daily caloric requirement on average. The deficit was

---

32 "Not Waving. Perhaps Drowning," *The Economist*, May 27, 2010, http://www.economist.com/node/16214349.

33 Ibid.

unlikely to have been fully covered by other foods due to low purchasing power of these households.[34]

Put directly, families with no access to farm production, no political power to command food, no products to trade on the markets for food, and no income went hungry or worse, died. These families typically were industrial workers and miners—where the factory or mine ceased to produce any outputs of any value—who had no relatives in rural areas with access to farm production. This severely food insecure population should give the Politburo pause because they live in urban areas where a large disaffected population can cause political instability. Historically and globally, most famines have been in rural areas, and sometimes have had cascading consequences in urban areas. In North Korea, however, the famine and food insecurity epicenter has been in the politically most destabilizing region: cities, where famines are more visible and where political power is concentrated.

What is most fascinating about the 2009 currency disaster is not why Pyongyang proposed the reforms, but the unprecedented public fury they unleashed among the new middle class, and the reaction of the government to that public outrage. Nothing like this reaction has ever occurred in North Korea since its founding in the 1940s; it implies that the structure of North Korean society had undergone profound change during the seven years after the 2002 reforms—the public were no longer so terrified of the State that they would acquiesce to these new policies that they understood would put them at risk of a new famine. A new, more independent middle class of merchants, small business people, and traders was now making its weight and influence felt. The fact that Pyongyang would propose such a disastrous set of economic policies showed how completely out of touch the aging senior party elite in Pyongyang were with public sentiment and the economic reality facing the population. Even more disturbing may be the possibility that the currency disaster was driven less by the party elite and more by the military and security apparatus, the most reactionary and resistant faction in the government to any reform movement and the most isolated from the outside world. The regime's attempt to reassert the dying old order may undermine the legitimacy of the state for the nascent middle class and new merchant class to such a degree that the ongoing and rocky transition to Kim Jong-un as North Korea's leader, may be seriously compromised.

34 FAO/WFP, *Special Report: FAO/WFP Crop and Food Security Assessment Mission to the Democratic People's Republic of Korea*, November 16, 2010, http://www.fao. org/docrep/013/al968e/al968e00.htm.

What is the Prospect for Improved Food Security
in the DPRK Over the Immediate Future?

It is dismal at best.

While it is possible some powerful, but secret North Korean acolyte of Deng Xiaoping or Mikhail Gorbachev is waiting to take over, the succession drama in North Korea suggests otherwise. Kim Jong-un does not appear to have the maturity, intellect, disposition, wit, or authority to understand or take the risks any reform effort would entail. In the event of a weak leader, the military and security apparatus will run the country and the currency manipulation scheme of 2009 may have been their handiwork. There is no evidence since Kim Jong-un's assumption of power that the regime is moving toward major reforms, and in fact the bellicose threats of war by Pyongyang against South Korea and the United States in the first half of 2013 may be evidence of an attempt by the new leader and his advisors to shore up the sclerotic old order.

What are the Political and Strategic Consequences
of the North Korean Food Problem?

The chronic food insecurity of North Korea has strategic consequences. The confrontational external behavior of the DPRK leadership may be directly connected to its preeminent objective, which is regime survival. It directs the attention of the military to an imminent external threat, even if that threat is entirely concocted by incidents North Korea itself creates. It directs the attention of the population to that same external threat instead of their own immediate food problems. When the country's food system is under the greatest stress, Pyongyang has often used its reputation for provocative behavior to command more food aid from donors. Typically it will cause a military incident, followed by appeals for food aid through the WFP or to its Chinese allies. Or, it will create military incidents as it launches economic reform measures. In the middle of the war scare in April and May 2013, the North Korean ambassador to Mongolia made a public appeal for food aid at the foreign ministry in Ulan Bator (Mongolia produces no food surpluses themselves). This may have been an indirect message to donor governments of a growing North Korean food deficit that Pyongyang has been unable to address.

The North Korean emergency food aid program has been in place since 1994, interrupted by occasional shutdowns when the leadership finds international food aid agencies' presence too intrusive or their rules too offensive. This is what happened in March 2009 when the DPRK expelled NGOs and cancelled the sizeable U.S. government aid program that had entailed much higher levels of monitoring than in any period in the past. The United States Agency for International Development (USAID) had pursued a wise policy of delivering food aid in monthly shipments (the DPRK insisted all the food aid be delivered up front, which USAID rejected) so that if the DPRK government violated the agreed-upon food monitoring protocols, future shipments could be cancelled. On two occasions in 2008 and 2009, the North Korean government violated these protocols and USAID stopped food aid shipments. The second time USAID redirected food aid shipment away from North Korea after violations of the protocols, Pyongyang announced on March 17, 2009, that it was cancelling the aid program entirely and expelling aid agencies.

The Shape of Food Aid Programs in North Korea

The currency reforms substantially increased the food insecurity of the North Korean population by destroying savings and thus the people's ability to command food on the markets. The weak leadership of the country since Kim Jong-il's death is a function of a rocky transition to power for Kim Jong-un. The power vacuum will be filled by the security apparatus and military, and this will ensure no constructive internal economic reforms will take place. Any hope of reform died with Kim Jong-il, who at least attempted reforms in 2002, however anemic they may have been. And thus the chronic food insecurity will continue, and will eventually pose a threat to political stability unless China steps in to fill the food deficit. And this will probably lead the DPRK leadership to make a new appeal for food aid from the World Food Programme. The WFP produced two reports in the summer of 2012 warning of a substantial decline in food production and the increased risk of a new famine. When the joint WFP/FAO fall harvest assessment was released a month after these dire predictions, it reported an improved harvest. One plausible explanation for this dramatic shift in the assessment is that the DPRK leadership could not afford to have a famine develop as Kim Jong-un completes his first year in office, so they doctored their harvest estimates for propaganda purposes—and then sent an indirect appeal out through the Mongolian government for food aid.

Should a new food aid program be undertaken, Pyongyang will try to manipulate it for its own purposes. While the international food aid program in North Korea is not the focus of this chapter, I will conclude with some final comments on the design of any future food aid programs in the country in light of the three shocks I described above.

Since the North Korean state was organized after the Korean War, it has fed the population based on the usefulness of classes of people to the survival of the state and the Kim family's hold on power. Despite claims of egalitarian Marxist ideology to the contrary, the North Korean people have never had an equal right to command food. Food has always been an instrument of political power in North Korea to control the population—to restrict their geographic mobility, to ensure their dependence on the political elite to get fed, and to reward through increased access to food (among other things) the security apparatus that manages the organized system of repression. While the 2002 economic reforms seemed to have moved the country away from the old command and control food security system embodied in the PDS, the 2009 reforms suggest elements of the old order were unhappy with the evolving system. It is likely they will try to use any outside aid, regardless of its source, to reestablish the connection between food security and political control. And thus any future food aid program that aggressively manages to conform to international humanitarian standards will directly clash with the North Korean effort to reestablish the old order.

Any new food aid program ought to be structured to avoid being used by the reactionary elements within the regime seeking to turn the clock back and crush the emerging new market economy. I have described below ten general guidelines that might accomplish this. If the North Korean authorities refuse to comply with these principles, no new food aid program should be undertaken as it would be counterproductive and undermine the new economy.

The WFP, the three principal bilateral donors—China, South Korea, and the United States (and possibly Japan as a fourth)—and NGOs ought to recognize this inherent conflict and plan accordingly. China has historically provided food aid for two purposes: to prevent the North Korean state system from collapsing, which would precipitate a potentially destabilizing political crisis on the Korean Peninsula; and, to end or at least limit large-scale refugee movements across the Korean-Chinese border. On the first count the Chinese aid program may have been marginally successful thus far in postponing the eventual collapse of the regime (though even that is debatable), but it has done nothing to encourage the North Koreans toward economic reform. On the second objective their efforts have failed; their food program has done nothing to change the internal incentives of refugees to try to get to China. This would have required the Chinese to target their food toward those most likely to move across the border and thus far they have refused to do that. Any future effort to use a humanitarian assistance program to increase food security will require all three major donors to agree to a common strategy, carried out through the WFP if it agreed to the conditions. We have one powerful older model for how this program should be run: Herbert Hoover's administration of the Volga River Famine program in the early 1920s in Russia. In that program, Hoover made clear to the new Bolshevik government that he—not they—would control the entire U.S. government food aid program, which he did very successfully, saving millions of Russian lives.[35]

Three options are available to international humanitarian policy makers: (1) capitulate to North Korean demands to control food aid, which the WFP has done too often (or use food aid to buy North Korean cooperation in nuclear talks, where both the talks and the effort to buy cooperation have been an abysmal failure); (2) refuse to provide any assistance given the inevitable clash; or (3) insist on the enforcement of an even more rigorous set of protocols that challenge the state system and avoid doing any damage to the nascent private economy now developing in the country. On the first option, any effort of bilateral donors, NGOs, and the WFP to return to conditions under which the food aid program operated beginning in 1995 is ethically indefensible given what we now know about the North Korean system and its current resistance to reform. On the second option, abandoning the country to a second famine is ethically indefensible in my view, though I would emphasize that the responsibility for the starvation of the North Korean people is entirely the fault of the Kim regime. On the third option, how might a food aid protocol be designed to challenge the state ideology or at least avoid undermining the evolution of the North Korean economy?

1. Under no circumstances should food aid be distributed through the public distribution system, a corrupt, politicized tool of state control and repression.
2. Under no circumstances should the food most preferred by the North Koreans—rice—be distributed, because it invites diversion by the elites. Maize and bulgur wheat should be distributed instead because their recipients are self-selecting. The poor eat maize now, and we know they will eat bulgur wheat if there are no other options.
3. No food aid should be delivered to west coast ports, as the western part of the country is the most food secure. Instead, food aid should be delivered in small amounts to the eastern ports, to as many smaller ports as possible, where it is likely to remain due to the continued paralysis of the transportation system.

35 See Benjamin Weissman's fine study of the Hoover effort, *Herbert Hoover and Famine Relief in Soviet Russia 1921–23* (Stanford, Calif: Hoover Institution Press, 1974).

4. Food aid ought not to be connected to any negotiations over any extraneous issues such as talks over the nuclear or any other issue, as rigorous monitoring will be the first thing the North Koreans insist be abandoned, which the ROK or U.S. government might be tempted to accede to.

5. All food aid shipments should be made on a monthly basis, so that should the North Koreans violate the agreed-upon aid protocols, future shipments can be cancelled.

6. Regular random nutritional surveys must be performed in sentinel surveillance sites to observe malnutrition rates, a drop in which would be one indication that food was actually getting to the poorest and most vulnerable people. If surveys showed no improvement in nutritional conditions, it would show that the food aid program was compromised and in my view should be shut down.

7. Food price monitors should be stationed at major markets around the country to report on any spikes in prices that could increase food insecurity. Should these price increases take place, food aid should be auctioned off at the port facilities to moderate the price increases.

8. Food should be targeted at unemployed factory workers and miners and their families who are destitute, or to any group the nutritional surveys show is food insecure and malnourished.

9. To the extent possible in schools, food should be cooked by NGO workers and distributed in school for children to eat. Food, once cooked, is not marketable and must be eaten quickly or it will spoil.

10. Finally, any aid protocol must insist on unlimited, unannounced, and random access and monitoring by international food experts who are Korean speakers. The aid community ought to insist that no limit be placed on the number of these monitors.

Food aid should, however, be a temporary measure, and is not viable as a long-term answer to North Korea's chronic food and agricultural problems. The fact that the food aid program in North Korea has been in operation since 1994 is testament to the DPRK regime's abysmal failure to constructively address its food insecurity challenge. The only long-term solution to North Korea's food insecurity is a combination of a privatization of the agricultural system, with investments in inputs such as improved seed stock, more and better-used fertilizer, gravity rather electrically driven irrigation systems, and better equipment and privatization and liberalization of their industrial sector. This would require the DPRK regime to reduce the funding for its military (as much as 25 percent of the GDP may be going to the military) to agriculture instead. Secondly, the chronic food insecurity of urban and mining areas can only be addressed by Chinese-style industrial market reforms that would produce marketable industrial products on international markets. This would require market liberalization, which the regime again is unlikely to initiate.

III   NORTH KOREA AND ITS NEIGHBORS

7 An Inconsolable Divide:
The Roots of the Korean Conundrum

Choe Sang-Hun

On the eve of Thanksgiving Day in 2010, I was strolling through Manhattan when the bizarreness of my home country, Korea, hit me with a neon-light glare. On the billboards of Times Square, Samsung and LG flashed their proud logos. Moments earlier, on my hotel room television, however, South Korea's Yeonpyeong Island was going up in smoke after North Korea pounded it with artillery. People rushing for cover as shells smashed their village, families mass-evacuating, homes gutted in flames—these were not scenes one would normally associate with a country that plays host to the G-20 summit of the world's wealthiest nations, floods the global market with fancy electronics, and exports "K-pop" and television dramas to mesmerized audiences around Asia and beyond.

Introduction:
A Korean Cat-and-Mouse Game

Six decades after the guns of the Korean War fell silent in an uneasy cease-fire and with the peninsula still divided, Korea remains a vexation. North Korea (or the Democratic People's Republic of Korea, DPRK) has survived decades of international sanctions, the collapse of the Soviet bloc, and a famine that killed millions of people. It has flouted the UN Security Council to conduct the world's three most recent nuclear tests. Time and again, it has sent its neighbors into a panic, with its missile tests and military and terrorist attacks. North Korea not only has defied the post–Cold War upheavals that changed the world around it, but it remains proudly isolated and fiercely focused on its ideology. While South Korea has moved on to build an export-driven global economy, North Korea has dug in, building and continuing to perfect a garrison state where malnutrition stunts children's growth, an unaccounted number languish in prison camps, and party slogans scream of a coming American invasion, exhorting people to become "human rifles and bombs." The country was so isolated, and its regime's control so pervasive, that when an estimated 10 percent of its population died in the famine of the 1990s, the outside world hardly heard a peep of protest from those starving. Still, tragically for its people, the regime remains defiant: "Let's live our own way!"

South Korea's policies toward North Korea—and the international efforts to end its nuclear program—have tried both engaging it with incentives and punishing it with sanctions. Neither approach has succeeded in changing the dictatorial regime or eliminating its nuclear weapons, perhaps not because one approach was worse than the other but because their implementation lacked support and persistence or because, as frustrated negotiators would say, North Korea was not ready for a deal that would give it a different future. Fractured domestic politics in South Korea, a shifting focus in U.S. foreign policy, a rising China with its own design for the peninsula, mistrust between Pyongyang and Washington, the North's intransigence—these are some of the elements of the Korean conundrum. Looking through lenses of domestic politics and national interests, neighboring powers see different pictures of North Korea's future. Nursing a visceral contempt for having to deal with such a rogue state as North Korea, Washington has so far responded with dialogue only when it faced crises, such as the DPRK's withdrawal from the Treaty on the Non-Proliferation of Nuclear Weapons (NPT) and its reprocessing of spent nuclear fuel. Such talks quickly bogged down in recriminations. They produced deals patched together with ambiguous wording on key disputes and fraught with promises the negotiators never intended to keep or were unable to sell to skeptical politicians at home. They were bound to break down. And they did.

Washington and Seoul had entered negotiations with Pyongyang demanding a "complete, verifiable, and irrevocable dismantling" of its nuclear assets. After years of talks, they have failed completely, verifiably, and almost irrevocably. After accomplishing its plutonium "breakout" during the Bush administration in Washington and the Kim Dae-jung and Roh Moo-hyun governments in Seoul, North Korea raced for a uranium breakout under the

Obama and Lee Myung-bak administrations. It came to the table with its own strident demands: an end to the "hostile U.S. policy," the signing of a peace treaty, the lifting of sanctions, and the opening of diplomatic ties. It chopped up and dragged out talks. It hedged its bets. It lied. It exploited Washington's distraction during the Iraq War to harvest nuclear fuel while never convincing its interlocutors that what it said it wanted was what it really wanted and that it would pay the price for it: the abandonment of its nuclear weapons and improvement in its human rights conditions. In the end, it won more sanctions. Both sides had expected a lot from a counterpart whom they didn't trust.

The Korean stalemate has created a cat-and-mouse game where all sides involved in the so-called Six-Party Talks are "just serious about playing the game as long as they can," while no one seriously believes that North Korea will abandon its nuclear weapons and hostile acts.[1] Cynicism and educated helplessness pervade.

What we face in Korea is not simply a problem of nuclear proliferation, but rather a problem as old as the divide of the peninsula and as complex as the unfinished business of the Korean War. This pestering problem known as North Korea, its nuclear weapons included, will not go away until Korea is unified again. Isolated and friendless, trapped in a dogma of Korea-vs.-imperialist, and still technically at war with the United States, North Korea will never face South Korea and its American ally without nuclear weapons. Tackling its nuclear threat without addressing the root cause of fear and hostility—the Korean divide—is like grappling with tendrils of smoke without reaching the fire. For now, we do not know how and in what form unification will come or for that matter, whether regional powers even want Korea unified.

Divided but Tangled:
Inter-Korean Relations in a Historical and Chronological Perspective

After three years of warfare, the Korean War was suspended in 1953, leaving the peninsula divided as it was when first partitioned by the Americans and the Soviets at the end of World War II. With Chinese and Soviet backing, North Korea invaded the South in 1950, trying but failing to unify Korea under a communist flag. American-led UN forces contained but tried and failed to "roll back" communism from the peninsula. For many,

1 The analogy and remarks are from the readers comments on "Talking to North Korea," *New York Times*, January 13, 2011, http://community.nytimes.com/comments/www.nytimes.com/2011/01/14/opinion/14fri1.html?sort=recommended.

the inconclusive conflict "marked the onset of the Cold War in Asia and established the ideological, political and strategic divisions that continue to dominate the international relations of East Asia to this day."[2] Indeed, a tension-provocation-reaction-stalemate cycle set by the war continues in Korea, as most recently demonstrated by the North Korean attack on Yeonpyeong, the North's nuclear test in February 2013, and the reactions of regional powers.

With their contest for the right to rule the whole of Korea unresolved, both Koreas kept up mutual enmity during the postwar decades. South Korean authoritarianism claimed legitimacy and popular support by reminding its people of the presence of the North Korean threat, just as the North Korean regime justified its totalitarianism with the need to liberate the South from "American imperialists." In the South, the government tortured and imprisoned political dissidents in communist witch-hunts; in the North, children learned to add and subtract by counting American soldiers they would kill.

A historic shift came when Kim Dae-jung flew to Pyongyang in 2000 for the first inter-Korean summit. In the ensuing decade, billions of dollars of South Korean investment, aid, trade, and long-term loans of food flowed into the North. Thousands of aging Koreans were allowed to hold temporary reunions with spouses and siblings they had not seen since the war. Kim's Sunshine Policy aimed to use economic goodwill to encourage North Korea to shed its ideological rigidity, political isolation, and military hostility while reducing the economic gap and the cost of eventual reunification. But the decades-old crust of misgivings proved hard to melt, and the road to reconciliation bumpy. North Korea opened the door to outside investors, but only to the fenced-off enclaves at the corners of its territory. Only one of them—the Kaesŏng industrial complex on the southwest—was successful, but only on a limited scale. Pyongyang imposed a litany of "mosquito-net" restrictions designed to keep the cash flowing in but keep outside influences from the rest of the population. Meanwhile, six-nation talks on ending North Korea's nuclear weapons program stalled. The regime held onto its nuclear weapons as the only key to survival that its ideological quandary at home permitted it to see. It confined its interaction with South Korea to satisfying its immediate needs for aid and using it as a tool to win the attention

2 John Swenson-Wright, "Contested History: Re-Examining The Korean War," review of *The Korean War: A History*, by Bruce Cumings, *Global Asia* 5, no. 4 (Winter 2010), http://www.globalasia.org/V5N4_Winter_2010/Bruce_Cumings.html?PHPSESSID=coefda8e06979f10c4d8208a89b7ae25.

of Washington. Kim Jong-il never kept his promise made in 2000 to visit South Korea for a return summit.

A political fault line deepened in the South. Kim Dae-jung and Roh Moo-hyun, who succeeded Kim in 2003 and inherited the Sunshine Policy, faced conservative accusations that their unconditional aid bolstered the Pyongyang regime that abused human rights and refused to give up nuclear weapons. The North's nuclear and missile tests, the naval skirmishes it triggered in 1999 and 2002, the friction the Sunshine Policy had created with the Bush administration, and North Korea's refusal to discuss denuclearization with the South or to allow outside monitors to ensure that food aid reached the needy, not its military—all these provided ammunition for right-wing enemies of Kim and Roh. In the waning days of his rule in 2007, Roh flew to Pyongyang for a second inter-Korean summit. The meeting produced a comprehensive deal for economic cooperation. But his feisty relationship with the conservative opposition and right-wing dailies at home ensured that his trip received more ridicule than hail. The pall was descending on the Sunshine Policy.

The political pendulum swung when Lee Myung-bak won the December 2007 election. His "Vision 3000: Denuclearization and Openness" challenged the core of the North's survival plan: it would need to give up its nuclear weapons if it wanted South Korean largess to continue. Inter-Korean relations spiraled down, tough-guy thinking on one side met with hard-line responses on the other. The South stopped all cross-border economic cooperation, except the Kaesŏng industrial park. The North cut off official dialogue, calling Lee a "traitor" and "rat." In Seoul, proponents of dogged engagement, who argued that the inter-Korean contacts painstakingly cultivated during the Sunshine period should be built and improved upon, found no room in official policy discussions. In the South's viciously divided politics, an us-or-them ideological rivalry and an ad hominem impulse to discredit the enemy often directed policymaking. Lee's North Korea policy no doubt reflected disillusionment with Kim Jong-il. But it was also driven by a political need to discredit the Sunshine Policy and Roh, the more temperamental and combative yet lesser of the conservatives' two archenemies at home. Inter-Korean relations chilled further after a South Korean warship, the *Cheonan*, sank in disputed border waters in March 2010 in what the South called a North Korean torpedo attack. In November 2010, American experts visiting North Korea were escorted to witness a stunning revelation: a brand-new industrial-scale uranium enrichment plant in the North Korean nuclear complex of Yongbyon, north of Pyongyang. North Korea was fast acquiring technology to build uranium bombs in addition to its plutonium weapons. Hardly had the world registered the shock when the North delivered another bombshell, literally. On November 23, its shoreline artillery rolled out of its tunnels and launched a barrage on Yeonpyeong. The attack stirred South Koreans' worst fears: North Korean artillery and rocket tubes clustered along the border only thirty-five miles north of Seoul, home to ten million South Koreans. Capable of turning the South Korean capital into what the North calls a "sea of fire," these tubes had already served as the North's weapons of mass destruction (WMD) long before its acquisition of nukes. The shelling indicated that nuclear weapons were emboldening the North to launch military provocations with impunity.

Conservatives had argued that shipping unconditional aid to North Korea to persuade it not to raise tensions was as useful as bribing a gangster for peace; it worked only until the next payment. Lee's tough approach brought a moral and ideological satisfaction to conservatives, and perhaps taught the Pyongyang regime a lesson: its blackmailing doesn't always work. But as his term neared the end, Lee faced growing accusations among progressive South Koreans that his approach did little to stop North Korea from expanding its nuclear capability or changing its behavior—it only worsened its bellicosity. Park Geun-hye, who won the presidential election in December 2012 and was inaugurated in February the following year, championed "Trustpolitik," a North Korea policy that she said would incorporate lessons learned from the previous liberal and conservative governments' dealings with North Korea.

Both the *Cheonan* sinking and the Yeonpyeong attack took place just south of the Northern Limit Line (NLL). Unilaterally imposed by an American general after the Korean War armistice was signed but never accepted by North Korea as a maritime borderline, the NLL symbolizes a war that has never officially ended and the festering instability of the peninsula. North Korea keeps rattling that weak link in Korea's fragile peace to wrangle peace talks with the United States, talks it said it would turn into a forum for regional nuclear arms reduction. It has a far bigger chess game in mind than trading its nukes for mere economic benefits. In September 2010, its vice foreign minister, Pak Kil-yon, told the UN General Assembly: "As long as U.S. nuclear aircraft carriers sail around the seas of our country, our nuclear deterrent can never be abandoned, but should be strengthened further." North Korea defined itself as a nuclear power in a revised constitution adopted in April 2012. In March 2013 its ruling Workers' Party adopted a new party line that called for expanding its nuclear arsenal while "simultaneously" rebuilding the economy. It has become increasingly clear that North Korea is now focused on making the rest of the world accept it as a nuclear weapons state.

Making North Korean Sense:
Why North Korea Behaves The Way It Does

Despite a growing heap of media reports and wordage from analysts, we know few hard facts about the Pyongyang leadership. "There is no such thing as a North Korea expert," a top national security aide to President Lee told foreign media on October 12, 2012, citing the paucity of reliable information on North Korea. Until the North's state-run media carried the photos of Kim Jong-un, Kim Jong-il's twenty-something son, attending a party meeting in September 2010, no outsider had seen him or any photos of him as an adult. Although he took over top leadership in Pyongyang following his father's abrupt death in December 2011, there is no credible profile of the young man who has inherited one of the world's most militaristic regimes. Kim Jong-il once said: "When the enemies peek into our republic, they only see a fog."

Kim Jong-il himself had been caricatured as an all-purpose menace: "a pygmy," "evil," "Satan," "Communist bandit chieftain," or a nutcase in a Mao suit with a bouffant hairdo, elevator shoes, and a lavish taste for top-label French cognac, Black Sea caviar, and pretty women. Or, he was a "smart" and "rational" leader with a sense of humor and a desire to negotiate. Taken alone, none of these labels did justice to a ruthless tactician who time and again fended off pressure from Washington and Seoul and forced them to talk, and ultimately haggle, with him while creating the world's newest and implacably bellicose nuclear weapons state. The media-driven perceptions of North Korea as a Cold War relic, capricious regime, or hermit kingdom encircled by global economies also fail to fully explain a regime that lost a sizeable chunk of its population during a war, endured another decimation of its people in a famine, and still stands, impoverished yet proud and defiant. The outside media focus on the quirkiness, illness, and (mostly imagined) "reform," "power struggles," and "political purges" in Pyongyang. That penchant reaches a fervor pitch during transfers of power in Pyongyang—first in 1994, when Kim Jong-il's father, founding president Kim Il-sung, died, and again in 2012, when Kim Jong-un inherited the regime after Kim Jong-il's death. The media cobble together whatever scraps of information and rumor they can get and ask analysts for what usually amounts to wild guesswork. Rival governments approach the North Korean imbroglio with their vision constrained by their own fear, ideology, and ignorance. Party slogans that imbue the daily life of North Koreans are disregarded for their comical simplicity, xenophobic bombast, and anachronistic unfamiliarity. The North's threats are trivialized as "rhetoric," "bluffing," "blackmail," or the squealing of an attention-hungry child. Yet, a careful examination of North Korean acts and statements reveals that the regime over the years has been remarkably consistent with its core principles.

Honor thy Father: North Korea as a Dynasty, a Family State, and a Gigantic Cult Church

Kim Il-sung led a group of Korean guerrillas fighting colonial Japanese troops in Manchuria before the Soviets installed him in Pyongyang at the end of World War II. The Kim family cult and North Korea's official history start there. Korea is the "Kim Il-sung nation," and Kim's guerrilla-day stories its founding myth. Korea was singlehandedly liberated by Kim, a figure comparable to a "secular Christ, or Christ-substitute" among North Koreans.[3] The North's propagandists credit Kim with miracles reminiscent of Biblical stories: Kim turning pine cones into bullets and making the crippled walk. Murals show Kim leading North Koreans through harsh Manchurian hills battered by a snowstorm, and then with his son, Kim Jong-il, beaming in a spring garden filled with flowers and well-fed North Koreans. It is the Exodus of the Kim Il-sung religion. Now, under the third-generation dynastic ruler, Kim Jong-un, North Korea is finally turning into a "strong and prosperous" country no "imperialist" superpower dare provoke because it bristles with nukes and missiles. So says its propaganda.

Lee Jong-seok, a former South Korean unification minister, says of North Korea: "While the system formally purports to have the outward appearance of socialism, it is actually a magnified image of the 'oriental family' in which the state is seen as an extended family."[4] Individuals enter a child-father relationship with the revolutionary leader and his dynastic successors. Newlyweds pay homage to the nearest Kim Il-sung statue. As filial children tend to a parent's tomb in traditional Korea, citizens sweep around the Kim monuments, some every morning. At the 2010 party meeting, when Kim Jong-un appeared before the public for the first time, he was packaged to look like his grandfather: a Mao suit, portly body, swept-back hair, and that casual aloofness when he clapped his hands. In murals,

3 Bruce Cumings, *Korea's Place in the Sun: A Modern History* (New York: W.W. Norton, 1997), 420.

4 Lee Jong Seok, "The Next Kim: Prospects for Peace in Korea," *Global Asia* 5, no. 4 (Winter 2010), http://www.globalasia.org/l.php?c=e353.

musicals, monuments, statues, and editorials, the memory of colonialism and Kim Il-sung's (and Korea's) struggle against imperialists is constantly reinvented, finding his son and now his grandson places in the ongoing saga of the Kim family and the Korean revolution.[5] In November 2010, at the Vietnam Football Federation Cup, An Jong-hyok, the team doctor of the North Korean national soccer team, chastised a South Korean reporter for referring to Kim Jong-un without the appropriate honorific of "Dear Young General": "How would you feel if I talked impolitely to your father? That's exactly how I feel now. . . . We consider General Kim Jong-il and Comrade Kim Jong-un our father."[6]

In the system, the son's legitimacy as national leader rests on his "bloodline" and the infallibility of the father. Then how can the son question or disrespect the earlier leader's policies by introducing reform? The term "reform" is an anathema to the North Korean regime. Here may lie a key difference between China and North Korea. The personality cult allows no countervailing force within the regime. Kim Jong-il sat, and now his son Kim Jong-un sits, like a spider at the center of a web of state, party, military, and secret police that do not necessarily communicate with each other and all ultimately report only to him. The monolithic leader supposedly wields an almost absolute power—but within the confines his forebears bequeathed to him.

The "Military-First" Policy:
Looking at the Outside World From a Military Bunker

In the 1990s, North Korea faced its worst crisis since the war. Old socialist friends drifted away, embracing market reform, cutting trade with the North and opening ties with the South. With its economy moribund and its military decaying, North Korea was lagging irrevocably behind South Korea in their long-running competition for legitimacy. Then came the spiritual crisis: Kim Il-sung, the only leader the North Koreans had known, a deified man they believed was rescuing them from subjugation to foreign powers to a promised land of independence and "white rice and meat soup," died of heart failure in 1994. Soon bad weather moved in. Famine hit. Many people

5 Heonik Kwon, "North Korea's Politics of Longing," *Critical Asian Studies* 42, no. 1 (2010): 3–24.

6 "[단독] 北대표팀 주치의 '월드컵 결과로 인민재판? 어이없다'" [Team doctor for the North Korean national squad denies a people's court punishment for World Cup performance], 일간스포츠 [Daily sports], November 10, 2010, http://isplus.live.joinsmsn.com/news/article/article.asp?total_id=4638200&cloc=.

died in silence as the regime denounced its former allies for succumbing to capitalists and vowed to carry the socialist revolution to its bitter end. "Don't expect change from me!" was a slogan under the new leader, Kim Jong-il, the late Kim's son. With the state ration system no longer able to feed them, North Koreans scrambled for their own ways of survival: foraging in the hills for edible herbs, cultivating private plots of vegetables, trading in nascent black markets, or fleeing to China and South Korea.

Around this time, Kim adopted his *songun*, or "military-first," policy, creating a military-centric control base that would oversee crisis management. He ordered the People's Army to become the main driving force in every sector of society, from building roads to policing the people to dictating foreign policy.[7]

Pushing the military to the forefront of political life jibed with the North Korean ideology. The Korean War, which Kim Il-sung started as a "fatherland liberation war," stopped after killing, maiming, widowing, and orphaning several millions of Koreans but with the fatherland devastated and still divided. Kim not only avoided taking responsibility for his catastrophic adventurism but instead he and his son and chief apostle, Kim Jong-il, used the blank sheet created by the utter destruction to "rewrite history" and create a personality cult that perpetuated the outlook of Korea vs. imperialists.[8] In its version of history, the South started the war at the behest of the Americans and the North Koreans took up arms to deter a ceaseless imperialist plot to subjugate the whole of Korea. When the regime exhorts its people to "live, study and fight like anti-Japanese warriors," it touches the core of the belief system. When the famine hit in the 1990s, Kim Jong-il called for an "arduous march," urging his people to endure the starvation as another heroic struggle against imperialists. Just as old Korean guerrillas chased into snowy Manchurian hills fought a debilitating hunger, North Koreans were now continuing that struggle, this time against the American imperialists' attempt to "stifle" their country with trade embargoes and military exercises in preparation for invasion. In the world of North Korean propaganda, the past justifies and glorifies the present. North Koreans must keep alert; the coming war will determine whether they will live as an independent nation or suffer the humiliation of being enslaved by another foreign power, as they were by Japan in the early twentieth century. The key

7 Bruce Kingner, "Steady as She Goes on North Korea," The Heritage Foundation, October 21, 2010, http://www.heritage.org/research/commentary/2010/10/steady-as-she-goes-on-north-korea.

8 Michael J. Seth, *A Concise History of Modern Korea: From the Late Nineteenth Century to the Present* (Lanham, MD: Rowman & Littlefield, 2010), 121, 139.

is to build a strong military and follow Kim Jong-il, who by the 1990s was most commonly referred to as "Great" or "Dear General." DPRK propaganda mocked the pangs of hunger as "peevish cries for food";[9] it asserted that true believers "can live without candies, but not without bullets"; and in North Korean schools textbooks glorified the image of North Korea as a cornered hedgehog, bristling with needles to deter an arrogant tiger. The North's state media reinforced this sense of victimization and a righteous path toward empowerment as the underpinning of the Kim family's grip on power:

> Our nation suffered the humiliation of falling victim to the regional powers' race for hegemony. . . . We were too weak to resist the gangsters and our grandfathers and grandmothers could do nothing but wail to the heavens. . . . Our nation must strengthen itself, no matter what price we will pay for it and no matter how many generations of us will have to sweat and bleed for it. . . . For sixty-five years, we have resisted imperialists' concerted pressure. . . . We are now among the few advanced powers that have achieved the grand feat of making and launching satellites and owning nuclear weapons. . . . Without the gun barrel and *songun*, we would never be able to live under the blue sky in dignity and prosperity. Without it, the dark cloud of war would have swept over this land hundreds of times. Without it, our streets and villages would be again ringing with the arrogant and savage boots of invaders.[10]

After Kim Jong-il's death, the first top leadership title his son, Jong-un, assumed was supreme commander of the North Korean military. The son inherited his father's *songun* legacy, as well as the military's elevated status. As he has consolidated his power, Kim Jong-un has moved to curtail the influence of the military and restore the party as the central tool of control. He dismissed Vice Marshal Ri Yong-ho, the army chief and rising star among the military elite. He deprived the People's Army of its lucrative rights to trade in some minerals and seafood and returned those rights to the Cabinet. Still, the "military-first" policy remains the country's guiding ideology.

North Korea is a bunker or guerrilla state built on one overriding belief—a belief the regime works relentlessly to implant in a populace whose everyday concern is food, not politics: the country is under siege and surrender is not an option.[11]

The Kim family's search for survival as a monolithic leadership—and the xenophobic fear and nationalistic pride it has cultivated—inexorably led to

9 From a North Korean epic poem, cited by Kwon in "Politics of Longing."
10 Dong Tae-gwan, "General Kim Jong-il," *Rodong Sinmun*, August 24, 2010.
11 The term "guerrilla state" was first popularized by the Japanese historian Wada Haruki.

its *songun* policy and its development of nuclear weapons as "deterrent."[12] It likely has learned from Saddam Hussein's and Colonel Gaddafi's fates, and determined that it should never face the United States without nuclear weapons. North Korea's self-perceived membership in the nuclear club was the biggest achievement Kim Jong-il could cite to his people as he began to extend his dynasty into the third generation. North Korea appears to have determined that nuclear arms will help it regain some confidence in confronting South Korea, secure its continued rule of the northern half of the peninsula, and boost its ability to play China and the United States against each other. Meanwhile, it reminds its people that the struggle to drive out imperialists from Korea—a Korean revolution begun with its messiah Kim Il-sung's anti-Japanese guerilla campaign and continued through the Korean War—has never ended. Kim Jong-il used to start the new year by visiting the Ryu Kyong-su crack tank division, famed in the North for being the first unit to roll into Seoul after the war started in 1950.[13] His *songun* policy, now inherited by son Kim Jong-un, and North Korea's nuclear nationalism explain why it makes little strategic sense for the regime to give up its nuclear arms any time soon if at all: they have become the source of regime stability.

While the personality cult and the *songun* policy were essential to the hereditary succession of power, they required "external threats" and tension to be sustainable. If there were none, they had to be created. In a region where most everyone else is preoccupied with growth and stability, North Korea has learned that it not only can raise tension but also can extract diplomatic and economic concessions by being a menace. It does not sit still when talks do not go as it planned, when its enemies ignore or try to punish it by withholding aid shipments, or when it needs to demonstrate a strong will for domestic purposes. It walks out of talks, expels UN nuclear monitors, fires missiles, makes more fissile materials, and detonates nuclear devices. It sends agents to kill South Korean leaders, bombs a South Korean passenger jet, or (in more recent years) triggers military skirmishes and shells a South Korean island. Once it creates tension and wins attention—even at the risk of adding a few more international sanctions to a long list of trade penalties

12 Jacques Hymans, author of *The Psychology of Nuclear Proliferation*, explained the role of "fear and pride" in a nation's nuclear weapons development. Cited in reference to North Korea in Scott Snyder, "Kim Jong-il's Successor Dilemmas," *The Washington Quarterly* 33, no. 1 (January 2010): 39.

13 Yonhap news agency, "北김정일, 탱크부대 훈련 보며 올해 마감(종합)" [Kim Jong-il of the North ends the year by watching a tank unit in a drill], December 31, 2010, http://news.naver.com/main/read.nhn?mode=LSD&mid=sec&sid1=100&oid=001&aid=0004846720.

endured so long, ever since the war, that such penalties are a given—it shifts gears and insists that its enemies talk with it if they want to avoid the worst. South Koreans call the gambit a "dialogue offensive." When the enemies come grumbling to the table or send delegates to Pyongyang, the regime advertises it internally as an enemy surrender.

One can argue that North Korea's tendency to use bellicosity toward real or imagined external foes as a way of consolidating domestic power and reaffirming leadership legitimacy has deepened its isolation and undermined its effort to revive the economy for its long-term survival. But it can also be said that its tactics "have worked repeatedly in the past, with Washington and Seoul buying their way back to a calmer status quo."[14] Since 1984, every North Korean provocation has been followed, sooner or later, by talks, many of which led to goodies for Pyongyang.[15] It is never long before the North shakes the equilibrium again; belligerence is built in its ideology. Even when the South was charming it with aid, North Korea never forgot to de-stabilize the peninsula, provoking naval clashes in 1999 and in 2002 during the Sunshine period. Kongdan Oh sums it up: "Unfortunately, as long as a dynastic North Korea continues to exist, especially as long as it is guided by 'military-first politics' and ruled by so-called 'great generals,' South Korea will be vulnerable to surprise attacks."[16]

Can't Live With Her, Can't Live Without Her: South Korean Attitudes Toward North Korea

A nighttime satellite image of the Korean Peninsula delivers an elo-quent testimony to which side has emerged victorious. The southern half is splotched with light, while the North is veiled in darkness; only a pinprick of light reveals the location of Pyongyang. To South Koreans, however, the divide has never been this black and white. They detest the North Korean regime for running gulags and starving millions of people to death. But their indignation is mollified by a compassion for fellow Koreans facing another harsh winter without heat or food, trapped in an ideological dead end that in their view was as much a result of history's cruel injustice to the Korean

14 Bruce Klingner, "Kim Jong Il: The Boy Who Cried Nuke?" *Los Angeles Times*, December 23, 2010, http://articles.latimes.com/2010/dec/23/opinion/la-oe-klingner-ko-rea-20101223.

15 Victor Cha, "Five Myths About North Korea," *Washington Post*, Decem-ber 10, 2010, http://www.washingtonpost.com/wp-dyn/content/article/2010/12/10/AR2010121002488.html.

16 Kongdan Oh, "Same Old News," *Korea Times*, December 27, 2010, http://www.koreatimes.co.kr/www/news/include/print.asp?newsIdx=78703.

nation as it was of the North's own making. South Koreans seldom dwell on the threat of North Korean nuclear bombs. Rather, ethnonationalism often compels young South Koreans to watch the North's nuclear standoff with Washington with both frustration and admiration. To them, North Korea is a gangster-like regime trying to make a living with nuclear blackmail, but it also represents their alter-ego: a small Korea struggling for an independent identity under high-handed pressure from bigger foreign powers.

Is Pyongyang a cornered beast whose hissing is really a cry for a way out? Or is it an evil regime that must be toppled so its people can be liberated? How to view North Korea remains a key dividing line between liberals and conservatives in South Korea. One school of thought is exemplified by the Sunshine Policy. The most vocal version of the other comes from Korean War veterans, North Korean defectors, journalists-cum-ideological pamphleteers, and flag-waging conservative Protestant churchgoers; they burn Kim Jong-il in effigy and launch leaflet-laden balloons urging North Koreans to revolt. But both camps rarely consider North Korea as a global proliferation threat, as Washington does, but rather see the country within the highly local context of how to cease the never-ending hostilities and possibly reunify the peninsula. The *Cheonan* sinking and the Yeonpyeong attack generated a South Korean fury against North Korea—Seoul officials called these events "our 9/11." But these incidents are eventually brushed away, with a sigh. To South Koreans, they are recurring episodes they have to live with as long as rival governments sit in Pyongyang and Seoul. In the face of the bloody North Korean attacks, the Seoul stock market hardly blinked. In contrast, when Washington contemplated bombing the North Korean nuclear complex in 1994, South Koreans panicked, hoarding food.

During the Cold War, Southern authorities stressed ethnic affinity with the North, but their take on the Pyongyang government was loud and focused, best captured by a common government poster: "the best treatment for Commies is the one for rabid dogs: the cudgel." Different sentiments filtered in during recent decades, particularly among the generations who did not witness the Korean War. Children of South Korea's postwar economic miracle, they did not carry their parents' emotional baggage from that vicious conflict. Those generally known as the 486 generation (so-called because they were mostly in their forties, were in college in the eighties, and were born in the sixties) formed their political perspectives when their college campuses were at the frontline of their country's bloody struggle for democracy. In the eighties, this generation spent less time criticizing North Korea and more time hating the military dictatorship at home and questioning the role of the United States, which they accused of supporting and condoning the brutalities of the tyrants in Seoul, such as political massacres during the war and a military crackdown on a 1980 pro-democracy uprising in Kwangju. From their vantage point, they considered the United States a progenitor of the Korean tragedy—the partitioning of the peninsula—rather than (or as well as) the savior older South Koreans thought the Americans were for defending their country from communist invaders. Many sympathized with North Korea's fiercely nationalistic *Juche* ideology, if not with its dictatorship. To them, the old North Korean leadership, many of whose members had fought as anti-Japanese guerrillas, carried more legitimacy than South Korea's founding elite, many of whom survived the colonial era as exiles and collaborators. North Korea was no longer an enemy to hate; it was a sibling to be pitied for its poverty and feared for its brutality against its own people, yet one to be admired at least for standing up to a massive foreign power. Back then, the light blue "Korea-is-one" flag adorned college campuses and the word "unification" filled the air. This romantic view of North Korea has largely dissipated. The outflow of North Korean refugees with their tales of famine, torture, and prison gulags, along with the mixed results of the Sunshine Policy, brought disillusionment to whatever North Korea had once meant for this group. Some of the old student leaders turned into "new-right" anti-North Korean activists. But with the postwar generations coming of age, the simplistic Cold War era right-and-wrong, good-and-evil assumptions of North Korea—and policies based on them—no longer sell in South Korea.

South Koreans in their twenties and thirties spent their college years under the uncertainty of regional or global economic meltdowns. They care more about jobs than about North Korea or the ideological strife from the past. But they too have inherited a nationalist mentality, though it is often masked and vitiated by their more pragmatic worldview. They have no trouble craving Japanese manga comics while despising Japan with an equal fervor for claiming a territorial right to South Korean–held islets or for enslaving Korean women in its World War II army brothels. Nor are they bothered by the seeming cognitive dissonance of denouncing Washington politically while choosing America as their top destination for graduate study abroad.[17]

The new mindset of postwar generations boiled to the surface during the liberal rule of Kim Dae-jung and Roh Moo-hyun, from 1998 till 2008, especially after George W. Bush took office in 2001. Bush rejected the Sunshine Policy, dismissing engagement as dangerous appeasement. Surveys

17 John Swenson-Wright, "Contested History."

at the time showed that South Koreans considered the United States a bigger threat to peace than North Korea. When Bush called North Korea one of America's three "axis of evil" archenemies and told the rest of the world to be "either with us or against us," many South Koreans felt puzzled, amused, and angered by the call's shockingly unexpected irrelevancy. No matter what North Korea does, ethnic affinity with the North lies at the heart of South Koreans' national identity. Although largely supportive of their country's alliance with the United States for practical reasons, the postwar generations smart at Washington's asymmetrical relationship with their country. They suspect that U.S. motives and priorities over security, North Korea, and the future of the Korean Peninsula differ from their own. These sentiments helped transform the death of two teenage girls by a U.S. armored vehicle in 2002 and a mad-cow beef protest in 2008 from what would have been a tragic yet simple traffic accident and a technical trade issue into massive political demonstrations with a streak of anti-American nationalism.

South Koreans also remain wary of China, which has a history of invading and subjugating Korea. Reports of growing Chinese investment in the North while inter-Korean relations deteriorate stoke fears that North Korea will become "Sinicized," making the dream of unifying the peninsula more distant. Many South Koreans may oppose unification, or rather the economic cost of absorbing the poor North, but they dread even more the prospects of ceding the North to China. Such a scenario, perhaps deemed ridiculous by the North Koreans themselves, represents a very real threat for nationalist-minded South Koreans. Koreans' attitude toward the powers surrounding it is still best summarized by an early twentieth-century Korean ditty: "Don't trust the Americans, don't be cheated by the Soviets and beware of the Chinese, or the Japanese will rise again."

2013: A Time for Change or for Staying the Course?

On December 9, 2010, South Korea's President Lee declared that "an unstoppable change is taking place among the North Korean people, and the time has come for South Korea to prepare for unification."[18] U.S. diplomatic cables released by WikiLeaks revealed that Seoul officials under Lee tried to convince Washington that North Korea was wracked by unrest, with Kim Jong-il in failing health and his plan to transfer power to his son in jeopardy.[19] The regime was becoming increasingly vulnerable, so hanging tough

18 From a speech made in Malaysia. See http://news.naver.com/main/read.nhn?mode=LSD&mid=sec&sid1=100&oid=001&aid=0004812589 (in Korean).

19 Mike Chinoy, "How S. Korea's Tough Policy on North backfired," CNN Opin-

with sanctions and perhaps highly conditional talks might force change or a collapse in Pyongyang. Or China will finally come around to twist North Korea's arm for better behavior. So went their argument. U.S. and South Korean diplomats had a name for the approach: "strategic patience" or "benign/malign neglect." Was the policy based on solid analysis of the North Korean situation and the Chinese leadership thinking? Or did it derive from wrong assumptions about the North Korean regime's durability and its people's mindset, mistakes spawned by wishful thinking and ideologically driven politics? The policy of strategic patience may be the most realistic there is. Or it may be just another name for rolling over an intractable problem from one administration to another, a strategy borne of a political need to find a plausible-sounding excuse not to have to deal with Pyongyang.

Meanwhile, North Korea celebrated 2012 as a landmark year, the centennial of Kim Il-sung, the year when his grandson was elevated to the top of military, party, and state leadership. Kim Jong-un's bloodline, his father's vaunted nuclear weapons, and his resemblance to his grandfather, still a god-like figure among North Koreans—all of these rendered an aura of legitimacy to the young man's succession. With his influential aunt and uncle serving as guardians, Kim Jong-un has moved swiftly to build his image as a youthful, vigorous, and more accessible leader. North Korean state media showed him hooking arms with factory workers and soldiers, chatting with kindergartners on his lap, and watching—with a fashionable wife and military generals at his side—a concert that featured Mickey Mouse, a film clip of Sylvester Stallone as Rocky Balboa, and a band of leggy string players in mini-skirts. In his first speech as leader, he vowed to ensure that his people would not have to tighten their belts again.

But his youth and lack of experience create potential challenges to the regime's internal cohesion. His father, Kim Jong-il, fought for his inheritance as much as it was bestowed upon him by his father. He terrorized and won a grudging respect among the older elite in a decades-long process of consolidating absolute power. His rule survived the famine of the 1990s partly because no one would dare challenge his authority. In comparison, Kim Jong-un had his inheritance delivered to him on a plate. The elites have so far closed their ranks around the new leader. They share a vested interest in maintaining the current system, their claims to wealth and their reputations legitimized by their connections to Kim Il-sung and his blood heirs. All signs indicate that Kim Jong-un is quickly securing his grip on power. But if

ion, January 1, 2011, http://www.cnn.com/2010/OPINION/12/31/nkorea.wikileaks/index.html.

the North Korean economy slides into a deeper crisis, can the young leader demonstrate, as his father did, the cunning and ruthlessness necessary to manipulate those generals and party insiders surrounding him—people thirty to forty years older than he is and all veterans of a political survival game? We hardly know anything about the old elites, whose ambitions and interpersonal rivalries were kept in check by Kim Jong-il's merciless power. The dynamics of power under Kim Jong-un, especially his relationship with his influential uncle and mentor, Jang Sung-taek, remain a mystery. If Kim Jong-un eventually turns out to be far less than the absolute leader his father and grandfather were, how would a people who have only known deified monolithic dictators react?

The North Koreans of today are not the North Koreans of the 1990s who died in silence during the famine. Tens of thousands have since crossed into China to find food and returned with news of the outside world. Many watch South Korean soap operas smuggled into the country on DVDs and computer memory sticks from China. Owning South Korean electronics has become a status symbol. A fundamental societal change has taken place: "In the very struggle people waged to survive the famine, the state lost much of its control over their daily lives."[20] School textbooks still teach that South Koreans are slaves toiling in an American colony, their marrow sucked out daily by "flunkey capitalists."[21] How long can the regime, regardless of its proud stockpile of nukes, justify its raison d'être when more and more North Koreans are realizing that the South is vastly better off than the North? Pyongyang's totalitarian grip makes outbursts of discontent sporadic and isolated at best and precludes organized dissent. But the power of the personality cult will decrease with each generation. Will North Korea adopt a gradual openness and a slow death to its personality cult, and evolve toward Chinese-style market authoritarianism, now that the regime may feel more confident with nuclear weapons? Do we know what North Koreans want? Here is one mid-level Pyongyang party official's take, as reported by Good Friends, a South Korean relief agency:

> No matter how difficult the situation is, [North Korea] is not going to collapse now, because the fate of the mid-ranking officials is connected to the leadership. Moreover, China does not want us to collapse. . . . Still, the question

20 Kay Seok, "North Korea's Transformation: Famine, Aid and Markets," Human Rights Watch, April 16, 2008, http://www.hrw.org/en/news/2008/04/14/north-korea-s-transformation-famine-aid-and-markets.

21 Excerpts of North Korean textbooks can be found on many South Korean blogs, such as http://kimyenna.blog.me/90102137786; http://nkinside.com/140102371561; and http://unibook.unikorea.go.kr/?sub_num=83&state=view&idx=64.

is whether the new leadership can be trusted. People are watching how Kim Jong-un . . . deals with the food problem. . . . The mid-ranking officials will welcome whatever changes are necessary to secure the lives of their children and themselves. It does not matter whether the changes are in the direction of China or the United States. However, South Korea is not an option. Their safety will not be guaranteed if they choose South Korea. . . . [O]ur most urgent priorities are national security and resolution of the food problem.[22]

Kim Jong-un must reconsolidate loyalty. In 2012, South Korean media reported that North Korea was introducing market-oriented incentives to boost the productivity at collective farms and factories. But true reform and openness, of the kind that could fix the North's economic mess, would require the courage to loosen political control and even give up nukes. The Kim family and its cohort of old generals must have watched—with dread and disgust—the execution of Nicolae Ceauşescu, the former Romanian dictator, and the recent uprisings in the Middle East. When they peek out with their military-bunker frame of mind, they see minefields everywhere. Unless the regime develops confidence in dealing with outside powers and maintaining its grip at home, it will see no option but to persist in nuclear weapons development and brutal control of its people. It will continue trying to use its military threats to win aid and recognition from its sworn enemies while cultivating closer, yet guarded, trade ties with China.

Victor Cha, a former White House official, says:

The dilemma for the Obama administration is that it knows Pyongyang wants to use negotiations to again extort assistance for its starving economy, but it also knows that Kim is not willing to give up his country's nuclear program verifiably and irreversibly. This is why U.S. diplomats often use the phrase "hold your nose and negotiate with them" in talking about the North Koreans—they know that discussions may bring an agreement and a temporary reprieve from the crisis at hand, but they also know that in time, that agreement will be broken by the North, only to be followed by another crisis. So why do we keep renegotiating with North Korea? Mostly because we have no other options.[23]

The joint U.S. and South Korean approach of "strategic patience" has failed to reach a critical mass partly because China remains an ambiguous partner in the process, if not deliberately scuttling it. To Beijing, bolstering an anti-American North Korea on its border is better than pushing that ally too far and too suddenly into reform. The latter option might trigger instability and a flood of refugees into its northeastern provinces, forcing Beijing

22 "평양 간부, '붕괴? 말도 안 되는 소리'" [Official in Pyongyang: collapse of the regime? Nonsense!], Good Friends, March 16, 2011, http://www.goodfriends.or.kr/n_korea/n_korea12.html?sm=v&b_no=11903&page=1.

23 Victor Cha, "Five Myths."

to choose between intervening militarily and tolerating a pro-American unified Korea with U.S. troops on its border.

So what we have on the peninsula is the continuation of the same dynamics that have defined geopolitics there since the division of the peninsula: the contest between the two Koreas, overshadowed by—and in turn stoking—the hegemony game between their bigger allies. The contest tipped in favor of South Korea with the collapse of the Soviet bloc, and North Korea has been trying to rebalance it by developing nuclear weapons. The North's nuclear program brought Seoul and Washington into their first serious dialogue with their former battlefield foe. Years of negotiations showed what doesn't work: insisting that North Korea give up its nuclear program before Washington improves relations with Pyongyang, applying half-hearted sanctions, or pursuing short-lived engagement. When President Lee demanded that North Korea first abandon its nuclear weapons program before expecting aid, that suggestion was tantamount to asking a bank robber to give up his guns so he may be given the cash. Meanwhile, the North's provocations and its repeated mendacity over such things as its uranium enrichment have made engagement with it more unpalatable in Washington and Seoul. Policy pundits wonder whether North Korea has ever intended to give up its nuclear weapons for a price acceptable to Washington and Seoul. No one, perhaps not even the North itself, will know the answer. Years of talks with the North make this much clear: unless this source of fear, pride, and hostility in Korea is removed, no lasting deal can be reached with North Korea, and the pattern of aggression, tension, and negotiation will repeat like a perpetual-motion machine.

This cycle can be broken either when North Korea collapses—with consequences hard to predict and probably so violent that they would make the Arab Spring uprisings look like an urban riot in comparison—or when the nations implicated in the Korean division and the war create a process of reunification that envisions gradual government change in Pyongyang. Elections and leadership reshuffles provide opportunities to rethink foreign policy. For many of those nations, 2013 is such a year. The United States and China both want stability in Korea. Washington and Seoul should shift the focus of their North Korea policy to convincing China and Russia that the dissolution of the North Korean regime would not weaken their influence in Northeast Asia and could ensure a stable unified Korean state on their borders. Minus differences over North Korea, China and South Korea are already as closely tied as any two neighbors can be. Their bilateral trade exceeds South Korea's combined trade with the United States and Japan. To persuade China, Washington and Seoul can link Korean unification with the withdrawal of U.S. military forces from Korea.[24] Even without an American military presence, South Korea would remain a strong U.S. ally, with so many Koreans studying, working, and living in the United States. A recent free trade agreement further cemented that relationship. South Korea is a triumphant example of what good American intervention can do overseas. If anything, the North Korean nuclear crisis is a wake-up call for the United States to bring an end to its longest war (sixty years old and counting) and cap one of its shiniest success stories of foreign intervention by helping create a democratic unified Korea. Until then, it will never have solved the problem it originally helped create.

For their part, South Koreans made their own arduous march toward democracy and economic development, believing that that would be the quickest and safest way to unification, which generations of school children were taught to consider National Wish No. 1. Somewhere on their way they got lost and squabbling erupted among their leaders over how to deal with North Korea. National reunification has become all but an empty slogan and the people have grown complacent with the status quo of a divided Korea. But events like the attack on Yeonpyeong and the scenes of starving North Korean children are crude reminders that as long as the Korean divide continues, with its inherent tension, South Koreans can never rest.

24 A similar argument is made by Jacquelyn Schneider, "Chinese Military Involvement in a Future Korean War," *Strategic Studies Quarterly* 4, no. 4 (Winter 2010): 50–67.

8 North Korea's Distorted View of the United States and Japan

David Straub and Daniel C. Sneider

In the North Korean worldview, the United States and Japan constitute its paramount major security threats. North Korea sees the United States as the primary supporter of South Korea, the North's existential rival for ultimate control of the Korean Peninsula and Korean nation. With the end of the Cold War and the collapse of the Soviet Union, however, North Korea engaged in a quixotic quest to persuade the United States to enter into a strategic relationship with it. The North's aims were two-fold: to reduce American support for South Korea, and to play the United States off against a rising China to maximize the North's security and autonomy. In response to the Obama administration's firm response to the North's second nuclear test, in 2009, North Korean leaders apparently abandoned hope that the United States would agree to a strategic relationship and are now relying almost exclusively on the PRC for external support.

As for Japan, North Korea historically has regarded it as primarily a source of hard currency, largely in the form of remittances from pro–North Korea ethnic Korean residents of the country, and a source of high-tech goods. North Korea also uses the history of Japan's colonization of Korea to inspire national solidarity among its people through incessant warnings that Japan is remilitarizing and will one day again seek to colonize the Korean Peninsula. The latter use has increased since Japan's government cut off most remittances and other economic flows between the two countries a decade ago in response to confirmation of revelations that North Korea had abducted numerous Japanese citizens. North Korea regards Japan as largely following the American lead in security policy. Along with the historical feelings against Japan, this has made North Korean leaders generally reluctant to engage Japan seriously.

This chapter describes how North Korea regards the United States and Japan in terms of its security. It begins with a discussion of the difficulties of assessing North Korean views and intentions and it presents our view that North Korea behaves, in many respects, in classic *realpolitik* fashion toward the United States and Japan. We review the history of North Korean dealings with the United States, arguing, however, that Pyongyang sees its vital national interests through an ideological and cultural lens that results in the regime leadership profoundly misjudging U.S. motivations and intentions, most notably in respect to the North Korean nuclear program. We also review the history of North Korea's relations with Japan, from Japan's role as a major source of economic support for the North to today's mutually extremely hostile relationship. Also in the case of Japan, the North Korean regime takes an ideologically based approach that has very much dimmed the prospect for any improvement in bilateral relations.

The Difficulty of Assessing North Korean Intentions

Assessing how North Korean leaders regard the United States and Japan, even more than most things North Korean, is a major epistemological challenge. Hassig and Oh quote Kim Jong-il as having said, "We must envelop our environment in a dense fog to prevent our enemies from learning anything about us."[1] In fact, direct access by the outside world to the actual top leaders of North Korea is extremely limited.

It is not, however, only the North Korean leaders' sense of vulnerability and thus self-isolation that makes determining their views and intentions so difficult. The division of the Korean Peninsula into two competing states since 1948 has ensured that there will almost always be two versions of events, and misinformation and disinformation spread by the two states and their supporters have proliferated through the decades. Most of the writings and statements attributed to the top leaders in Pyongyang are heavily

---

1 Ralph C. Hassig and Kong D. Oh, *The Hidden People of North Korea: Everyday Life in the Hermit Kingdom* (Lanham, MD: Rowman & Littlefield Publishers, 2009), page following the copyright page.

propagandistic and thus of relatively little use in assessing their actual views and intentions.

Outside the peninsula, journalists have often reported on North and South Korean statements and media stories without having sufficient grasp of the complexities of inter-Korean relations to make sense of the situation for their readers. Officials as well as journalists, in the United States and other countries, have often engaged in wishful thinking rather than informed, careful analysis of North Korea—witness the widespread speculation about regime collapse after Kim Il-sung's death in 1994, which was based on superficial and fallacious analogies between North Korea and the former Soviet Union and its satellite states in Eastern Europe.

The international community does, however, know considerably more about North Korea now than just a couple of decades ago. One source of valuable information is the diplomatic archives of the former Soviet Union and its satellite states. Opened up after the Cold War, they reveal the confidential observations and judgments of diplomats from friendly countries living and working in Pyongyang since the state's founding until the collapse of communism in Europe.[2]

More recently, most European Union (EU) member states normalized relations with the Democratic People's Republic of Korea (DPRK) at the turn of this century; three Western European governments maintain resident embassies in Pyongyang and so are able to obtain current, firsthand assessments of conditions and attitudes from reliable observers.[3] Although the United States does not have formal diplomatic relations with North Korea, much less a resident presence in the country, U.S. officials are increasingly well-informed about North Korea, especially about its negotiating tactics, in part due to the accumulation of experience in direct contacts with DPRK counterparts since 1992.[4]

---

2 See especially the work of the Cold War International History Project at the Woodrow Wilson International Center for Scholars and work by Kathryn Weathersby: http://www.wilsoncenter.org/index.cfm?fuseaction=topics.home&topic_id=1409.

3 For an excellent example of the value of such opportunities, see "Relations with Europe," chapter 9 in this volume, by John Everard, British ambassador to Pyongyang, 2006–2008. See also his book, *Only Beautiful, Please: A British Diplomat in North Korea* (Stanford, CA: Shorenstein Asia-Pacific Research Center, 2012).

4 The 1992 meeting of U.S. Under Secretary of State for Political Affairs, Arnold Kanter, and [North] Korean Workers' Party Director for International Affairs Kim Yong-sun was the first ever held between senior civilian officials of the two countries. See Don Oberdorfer, *The Two Koreas: A Contemporary History* (New York: Basic Books, A Member of the Perseus Books Group, 2001), 266–67.

Other sources of information may be useful in understanding the broader context in which top North Korean leaders operate. For example, Myers' analysis of North Korean propaganda directed at its own people suggests that North Koreans are imbued with an ethnic nationalism derived in part, ironically, from prewar Japanese fascism, and that this attitude colors the DPRK's relations with all countries, including the United States and Japan.[5] Academic scholarship about North Korea has drawn on an increasingly broad range of information sources and used sophisticated methodologies in an attempt to understand the country better. Nongovernmental organizations (NGOs) and academics from the United States and other countries have had increased, if still limited, direct access to North Korea, especially since the famine of the mid-1990s.[6] Refugees from North Korea and even some North Koreans still resident in the country are increasingly being heard (although this is an area where great caution must still be exercised since such sources will have an uncertain quotient of unrepresentative information and even disinformation).[7]

Ultimately, given the extreme limitations on outside access to the frank, detailed, and timely views of North Korea's top leaders, our soundest and most useful source of understanding North Korea's leaders is their actual behavior as state managers over the past six decades. Because the regime has been ruled by one family and its close associates since its founding, we can identify basic patterns of state behavior and from these infer, with some confidence, current leadership attitudes, strategies, and motivations.

5 B. R. Myers, *The Cleanest Race: How North Koreans See Themselves and Why It Matters* (Brooklyn, NY: Melville House, 2010).

6 To name just a few, see Scott Snyder, *Negotiating on the Edge: North Korean Negotiating Behavior* (Washington, DC: United States Institute of Peace Press, 1999); Gi-Wook Shin and Karin Lee, eds., *U.S.-DPRK Educational Exchanges: Assessment and Future Strategy* (Stanford, CA: Shorenstein Asia-Pacific Research Center, 2011); L. Gordon Flake and Scott A. Snyder, eds., *Paved with Good Intentions: The NGO Experience in North Korea* (Westport, CT: Praeger, 2003).

7 See, for example, Barbara Demick, *Nothing to Envy: Ordinary Lives in North Korea* (New York: Spiegel & Grau, 2010); Marcus Noland and Stephan Haggard, *Witness to Transformation: Refugee Insights into North Korea* (Washington, DC: Peterson Institute for International Economics, 2011); and the website and publications of *Rimjingang: Reports by North Korean journalists within North Korea*, http://www.asiapress.org/rimjingang/english/.

A *Realpolitik* Perspective on North Korea

Some facts about North Korea are basic but often ignored or glossed over, perhaps because they are so obvious. *Fundamentally, North Korea is one of two Korean states on the Korean Peninsula, each of which regards itself as the only legitimate Korean state. The two states have radically different systems, and neither is willing to consider unification on the other's terms. Each hopes for unification eventually but only on its terms.* North Korean leaders' attitudes and policies, including toward the United States and Japan, are shaped within this existential framework.

Commentators on North Korea tend to fall into two camps. One camp argues that the nature of the regime itself is "evil" and that all issues stem from that fact. They note that the North Korean regime has one of the world's worst records of lack of respect for human rights.[8] They cite also that North Korea ranks at or near the bottom in terms of economic freedom.[9] They conclude accordingly that only regime change will resolve the North Korea problem. The other camp argues that North Korea is, to a significant extent, a "victim" of others, above all the United States and South Korea. Members of this camp do not deny North Korea's lack of freedom and respect for human rights, but argue that the situation would be much better if the outside world were less threatening.[10] This camp argues that an engagement policy similar to that of President Kim Dae-jung's Sunshine Policy can successfully address the North Korea problem, although it may take considerable time to do so.

We believe that neither of these viewpoints aids understanding or helps to predict North Korean regime behavior. It is certainly correct to say that North Korea's regime is one of the worst, if not the worst, in the world in terms of lack of respect for basic human rights and economic freedoms. The way it treats its own people is appalling, constituting a twenty-first-century humanitarian tragedy of historic proportions. It is also true that

8 See, for example, "Human Rights Abuses by Country," *The Guardian*, http://www.guardian.co.uk/Tables/4_col_tables/0,,258329,00.html; "Freedom in the World 2012: North Korea," *Freedom House*, http://www.freedomhouse.org/report/freedom-world/2012/north-korea; and "World Report | 2013," *Human Rights Watch*, http://www.hrw.org/world-report/2013/country-chapters/north-korea.

9 See, for example, "2013 Index of Economic Freedom," *The Heritage Foundation*, http://www.heritage.org/index/Ranking.

10 See, among others, Selig S. Harrison, *Korean Endgame: A Strategy for Reunification and U.S. Disengagement* (Princeton, NJ: Princeton University Press, 2002), and Leon V. Sigal, *Disarming Strangers: Nuclear Diplomacy with North Korea* (Princeton, NJ: Princeton University Press, 1998).

North Korean leaders feel threatened by the outside world and respond to external pressures with calculated brinkmanship.

We, however, agree with Lawson: to best understand North Korea, *we should neither demonize nor infantilize it.*[11] North Korean leaders do not deal with the outside world as they do primarily because they are evil or primarily because they are victims. They act as state leaders in classic *realpolitik* terms. They seek to preserve their regime and their state and, as Korean nationalists fixated on national-ethnic purity, to keep open the option eventually of unifying the Korean Peninsula on their terms.

Of course, the nature of the regime is a very important factor: North Korean leaders undoubtedly recognize that the existence of radically different systems in the two halves of the peninsula precludes a unification that would be a win-win situation for the elites in both countries. As mentioned above, neither Korean state will accept the other system. Moreover, as Lankov has pointed out, North Korean leaders must be aware that they, their families, and their associates would be at substantial risk if unification occurred on South Korean terms, since there can be no credible guarantee that they would not be subject to trial and punishment for crimes against their own people.[12] For this and other reasons, top North Korean leaders must believe it essential to preserve their state. It is on that basis that we can best interpret their foreign and security policies.

Similarly, the victimization narrative falls short in explaining North Korean behavior. No doubt, one can trace a chain of events that links every American or South Korean failing or misdeed to a North Korean response, but such a viewpoint misses the forest for the trees.[13] Such a narrative can offer only partial, superficial explanations for North Korea's behavior. The North Korean regime has survived for over six decades under extremely difficult internal and external conditions. It has its own history, its own ideology, and its own strategy for survival and for attempting to make progress as it defines progress. While North Korea makes heavy use of the victimization narrative in its own propaganda, the regime does not act as a victim; it acts

11 Konrad Lawson, "The North Flank Guard: A Military Exercise Escalated into Artillery Exchange," December 12, 2010, http://www.froginawell.net/korea/2010/12/the-north-flank-guard-a-military-exercise-escalated-into-artillery-exchange/. We are grateful to Aidan Foster-Carter for the reference.

12 Andrei Lankov, "Challenges in Post-Kim Jong-il Era," *The Korea Times*, December 25, 2011, http://www.koreatimes.co.kr/www/news/opinon/2013/01/304_101506.html.

13 See, for example, Sigal, *Disarming Strangers*.

to control its fate, including by such bold measures as developing nuclear weapons and long-range missiles.

How North Korea Has Viewed the United States

In the thinking of the North Korean leadership, the United States has been a major external factor since the Pyongyang regime's founding in 1948. Many American and South Korean observers say that the United States has, in fact, been the *greatest* external factor in North Korea's thinking. They note, among other things, North Korea's own statements that the United States is the main threat to its security, and, like North Korea, they argue that it would not have developed nuclear weapons if the United States had not posed a threat to it. Actually, however, North Korean leaders' statements to this effect reflect less their genuine belief in the existence of a direct threat from the United States than a calculated effort to improve their overall strategic situation vis-à-vis their neighbors, especially China and South Korea.

For North Korean leaders, the United States as an external strategic factor can be divided into two long historical periods: the Cold War period (1948–1991) and the post–Cold War period (1992–present). It is clear that from the founding of the DPRK in 1948, its leader Kim Il-sung was intent on unifying the Korea Peninsula, by military force if necessary. It is also clear that his motivation was less ideological than nationalistic. In his own mind a Korean patriot, he sought to accomplish the historic task of unifying the peninsula and the Korean nation after its division by the United States and the Soviet Union in 1945 and the subsequent establishment of explicitly competing states in north and south in 1948. In other words, his main external concern and object was not the United States, but South Korea. We believe that South Korea remains the primary, long-term security concern of North Korean leaders today.

With the United States having already removed all of its forces save advisers from South Korea in 1949 and with official U.S. government statements downplaying South Korea's strategic importance, Kim Il-sung persuaded Stalin and then Mao that the United States' role would not be decisive if he invaded the south with their support. Kim completely misjudged the U.S. response. Not only did the massive U.S. military intervention shortly after Kim's invasion on June 25, 1950, succeed in ensuring the survival of the regime in Seoul, but North Korea itself was nearly overrun and U.S. bombing left little standing there by war's end in 1953.

This was but the first of several examples of top North Korean leaders' wishful thinking and disastrous misjudgments about the United States, perhaps not surprising given that neither Kim Il-sung nor Kim Jong-il ever visited the West, much less the United States. Their pronounced recurring tendency to misunderstand the United States, despite knowing far more about its leaders' intentions than American officials know about North Korean leadership thinking, is likely the result of a dictatorial system in which those North Korean officials who may know better must be wary of contradicting the views and wishes of the top leaders.

After the Korean War ended, Kim Il-sung naturally aimed to rebuild his country, and by most accounts was able to make good progress using Stalinist methods of domestic control and receiving large amounts of aid from the USSR and its satellite states. He was not focused on the United States or South Korea, but on domestic reconstruction and maintaining his autonomy vis-à-vis his giant neighbors, the PRC and the USSR. He did this in part by playing the two communist powers off against each other, and by purging domestic supporters of the USSR and the PRC in succession.[14] While tensions remained high along the Demilitarized Zone (DMZ), North Korean provocations against the South and U.S. forces there were fairly limited in the first decade after the Korean War.

With domestic reconstruction in North Korea having made progress, the United States bogged down in Vietnam, and anti-Americanism spreading internationally, North Korea stepped up military provocations along the DMZ and off both the eastern and western coasts from the mid-1960s through the first years of the 1970s.[15] It was during this period that North Korean commandos infiltrated South Korea aiming to assassinate President Park Chung-hee, Pyongyang initiated other major provocations, and North Korea launched its first major political-military campaign to undermine the Northern Limit Line between North and South Korea in the Yellow Sea.[16] Kim Il-sung's motivations have been variously ascribed to bolstering his campaign to assume a leadership role in the Nonaligned Movement;

14 Andrei N. Lankov, *Crisis in North Korea: The Failure of De-Stalinization, 1956* (Honolulu: University of Hawai'i Press, Center for Korean Studies, University of Hawai'i, 2007).

15 For a tabulation of the history of clashes on the Korean Peninsula, see Stephen Wittels, "Korean Peninsula Clashes (1955–2010)," an appendix to Paul B. Stares, "Military Escalation in Korea CPA Contingency Planning Memorandum No. 10," Council on Foreign Relations Center for Preventive Action, November 2010, http://www.cfr.org/conflict-prevention/military-escalation-korea/p23344.

16 Narushige Michishita, "The West Sea Incident," chap. 4 in *North Korea's Military-Diplomatic Campaigns, 1966–2008* (London: Routledge, 2010). See also appendices A–C for historical tables of military incidents and casualties on the Korean Peninsula.

assisting North Vietnam by opening another front to which the U.S. military had to pay attention; and enhancing support for his regime at home.

In May 1972 North and South Korea held secret talks. Both sides had been unnerved by the dramatic U.S.-Chinese rapprochement of 1971–1972. Moreover, South Korean concerns about possible U.S. abandonment had increased following Nixon's enunciation of the Guam Doctrine in 1969, the U.S. debacle in Vietnam, and the withdrawal from Korea of the U.S. Seventh Infantry Division. The secret North-South talks produced a joint statement by Kim Il-sung and Park Chung-hee on July 4, 1972, promising "unification…without …external…interference…through peaceful means…transcending differences in ideas, ideologies, and systems."[17]

It was a thoroughly cynical effort on both sides. As Oberdorfer recounts,[18] the North Koreans told the East Germans confidentially that they had "undermined the attempts of the U.S. imperialism [sic] to retain its troops in Korea" and that the "Park Chung-hee clique will capitulate to this peace offensive. The tactical measures we adopted proved successful with the holding of talks with the enemy." In the South, meanwhile, President Park's longtime aide later said that Park "saw the dialogue as a helpful tactic in a harsh environment in which North Korean military power was a serious threat. Park had no belief or interest in unification in his lifetime. . . ."

This basic state of affairs continued until the collapse of the Soviet Union in 1991, bringing with it the end of the Cold War. North Korean leaders, who had relied on competition between the USSR and the PRC over their country to maximize both their autonomy from each and aid from both, faced a fundamentally new strategic situation. Russia was now a capitalist democracy, and the PRC was a reforming, much more open system that was enjoying rapid economic development; ideological contamination from the two countries now became a North Korean concern. China's switch more than a decade before to greater reliance on a market economy also threatened the flow of PRC aid to Pyongyang, and Russia no longer felt a need to compete with the PRC for Pyongyang's affections.

Meanwhile, South Korea had continued to enjoy dramatic economic growth, far outpacing Pyongyang, and in 1987 the nation democratized. North Korea could no longer plausibly claim that it was superior to the supposedly benighted South in any respect—economically, technologically, politically, diplomatically, or culturally. Its only, if rapidly fading, appeal was

17 Full text at "July 4th North-South Joint Statement," http://www2.law.columbia.edu/course_ooS_L9436_oo1/North%20Korea%20materials/74js-en.htm.
18 Oberdorfer, *Two Koreas*, 23–26.

nationalistic—that it, unlike the South, was not beholden to foreign powers. Even that was blatantly untrue. While North Korea had long proudly proclaimed an ideology of *Juche* or national autonomy, the fact was that it had relied very heavily on aid from the USSR, its satellite states, and the PRC. When that dried up in the early 1990s, North Korea's economy essentially collapsed, and by the mid-1990s the country was suffering a devastating famine.

The Quixotic Quest for a Strategic Relationship with the United States

It was this unexpected, catastrophic set of events that prompted North Korea to seek a strategic relationship with the United States in the early 1990s. Beginning with North Korea's first high-level political exchange with the United States—Korean Workers' Party (KWP) Secretary Kim Yong-sun's January 1992 meeting with Under Secretary of State Arnold Kanter—senior North Koreans have more or less continuously told official and private American interlocutors that they aimed for a strategic relationship with the United States. In 2002, a North Korean official told Robert Carlin and John W. Lewis that "You [Americans] must look at the strategic picture—the big picture—as we have to in order to survive."[19] As recently as January 2011, Kim Jong-il's eldest son told a Japanese reporter: "North Korea's foremost wish is to normalize relations with the United States and [achieve a] peaceful settlement on the Korean Peninsula."[20]

Most American officials did not take the North Korean statements seriously, coming, as they did, even as North Korea was developing its nuclear weapons program and proving to be an extremely difficult negotiating partner. Many U.S. officials assumed that the North Koreans were simply trying to gull them with such blandishments about a strategic relationship. While every U.S. administration since that of President George H. W. Bush (1989–1993) has expressed a willingness to normalize relations with North Korea if it abandons its nuclear weapons programs, none has ever remotely contemplated forging a strategic relationship with the regime.

North Korea's top leaders evidently did not understand basic factors in American thinking about the Korean Peninsula. Above all, the United

19 Robert Carlin and John W. Lewis, *Negotiating with North Korea: 1992-2007* (Stanford, CA: Center for International Security and Cooperation, Stanford University, January 2008).

20 Yoji Gomi, "Interview with Kim Jong-il's Son Jong Nam: Father Was Against Hereditary Succession," *Tokyo Shimbun*, January 28, 2011.

States is profoundly committed to the security and success of the Korean regime—the Republic of Korea (ROK)—that it helped to establish and for which it sacrificed over 33,000 American lives to defend. Americans regard South Korea as one of the United States' greatest foreign policy successes. From an economic basket case and an autocratic system, the ROK, with U.S. support, emerged in less than two generations as the world's twelfth-largest economy, a dynamic democracy, and a major American ally. To put it in its starkest and most simple political terms: any American president who "lost" South Korea could anticipate with virtual certainty that he or his party's candidate would not win the next election. As long as the regimes in Seoul and Pyongyang are competing against one another as representatives of the Korean nation, there is no chance that the United States would ever forge a strategic relationship with North Korea.

Even if South Korea were not immeasurably more successful than North Korea, the United States would not seek a strategic relationship with Pyongyang. In an era of nuclear weapons, intercontinental missiles, aircraft carriers, and "smart" weapons, of what possible use to the United States would a strategic relationship with a failed economy such as North Korea be? Even toying with such an idea would be counterproductive: the PRC would undoubtedly react with anger and dismay and respond in ways that would threaten American interests, including in South Korea.

Finally, North Korean leaders evidently do not understand how Americans, not only the public but also officials, regard the nature of the North Korean regime, despite the constant North Korean propaganda refrain about American "hostility." While the United States has collaborated with authoritarian regimes at times and under certain circumstances, Americans genuinely find totalitarian systems abhorrent. According to major opinion surveys, North Korea is one of the countries Americans like least in the entire world. In Gallup's 2011 annual world affairs poll, 84 percent of Americans said they held an unfavorable view ("mostly unfavorable" + "very unfavorable") of North Korea, which was exceeded only by the 85 percent for Iran.[21] Closer examination of the results in table 8.1, however, shows that the *intensity* of American feelings about North Korea is

21 Jeffrey M. Jones, "Iran, North Korea Still Americans' Least Favorite Countries," Gallup, February 11, 2011, http://www.gallup.com/poll/146090/iran-north-korea-americans-least-favorite-countries.aspx.

stronger: 53 percent of respondents said that they felt "very unfavorable" toward North Korea, as compared to only 43 percent against Iran.

TABLE 8.1

American views of North Korea and Iran (%)

	Very favorable	Mostly favorable	Mostly unfavorable	Very unfavorable	No opinion
North Korea	3	8	31	53	5
Iran	2	9	42	43	4

Source: http://www.gallup.com/poll/File/146096/Am_Views_Different_Countries_Feb_11_2011.pdf.

There is also strong evidence that, in actuality, Americans probably dislike North Korea even more than Iran. A Gallup breakdown of the results of its 2010 survey by the age group of respondents found young Americans nearly twice as likely as middle-aged Americans to hold "favorable" views of North Korea.[22] The most probable explanation for such a disparity is that young people are likelier than older Americans to confuse the "good" Korea with the "bad" Korea. In other words, a significant percentage of young Americans quite likely do not know if North or South Korea is the United States' ally.

TABLE 8.2

Americans holding favorable views of North Korea and Iran, by age (%)

	18 to 34 years	35 to 54 years	55 and older
North Korea	30	11	6
Iran	18	10	6

Source: Lydia Saad, "In U.S., Canada Places First in Image Contest; Iran Last," Gallup, http://www.gallup.com/poll/126116/canada-places-first-image-contest-iran-last.aspx.

Moreover, American dislike of North Korea has been consistent. From 2003 through 2013, the percentage of Americans expressing a "favorable" view of North Korea in the Gallup series ranged from only 8 to 15 percent.[23] The total "unfavorable" figure for North Korea never fell below 59 percent, even in the period just after the first-ever North-South Korean summit of

22 Lydia Saad, "In U.S., Canada Places First in Image Contest; Iran Last," Gallup, February 19, 2010, http://www.gallup.com/poll/126116/canada-places-first-image-contest-iran-last.aspx.

23 Lydia Saad, "Americans Give Record-High Ratings to Several U.S. Allies," Gallup, February 16, 2012, http://www.gallup.com/poll/152735/americans-give-record-high-ratings-several-allies.aspx; "Country Ratings," Gallup, February 7–10, 2013, http://www.gallup.com/poll/1624/perceptions-foreign-countries.aspx.

2000. In the annual surveys from 2003 through 2013, the total "unfavorable" figure ranged from 77 to 86 percent.[24]

A concrete example of North Korea's top leaders misunderstanding the United States involves the country's Arirang mass games. When Madeleine Albright visited Pyongyang in 2000 for the first-ever and still only trip to North Korea by a U.S. Secretary of State, Kim Jong-il unexpectedly invited her to attend a mass games performance. She defended her decision to accept, arguing that rejecting the invitation would have offended her host and put U.S. interests at risk.[25] In response, the *Washington Post* wrote a scathing editorial that seemed to reflect most American media and public sentiment. It began: "Secretary of State Madeleine Albright said she found 'amazing' the pageant she watched in Pyongyang alongside North Korean leader Kim Jong-il. We found it amazing, too, but not for the same reason. We were amazed that the secretary of state would allow herself to be photographed, smiling, as 100,000 essentially enslaved laborers performed for her and one of the world's most repressive dictators."[26] In a word, when most Americans think of the North Korean mass games, they are reminded of something like Nazi Germany's Nuremberg rallies.

In spite of the enormous criticism Secretary Albright had received for accompanying Kim Jong-il to the mass games in 2000, journalist Laura Ling quoted former President Bill Clinton as telling her that Kim Jong-il invited him to attend the Arirang mass games when Clinton visited Pyongyang in August 2009 to retrieve the imprisoned Ling and her colleague Euna Lee.[27] In spite of North Korean leaders' ready access to publicly available information in and about the United States, it seems likely that no North Korean official had briefed the North Korean leader on American attitudes toward the mass games in general or on the reaction in particular to Albright's attendance at the games, and thus on the likelihood that Clinton would decline the invitation—as he did. Perhaps, in view of Kim Jong-il's reported personal sponsorship of the mass games, North Korean officials feared offending him if they told him about such American attitudes.

24 "Country Ratings," Gallup, February 7–10, 2013, http://www.gallup.com/poll/1624/perceptions-foreign-countries.aspx, and preceding annual reports.

25 Madeleine Albright and William Woodward, *Madam Secretary: A Memoir* (New York: Miramax Books, 2005), 455–72.

26 "Toasting Kim Jong-il," *Washington Post*, October 27, 2000.

27 Laura Ling and Lisa Ling, *Somewhere Inside: One Sister's Captivity in North Korea and the Other's Fight to Bring Her Home* (New York: William Morrow, 2010), 207–08.

The Nuclear Card—Misplayed

Even as North Korea apparently genuinely hoped for some sort of a "strategic relationship" with the United States in the post–Cold War era, it continued to pursue a nuclear program begun during the Cold War that was antithetical to American security interests. Were the North Koreans at any point really prepared in principle to give up their nuclear program in exchange for American concessions? Or were they always planning to take a "have your cake and eat it, too" approach, i.e., play the nuclear card to extract maximum foreign aid and concessions without ever completely giving up the nuclear program?

Expert opinion is divided on whether North Korea would have developed nuclear weapons at all costs or whether a different U.S. approach might eventually have persuaded it to abandon the program. In either case, the record shows that the North Korean leadership again seriously misjudged the United States. If North Korea truly wished for a diplomatic resolution to the nuclear program, its demands reflected a lack of understanding of the limits imposed by political, strategic, and security interests on possible U.S. concessions. From an American perspective, North Korea should not have pursued nuclear weapons in the first place; thus, economic assistance and other concessions to North Korea in exchange for promises to end its nuclear programs were widely regarded in the United States as tantamount to blackmail payments. Moreover, as explained above, American dislike and distrust of North Korea were profound, yet North Korean authorities gave the Americans little reason for increased confidence in Pyongyang.

Even if North Korea never intended to give up its nuclear weapons program, it arguably played the nuclear card cleverly for years, only to overplay its hand recently. By leaving Americans with the hope that it might be persuaded eventually to abandon nuclear weapons, North Korea was able to obtain aid such as oil, food, and medicines; cash payments (for assisting in the return of the remains of Americans missing in action from the Korean War), and political concessions such as visits by senior Americans, bilateral joint statements, the easing of sanctions, and the removal of Pyongyang from the U.S. list of state sponsors of terrorism. Even after it tested its first nuclear device on October 9, 2006, Pyongyang soon obtained greater concessions from a suddenly much more forthcoming George W. Bush administration.

With the election of Barack Obama as president, who as a candidate had taken the controversial position that he was willing to sit down with leaders such as Kim Jong-il should they "unclench (their) fist," North Korea had a significant opportunity to pursue a comprehensive diplomatic settlement with the United States, using its 2006 nuclear test as leverage. Following his inauguration, President Obama sent confidential and public messages to Pyongyang underlining his readiness to explore a diplomatic resolution. To set the stage for such talks, the United States called on North Korea to suspend further tests of nuclear devices and long-range missiles. Nevertheless, on April 5, 2009, North Korea launched a Taepodong-2 rocket, and on May 25, 2009, conducted its second test of a nuclear device. The United States reacted sharply to the tests, and the Obama administration has since maintained a very skeptical attitude toward Pyongyang.[28]

Did Pyongyang not anticipate the Obama administration's tough reaction, or did it believe that a successful nuclear test (the first test was only partly successful) would strengthen its negotiating position? Did Pyongyang, based on its experience with the Clinton and George W. Bush administrations, believe that a Democratic president would take a "softer" approach toward North Korea? Did George W. Bush's dramatically softer approach after the first nuclear test encourage North Korean leaders to believe that President Obama would take a much softer approach after a second, successful nuclear test? Was North Korea confident that, in any event, sooner or later the United States would accommodate itself to a nuclear-armed North Korea, recognizing it and removing sanctions against it? After all, it took decades, but the United States eventually accommodated itself to India's nuclear weapons program and deals with Pakistan as a regional ally in spite of that country's nuclear weapons.

We cannot be certain of the answers to these questions. In any event, it appears clear that North Korea has misjudged the United States on the nuclear issue. North Korea's optimal negotiating position was after the first nuclear test, which had shocked American leaders. The test was largely a failure and indicated that North Korea still lacked a credible nuclear device. By testing a second device, and successfully doing so, especially after President Obama's entreaties, North Korea convinced most American observers that it had no intention of abandoning nuclear weapons in the foreseeable future on terms that might be acceptable to the United States. Numerous public and private statements by North Korean officials that Pyongyang has no intention of giving up nuclear weapons removed all doubt in the minds of most Americans in government and the academic community.[29]

28 See Jeffrey A. Bader, "North Korea: Breaking the Pattern," chap. 4 in *Obama and China's Rise: An Insider's Account of America's Asia Strategy* (Washington, DC: Brookings Institution Press, 2012), 26–39.

29 For example, North Korea's most senior nuclear negotiator, Kang Sok Ju, said in 2006, ". . . how can we abandon our nuclear weapons? Do you mean that we conducted a

With Americans now deeply skeptical about North Korean intentions, there is little incentive for any American president to explore a diplomatic solution with North Korea, and much domestic political risk in doing so. Concessions to North Korea in exchange for partial nuclear agreements will be regarded today as blackmail even more than they were in the past, and as profoundly naïve. Any concessions to North Korea that are not fully and verifiably reciprocated by North Korea will make any further U.S. concessions all the more difficult to offer. At least as long as the United States' South Korean ally is governed by conservatives, U.S. concessions to a nuclear-armed North Korea would create great difficulties for alliance management.

Finally, even if the United States, in spite all of these obstacles, pursued and achieved a diplomatic settlement of the nuclear issue, the North Koreans' revelation that they had built an advanced uranium enrichment facility ensured that there could be virtually no political support in the United States for any nuclear agreement. Hitherto, North Korea had stoutly maintained that U.S. charges that it was pursuing uranium enrichment capability were a lie. That Pyongyang was able to construct its uranium enrichment facility between the time that International Atomic Energy Agency (IAEA) inspectors departed Yongbyon in April 2009 and the North Koreans' revelation of its existence there in November 2010 has undoubtedly persuaded any remaining skeptics of North Korean capabilities within the U.S. government that North Korea has other uranium enrichment locations and that it has long pursued the capability. In other words, as former Bush administration North Korea negotiator Christopher Hill has since declared, North Korea simply "lied."[30]

When North Korea no longer has any credibility with the United States, verification of any nuclear agreement becomes vital. But the fact that North Korea was able to construct the uranium enrichment facility in Yongbyon, which the United States monitors as closely as possible, apparently without the United States knowing what was happening, means that Congress and the American public would demand extraordinarily intrusive, nationwide inspections of North Korean territory before approving any nuclear deal. No one believes North Korea is prepared to accept such inspections.

nuclear test to give them up?"; "Official Says North Korea Won't Give Up Nuclear Weapons," AFP, November 22, 2006, referenced at Space War: Your World at War, http://www.spacewar.com/reports/Official_Says_North_Korea_Wont_Give_Up_Nuclear_Weapons_999.html.

30 Christopher R. Hill, "Food for Thought in North Korea," *Project Syndicate*, February 22, 2011, http://www.project-syndicate.org/commentary/food-for-thought-in-north-korea.

Even if North Korea understood all of the above before conducting its second nuclear test, it apparently believes that the United States and the international community as a whole will eventually accept its nuclear weapons program, as the world has adjusted to those of Israel, India, and Pakistan. But for the reasons explained above—the priority of alliance relationships with South Korea and Japan and the domestic political calculus—along with the negative precedent that accommodation would send to countries such as Iran that may also seek nuclear weapons, the United States will undoubtedly opt for a continuation of increasing sanctions and pressure against a nuclear North Korea for the indefinite future.

Some observers propose that, since a deal ending North Korea's nuclear weapons program no longer appears possible, the United States should satisfy itself for now with a North Korean promise to suspend its nuclear weapons development and to end its involvement in nuclear proliferation, such as its covert export of a nuclear facility to Syria that was destroyed by Israeli bombers in 2007.[31] But with North Korea lacking any credibility in the United States and in the absence of any feasible means to verify a North Korean nonproliferation agreement, that approach has no prospect of adoption. The United States' "Leap Day Deal" with North Korea in early 2013 collapsed almost immediately when Pyongyang broke its pledge to suspend long-range missile tests by proceeding with what it termed a satellite launch. In exchange for that promise, the United States had undertaken to deliver to the North 240,000 tons of food aid, the only type of gesture to the North that remained, albeit marginally, politically acceptable in the United States. After North Korea broke its pledge, some American legislators even moved to statutorily forbid further food aid to North Korea. Thus, for the foreseeable future, any U.S. administration is virtually certain to maintain a policy of "strategic patience," actually containment, toward North Korea, even if it does not use the terms.

In sum, North Korean leaders went from a point of maximum negotiating leverage against the United States in 2006 after their first nuclear test to the current situation in which they have no credibility and virtually no leverage against the United States—and no prospect of regaining leverage. This appears to be the result of North Korean leaders' lack of a basic understanding of American leaders' perceptions, motivations, and interests in regard to the Korean Peninsula. Because they were not realistic about the

---

31 Siegfried S. Hecker, "What I Found in North Korea," *Foreign Affairs*, December 9, 2010, http://www.foreignaffairs.com/articles/67023/siegfried-s-hecker/what-i-found-in-north-korea.

"American card," North Korean leaders have lost any chance of reaping even the limited benefits they could have gained from improved relations with the United States, including an end to most sanctions and the provision of humanitarian aid and basic developmental assistance.

Japan and North Korea: Yen and History

For North Korea, Japan has historically meant only two things—a source of much-needed hard currency and technology and a means of asserting the North's status as the true repository of Korean national identity.

Japan was North Korea's most important economic partner in the capitalist world until the beginning of the past decade. For the largely isolated DPRK, Japan played an invaluable role as a significant source of hard currency acquired through legal trade, the flow of remittances from Korean residents of Japan, and from illicit activities such as gambling and the sale of illegal drugs. At its height, in the mid-1990s, the money pipeline from Japan to North Korea may have funneled around $100 million a year into Pyongyang's coffers, though some estimates put that number much higher. Beyond that flow, Japan held out the lure of an even bigger payday in the form of a massive multibillion dollar de facto reparations payment, in the form of loans and investment, that was envisioned to accompany the normalization of relations between Japan and the DPRK.

Instead, the pipeline from Japan to North Korea began to shut down in the mid-2000s, with Japan's role replaced by that of South Korea and China. By now, the flow has been reduced to a trickle, mostly channeled indirectly from Korean residents through China, Hong Kong, and Macao. The significance of Japan as a vital source of hard currency and technology has come to an end.

Now Japan has reverted to its second, but perhaps more enduring, function for the North Korean state, i.e., as a target of propaganda attack as the historic enemy of Korean national independence. For Pyongyang, Japan is now more important as a means of asserting its status as the true defender of the Korean nation in its unending contest with the South for legitimacy.

The Money Pipeline from Japan to North Korea

The money pipeline from Japan to North Korea has its origins in a not well-understood legacy of Japanese colonial rule in Korea. At the end of World War II, approximately two million Koreans were on the Japanese mainland where they had been brought as laborers to work in the mines and factories of wartime Japan (many other Koreans were also forced to labor in other parts of the Japanese empire from Sakhalin island to Southeast Asia). The majority of Koreans returned to their homeland after liberation from colonial rule in 1945 but about six to seven hundred thousand Koreans remained in Japan, where they were technically stateless. They were pressed after the division of Korea to declare their affiliation with one of the two Koreas, each represented in Japan by residents organizations.

Though it may seem curious today, in the 1950s most Korean residents of Japan chose to affiliate with the pro–North Korean General Association of Korean Residents in Japan (*Chongryon* in Korea, *Chosen Soren* in Japanese). It was far better organized and offered a sophisticated system of Korean-language schools, high schools, even a university, as well as its own banks, credit unions and successful businesses, sometimes in gray areas such as pachinko gambling parlors and in the ranks of organized crime. As a result, more than two-thirds of ethnic Koreans in Japan chose to identify with the pro–North Korean group, with membership reaching as high as 470,000 in the 1950s (though it has declined to 150,000 or fewer today).[32]

Chosen Soren was the main facilitator of trade between Japan and the DPRK, and the remittances made by members appear to have been a significant source of income for the regime. Some of that took place through organized legal trade, and some through a largely unregulated flow of cash, for example, from gambling profits, that was hand-carried by North Korean residents to Pyongyang on a cargo and passenger ferry that sailed back and forth across the Sea of Japan on an average of two trips each month for decades. The estimates of remittances from Japan to North Korea, dating from the early 1990s, have varied widely—from a low of $10 million annually to as high as $2 billion.[33]

Japanese police authorities told the Diet in March 1994 that they believed *Chosen Soren* was funneling 60–80 billion yen a year to Pyongyang (about $650–$850 million at prevailing exchange rates). But scholars and experts have questioned those higher-end estimates. In a study published in 1996, based on looking at DPRK spending patterns and balance-of-trade figures, Nicholas Eberstadt concluded that annual transfers from Japan averaged less than $100 million a year after 1990.[34] A decade later, taking into

32 James L. Schoff, *Political Fences & Bad Neighbors: North Korea Policy Making in Japan & Implications for the United States* (Cambridge, MA: Institute for Foreign Policy Analysis, Inc, 2006), 2.

33 Stephen Haggard and Marcus Noland, *North Korea's External Economic Relations* (Washington, DC: Peterson Institute for International Economics, 2007), 15.

34 Nicholas Eberstadt, "Financial Transfers from Japan to North Korea: Estimating the Unreported Flows, *Asia Survey* 36, no. 5 (May 1996): 523–42.

account the dramatic slowdown of the Japanese economy which also impacted Koreans resident in Japan, the flow had dropped to less than $40 million, experts concluded.[35]

The declining role of Japan in propping up the North Korean regime and its economy is also reflected in the dramatic drop in official, bilateral trade. Trade was actually at its height in the early 1980s. But as recently as 1995, Japan was North Korea's largest trading partner, outstripping China and the ROK. At that time, trade with Japan constituted slightly more than 25 percent of North Korea's total trade. North Korean residents and their businesses sent electronic components and clothing materials to North Korea for assembly, with the finished goods then reexported to discount stores in Japan. Seafood and mushrooms were also exported from North Korea, with vehicles heading back the other way. A decade later bilateral trade had dropped more than 80 percent and constituted a little less than 5 percent of North Korea's total trade.[36]

The decline is partly a reflection of the collapse of the North Korean economy in the wake of the cutoff of aid from the Soviet Union at the end of the Cold War and the famine of the mid-1990s. But it is also attributed to the deterioration of relations following the abortive attempt by Prime Minister Junichiro Koizumi to normalize relations in 2002 and the emergent crisis over North Korea's nuclear program. At the time of Koizumi's first trip to Pyongyang in September 2002 (a second visit took place in 2004), the two governments issued a joint declaration that promised large-scale Japanese economic assistance following normalization, including grant aid, long-term loans, and humanitarian assistance. The package was intended to mirror that given to the ROK at the time of normalization of relations in 1965. The value was not set but reports put it in the $5–$10 billion range, which would have been a huge sum for North Korea.[37]

Those intentions disappeared in the cloud of controversy that followed the North Korean admission of its abduction of numerous Japanese citizens and its refusal both to account for all the abductees and to release all of them and their families.

Beginning in 2003, the Japanese government has imposed a series of sanctions that have targeted the trade and remittance flows from Japan to North Korea. In May 2003 the government announced a reinterpretation of

35 Schoff, *Political Fences*, 2.

36 Ibid., 17.

37 Mark E. Manyin, *Japan-North Korea Relations: Selected Issues* (Washington, DC: Congressional Research Service, Library of Congress, 2003).

the Foreign Exchange and Foreign Trade Law that would allow it, in principle, to ban all remittances to Pyongyang. The following year the Diet passed laws giving the government power to not only interrupt money transfers but also to ban port calls by North Korean vessels if they lacked proper insurance. The regular ferry service was suspended in 2003 and by 2006 had been effectively ended.[38]

The Japanese government also began to target *Chosen Soren* and its ability to function as an arm of the North Korean state. The authorities put pressure on the privately owned Ashikaga Bank that was the main channel to move remittances for the organization. According to some reports, however, money was sent through Chinese banks instead.[39] National and local authorities also moved later to remove tax exemptions from the organization and to block public support for the association's schools.

Those sanctions have only gotten stiffer since the North Korean missile and nuclear tests beginning in 2006 and other North Korean escalatory provocations. The cap on remittances that is allowed without reporting has been steadily lowered from 30 million yen to 3 million yen and the limit on cash that can be carried to North Korea was reduced from three hundred thousand yen to one hundred thousand yen in May 2010.[40] About 438 million yen in cash was taken to North Korea in 2009, compared to more than 2.7 billion yen in fiscal year 2005. Declared remittances were 55 million yen in 2009, about a quarter of the level from four years earlier.[41]

The shutdown of the money pipeline from Japan to North Korea was compensated for by the expansion of economic activity with China and the ROK. But the loss could not have failed to have some impact on the North Korean leadership, particularly in cutting off a key source of hard currency and access to electronic and other technology that has been utilized in North Korea's nuclear and other military-related programs.

Japan as a Target of Propaganda Attacks

If Japan no longer serves as a major source of economic and technological support, its importance as a means of mobilizing nationalistic feelings remains fully intact. North Korean official propaganda continues to keep

38 Schoff, *Political Fences*, 11.

39 Bertil Lintner, "North Korea: It's Hard to Help Kim Jong-il," *Far Eastern Economic Review* 166, no. 12 (March 27, 2003): 20–22.

40 Reuters, "Japan to Step Up North Korea Sanctions After Sinking," May 28, 2010, http://in.reuters.com/article/2010/05/28/idINIndia-48870320100528.

41 Ibid.

up a steady stream of attacks on Japan—in sheer volume greater than the verbiage directed against the United States.

The themes of North Korean assaults on Japan are multiple. Modern Japan is portrayed as an unreconstructed descendent of imperial, wartime Japan, a state that harbors ambitions to resume its colonial domination of Korea. In this context, the North Korean propaganda machine links Japanese militarism to the United States, but also uses this issue to assail officials of the allegedly pro-Japanese conservative government in the ROK as "traitors" who are willing to sell out the nation to the hated historic enemy. North Korea also comes to the rhetorical defense of the Korean residents in Japan against Japanese government measures to limit the organization.

A public statement issued by a North Korean front organization, the Central Committee of the Democratic Front for the Reunification of Korea, timed to the anniversary of the Japanese annexation of Korea in 1910, summed up all these themes:

> The Japanese reactionaries have become evermore undisguised in their moves to hatch plots and apply sanctions against the DPRK and persecute and crack down upon the General Association of Korean Residents of Japan, in pursuance of the U.S. hostile policy toward it. They are taking part in the anti-DPRK war maneuvers of the U.S. and the south Korean puppet authorities in a bid to realize the old dream of the "Greater East Asia Co-Prosperity Sphere." The Japanese reactionaries' moves for reinvasion and anti-DPRK campaign are encouraged by the Lee Myung-bak group's sycophancy and treachery to serve Japan.[42]

Some of the attacks on Japan are more specific. Recent discussion of increased military cooperation between Japan, the ROK, and the United States prompted, for example, a stiff retort from the North Koreans. The dispatch of observers from the Japanese Self-Defense forces to joint U.S.-ROK exercises in late 2010 was an indication "that the Japanese reactionaries' scenario to stage a comeback to Korea has reached a grave phase," a Korean Central News Agency (KCNA) dispatch warned. Citing Japanese involvement in the Korean War, KCNA told its readers that "the Japanese militarist forces with such crime-woven history behind [them] are working hard to stage a comeback to Korea under a war umbrella of the U.S. again in the new century."[43]

The North Koreans frequently invoke the crimes of Japanese colonialism, asserting their status as the true defenders of the Korean nation. The

42 Korean Central News Service of DPRK (KCNA), "Japan Urged to Make Apology for Its Past Crimes," August 22, 2010.

43 KCNA, "Japanese Reactionaries' Moves to Stage Comeback to Korea Disclosed," December 1, 2010.

other side of that campaign is the characterization of the conservative government and political forces in the South as "pro-Japanese lackeys" akin to those Koreans who collaborated with Japanese colonialism in the past. One recent article in the party daily *Rodong Sinmun* linked Lee Myung-bak to the "five traitors of 1905," who had agreed to the first stages of imposition of Japanese rule on the peninsula. "It is only two and a half years since the Lee Myung-bak group came to power but they committed bigger and more intolerable sycophancy and treachery to serve Japan than any preceding ruling quarters perpetrated in the whole period of their office," the signed article in the party daily declared.[44]

Japan thus offers only marginal assistance to the North Korean leadership as it tries to cope with the multiple challenges to its continued rule. Japan no longer provides a vital source of economic sustenance and there is no prospect that it will resume that role, short of a dramatic improvement in bilateral relations leading to normalization. On the other hand, Japan continues to offer a convenient means for Pyongyang to wrap itself in the flag of the Korean nation in the unresolved competition for legitimacy on the peninsula with its enemies to the South.

Post-Succession Prospects

On December 17, 2011, Kim Jong-il died suddenly of a heart attack. The North Korean media immediately made it clear that his third son, Kim Jong-un, would be his successor, and soon thereafter the younger Kim was installed in all of the top positions in the North Korean regime. Kim Jong-un's youth, his schooling in Switzerland, his more engaging manner, and his talk about the need to ensure the prosperity of the people of North Korea initially heightened hopes and speculation that he might have a more informed and balanced view of the world and that he might therefore eventually undertake major reforms of both domestic and foreign policies. Unfortunately, the new leader has shown little propensity so far for domestic reform, and North Korea's foreign and security policies have become even more belligerent since he has taken the helm. Kim astounded international public opinion by his decision to party with the visiting former American basketball player Dennis Rodman in early 2013, even as he and his top officials were repeatedly threatening war against the United States and its South Korean ally. The younger Kim has repeatedly underlined that North Korea does not see itself as a victim but as a powerful actor in international affairs,

---

44 KCNA, "All Koreans Called Upon to Eliminate Pro-Japanese Lackeys," September 3, 2010.

but his words and deeds suggest an even deeper lack of understanding of the United States, Japan, and the rest of the international community than his late father held. All but ignoring the transformation that has spread across most of East Asia over the last few decades, the new North Korean leadership appears intent on clinging to the regime's anachronistic worldview that makes a near-term resolution of the long-standing tensions on the Korean Peninsula unlikely, if not impossible.

9 China's Growing Presence in the DPRK: Origins, Objectives, and Implications

Thomas Fingar

China's arm's length, "lips and teeth" relationship with North Korea (the Democratic People's Republic of Korea or DPRK) appears to have entered a new phase in about 2009. Since then, Chinese firms, certainly with approval and perhaps encouragement from Pyongyang and Beijing, have been building infrastructure and facilities in the DPRK at an accelerating pace.[1] Chinese-invested enterprises clearly are not confined to the Special Economic Zones established to contain foreign influence and limit interaction with ordinary people and the broader economy.[2] Many of the known

1 Statistics from China's Ministry of Commerce indicate that aggregate Chinese investment in the DPRK increased from $120 million in 2008 to $260 million in 2009 and $300 million in 2011. Much of the investment was in infrastructure, mining (coal and several metallic minerals), and metallurgy. For additional detail, see Jin Moo Kim, "North Korea's Reliance on China and China's Influence on North Korea," *Korean Journal of Defense Analysis* 23, no. 2 (June 2011): 257–71, http://www.kida.re.kr/data/kjda/07_Jin%20Moo%20Kim.pdf; Li Xiaokun, "Neighbors Explore Cooperation," *China Daily*, August 18, 2012, http://www.chinadaily.com.cn/china/2012-08/18/content_15685431.htm; and Daniel Gearin, "Chinese Infrastructure and Natural Resources Investment in North Korea," U.S.-China Economic and Security Review Commission Staff Backgrounder, October 20, 2010, http://www.uscc.gov/researchpapers/2010/ChineseInfrastructureandNaturalResourcesInvestmentsinNorthKorea.pdf.

2 See Andrei Lankov, "North Korea Not Quite in the Zone," *Asia Times*, June 21, 2011, http://www.atimes.com/atimes/Korea/MF21Dg01.html; and Bradley O. Babson,

projects are located near the joint border but reporting indicates that they can be found in Pyongyang and seven of the North's nine provinces.[3] These developments are noteworthy because they stand in such marked contrast to the recent past as well as previous decades of PRC-DPRK relations.[4]

The magnitude of the increase in Chinese activity in the North, which has occurred largely without fanfare or formal policy statements from either capital, raises many questions about why it is happening and what it might tell us about PRC-DPRK relations and the intentions of Kim Jong-un. Thus far about the only judgment one can render with confidence is that DPRK behavior—and possibly that of China—appears to have changed in significant ways. Why it has changed and what it portends is even less clear because we know little about the origins, objectives, and implications of what we are able to observe. This essay attempts to provide a framework and suggestive hypotheses to explore questions about objectives, perceptions, and implications, but it stops far short of providing an empirical analysis or theoretical model. It is, in other words, a modest step designed to enhance understanding by eliciting information and insights from others intrigued by the latest turn in DPRK policy and China-DPRK relations.

Setting the Stage

The recent upsurge in Chinese investment and other activities in the North antedates the ascension of Kim Jong-un and the personnel and policy changes announced in the months since the death of his father. What we are witnessing now was initiated by Kim Jong-il and should be understood as part of the legacy bequeathed to his successor. This gives the change in policy a stature and a legitimacy that render it relatively immune, at least for a while, to criticism and attempts to reverse course. Indeed, one of the ways we learned about the Chinese activities is from Chinese media coverage of site visits by Kim Jong-il, often accompanied by Kim Jong-un. Allowing greater scope for Chinese penetration and integration into the DPRK economy may be an experiment or expedient, but it is likely to continue for some

"Will North Korea's Plans for Foreign Investment Make it a More Prosperous Nation?" *38 North*, May 2, 2012, http://38north.org/2012/05/bbabsono50212/.

3 See, for example, Dick S. Nanto, "Increasing Dependency: North Korea's Economic Relations with China," in *Korea's Economy 2011*, vol. 27 (USA: The Korea Economic Institute of America, 2011), 75–83, http://www.keia.org/publication/increasing-dependency-north-korea's-economic-relations-china.

4 See, for example, Robert Sutter, "China's Recent Relations with North Korea—Look Beyond 'Stability'," *International Journal of Korean Studies* 15, no. 2 (Fall 2011): 1–15, http://www.icks.org/publication/pdf/2011-FALL-WINTER/2.pdf.

time because abrupt curtailment would be a dramatic refutation of decisions attributed to Kim Jong-il and, presumably, endorsed by other top leaders.

If this analysis is correct, the new policy will remain in place long enough to begin showing results. Some of the results will benefit the regime and may benefit local communities and their inhabitants. They will probably also be in place long enough to begin manifesting negative or problematic consequences for Pyongyang. To use a Chinese aphorism employed by Deng Xiaoping to explain negative consequences of his reform and opening policy, "Opening the window to admit fresh air invariably also allows a few flies and mosquitoes to enter." His point was that one had to put up with some things that were undesirable or problematic in order to achieve higher priority objectives. What is now playing out in the DPRK is likely to remain in place long enough to clarify the advantages and disadvantages for both the DPRK and for China.

The new policy appears to have emerged gradually over a number of years, probably beginning in the mid-2000s. Pyongyang had tried for years to develop a relationship with the United States to buffer and counterbalance its always somewhat-fraught relationship with China. Those efforts achieved a measure of success in the 1990s and through 2000 but progress stalled and relations worsened dramatically during the George W. Bush administration.[5] By 2009, a physically ailing Kim Jong-il apparently had decided that smooth transfer of power to his son, and possibly even preservation of the regime, required prompt action to improve the DPRK economy. Experience had taught him that restarting the normalization of relations with the United States would at best be slow—too slow—even if the new American administration wanted it to happen, and that he would have to reach an acceptable modus vivendi with China if he were to achieve the economic performance and political stability required for the succession of Kim Jong-un.[6]

Decisions to launch the new policy were made in the context of poor relations and worsening tensions with the Republic of Korea (ROK), the United States, Japan, and most of the developed world. Japan began to cut

5 See Robert Carlin and John W. Lewis, *Negotiating with North Korea: 1992–2007* (Stanford, CA: Center for International Security and Cooperation, 2008); and David E. Sanger, *The Inheritance: The World Obama Confronts and the Challenges to American Power* (New York, NY: Harmony, 2009).

6 Kim Jong-il signaled the tilt toward Beijing by greeting Chinese Premier Wen Jiabao at Pyongyang airport, a break with his normal practice, when Wen arrived on October 4, 2009. See, for example, "Chinese Premier Arrives in Pyongyang, Greeted by Kim Jong Il at Airport," Xinhuanet, October 4, 2009, http://news.xinhuanet.com/english/2009-10/04/content_12179189.htm.

off all trade with the DPRK after the effort to resolve the abductee issue backfired.[7] UN sanctions imposed after the first (2006) and second (2009) nuclear tests severely limited possibilities for economic growth through cooperative arrangements with other nations.[8] New ROK president Lee Myung-bak's government abandoned his predecessors' Sunshine Policy in 2008 and stated that it would not provide further large-scale humanitarian aid unless the North abandoned its nuclear weapons program.[9]

Without giving up its nuclear weapons, something that Pyongyang was unwilling to do, the regime had no real option but to rely more heavily on China. The context for the decision or decisions to expand the scale and scope of Chinese penetration also included a perceived DPRK need to solidify relations with Beijing in preparation for the succession, one that took on greater urgency after Kim Jong-il's stroke in 2008. Increased DPRK dependence on its relationship with China probably inclined Pyongyang to solidify the relationship. Increased dependence also gave Beijing leverage to press for changes in DPRK policy that would move Pyongyang in the direction of China's own successful path to growth via reform and opening to the outside world while also bringing economic and political benefits to the PRC. Lee Myung-bak's strong tilt toward the United States may also have been a factor, albeit at the margins, influencing Beijing to respond positively to new initiatives from the North.

The decisions were also made in the context of increasing movement of people and goods across the PRC-DPRK border and the spread of cell phones, DVDs, and other means of communication that increased North Korean citizen knowledge of life in China and the ROK and awareness of the gap between regime rhetoric and reality.[10] Though still manageable, the

7 For a brief summary of the issue see, "DPRK-Japan Relations: An Historical Overview," December 1, 2011, The National Committee on North Korea, http://www.ncnk.org/resources/briefing-papers/all-briefing-papers/ncnk-issue-brief-dprk-japan-relations-an-historical-overview.

8 See "Security Council Condemns Nuclear Test by Democratic People's Republic of Korea," UN Security Council Resolution 1718 (2006), http://www.un.org/News/Press/docs/2006/sc8853.doc.htm; and "Security Council, Acting Unanimously, Condemns in Strongest Terms Democratic People's Republic of Korea Nuclear Test, Toughens Sanctions," UN Security Council Resolution 1874 (2009), http://www.un.org/News/Press/docs//2009/sc9679.doc.htm.

9 See, for example, Aidan Foster-Carter, "North Korea-South Korea Relations: Still Stalemated," *Comparative Connections* 10, no. 3 (October 2008): 83–99, http://www.isn.ethz.ch/isn/Digital-Library/Publications/Detail/?ots591=cab359a3-9328-19cc-a1d2-8023e646b22c&lng=en&id=97484.

10 Katharina Zellweger, "Accelerating Social Change in North Korea" (unpublished

magnitude of this challenge was certain to grow and might begin to pose real problems for the regime in the midst of the transition from Kim Jong-il to his young and untested successor. This added incentive, indeed urgency, to the search for ways to modernize the country and provide tangible benefits to the people.

Relevant developments were occurring at two levels during this period.[11] Kim Jong-il made formal policy decisions, but a kind of de facto policy also emerged from the explosion of contacts, legal and illegal, across the PRC-DPRK border. Pyongyang was distressed by the magnitude of smuggling activity and made recurring efforts to bring it under control. Individuals and organizations (e.g., the Korean People's Army) were benefiting from these activities and corruption was eroding whatever discipline remained after years of famine and food shortages. Even if Kim had insisted on a harsh crackdown, it is doubtful that he could have ended all such activity.

Despite the existence of illegal and informal cross-border activity, China's activities and unprecedented penetration of the DPRK are happening because Pyongyang authorized and endorsed them. This is not a case of unwanted or hostile penetration by a stronger power. Pyongyang could have continued to reject PRC offers and rebuff its requests to emulate China's strategy of reform and opening. China would not have forced the DPRK to allow the activities we are witnessing because China had more important interests elsewhere in the world and did not wish to tarnish its image and pursuit of acceptance and influence as a responsible member of the international community by flagrantly disregarding its calls for a more "harmonious world" by appearing to bully the North.[12] Pyongyang could have said no but to do so probably was perceived, under the circumstances, as entailing more immediate risks.

DPRK Objectives and Calculus

As is often the case with North Korea, the paucity of information about the origins and objectives of Chinese activities in the country makes it

paper, August 2012).

11 See Stephen Haggard and Marcus Noland, "Networks, Trust, and Trade: The Microeconomics of China-North Korea Integration" (Washington, DC: Peterson Institute for International Economics Working Paper WP 12–8, May 2012), http://www.iie.com/publications/wp/wp12-8.pdf.

12 See, for example, Hu Jintao, "Report to the Seventeenth National Congress of the Communist Party of China on Oct. 15, 2007, Part XI, Unswervingly Following the Path of Peaceful Development," China.org.cn, October 15, 2007, http://www.china.org.cn/english/congress/229611.htm#11.

necessary to rely on conjecture and logical constructs to develop alternative hypotheses to explain what has happened and predict what to expect. We do not know why Pyongyang decided to invite or allow Chinese firms to play a much larger role in the DPRK economy, but we do know that the decisions were made in the context of the clear failure to achieve a relationship with the United States that would have increased Pyongyang's sense of security through a balance of power arrangement. Lacking the ability to use the United States as a counterbalance to the PRC, Kim Jong-il decided, perhaps with considerable encouragement from Beijing, that the best way to limit Chinese interference was to foster a closer bilateral relationship with the PRC.

Since we do not have authoritative statements and conclusive evidence, it seems prudent to explore a number of different hypotheses to explain observed and inferred behavior. Three that will be outlined here may be summarized as follows:

Acting from strength. Pyongyang assessed that its partially successful nuclear detonation had enhanced DPRK security and bargaining leverage sufficiently to take risks with respect to foreign participation in its economy, risks that had previously been judged unacceptably high.

Acting from necessity. Pyongyang assessed that its strained relations with all nations following the first nuclear test and the prospect of domestic instability during the pending transition from Kim Jong-il to Kim Jong-un made it necessary to improve economic performance and the condition of ordinary people by allowing foreign interests, beginning with Chinese firms, to play a much larger role in the DPRK economy.

Acting from conviction. After years of encouragement from Beijing to emulate China's successful self-strengthening strategy, its own numerous experiments and partial efforts to take advantage of market mechanisms and foreign (including ROK) desire for access to DPRK resources and labor, and recurring debate within the political elite, Pyongyang—Kim Jong-il—was finally persuaded that the risks of acceding to Chinese pressure were less dangerous than the risks of sticking with policies that had not worked. He may have persuaded himself that the best way to protect DPRK identity and independence was to allow a greater role for foreign—Chinese—firms.

These hypotheses are not mutually exclusive and it is possible, even likely, that the third is mainly a rationalization for one or both of the first two. However, exploring them as distinct alternatives helps to illuminate different sets of considerations.

Acting From Strength

Kim Jong-il (like his father) seems to have employed a two-track approach to increase DPRK security. One track was to reduce the danger of attack by the United States and/or its allies through diplomatic means (e.g., securing acceptance of the DPRK's right to exist through membership in the United Nations, negative security assurances and formal diplomatic recognition from the United States, and a degree of rapprochement with the ROK). Success on this track would have had the added advantage of enabling Pyongyang to use the United States and others to balance and check Chinese influence and mercantilist ambitions in the North. The diplomatic track achieved only partial results. These results were unacceptable to Pyongyang, largely because of what was happening on the second track.

That second track was the pursuit of security through the acquisition of nuclear weapons. For Kim, the bomb was the ultimate insurance policy. If he had it, the DPRK could deter aggression from any and all directions. Moreover, employing a variant of the Eisenhower administrations "bang for the buck" argument, Kim sometimes implied that possession of nuclear weapons would enable him to reduce the military and focus more on promoting economic growth. The partially successful nuclear detonation in 2006 and more successful nuclear test in 2009 gave credence to the DPRK's declaration in early 2005 that it had become a nuclear weapon state.[13] The tests and conclusions about the efficacy of the North's nuclear "deterrent" may also have given Kim the confidence, or the arguments, he needed to expand the parameters of acceptable foreign participation in the country's economy.

At the time when Pyongyang may have conducted the type of security and policy review suggested above, only China was willing to commit substantial resources to the development of facilities in the North. Giving China alone expanded access to DPRK resources was probably troubling to the intensely nationalistic Koreans, especially so given the disparity in size, long history of Chinese assertions of suzerainty over Korea, and recent publication of maps describing portions of Korean territory as having been, at one time, part of the Chinese empire.[14] Pyongyang, or some officials in

13 Anthony Failoa, "N. Korea Declares Itself a Nuclear Power," *Washington Post*, February 10, 2005, http://www.washingtonpost.com/wp-dyn/articles/A12836-2005Feb10. html.

14 See, for example, "S. Korea-China History Dispute over Ancient Kingdoms," *The Hankyoreh*, September 6, 2006, http://english.hani.co.kr/arti/english_edition/e_international/154761.html; and Choe Sang-Hun, "Tussle over a Vanished Kingdom," *New York Times*, October 12, 2006, http://www.nytimes.com/2006/10/12/world/asia/12iht-histo-

Pyongyang, may have hoped or speculated that concern about China's rise and capitalist hunger for DPRK resources would convince the United States, ROK, and Japan to put aside their concerns about DPRK nuclear weapons to constrain Chinese influence in the North and gain access for their own firms. If that was part of the calculation, it misread the intensity of external concern about the DPRK nuclear program and human rights situation, and badly overestimated other countries' interests in access to resources and cheap labor in the North.

Acting From Necessity

This is, in many ways, the "glass half empty" counterpart to the hypothesis that acquisition of nuclear weapons gave Pyongyang the confidence required to shift attention to the economy and allow China to play a much larger role inside the DPRK. It posits that increased isolation and international opprobrium after the nuclear tests made Pyongyang feel even more insecure because possession of a few nuclear weapons tempted powerful states to seek regime change and perhaps even contemplate use of military force to eliminate the nuclear threat from the North before it became greater.[15] These concerns may have been compounded by uncertainties with respect to Kim Jong-il's health and the efficacy of succession arrangements apparently put on a faster track after he suffered a stroke in fall 2008, and further compounded by the combination of poor economic performance, continuing popular deprivation, and growing public awareness that life was better in China and the ROK than in the DPRK. If the "acting from strength" explanation is understood to mean, "doing something because we can," this alternative should be understood as "doing something because we must."

Lacking a better alternative and unable, under the circumstances, to attract investors from multiple countries by opening the DPRK to new forms of investment by any nation wishing to take advantage of the opportunity, Pyongyang may have offered China special access and conditions. Given the relatively close relationship between Beijing and Pyongyang, the invitation, if that is what it was, probably built upon discussions occurring over a number of years. It may well have built upon proposals from the Chinese describing what they were prepared to do if Pyongyang relaxed its restrictions on foreign involvement in its economy. In other words, the DPRK may have picked up an offer that had been on the table for a long time because it felt that it had no better option.

A variant of the scenario sketched out above accords greater importance to Chinese recognition that the North was in a very weak position and thus increased Chinese willingness to use their leverage to press for greater access with fewer conditions than had been considered previously. This need not have been as exploitative as the preceding sentence suggests because for many years Beijing had been pressing Pyongyang to alleviate its economic problems and accelerate self-strengthening efforts by taking advantage of opportunities resulting from globalization.[16] DPRK reticence probably caused Chinese officials to emphasize that they had employed a step-by-step approach ("crossing the stream by feeling for stones") with numerous opportunities to review and revise policies to correct problems and capture new opportunities. The implicit and explicit message would have been that the most important thing was to get started in order to gain concrete experience. Regardless of the specific content and character of these discussions, both sides understood that doing so would give the Chinese more than they had been offered or were able to achieve previously.

If the above scenario is more or less the way this played out, DPRK officials may have been as resentful and suspicious as their Chinese counterparts were sixty years earlier when China felt compelled to accept Stalin's conditions for providing protection and assistance to the newly established People's Republic.[17] Indeed, the North Koreans may have had the Sino-Soviet example in mind when accepting the Chinese conditions and taken comfort from the fact that the Soviets were ultimately forced to leave but the facilities they built remained in China. Officials in the North could have argued to domestic opponents of the new policy that everything being built would be in the DPRK, making the facilities hostage to the North while increasing the incentive for China to ensure that they were successful. As noted above, they may also have seen accepting the Chinese investments as a way to entice the United States and others to shelve concerns about nuclear weapons in

16 See, for example, Gong Keyu, "Current China-DPRK Relations," *Global Review* (Spring 2012): 73–87, http://www.siis.org.cn/Sh_Yj_Cms/Mgz/201201/20124615 3155AT98.DOC.

17 See, for example, Thomas P. Bernstein, "Introduction: The Complexities of Learning from the Soviet Union," in *China Learns from the Soviet Union, 1949–Present,* ed. Thomas P. Bernstein and Hua-Yu Li (Lanham, MD: Lexington Books, 2010), 1–26; and John W. Garver, *Foreign Relations of the People's Republic of China* (Upper Saddle River, NJ: Prentice Hall, 1993), 39–43.

favor of containing China by getting a piece of the action through reengaging with the DPRK. Regardless of the specifics of this scenario, it is virtually certain that it would not have led to the Chinese activity we now know to be occurring if Pyongyang had not been confident that it could "manage" and control the Chinese presence.

Acting From Conviction

Each of the motivations and scenarios outlined above may overstate the importance of perceived strengths and vulnerabilities. It is possible that Kim Jong-il was finally persuaded to adopt a variant of the Chinese model by the success he saw on his trips across the border. Situational factors may have influenced his decision, but he seems to have determined that half measures and attempting to confine foreign activity to special zones on the periphery were not producing desired—or necessary—results.

We know that individuals and groups within the North Korean elite had long debated alternative proposals to preserve security, develop the economy, and meet the needs of the nation. Although we have only a dim and partial view of the institutions, individuals, and arguments in these debates, it is possible that those championing more extensive, more rapid, and higher-risk strategies finally prevailed because changed conditions provided both incentives and opportunities to seek higher payoffs by adopting a somewhat riskier approach.[18]

Such a change of mind or recalculation of costs and benefits is theoretically possible but seems unlikely unless one factors in the considerations summarized in the "strength" and "necessity" scenarios. Such decisions are not made in a vacuum and it would be illogical—and politically impossible—to disregard the factors creating both opportunities and the necessity for a change of course. Pyongyang may have adopted the new policy granting China greater access to the country because it became convinced that it was the least-bad option as much as out of a newfound conviction that what the Chinese had been telling them for two decades was the right course to take.[19]

18 Robert L. Carlin and Joel S. Wit, *North Korean Reform: Politics, Economics and Security* (Abington [England]: Routledge for the International Institute for Strategic Studies, 2006).

19 Despite the acquisition of nuclear weapons, lack of better alternatives, and example of Chinese success, this could not have been an easy decision because it was made in the context of growing discomfort about the amounts of coal and other resources being shipped to China and concern that cheap goods from China were bad for efforts to develop indigenous industry.

China's Objectives and Calculus

China's top priority with respect to the DPRK is to prevent developments triggered by or directed toward the North from jeopardizing stability in the region or China's ability to sustain high rates of economic growth.[20] War in the neighborhood, regardless of how it started, would not be good for China. Pyongyang knows this and uses the leverage it has from Beijing's judgment that it has a substantial stake in preventing regime collapse (which could trigger intervention by the ROK and perhaps the United States) as well as large numbers of refugees fleeing to China. Much of the time, Beijing responds to the actions of its "close as lips and teeth" partner and only formal military ally by providing fuel and food aid as well as political cover in the United Nations Security Council.

The generation that shed blood together in the Korean War is mostly gone from the scene and many Chinese, particularly younger generations, view the North with dismay and even abhorrence. Chinese leaders cannot ignore public attitudes but policies toward the DPRK are governed primarily by *Realpolitik*.[21] Geography shapes destiny and Beijing's fate, in some respects, is tied to that of North Korea. Chinese may be unhappy about having to prop up the regime in Pyongyang but see no alternative to doing so. They believe what they have been telling the North for two decades, namely, that the regime can—perhaps can only—survive if it adopts measures similar to Deng Xiaoping's policy of reform and opening.

We do not know whether the North came to China with a proposal to allow deeper Chinese involvement in the DPRK economy, or if China saw an opportunity to propose new forms of cooperation. Regardless of how the process began, it seems likely that Beijing saw an opportunity to pursue a number of objectives simultaneously. One objective was to persuade the DPRK to adopt the kind of reforms that China considered necessary to prevent regime collapse. Whether by playing to DPRK convictions that nuclear weapons had given it the security it needed to attempt more extensive reform or by taking advantage of Pyongyang's weakness to extract concessions in exchange for continued assistance, Beijing seized the chance to demonstrate the benefits of reform and opening by building infrastructure

20 See, for example, Bates Gill, *China's North Korea Policy* (United States Institute of Peace, Special Report 283, July 2011), http://www.usip.org/files/resources/China's_North_Korea_Policy.pdf.

21 See, for example, Stapleton Roy, "Response to *PacNet* #32R—The Illogic of China's North Korea Policy," *PacNet* Number 32R-A, June 7, 2012, http://csis.org/files/publication/Pac1232RA.pdf.

and establishing Chinese enterprises in the North. One objective, therefore, was to demonstrate the benefits and manageability of greater reliance on foreign firms.

A second objective may have been to reduce the need to subsidize and prop up the regime in Pyongyang, reducing both the economic and, more importantly, the political costs to Beijing. A better-functioning DPRK economy would need less assistance and there would be less incentive for economic migrants to cross the border into China. A better-functioning economy could also make it possible to improve opportunities and living standards and renew confidence in the regime, thereby reducing the danger of external intervention triggered by domestic unrest. Improving the ability of the regime to satisfy internal demands presumably would prolong its tenure and delay reunification of the peninsula. For those Chinese who still think in such terms, this would preserve the DPRK as a buffer between China and the ROK and its U.S. ally, and prevent the emergence of an even more formidable Korean economic competitor.

China's objectives also include gaining access to minerals and other resources needed to sustain its economic rise. Even though its huge foreign exchange reserves and large volume of foreign trade enable China to purchase pretty much anything that it needs in international markets, significant numbers of Chinese distrust markets and fear that the United States and its allies might use military and political power to prevent China from obtaining the fuel and other resources it needs for sustained growth.[22] This makes them partial to mercantilist or quasi-mercantilist arrangements for captive sources of supply. The DPRK has the added advantage, from Beijing's perspective, of being an adjacent country with "interior," and therefore more secure, transport routes to the PRC. Building Chinese-owned extractive and processing facilities in the DPRK and constructing modern road and rail links to China has the triple advantage of Chinese control, more secure access, and lower costs.

Attainment of the objectives noted and advantages for China that are expected to flow from its investments in the DPRK provide substantial incentive, but Beijing must have considered potential downsides as well. One potential downside is vulnerability to DPRK retaliation for some future offense and the attendant increased ability of Pyongyang to use threats to the facilities to elicit or ensure PRC support on future issues. This hazard seems

22 See, for example, Erica Strecker Downs, *China's Quest for Energy Security* (Santa Monica, CA: RAND, 2000), chapter 4, http://www.rand.org/content/dam/rand/pubs/monograph_reports/MR1244/MR1244.ch4.pdf.

more theoretical than real because, for the foreseeable future, the DPRK will remain dependent on assistance and support from China. China will feel compelled to provide support for reasons other than—and arguably more important than—protecting particular investments in the North. Moreover, China appears to have hedged this vulnerability by subcontracting it to private investors. Investors stand to profit economically, but it is also they who are exposed to expropriation, curtailment of electricity or water for political reasons, or violence from unhappy Koreans. Insurance and the expected desire of the DPRK to attract other foreign investors presumably reduce the risk even further.

In addition to discounting the risk to hostage firms from adverse action by Pyongyang or groups of Koreans, Beijing (and Pyongyang) may calculate that the existence of a number of Chinese facilities in the North will serve as a deterrent to attack by conventional forces. A factory or mine is not an official presence, but Chinese (and North Koreans) probably calculate that American drones and bombers constitute the greatest danger to the facilities, and that reaction to the U.S. bombing of China's embassy in Belgrade will make the United States reluctant to attack a known Chinese facility, even if it is a commercial enterprise in a third country.[23] Koreans may calculate that Chinese ownership will make the United States more, not less, hesitant to attack the North.

ROK Perspective and Concerns

Officials and other observers in the ROK probably have mixed and somewhat contradictory feelings about the North's opening to China. On the one hand, Chinese investments and efforts to persuade the DPRK to participate more extensively in the global economy might result in higher rates of growth, a larger DPRK stake in peace and stability, and lasting improvements in living conditions. To the extent the regime valued the investments and such benefits, it might be less willing to put them at risk by engaging in provocative behavior.[24]

ROK observers will be less positive about changes that bolster the legitimacy of the regime. However, if the process forestalls regime collapse and

---

23 See Kerry Dumbaugh, *Chinese Embassy Bombing in Belgrade Compensation Issues* (Washington, DC: Congressional Research Service, April 12, 2000), http://congressionalresearch.com/RS20547/document.php.

24 See, for example, Jin Moo Kim, "North Korea's Reliance on China and China's Influence on North Korea," *Korean Journal of Defense Analysis* 23, no. 2 (June 2011): 257–71, http://www.kida.re.kr/data/kjda/07_Jin%20Moo%20Kim.pdf.

its attendant dangers to people on both sides of the DMZ, especially if the process ultimately makes the regime more like the one in China, those developments would be welcomed by many in the South. Conversely, if improved economic performance and enhanced legitimacy emboldened the regime to undertake more repressive or provocative actions, ire in the ROK probably would be directed more at China than at the policies of the South Korean government. At this point there is little basis for predicting how events will play out, but progressives, and perhaps others, will want to lock in positive changes through reengagement with the North. Whether reengagement takes the form of an updated Sunshine Policy or is more cautious and limited will depend on the outcomes of electoral politics in the ROK.

In addition to concerns and considerations centered on the future of the regime and the lot of ordinary people in the North, ROK observers will view the growing Chinese presence in the North through nationalistic lenses. Some will suspect that the investments are the leading edge of a move to reassert "middle kingdom" influence in the northern part of the peninsula and will be troubled by expansion of the Chinese presence. This may evolve into something of a dilemma for the ROK. If Chinese penetration improves the economy and lot of the people and reduces the likelihood of provocations, instability, and regime collapse, it will be regarded as a good development. However, if the initial experiment is regarded as successful and Pyongyang agrees to allow an even larger and geographically broader Chinese presence, concerns about Chinese influence and aspirations will increase. Along the way, pressure will increase for the ROK government and ROK firms to invest in the North to contain Chinese influence and reap benefits perceived as flowing to Chinese rather than Koreans. Whether Pyongyang would allow ROK firms access or terms comparable to those for China is unknown but now seems unlikely without a quid pro quo.

Japan's Calculus and Concerns

Japanese will see China's expansion into the DPRK through lenses colored by their perception of growing Chinese assertiveness on territorial issues in the Sea of Japan and the South China Sea.[25] For some, it will confirm fears that a rising China will become an expansionist power determined to reassert Chinese suzerainty in the region. In addition, some will remember

25 See, for example, Martin Fackler, "Dispute Over Islands Reflects Japanese Fear of China's Rise," *New York Times*, August 21, 2012, http://www.nytimes.com/2012/08/22/world/asia/dispute-over-islands-reflect-japanese-fear-of-chinas-rise.html?ref=territorialdisputes.

that Japan occupied Korea a century ago because it judged that doing so would secure valuable resources and enhance its own security. That, of course, turned out badly for Japan, but some will suspect that China employs a similar calculus and pursues similar objectives, albeit updated for conditions in the twenty-first century. To state these concerns is probably to overstate them, however, because those who harbor them likely already are convinced of malign PRC intent and would view developments in the PRC as confirmation of what they already believed rather than as a fundamentally different type of development.

China's engagement in the DPRK could trigger three additional Japanese reactions. One may be rekindled Japanese interest in reengaging the North in order to gain access to nearby resources and disciplined labor needed by Japanese firms and, in the process, to counter the Chinese monopoly of influence on the North. The hypothetical scenarios in the section on DPRK objectives envision such a response. A second additional response is likely to be reduced interest in a "balanced" relationship with China and the United States and greater reliance on the alliance and extended deterrence. Greater interest in the U.S. nuclear umbrella will be reinforced by a third additional response, namely, the conviction that closer ties between China and the DPRK will make it even more likely that the North will retain its nuclear weapons for a very long time.[26]

Should the United States Welcome or Worry About What is Happening?

The prudent answer to this question is that we probably do not yet know enough to determine the balance of positive and negative possibilities. That said, we know from experience that Washington's assessment will be significantly influenced—but not determined—by reactions in Seoul. Though inclined to defer to the wishes of its ally on questions involving the peninsula, the United States has its own interests which may at times be even more important than considerations of alliance maintenance.[27]

---

26 See, for example, Yuki Tatsumi, Editor, *North Korea: Challenges for the U.S.-Japan Alliance* (Washington, DC: The Henry L. Stimson Center, 2010), http://www.stimson.org/images/uploads/research-pdfs/Full_-_North_Korea_Challenge_for_the_U.S.-Japan_Alliance.pdf.

27 On the range of U.S. interests, see Kurt M. Campbell, "Asia Overview: Protecting American Interests in China and Asia," Testimony Before the House Committee on Foreign Affairs Subcommittee on Asia and the Pacific, March 31, 2011, http://www.state.gov/p/eap/rls/rm/2011/03/159450.htm.

In the United States, advocates of engagement and its putative transformative power will welcome China's activities in the North on grounds that transforming the DPRK into something more like the PRC would be positive development. The PRC has many defects, from an American perspective, but even its authoritarian system is far preferable to that of the regime in Pyongyang. A Chinese-led transformation of the North would not be as desirable as one led by the ROK because it would entail less impetus for political reform. But under current conditions, it is difficult to imagine a scenario that would assign the lead to Seoul. The United States has demonstrated its ability to facilitate transformations from authoritarian to democratic governments, notably in the ROK and Taiwan, but there is very little likelihood that U.S.-ROK alliance politics or domestic politics in the United States would allow Washington to take the lead, even if the DPRK were to become a willing partner.

If China's involvement in the North's economy enhances the well-being of ordinary people, Americans would regard it as a positive development. However, some, perhaps many, in the United States will argue that China's actions will strengthen and prolong the life of a noxious regime that will continue to reward the ruling elite at the expense of ordinary people while allowing the North to continue its nuclear weapons programs and other threats to the United States and its allies. Those holding this view will likely also argue that Beijing lacks the will to transform the regime in Pyongyang in positive ways, and that even if it could do so, the result would be only to change one type of repressive system into another.

One could easily extend the list of diametrically opposed American (and other foreign) assessments of China's involvement in the DPRK. For example, some will see the proliferation of Chinese facilities in the North as likely to increase Chinese incentives and leverage to prevent "bad behavior" by the DPRK. The reasoning would be that such behavior would endanger both regional stability and China's "macro" developmental objectives as well as the "micro" interests of particular Chinese firms. Others will argue that the presence of "hostage" Chinese firms will tie the PRC even more tightly to the DPRK and allow Pyongyang to undertake even more reckless actions without fear of Chinese retribution. My own view is that any increase or decrease in Chinese incentives and leverage is likely to be marginal. The PRC macro objective—preserving a peaceful regional and global environment conducive to China's continued rise—trumps the importance of its micro interests and objectives on the Korean Peninsula. Similarly, U.S. interests accord far higher priority to relations with China than to the DPRK;

Washington is unlikely to do anything with respect to the DPRK without serious consideration of the implications for U.S.-China relations.

The United States will remain most concerned about nuclear weapons in the North and the danger that Pyongyang will sell fissile material or nuclear know-how to rogue states or nonstate actors.[28] Though uncomfortable with the prospect of having to live with a nuclear North Korea for years of peaceful transformation, there is no better alternative for Washington at the current time. A key U.S. concern is that even if one accepts the premise that engagement will ultimately transform the DPRK and lead to the surrender of its nuclear weapons, there is no way to be certain that the North will not sell or transfer fissile material during the interim period.

Despite the predictions embodied in the scenarios in the section on DPRK objectives, the United States is unlikely to be drawn into a competition with China for influence in the DPRK because it does not have territorial or economic ambitions there and is not motivated by desire to pull the DPRK to its side (as was the case with China in the 1970s). Depending on circumstances at the time, the United States might—or might not—attempt to discourage efforts by the ROK and/or Japan to compete for investment opportunities in the North.

Net Assessment

The factors and considerations outlined above will shape perceptions and influence policy decisions in the DPRK, China, the ROK, Japan, and the United States, as will other factors, but there is no way to determine, yet, which will be most influential in individual countries or how the factors will interact in bilateral and multilateral combinations. Domestic politics will play a very important role, perhaps a more important role than Realpolitik strategic considerations, in shaping the perceptions and responses of the ROK and Japan. They will also be important shapers of U.S. perceptions and policies.

The way events play out will also be influenced by how China conducts itself in the North. Elsewhere in the world, Chinese attitudes and actions have eroded enthusiasm for their presence. Whether the Chinese have learned from such experiences or are likely to be more sensitive to DPRK concerns because of cultural affinity and decades of political interaction, or will act in ways that persuade Pyongyang that the pilot activities had failed

28 See Joshua Pollack, "North Korea's Nuclear Exports: On What Terms?" *38 North*, Special Report 9, October 14, 2010, http://38north.org/wp-content/uploads/2011/08/38North_SR9_Pollack2.pdf.

is by no means self-evident. How well or badly China manages its increased presence in the DPRK will influence North Korean attitudes to reform and opening. It may also influence DPRK willingness to make concessions calculated to attract investment and involvement by nations that might counter Chinese influence.

The bottom line is that it is too soon to tell what this means and how it will play out. Personalities and politics shape perceptions and policies in each of the major actors and we are on the cusp of unprecedented interaction among new players with unknown preferences and untested abilities to shape and respond to events. Kim Jong-un appears firmly in command in the DPRK, but he is still assembling "his" team and implementing decisions made by his father. China's once-in-a-decade leadership changes are still unfolding and are certain to bring to power many new people. Whether, or in what ways, their perceptions and policy preferences may differ from those of their predecessors remains to be seen. President Xi Jinping seemed to take a harder line on North Korea when he called for denuclearization during his May 24, 2013, meeting with DPRK Special Envoy Choe Ryong-hae, but what, if anything, this means for economic dimensions of the relationship is unclear.[29] The proclivities and priorities of those elected in the United States and the Republic of Korea are almost as uncertain. American presidents normally enjoy greater freedom of action during a second term, but President Obama's will and ability to explore new possibilities with respect to Northeast Asia will be constrained by domestic politics, competing priorities, and events around the globe. Similar uncertainty exists with respect to the priorities and possibilities of newly elected ROK president Park Geun-hye. The return to power and early actions of Shinzo Abe in Japan add yet another layer of uncertainty. Even if Obama is reelected with the greater freedom of action normally enjoyed by a second-term president, his will and ability to explore new possibilities with respect to Northeast Asia will be influenced by the outcome of congressional elections, domestic developments, and events around the globe. Similar uncertainty exists with respect to the outcome of elections in the ROK. The likelihood of early elections in Japan adds yet another layer of uncertainty.[30] Leaders in each of the five countries will make calculations about the objectives and likely actions of

29 Foreign Ministry of the People's Republic of China, "President Xi Jinping Meets with Choe Ryong Hae, Special Envoy of Kim Jong Un," May 24, 2013, http://www.fmprc.gov.cn/eng/zxxx/t1044747.shtml.

30 See "U.S. Briefed on Abe Aide Iijima's Surprise Pyongyang Visit," *The Japan Times*, May 17, 2013, http://www.japantimes.co.jp/news/2013/05/17/national/u-s-briefed-on-abe-aide-iijimas-surprise-pyongyang-visit/#.UaaZmOD88so.

counterparts in the other capitals. Some of those calculations will be wrong, and "stuff" will happen that forces all players to review the bidding. The only safe prediction is that what happens will be interesting to watch and challenging to manage.

Watch this space.

10 North Korea's Relations with Europe

John Everard

European government-to-government relations with the Democratic People's Republic of Korea (DPRK, or North Korea) are an amalgam of two quite different historical experiences. Eastern European countries established diplomatic links with the DPRK soon after its creation in 1948, while Western European countries did so only at the turn of this century. This has meant, for example, that in 2008 several Eastern European countries celebrated (or at least noted) sixtieth anniversaries of their diplomatic relations with the DPRK, while in 2010 various Western European nations celebrated tenth anniversaries of theirs. This split inheritance gives rise to two quite different approaches to the DPRK. At least until quite recently the DPRK has seemed to many in Western European foreign ministries to offer the lure of the exotic, whilst their Eastern European colleagues are more likely to regard it with a weariness born of a long and problematic acquaintance. Similarly, while some staff in Eastern European embassies in Pyongyang are battle-hardened veterans of the DPRK, no Western European diplomat has ever served a second tour there and very few speak Korean.

Alongside these different governmental perspectives, European nongovernmental organizations (NGOs) strive to relieve the DPRK's poverty and suffering (of which there is plenty). Few NGOs have any sympathy with sanctions against the DPRK, let alone with possible military responses to DPRK misbehavior. Then, too, there is the perspective of European business people. Few mainstream companies have shown any appetite for commercial engagement with the DPRK and the business people who have become involved with this precarious market are often colorful characters. They tend to exercise less influence on their governments than do NGOs, but like NGOs are often sharply critical of European governments' policies toward the DPRK. On one occasion a European business representative went so far as to distribute leaflets at a Pyongyang party, condemning UN sanctions against the DPRK.

The upshot of these different perspectives is constant debate, both within the European Union (EU) and between governments, NGOs, and executives. This chapter attempts to consider some of these strands.

Government-To-Government Relations

Historical Perspective: Eastern Europe

Most Eastern European countries (Albania, Romania, Czechoslovakia, Poland, Yugoslavia, and Hungary)[1] established embassies in Pyongyang and had extensive diplomatic cultural and trade relations with the DPRK from soon after the DPRK's foundation in 1948. Many of these embassies were huge. That of impecunious Bulgaria was a multistory gray marble palace (now occupied by the World Food Programme [WFP]) while the German Democratic Republic (GDR) maintained a large site on which over forty families lived in tiny flats, with its own shop and bar. In addition to their embassies, Eastern European countries also maintained well-staffed trade missions to the DPRK which were needed to lubricate the complex and intricate system of state trading of the Council for Mutual Economic Assistance (Comecon).[2]

With greater or lesser degrees of willingness, the Eastern European countries contributed large amounts of aid to the DPRK, especially after the Korean War. The levels of aid seem to have been very high; between 1970 and 1997 the DPRK's cumulative foreign trade deficit (the value of its

---

1 This chapter refers for convenience to all countries that once had socialist regimes as Eastern Europeans, although, for example, the Czech Republic is a Central, not an Eastern, European nation.

2 Although the DPRK never joined Comecon it was invited to participate as an observer in its sessions (see "COMECON" at *wordiq*, http://www.wordiq.com/definition/COMECON). Trade between the DPRK and the Comecon countries seems to have been conducted almost as if the DPRK had been a full Comecon member.

imports not paid for by exports—effectively aid received)[3] was $12.5 billion.[4] The German Democratic Republic, which seems to have been paired with the DPRK under socialist bloc arrangements,[5] was particularly generous. Its flagship project was the reconstruction of the wrecked city of Hamhung,[6] at huge cost. In later years the cities of Leipzig, Dresden, and Magdeburg, when they acquired new trams for their urban transport networks, donated the old ones to Pyongyang. These elderly vehicles continue to run today. (They were supplemented in 1994 by trams formerly from Zürich, which the city had planned to scrap but which the DPRK bought at the knock-down price of 250,000 francs for eighteen vehicles,[7] and again in 2008 by twenty used trams bought for $800,000 from Prague).[8]

It is clear from the diplomatic papers that are now available, especially from the Pyongyang embassies of Hungary and the GDR, that Eastern European diplomats found the DPRK an intensely frustrating partner.[9] The reports on Kim Il-sung's regime that they sent back to Eastern European capitals were less than flattering and sometimes drew direct comparisons

3 And also external debt, but as the DPRK has never honored external debt—effectively treating loans as grants—there seems little point in distinguishing between the two.

4 Nick Eberstadt, *The End of North Korea* (Washington, DC: AEI Press, 1999), 99–100. This figure includes not only aid from Eastern Europe but also Chinese aid, Soviet aid, loans from Western countries that were not repaid, and Western aid in response to the famine of the 1990s (although up to 1997 this last element was not large). It is similarly difficult to disaggregate Eastern European from other aid during the period immediately after World War II, but again the overall amounts gifted were extremely large—perhaps the "biggest bailout in history" (James Person, "Knowing the North: Intelligence and Intentions of the DPRK" [presentation at Woodrow Wilson International Center for Scholars, September 8, 2010], http://www.wilsoncenter.org/event/knowing-the-north-intelligence-and-intentions-the-dprk). Even a modest percentage of such huge amounts would have represented a major outlay for the impecunious countries of Eastern Europe.

5 I was told this by former GDR diplomats in Pyongyang. I have not traced documentation to support this assertion but it appears to be borne out by the huge amounts of GDR money that flowed to the DPRK at this time.

6 This is detailed by Rüdiger Frank in *Die DDR und Nordkorea. Der Wiederaufbau der Stadt Hamhŭng von 1954–1962* (Aachen: Shaker,1996).

7 "Trams," *The Pyongyang Metro*, http://www.pyongyang-metro.com/metrotrams.html.

8 "Iconic Red and Cream Prague Trams Get New Lease of Life in Pyongyang," Radio Prague, June 5, 2008, http://www.radio.cz/en/section/curraffrs/iconic-red-and-cream-prague-trams-get-new-lease-of-life-in-pyongyang.

9 Scholars at the Wilson Center such as Bernd Schäfer and Balazs Szalontai have analyzed these archives. The diplomats' frustrations are also made clear by Hans Maretzki, the last GDR Ambassador to the DPRK, in his book *Kim-ismus in Nordkorea: Analyse des letzten DDR-Botschafters in Pjöngjang* (Böblingen: A. Tykve, 1991).

with European fascism. For example, the GDR ambassador described a speech by Kim ordering the dissolution of all marriages between Koreans and foreigners as "Goebbelsian."[10] Some of the staff of Eastern European embassies were Korean specialists who seem to have been doomed to spend half their careers in their own capitals and the other half in Pyongyang. (It is unlikely that any group greeted with more enthusiasm than these people the establishment of relations between the Republic of Korea [ROK, or South Korea] and Eastern Europe, which offered postings to Seoul as a third option).

The fortunes of these embassies during the tumultuous 1990s varied. The Hungarian ambassador was thrown out by the DPRK following Hungary's recognition of the Republic of Korea during the Seoul Olympic games (the new Hungarian embassy in Pyongyang, which was never occupied by the Hungarians, is now used by the Swiss Development Corporation). The Czechs closed their embassy but reopened one in 2005. The Poles stayed on, though with a much reduced staff. The Bulgarians kept their embassy open but with a staff of only one person, who in addition to his many other duties was (and is) entrusted with leasing and collecting rent for the Bulgarian-owned properties around Pyongyang (both the embassy building and several former diplomatic flats). The Romanians still inhabit part of their vast Ceaușescu-era palace but much of it is mothballed, and following an argument over their limited levels of access to the DPRK regime their mission is now headed by a chargé d'affaires rather than by an ambassador. Neither the Yugoslav successor states nor Albania any longer maintain missions in Pyongyang.

This history has bequeathed to most Eastern European countries a cadre of people who are experienced in working in the DPRK, who sometimes speak good Korean, and who have networks of contacts there. Moreover the decades of contacts left their mark on DPRK language skills. Many North Koreans studied in the German Democratic Republic before 1990 and there are still Koreans in middling and senior positions of the administration who speak good German.[11] (From time to time the German Embassy in Pyongyang is able to arrange reunions of these people.) This is particularly true in the medical profession because many Koreans were trained in the Charité Hospital in Berlin—which provided the team of heart surgeons who

10 Jasper Becker, *Rogue Regime: Kim Jong Il and the Looming Threat of North Korea* (Oxford: Oxford University Press, 2005), 66.

11 For example, Choe Tae-pok, Chairman of the Supreme People's Assembly. (Kim Jong-un was partially educated in Switzerland and may also speak German—but this of course is not a fruit of socialist era cooperation.)

are reported to have operated on Kim Jong-il in 2007. Numbers of Koreans also speak Czech and Polish, and some speak Bulgarian (e.g., Kim Chun-guk, formerly Director for Europe in the DPRK Ministry of Foreign Affairs [MFA] and now DPRK ambassador to Italy). Many more Koreans have visited these countries than have visited Western Europe. Also the new democracies of Eastern Europe inherited exchange programs with the DPRK that have, by and large, continued. The Czech Republic (and its Czechoslovak predecessor) has hosted more than 2,000 DPRK students since 1948, and currently hosts about twenty-five of them at any one time. (It currently annually offers two to five scholarships for four to six years study,[12] and four scholarships a year for five-week study visits. The Czech Republic also organizes economic seminars for groups of seven to ten experts). Thus there are more DPRK students in the Czech Republic than study in the whole of Western Europe. Large numbers also study in Poland, a program that has run since 1954.[13]

Their history gives Eastern European diplomats access to places in the DPRK banned to Westerners. A Czech ambassador was once invited to visit an underground engineering factory, from which the workers hardly ever seemed to surface, because it had been fitted out with Czech equipment during the days of socialist brotherhood (he found that the workers did not know that Czechoslovakia had split and wondered how much else they did not know about recent history).

Historical Perspective: Western Europe

In sharp contrast to the Eastern European experience, few Western European countries had any significant relationships with the DPRK until the late 1990s. There were occasional earlier contacts, including famously the DPRK's national soccer team's participation in the 1966 World Cup in England. The team's success in qualifying presented the British Foreign Office with some thorny problems but in the event the North Koreans played memorable football and forged lasting friendships with communities in the northeast of England where the matches were played.[14]

---

12 In 2010 this program was in doubt after a North Korean student refused to return home after his studies and Pyongyang refused to send any more students to the Czech Republic.

13 Stanislaw Bednarek, "Foreign Students in Poland: Their Preparation and Problems," *International Review of Education* 37, no. 4 (1991): 489.

14 "World Cup Fears over North Korea in 1966," *BBC News*, June 14, 2010, http://www.bbc.co.uk/news/10305374.

Formally most Western European nations took the view that the UN resolution of October 27, 1950, which established the United Nations Commission on the Unification and Rehabilitation of Korea (UNCURK), made any formal recognition of the DPRK inappropriate. It was only after November 21, 1973, when UNCURK came to an end, that some nations took the view that diplomatic links with Pyongyang would be legally possible. Even so, few countries acted. The Nordic countries and Austria established diplomatic relations with the DPRK in 1974 and were followed by Portugal (and Australia) in 1975. But these formal relations rarely grew into anything of substance. Austria and Finland established trade offices (the Finnish trade office, though unoccupied for many years, was formally closed only in 2006).

The striking exception to this dearth of contacts was Sweden, which has maintained an embassy in Pyongyang since 1974 (with a brief break in late 1994–95). The decision to do so seems to have been prompted by a Swedish decision to extend a trade credit of one billion kroner to the DPRK (which has still not been repaid)[15] and the ensuing realization by Swedish businesses that they needed support in doing business in Pyongyang.[16] But the embassy rapidly became a vital channel of communication between the DPRK and the West, especially once it represented U.S. interests in the DPRK. Until Eastern European countries changed the staff of their Pyongyang embassies from the former communists to newly trained diplomats in the 1990s, and NGOs and UN agencies started to arrive in force during the famine, Pyongyang was one of the loneliest and perhaps the strangest posting in the Swedish diplomatic service. I recall meeting a member of staff from the Swedish embassy in Pyongyang in Beijing in 1978, where she had come for rest and recreation. Those who knew Beijing at the time will recognize what this says about life in Pyongyang.

But few nations took part in these early contacts, and most Western European nations did not start to develop their relations with Pyongyang until the late 1990s when several of them held exploratory talks with the DPRK on this, encouraged by the government of the Republic of Korea, which was keen to promote wide international engagement with the DPRK. The first EU country to normalize relations with the DPRK was Italy, on

15 Part of this money was used to purchase one thousand Volvo cars. Many of these can still be seen driving around Pyongyang, a testament both to Swedish engineering and to the ability of North Koreans to maintain vehicles with the most rudimentary materials and tools.

16 Erik Cornell, *North Korea under Communism: Report of an Envoy to Paradise* (London: RoutledgeCurzon/Taylor & Francis, 2002), 9.

January 4, 2000.[17] The United Kingdom (UK) followed on December 7 that year and Germany on March 1, 2001. Two EU countries—the UK and Germany—decided to open embassies in Pyongyang. Germany found that it had inherited the huge, echoing compound of the former embassy of the GDR. It had already agreed that the Swedish embassy should establish offices there and soon the compound housed the UK embassy too, so that three of the seven EU embassies in Pyongyang are on one site—a great aid to communication. The newness of the Western Europeans' relationships with the DPRK has meant that their diplomatic staff are relatively inexperienced. As I noted earlier, no Western European diplomat has ever served a second tour in Pyongyang, and very few speak Korean.

France, though, did not establish relations with the DPRK (diplomatic anecdotes suggest that this was partly because of irritation that other EU countries had done so during a French EU presidency without either consulting Paris or attempting to create an EU consensus before acting). Estonia's parliament refused to ratify an agreement to open diplomatic relations, and Estonia and France remain the only EU countries without formal links with the DPRK. (In October 2009, however, President Sarkozy appointed a presidential envoy to the DPRK, Jack Lang.[18])

Apart from the seven European countries that maintain embassies in Pyongyang and the two that have no diplomatic relations, the others have diplomatic relations with the DPRK but have not opened missions there. At first most of these countries cross-accredited their ambassadors in Beijing to Pyongyang (for reasons of proximity and convenience—it is much easier to reach Pyongyang from Beijing than from anywhere else), but there has been a steady move to shift these cross-accreditations to embassies in Seoul. Some, but not all, of these cross-accredited ambassadors visit Pyongyang frequently. Italy maintains an aid office, but no embassy, in Pyongyang.

At DPRK instigation in 2000 there were occasional discussions about establishing a full mission of the European Commission too, but this idea was shelved in the wake of the 2006 missile and nuclear tests. This has meant that the only formal interactions between the DPRK and the European Union as such, rather than with its constituent states, are the occasional demarches by the local EU troika or presidency in Pyongyang on instructions from Brussels rather than from national capitals, and the frequent (in

17 At the time no Eastern European country had joined the EU.

18 "French Envoy Jack Lang Arrives in Pyongyang," *France 24*, September 11, 2009, http://www.france24.com/en/20091109-french-envoy-jack-lang-arrives-pyongyang. France has recently opened a cultural office in Pyongyang.

practice, roughly annual) visits to the DPRK by the EU troika at the director level that are (again, approximately annually) reciprocated by the DPRK.

The motives of EU countries for establishing relations appear to have varied, and are not well documented. Although anecdotal evidence suggests that in many, perhaps all, cases urging by the ROK seems to have played a role, no EU country has acknowledged this publicly. Only a few countries publicly explained why they established relations. Germany stated that "diplomatic relations are aimed at securing the non-proliferation of weapons of mass destruction, advancing inner-Korean dialogue and improving the human-rights situation in North Korea."[19] Italy "has sought not just to encourage a more active EU role to support the six-way negotiations, but also to take forward the inter-Korean dialogue and prevent North Korea from being totally cut off from the international community."[20] For its part, the DPRK seems to have wanted to show that it was not isolated (in negotiations with some Western Europeans, the DPRK MFA pressed hard for the establishment of embassies in Pyongyang as a physical symbol of the DPRK's status in the world), and it probably wanted the presence of foreign diplomats in town to flatter the egos of the regime.

With the establishment of relations came other areas of contact. Modest academic exchanges were initiated (even France, with no diplomatic relationship, receives two DPRK students a year). Some cultural exchanges started. West Europeans started to appear in the Pyongyang Festival—the British opera singer Suzannah Clarke became a well-known figure[21]—and European nations started to participate in the Pyongyang film festival. (They found that even daring choices of film could be shown. In 2008 Germany presented "Downfall," a film about the last days of Hitler that portrayed a deranged dictator barking incomprehensible orders as his country collapsed about him.) An exhibition of Berlin's Buddy Bears (large fiberglass bear sculptures) in Pyongyang in October 2008 drew between two and three hundred thousand visitors. The United Kingdom succeeded in having the film *Bend It Like Beckham*, which deals with quite sensitive race and gender issues, broadcast on DPRK television on December 26, 2010, to mark the tenth anniversary of UK-DPRK diplomatic relations.

19 "Korea (Democratic People's Republic of)," *Federal Foreign Office,* last updated March 2012, http://www.auswaertiges-amt.de/EN/Aussenpolitik/Laender/Laenderinfos/01-Nodes/KoreaDemokratischeVolksrepublik_node.html.

20 Italian Ministry of Foreign Affairs, http://www.esteri.it/MAE/EN/Politica_Estera/Aree_Geografiche/Asia/Rapporti_bilaterali_Asia_orientale/Corea_Nord.htm.

21 Suzannah Clarke's website, http://www.suzannahclarke.co.uk/.

The DPRK had maintained a presence in various Western capitals as representations to international organizations (e.g., to the International Maritime Organisation in London), which would from time to time attempt to act as bilateral embassies, usually to find these efforts firmly rebuffed by their host governments. But as Western European countries started to open embassies in Pyongyang, so the DPRK started to establish new embassies in Western capitals. Its embassy in London opened on April 30, 2002 (the North Koreans seem to have wanted to open earlier but struggled to find affordable property). The DPRK's embassy to the former GDR was reopened in Berlin, and an embassy in Rome opened on July 27, 2000.

The DPRK seems to have judged that it could leverage its new relationship with the EU as a counterbalance to its relationships with the United States, China, and the ROK. It also seems to have seen the EU as a possible lever over the United States, and for years EU ambassadors in Pyongyang would be asked to use their influence to change this or that aspect of U.S. behavior that the DPRK found objectionable. From the early years of this century to 2005, relations with the EU were supervised by vice foreign minister Choe Su Hon, considered a relative heavyweight within the regime, but in 2005 he was replaced. It was widely thought by Pyongyang-based diplomats at the time that this signaled an abandonment of the regime's efforts to take advantage of their relationship with the EU to affect their relationship with the United States, and so represented a downgrading of the EU's importance to the regime. The change in supervising vice foreign minister also seemed to coincide with a general deterioration both in the access enjoyed by EU heads of mission and the treatment they were accorded.

From the outset there were debates within the European Union over how to deal with the DPRK, both in terms of underlying policy and in terms of the mechanics of diplomacy. Neither issue has yet been satisfactorily resolved. Discussion continues, for example, over the relative effectiveness of sanctions and of engagement. The internal conversations became more acute with the accession to the EU on May 1, 2004, of several Eastern European countries, who brought to the European debate trenchant criticisms of the DPRK informed by their own bitter experiences of life under dictatorships. Meanwhile there is continued confusion over Union versus national approaches in dealing with the DPRK. There have been several occasions (e.g., after the 2006 nuclear test) when the EU has issued a declaration on events on the Korean Peninsula, with several EU member states then issuing separate national statements. There seems little sign that this will be resolved in the near future. But by and large EU decisions on overall policy, once reached, have been upheld. For example the EU Common Positions that, until the nuclear issue has been resolved, EU states will offer no development aid but only humanitarian aid to the DPRK, and that political visitors should not be at a higher level than vice-minister, have been honored.

Non-EU Countries

Switzerland has developed quite a different relationship with the DPRK than the European Union. Although Switzerland does not maintain an embassy in Pyongyang, it had since 1997 run an aid program in the DPRK coordinated by the Swiss Development Corporation (SDC), whose office is located in the old Hungarian embassy. Swiss objectives in the DPRK have been sharply different from those of the European Union, as once stated on the SDC website: "As a neutral and trusted partner, Switzerland continues to engage with the Democratic People's Republic of Korea (DPRK) in order to reduce poverty, improve people's livelihoods and build capacity of local and national institutions."[22] The DPRK has frequently suggested that EU nations too should follow this line (which is, of course, incompatible with the EU ban on development aid). But in 2008 a Swiss parliamentarian criticized development aid for the DPRK while that country practiced nuclear blackmail, and the Swiss government announced in 2010 that this program would cease by the end of 2011. Aid has been purely humanitarian since the beginning of 2012.

Another important strand of Switzerland's relationship with the DPRK has been the presence in Swiss banks of large amounts of the regime's foreign currency holdings. Press reports suggested that this might amount to $4 billion[23] and that it was held in Switzerland until the regime's funds in Banco Delta Asia (Macao) were frozen at the instigation of the United States in September 2006, at which point the regime moved its money from Switzerland to Luxemburg and Liechtenstein.[24] The Swiss authorities have said that they will investigate any clear evidence that the DPRK holds money

22 Swiss Agency for Development and Cooperation website, http://www.swiss-co-operation.admin.ch/northkorea/.

23 See, for example, "Kim Jong-il Keeps $4bn 'Emergency Fund' in European Banks," *The Telegraph*, March 14, 2010, http://www.telegraph.co.uk/news/worldnews/asia/northkorea/7442188/Kim-Jong-il-keeps-4bn-emergency-fund-in-European-banks.html. It is not, however, clear on what this figure is based, and there have been suggestions that it may exaggerate the regime's holdings by an order of magnitude.

24 "The Tangled Web of the N. Korean Regime's Slush Funds," *Chosun Ilbo* (English edition), November, 10, 2010, http://english.chosun.com/site/data/html_dir/2010/11/10/2010111001018.html.

in Swiss banks, but to date no such funds have been discovered.²⁵ It has also been reported that Kim Jong-un, Kim Jong-il's son and current leader of the DPRK, as well as his elder brothers Jong-nam and Jong-chol and his sister Yo-jong were educated at a Swiss boarding schools (the last three all at the International School of Berne). Ri Chol, who left Switzerland in 2010 after nearly thirty years there as the DPRK's ambassador first in Geneva and then in Berne,²⁶ is believed to have been one of Kim Jong-il's oldest friends and a vice-director of his personal secretariat.²⁷

Other than Switzerland, most non-EU European states have maintained diplomatic relations with the DPRK but these have translated into little of substance. One small exception was a decision by the Norwegian government to give the famous Pyongyang "traffic girls" reflective clothing to make their work safe at night. They were using this very visible gift until they were replaced by traffic lights in August 2010.

Neutral Nations Supervisory Commission

The Neutral Nations Supervisory Commission (NNSC) was brought into being by the armistice of July 27, 1953. It comprised four senior officers, two from neutral nations nominated by the DPRK, which chose Poland and Czechoslovakia, and two from neutral nations nominated by the UN, which chose Switzerland and Sweden. Thus all four officers and their staffs were Europeans, who for several decades exercised a significant role in maintaining the ceasefire and gained an intimate knowledge of its workings. The NNSC also required a significant physical presence at Panmunjom—the original Swiss contingent was ninety-six members, although this has been steadily reduced over time to five members at present (Sweden also currently fields five members). Following the changes in Eastern Europe, the DPRK forced the Czechs out of their building in 1993 and the Poles in 1995 (finally making their building uninhabitable by cutting off all power and water), since when the Korean People's Army has taken over these buildings and now uses them for other purposes. Even though the NNSC is now a shadow of its former self, over the more than fifty years that it has operated all four

25 "Switzerland to Look into N. Korean Bank Accounts," *Chosun Ilbo* (English edition), August 2, 2010, http://english.chosun.com/site/data/html_dir/2010/08/02/2010080200459.html.

26 "Ri Chol to Leave as UN & CH Diplorep," *North Korea Leadership Watch*, March 10, 2010, http://nkleadershipwatch.wordpress.com/2010/03/10/ri-chol-to-leave-as-diplorep-to-un-switzerland/.

27 "Yi Chol (a.k.a. Ri Chol), *North Korea Leadership Watch*," http://nkleadership-watch.wordpress.com/leadership-biographies/ri-chol/.

countries have built up a cadre of military personnel with experience of the problems of the peninsula (in the Swiss case this had already reached 700 people by 1987).[28] Both the Swiss and Swedish staff continue their presence at Panmunjom and visit Pyongyang periodically.

Unofficial and Semi-Official Links

NGOs and Aid

Unofficial links between European NGOs and the DPRK preceded formal diplomatic relations by some years. European NGOs became deeply engaged with the DPRK after the regime appealed for famine relief aid in 1995 and the NGOs in many cases provided humanitarian aid to relieve this disaster before their own governments and the international organizations reacted. The first to enter the DPRK was Médecins sans Frontières, which ran a health-assistance program in the country from 1995. The NGO presence in the DPRK grew rapidly after nine NGOs were allowed to establish a permanent presence in Pyongyang in 1997. These were Campus für Christus, (Switzerland), Children's Aid Direct (UK), Concern Worldwide (Ireland), Cooperazione e Sviluppo (Italy), Médecins du Monde (France), Médecins sans Frontières (various), German Agro Action (Germany), Action contre la Faim (France), and Oxfam (UK). The first seven set up their offices in 1997, the last two in 1998. In 1999 they were followed by ADRA (Switzerland) and PMU Interlife (Sweden) and then by Triangle (France) in 2000. In 2001 Handicap International (Belgium) and Hungarian Baptist Aid (Hungary) set up offices in Pyongyang, then Première Urgence (France) in 2002 and finally Save the Children Fund (UK) in August 2003.[29] But the operating conditions, the constraints on monitoring, and concerns that the regime was stealing aid supplies caused several NGOs to withdraw. Between 1998 and 2002 Médecins du Monde, Médecins sans Frontières,[30] Oxfam, Action contre la Faim, and Children's Aid Direct had all left, as had Cap Anamur (German doctors). (Dr. Norbert Vollertsen of Cap Anamur was so angered by his experiences in the DPRK that he has become one of the regime's most vocal

---

28 "Neutral Nations Supervisory Commission," *Wikipedia,* http://en.wikipedia. org/wiki/Neutral_Nations_Supervisory_Commission.

29 L. Gordon Flake and Scott A. Snyder, *Paved with Good Intentions : The NGO Experience in North Korea* (Westport, Conn.: Praeger, 2004), 47ff; updated by reference to NGO websites and through correspondence with their Pyongyang offices.

30 Jean François of MSF came under such stress over the moral dilemmas of working in the DPRK that he committed suicide. Becker, *Rogue Regime,* 222.

critics.) By 2003 therefore there was a caucus of eleven European NGOs resident in Pyongyang. The staff of these organizations, running projects often long distances from Pyongyang, were frequently the only foreigners with which Koreans in the provinces came into contact.

Once an office of ECHO, the EU humanitarian relief organization, was established in Pyongyang the NGOs were able to receive institutional support, and ECHO became a principle source of funds for the NGOs' DPRK programs. In 2005 the DPRK security authorities, who had been showing signs of nervousness at the numbers of NGO staff travelling around the country, sought to have the NGO presence removed. After much negotiation, both between the NGOs and ECHO on the one hand and the FDRC[31] on the other, and doubtless also between the FDRC and the security authorities, this ban was softened in early 2006 into an expulsion of five of the eleven and agreement that the remaining six (Concern, Triangle, Première Urgence, Save the Children Fund, German Agro Action, and Handicap International) should formally be drawn under the EU's wing as EU Programme Support units (EUPS) and accept limits on their expatriate staffing levels, while the FDRC was disbanded and the coordination of European aid taken over by the Korea-Europe Cooperation and Coordination Agency (KECCA), within the Ministry of Foreign Affairs. This arrangement continues to this day, so that formally the European NGOs in the DPRK are an extension of the EU's official presence there. Because NGO staff often do not rotate as rapidly as diplomats there are members of the NGO/EUPS community in Pyongyang whose experience of the DPRK is far greater than that of the European embassies—in at least one case extending back over seven years of permanent residence there.

The ECHO office in Pyongyang closed in 2007 because ECHO's mandate allows it to work only in emergency and postemergency situations, and it was decided that the DPRK could no longer be so described. Instead an office of Europeaid now operates.

Both through the NGOs and through other programs the European Union continues to give humanitarian assistance to the DPRK. At last count this totaled over 366 million euros.[32] (This is in addition to the over $129 million of European money from various sources that went to support the

---

31 FDRC—Flood Damage Rehabilitation Committee, the DPRK body established in the 1990s to coordinate foreign aid. It was disbanded in 2006.

32 "Political and Economic Relations with DPRK," Delegation of the European Union to the Republic of Korea, http://eeas.europa.eu/delegations/south_korea/eu_dprk/political_relations/index_en.htm.

aborted Korean Peninsula Energy Development Organization [KEDO] project between 1995 and 2005.[33])

Stiftungen

Two German political foundations—*Stiftungen*—have established long-term relationships with the DPRK. These are the Friedrich-Naumann-Stiftung and the Hanns-Seidel-Stiftung, the former associated with the Free Democrat party and the latter with the Christian Socialist Union. The Friedrich-Naumann-Stiftung is particularly active, organizing travel outside the DPRK for DPRK students and seminars and conferences in the DPRK itself, concentrating on the financial and banking sectors. It has been involved in the DPRK since 2002, and this long-standing relationship, together with the fact that it is a party and not a government body, has enabled it to develop a relationship of trust with the Korean Workers' Party (KWP).[34] The Hanns-Seidel-Stiftung has had a shorter relationship (since 2006) and has supported the development of North Korean business intermediary organizations through capacity building. Together with the EU–Korea Industrial Cooperation Agency, they have organized seminars and workshops with invited specialists in North Korea. They have also carried out projects on organic agriculture and sustainable forestry in North Korea. Few if any political parties in other European countries have matched this degree of involvement.

Educational Links

Several European nations maintain language teachers or teacher-trainers in Pyongyang. The British Council established two teacher-trainers in Kim Il-sung University and in Pyongyang University of Foreign Studies (PUFS) even before the United Kingdom and the DPRK established diplomatic relations. Shortly after relations were established this was increased to three (the third was allocated to Kim Hyong Jik University) and in 2008 they were joined by a senior trainer/coordinator. The Italians maintain an Italian teacher at PUFS, and the French a language teacher who works both in Kim Il-sung University and in PUFS. Germany has since 2002 maintained an academic lecturer from the German Academic Exchange Service (DAAD)

33 Korean Peninsula Energy Development Organization, "Deputy Executive Directors' Statement," http://www.kedo.org/pdfs/KEDO_AR_2005.pdf.

34 Friedrich Naumann Foundation, "Generational Change on all Levels in North Korea on the Way," http://www.fnfkorea.org/en/news/generational-change-on-all-levels-in-north-korea-on-the-way.

working at Kim Il-sung University's department of German studies (approximately 15–20 students). German is also taught at PUFS.

European countries also arrange for numbers of North Koreans to study in Europe.[35]

Trade

EU trade with the DPRK remains tiny, and is falling. In 2006 total two-way trade seems to have peaked at 280 million euros but by 2008 this had fallen to 206 million euros (so substantially less than the cost of EU humanitarian assistance to the DPRK); in 2009 trade fell again to 136 million euros, and in 2010 total trade rose slightly to 175 million euros.[36] The EU's main exports were machinery of various kinds, whilst the DPRK's main export to the EU has been textiles. The DPRK does not benefit from provisions extended to many other developing countries under the EU's General System of Preferences, and goods produced in the Kaesŏng Industrial Zone are not included under the EU-ROK Free Trade Agreement.[37]

Trade has, however, given birth to the European Business Association (EBA) in Pyongyang.[38] This was largely the initiative of the Swiss businessman Felix Abt, who first came to Pyongyang in 2002 to represent the interests of ABB but stayed on when that work came to an end until 2009. The EBA acts as a chamber of commerce and facilitates the presence of the (few) European companies who wish to attend trade fairs in Pyongyang.[39] Trade also led to the establishment of the EU-DPRK Trade Capacity Project, which ran from 2006–09 and aimed to demonstrate to DPRK officials the benefits of participation in international trade and to impart an understanding of how to do so. Those close to the project generally judge that it achieved considerable impact.

Very few European businesses maintain a presence in the DPRK. The UK company Spirax Sarco (a manufacturer of steam valves) has kept a small office, staffed entirely by Koreans, for some years. The Daedong Credit Bank,

35 There have been moves to enable European (and other) students to study in the DPRK, but it is not clear whether these have yet borne fruit. See, for example, the Pyongyang Project, http://www.pyongyangproject.org/.

36 "EU-DPRK Trade Relations," Delegation of the European Union to the Republic of Korea, http://eeas.europa.eu/delegations/south_korea/eu_dprk/trade_relation/index_en.htm.

37 "North Korea: EU Bilateral Trade and Trade with the World," http://trade.ec.europa.eu/doclib/docs/2006/september/tradoc_113428.pdf.

38 European Business Association, Pyongyang, DPRK, http://eba.nosotek.com/.

39 Wikipedia, "Felix Abt," http://en.wikipedia.org/wiki/Felix_Abt.

a joint venture with the DPRK Korea Daesong Bank, was once headed by a UK expatriate manager, but he left in 2011.[40] The law firm Hay, Kalb and Associates maintains a Pyongyang office headed by a Scottish lawyer, and an Italian law firm, Birindelli and Associates, visits frequently. The Swiss company Datactivity runs a joint venture in Pyongyang typing data onto disks for storage.[41] The only European news organization with a permanent presence in Pyongyang is APTN, a UK subsidiary of the Associated Press. Its office there is staffed by Koreans who are visited regularly by UK expatriate staff.[42]

Other Issues in the Relationship

Immigration

Immigration from the DPRK into Europe is still very low in absolute terms—most European countries measure only in hundreds the numbers of former DPRK citizens who now live there. But emigration from the DPRK is increasing fast—the twenty thousandth recorded person (these statistics are unlikely to be complete) from the DPRK arrived in the ROK in November 2010.[43] Already there are sufficient DPRK immigrants in the United Kingdom for them to have formed an association (which holds demonstrations and has written at least one letter to a national newspaper) and if numbers of emigrants from the DPRK continue to rise then immigration into Europe is likely to rise, too.[44]

DPRK Workers

There have been concerns, too, about North Koreans working in Europe under the control of their government, representatives of which appear to control the workers. There have been suspicions that the workers' earned wages were siphoned off by "minders" and sent directly to the DPRK. Two

40 "Foreign Shareholding in Daedong Credit Bank Sold," *North Korea Economy Watch*, August 28, 2011, http://www.nkeconwatch.com/category/organizaitons/daedong-credit-bank/.

41 The Datactivity website (http://www.datactivity.com/) does not mention this.

42 The only two agencies that are permitted to use expatriate staff are Russia's Intertass and China's Xinhua, both under arrangements dating from a bygone age.

43 "Number of N. Korean Defectors Exceeds 20,000," *Chosun Ilbo*, November 16, 2010, http://english.chosun.com/site/data/html_dir/2010/11/16/2010111600317.html.

44 "Defectors Protest at London Embassy," *DailyNK*, September 10, 2010, http://www.dailynk.com/english/read.php?cataId=nk03100&num=6789.

cases of particular concern have been the conditions of about seventy-five DPRK workers in Polish shipyards in Gdansk[45] and that of DPRK workers in the Czech Republic, where in 2006 the Czech Ministry of Labor reported that about 400 North Korean women were working in textile and leather factories, and described their situation as "troubling."[46] These activities, while apparently involving many fewer DPRK workers than the work camps in Russia, which may employ as many as 20,000 Koreans,[47] have the potential to embarrass European governments, especially as both the Polish and the Czech cases came to light only through the efforts of investigative journalists—which suggests that other similar operations may continue undetected.

Forward Look And Conclusion

The Future

Government-to-government relations between Europe and the DPRK will depend heavily on two factors. First, the effect of the financial crisis on European governments' ability to pursue diplomatic objectives in the DPRK, and second on the DPRK's own actions.

Embassies in Pyongyang are expensive and fraught. All EU countries that maintain a presence there face constant difficulties in recruiting staff and in ensuring their welfare, and almost all pay staff extra for the inconvenience of serving in the DPRK. Breaks outside the DPRK, at least to China and preferably to home countries, are essential. Security is a constant and expensive concern. Most EU embassies are housed in buildings inherited from the era of socialist brotherhood that were not well built in the first place and now are old and require frequent maintenance and repair. All this costs money at a time when foreign ministries' budgets are under extreme pressure.

At first it was possible to point to clear benefits from this expenditure. There was a period soon after the Western Europeans established relations with the DPRK when they seemed to be making real progress on core concerns. For example, the Swedes were able to engage in a human rights dialogue with the DPRK, and the DPRK agreed to send two students on a UK human rights course. But the atmosphere changed in 2005, perhaps

45 *Gazeta Wyborcza,* January 24, 2007.

46 Quoted by the U.S. State Department, March 6, 2007, http://www.state.gov/g/drl/rls/hrrpt/2006/78777.htm.

47 Shaun Walker, "Expats Recalled as North Korea Prepares for War," *The Independent,* November 27, 2010, http://www.independent.co.uk/news/world/asia/expats-recalled-as-north-korea-prepares-for-war-2145018.html.

partly because the DPRK seems to have decided at about that point that the EU could not after all be used as a counterweight to the United States, and partly as a result of the general security crackdown of that year which led to the expulsions of many NGOs the next year. From then on it became markedly more difficult to engage the DPRK in any meaningful way on subjects of concern to Europe. At present European diplomats in Pyongyang (unlike their Russian and Chinese colleagues) are denied access to senior levels of the DPRK hierarchy—usually access is capped at the vice-ministerial level, with occasional access to ministers.

Also, over the past decade DPRK behavior, never good, has deteriorated further. European governments have made clear their disgust at the DPRK's actions, including missile and nuclear tests and most recently the revelation of a highly enriched uranium program and the shelling of Yeonpyeong.[48] It is hard to demonstrate that a decade of expenditure of senior European time, treasure, and heartache has had any effect either on the DPRK regime's appalling human rights record or on its habit of threatening its neighbors with a growing arsenal of weapons.

Against that, European engagement with lower and middle levels of the regime has been much more successful. Europeans have built contacts with reasonable numbers of North Koreans. They have exposed some DPRK officials to Western thinking and many more North Koreans to Western culture. If (a big if) the DPRK lasts long enough for some of these people to attain positions of influence, it may be that there will be a significant return on this investment. Also, European embassies have provided eyes on the ground in this most secretive of countries. And maintaining embassies in Pyongyang at least prevents the total isolation of the DPRK and may be an investment against the day when the DPRK finally decides to engage seriously with the international community.

The cost-benefit ratio of continued engagement with the DPRK is difficult to compute. So far, in the face of all these difficulties, European foreign ministries have proved determined to maintain their missions in Pyongyang. It is difficult, however, to believe that some of them have not sometimes asked themselves why so much money should be spent on talking to a state that does not seem inclined to engage in any kind of dialogue, when there is such a desperate need for these resources elsewhere.

48 See, for example, Piet Baunø, "Lokke Condemns North Korean Attack," in the Danish tabloid *Ekstra Bladet* (http://ekstrabladet.dk/nyheder/krigogkatastrofer/article1456730.ece), or "As it Happened: Korean Artillery Clash," *BBC News,* http://news.bbc.co.uk/2/hi/asia-pacific/9218848.stm.

Of nonofficial links, the European NGO presence in the DPRK has remained stable since the expulsions of 2006, and none of the resident NGOs have indicated a desire to withdraw. On the other hand, few NGOs that are not currently in the DPRK have expressed any wish to establish a presence there (even if they were permitted to do so). It seems likely that the six resident NGOs will remain for the time being, but not that they will be joined by others. There seems little reason to think that there will be any early change to current low levels of trade between Europe and the DPRK.

Conclusion

There is a Cinderella quality to Europe's relations with the DPRK. Although in the first years of this century European contacts were important to the limited opening that took place at that time, Europeans now find themselves at the margins of the big debates, with no traction on human rights issues, no seat on the Six-Party Talks, and with Pyongyang fixated on its relations with Seoul, Beijing, and Washington to the exclusion of Europe. And almost all European countries, East or West, find themselves managing relationships with the DPRK that were established in quite different circumstances from today and for reasons that may no longer apply.

For all these drawbacks European engagement with the DPRK, particularly people-to-people contacts, may prove to be of vital importance to the return of that country to international normality. The frequent conversations between EU diplomats in Pyongyang and their host government (and with DPRK diplomats in European capitals), like the steady dripping of water on a stone, may already be shaping the private opinions of some North Koreans and may in time affect the thinking of the regime as a whole. It is a slow process and it does not address the immediate threat that the DPRK poses to its neighbors. But European-style slow-burn engagement seems at present to be one of the few strands of overall Western policy toward the DPRK that offers a reasonable prospect in the long term of bringing about nonviolent change there.

IV SCENARIOS FOR CHANGE IN NORTH KOREA IN COMPARATIVE PERSPECTIVE

11 The Political Economy of Unification: North Korea and Implications of the German Experience

Rüdiger Frank

Despite the large number of studies of varying style, form, and quality that have been written on German unification and its lessons for Korea, surprisingly little seems to have been learned by policymakers in Seoul. This is my conclusion from a series of interviews I conducted in 2009 with leading politicians, nongovernmental organizations (NGOs), think tanks, and academics in the Republic of Korea (ROK, or South Korea).[1] Two factors stood out among possible explanations for this phenomenon. First and foremost, it seemed that thinking about the German case often stopped at the recognition of the high costs of the unification process, which is now accepted as unchallengeable common wisdom. This was regarded as such an important

1 Rüdiger Frank, *Demokratie, Marktwirtschaft, Annäherung: Die Tätigkeit der Konrad-Adenauer-Stiftung in Korea 2006–2008* (Berlin: Konrad-Adenauer-Foundation, 2009).

This chapter is a revised version of papers presented at the international conference on "Dealing with North Korean Instabilities," Seoul, December 17, 2010, and at the Koret Conference "DPRK 2012" at the Walter H. Shorenstein Asia-Pacific Research Center, Stanford University, February 23–24, 2011. The author is obliged to the organizers and participants of the two events, in particular Yoon Young-kwan, Gi-Wook Shin, and David Straub for having provided and facilitated helpful comments.

lesson that the search for further insights was often discontinued. The second most frequently presented argument concerned the comparability of the Korean and the German cases. Heavy doubts were voiced regarding the relevance and expressiveness of such a comparison.

An analysis of the existing literature suggests that the authors of studies on German unification and its lessons for Korea mostly belong to two groups: experts of Germany,[2] or South Koreans and Korea experts from various disciplines, mostly economics and political science.[3] Often, we find coauthorships.[4] In far fewer cases is there a mix of expertise in a single author; if so, it mostly consists of knowledge about South Korea and Germany. However, and this is both surprising and troubling, it is very difficult to find a study that combines sufficiently deep insights into the process of German unification, the situation on the Korean Peninsula, and knowledge of the North Korean (Democratic People's Republic of Korea, DPRK) system.[5] In particular the latter seems to be the bottleneck, which is understandable as the overall number of DPRK experts is relatively small and the entry barriers (language, access) into the field are high. Some very insightful studies have been written by authors from former socialist countries, mostly the Soviet Union.[6] Particularly revealing are semi-autobiographical accounts written

---

2 See Gerlinde and Hans-Werner Sinn, "What Can Korea Learn from German Unification?" in *Middle Powers in the Age of Globalization. Implications for Korean Political Economy and Unification*, ed. Byong-Moo Hwang and Young-Kwan Yoon (Seoul: The Korean Institute of International Studies, 1996), 357–63; Holger Wolf, "Korean Unification: Lessons from Germany," in *Economic Integration of the Korean Peninsula*, ed. Marcus Noland (Washington: Institute for International Economics, 1998), 165–89; and Daniela Dahn, *Wehe dem Sieger: Ohne Osten kein Westen* (Hamburg: Rowohlt, 2010).

3 See Goohoon Kwon, "Experiences with Monetary Integration and Lessons for Korean Unification," *MOCT-MOST: Economic Policy in Transitional Economies* 10, no. 1 (2000): 111–36; and Un-Chul Yang, "Twenty Years of German Unification: Lessons for South Korea," *Sejong Policy Studies* 6, no. 2 (2010): 551–78.

4 See Jin Min Chung and John D. Nagle, "Generational Dynamics and the Politics of German and Korean Unification," *The Western Political Quarterly* 45, no. 4 (December 1992): 851–67; Marcus Noland, Sherman Robinson, and Li-gang Liu, "The Costs and Benefits of Korean Unification: Alternate Scenarios," *Asian Survey* 38, no. 8 (August 1998): 801–14; implicitly also Nak-chung Paik, "Habermas on National Unification in Germany and Korea," *New Left Review* I, no. 219 (September–October 1996): 14–21.

5 Among the exceptions are Bernhard Seliger "German Unification after 20 Years: Achievements and Challenges," *SERI Quarterly* 4, no. 1 (January 2011): 29–38; implicitly also Brian Myers, *The Cleanest Race: How North Koreans See Themselves and Why It Matters* (Brooklyn, NY: Melville House, 2010).

6 See Andrej Lankov, *Crisis in North Korea: The Failure of De-Stalinization, 1956* (Honolulu: University of Hawaii Press, 2005).

by former active participants in the unification process.[7] In this chapter, I draw heavily on the results of two recently published analytical studies of German unification.[8] These belong to a large body of literature that covers the economic side of unification, in close combination with political and social aspects, thus responding to the still-large interest by Germans in learning more about the process that they have been observing for two decades.

Aim and Structure of This Study

The German case has taught us that unification is a complex task. I hence apply a politico-economic perspective in this chapter, thus hoping to duly consider not only the economic logic but also the options and limitations posed by the specifics of time and place. As we do not know at what point in time Korean unification will occur, the only way to define the Korean part of the comparison is to use the status quo, which is not stable and thus limits the lifespan of specific conclusions and recommendations.

I will therefore not attempt the impossible. Rather than outlining discussion scenarios and presenting concrete solutions, the goal of this chapter is to *identify the issues* that will have to be dealt with in the course of Korea's unification. I focus on economic aspects, in particular on financing the unification process. The analytical framework is determined by the German case, a mostly concluded and well-documented example. The results will be weighted and filtered using current knowledge about both Koreas. By focusing on issues rather than solutions, I will avoid the normative bias that characterizes many policy-driven studies, and my results will have a less imminent expiration date.

The structure of this chapter follows the logic as outlined above. I start with a discussion of the comparability of the two cases to identify the limitations for my analysis. Combining standard literature on the transformation of state socialist systems with the experience of the German case, I identify those core issues that we can expect to matter for Korea. These issues will then be discussed in some more detail and tested for their relevance.

7 Very rich in detail is Egon Krenz, *Herbst 89* [The autumn of 1989] (Berlin: Edition Ost, 2009); substantially more polemic is Günter Schabowski, *Wir haben fast alles falsch gemacht. Die letzten Tage der DDR* (Berlin: Ullstein, 2009).

8 Karl-Heinz Paqué, *Die Bilanz. Eine wirtschaftliche Analyse der Deutschen Einheit* (München: Hanser Verlag, 2009); and Gerhard A. Ritter, *Der Preis der Deutschen Einheit: Die Wiedervereinigung und die Krise des Sozialstaates* (München: C.H. Beck, 2007).

Relevance and Comparability

Considering that German unification took place over twenty years ago, in Europe, and while the Cold War was still ongoing, it is a valid question to ask about the relevance of that experience for Korea. Wouldn't we be comparing apples and oranges? Reasoning by analogy is tempting but dangerous. However, completely dismissing the German experience as having nothing to teach at all would be equally wrong. As it is often the case, the truth lies somewhere in the middle.

It goes beyond the scope of this chapter to extensively analyze all the external and internal political, economic, and social conditions in Germany during 1989–1990 and Korea in 2013. However, even a superficial glance reveals a number of significant similarities and marked differences. If we summarize and generalize these, the most important conclusions regarding the internal and external conditions in 1989–1990 Germany and 2013 Korea are:

1. In Germany, division was a direct consequence of the lost war. Unification as a political question was a multilateral issue and lost official support over the years. In the Korean case, it is essentially bilateral. Powerful external interests are involved and the yet-unresolved Korean War implies a legal role for outsiders. In both Koreas, unification is officially on top of the agenda.
2. The gap between levels of development seems to be bigger in the two Koreas than it was in Germany. To illustrate this: in East Germany (German Democratic Republic, GDR), there was a shortage of luxury items—whereas in North Korea, staple food is missing.
3. The ideological, historical, and emotional barriers to overcome are bigger in Korea than in Germany. The main argument for this is the legacy of a hot war. Increasingly, the duration of division also emerges as a key difference. On the other hand, a potentially unifying nationalism is strong in Korea, while for historical reasons it was not allowed to play a role in Germany.
4. The GDR was one of the richest countries of the Eastern bloc, whereas the DPRK is one of the poorest. This affects the amount of necessary transfers but also the population's expectations regarding postunification achievements.
5. East Germans were much better prepared for life in a capitalist society than North Koreans. Their society was more sophisticated and information on the other side was accessible broadly and for a prolonged period of time. Even private visits to West Germany took place regularly and on a massive scale. The absence of any equivalent in North Korea is striking. In addition, the number of refugees from North Korea is much lower (thousands) than it was in the case of East Germany (millions).
6. East Germany was part of a crumbling system, with its major ally (Soviet Union) being on the brink of collapse and hence not very supportive; North

Korea, on the other hand, can count on assistance from China, which is internationally respected and economically successful.

7. Regarding the external economic environment of unification, the German case proceeded while globalization was still an ongoing process.[9]

This list is not complete. However, it points at the core of the problem of comparing the two cases. Differences are in many regards substantial; however, they are rarely of a principal nature. Germany and Korea share(d) many of the same problems that had or have to be solved, including the task of unifying two very different economic systems and societies, and operating within the larger context of world politics.

Merging Two Systems

German unification in 1990 essentially was the merging of a socialist and a capitalist system. This was a relatively one-sided process and meant the quick transfer of the institutional and legal structure of the West to the East while maintaining the now-unified state's economic, political, and social stability. Accordingly, most problems emerged in the formerly socialist part that was transformed. At least according to the present status of the Korean Peninsula, we have to expect a similar development there. The more the indigenous transformation of North Korea's society based on Chinese influence proceeds, however, this argument will become less valid. In fact, at some point the pressure to adjust might be much more equally divided between the two Koreas than it was the case in Germany.

I therefore begin my analysis by looking at the larger issue of socialist transformation. The process of German unification started with the long-term internal decay of the GDR. In the decades before 1989, the country went through a typical process of socialist development as described by János Kornai, in particular what he calls the classical stage.[10] Although the wording is different, it is striking to see how Kornai's more general observations made for socialist systems correspond with Ritter's list of East German economic problems shortly before unification. They include steering by an inflexible planning bureaucracy, the absence of competition and any effective pressure for cost reduction, the waste of resources through massive subsidies, wrong decisions regarding strategic sectors (e.g., pro-primary industry

9 This point is suggested by Ritter, *Preis*, 102.

10 János Kornai, *The Socialist System. The Political Economy of Communism* (Princeton, NJ: Princeton University Press, 1992); see also Rüdiger Frank, "Classical Socialism in North Korea and its Transformation: The Role and the Future of Agriculture," *Harvard Asia Quarterly* X, no. 2 (2006): 15–33.

and against light engineering), overemployment and hidden employment, a massive shortfall in labor productivity, a lack of capacity for innovation, the obsolescence and aging of capital stock, massive investment deficits, an underdeveloped infrastructure, large combines with vertical integration and a broad product diversification, no experience with effective marketing, and a strategic priority on hard currency acquisition though exporting at dumping prices.[11]

Most importantly, we observe these characteristics in the case of North Korea, too.[12] The DPRK is without a doubt very special, but not (yet) so different from East Germany or any of the Eastern European states that it would belong in another category. Moreover, in particular since the 2002 reforms,[13] we observe a "normalization" of North Korea in the sense that it increasingly develops features that make it more similar than ever to classical socialist systems in Kornai's sense. North Korea is not East Germany or Poland, and it never will be. But it is getting closer.

This perspective helps us to generate a list of formal steps that have been taken in the course of German unification. These correspond with the theoretical literature on economic systems. A market economy requires a number of mechanisms and institutions to function, such as price liberalization; introduction of a reliable, convertible currency; private ownership of enterprises and companies; a modern legal system; a reliable public administration; a well-developed transportation network; a well-developed telecommunications network; a comprehensive system of banking and financial services; the modernization of housing; and a comprehensive system of education at schools and universities.[14]

However, we should beware of what Paqué calls the illusion of feasibility: "Building up the East was seen [in 1990] as a comprehensive modernization of machinery, people, and country. This was a fundamental mistake."[15] As I will discuss below, many less tangible problems have emerged in Germany. Similar and new, hitherto unknown challenges will arise in Korea, too.

---

11 Ritter, *Preis*, 110 ff.

12 For an overview, see Rüdiger Frank, "The North Korean Economy," in *Handbook on the Northeast and Southeast Asian Economies*, ed. Anis Chowdhury (Cheltenham and Northampton: Edward Elgar, 2007): 298–316.

13 For a discussion of the 2002 reforms, see Rüdiger Frank, "Economic Reforms in North Korea (1998–2004): Systemic Restrictions, Quantitative Analysis, Ideological Background," *Journal of the Asia Pacific Economy* 10, no. 3 (August 2005): 278–311.

14 Paqué, *Bilanz*, 6.

15 Ibid., 7.

Using the general points made so far, we can generate a hypothetical list of issues that deserve to be analyzed in more detail. Mindful of Paqué's warning, I focus on tangible economic aspects but also consider political and social issues on various levels. As a result, I will look in more detail at the following list of topics that are relevant in a comparison of German and Korean unification: currency union, domestic production, wages and work-force mobility, privatization, property and capital, foreign trade, business promotion, welfare and social policies, pensions, and political campaigns and promises. Bearing in mind my brief discussion of the comparability of the Korean and the German cases and the latter's relevance, this list should be approached as a hypothesis that is to be tested systematically.

German Experiences and Their Application to Korea

Currency Union

It is no coincidence that establishing a monetary and currency union was the first step in the long process of economic unification in Germany—three months *before* formal unification. "Stable money is not everything. But without stable money, nothing is anything."[16] Money in a market economy plays an important steering role—but much less so in socialist economies.

In Germany, the currency union was initially discussed as an economic issue but quickly developed into a political question. Many East Germans were driven by economic motives in their enthusiasm for unification, an attitude that was fanned by West German Chancellor Kohl. This made the most economically logical option—free floating of the East German mark—unthinkable at that time as this would have led to a dramatic loss in its value. A strong devaluation of the East German mark was seen as particularly problematic as this would have reduced the household savings of East Germans almost to zero.[17]

In hindsight, doubts over this assessment emerged. Over time it became clear that what mattered most for East Germans and their decisions about consumption were not their savings,[18] but regular monthly wages in hard currency—in other words, job security. Accordingly, the negative effect for

16 Ibid., 27.
17 Ibid., 31.
18 These were relatively large; in 1989, cumulative savings of East Germans were 175 billion marks, i.e., about 100,000 marks on average (Krenz, *Herbst 89*, 225). With monthly wages usually below 1,000 marks, this was an enormous amount. However, it also shows the limited value of money in a shortage economy.

private households would have been one-time, and relatively minimal. By contrast, a devaluation of East German currency would have reduced enterprise debt to almost zero, thus allowing businesses to make a fresh start under the new conditions of a market economy. But with the actual conversion rate set, in various stages, at 1:1 and 1:2, many enterprises were burdened with debt that quickly led to their bankruptcy.

For Korea, the same problem can be expected as long as North Korean currency is not convertible. Accordingly, a great deal of uncertainty and loss of money can be prevented by establishing a weak but convertible currency in North Korea *before* unification. The German case has also shown that it is useful to have a respected and trusted financial institution to manage the currency reform. The West German central bank (Bundesbank) would thus serve as a model for the Bank of Korea, which will likely face a similar task.

Domestic Production

In the course of German unification, East German producers lost their domestic and international customers very quickly. Even before unification and increasingly after the currency union in July 1990, Western-made products replaced East German goods. To the surprise of many economists, this applied not only to products with inferior quality but to virtually every East German product, including even staple food such as bread and milk. In some cases, a few years later there was a rebound amidst a so-called "Ostalgie."[19] However, during the crucial first years after unification, domestic demand for East German products collapsed almost overnight.

Something similar happened to East Germany's foreign trade, although for different reasons. The monetary and currency union meant that GDR products were suddenly available only at hard currency prices. Thus they would directly compete with superior Western products. Whole business models became obsolete, such as the production at any cost (in GDR marks) for the earning of chronically scarce hard currency. The result was an almost complete and sudden collapse of foreign trade.

With regard to Korea, this implosion of the foreign trade structure already took place in the North around 1990 and hence is an effect that will not be part of a Korean unification process. On the other hand, market-based trade relations that have newly developed with China and others will most likely survive the shock of unification and contribute to the rehabilitation of the post-unification North Korean economy. However, for

---

19 A wordplay with the words *osten* (east) and *nostalgie* (nostalgia).

the domestic market, we can expect a similar development as observed in East Germany. This will have to be considered when calculating the value of North Korean enterprises. It will also play a major role regarding the labor market and the expected unemployment rate.

East German enterprises faced the difficult task of developing new, competitive products and selling them in a market that was saturated and occupied by big, experienced, and powerful competitors. Accordingly, it would be advisable to expose North Korean enterprises to a market environment *before* unification. This could be done by domestic reforms, i.e., the introduction of a managed market economy along the Chinese example, or by intensifying economic cooperation with between the two Koreas and thus implicitly engaging in capacity building.

Labor, Wages, and Workforce Mobility

Labor was one of the most pressing and costly problems of German unification. Two labor-related issues have dominated the debate before and after unification: employment and wages.

The GDR knew no unemployment and wage differences were relatively small. East German enterprises tended to "hoard" labor because costs did not play a role, there was no labor market, other resources except labor were often not available, and short-term demand for production increases had to be hedged against.[20] In addition to being a very inefficient use of human resources, this practice led to a significant "hidden unemployment." The situation in North Korea is very similar.

But as soon as the market economy was introduced in East Germany, this hidden problem suddenly became visible and employers started shedding jobs. Many enterprises collapsed, thus adding to pressure on the labor market. Within a very short period of time, the number of unemployed in East Germany jumped from zero to 240,000 in 1990 and then to 1.1 million in 1992. If we include those who received job training and other forms of state support, the number of underemployed East Germans was 783,000 in 1990 and 3.2 million in 1992. The official unemployment rate grew from zero to 2.7 percent at the end of 1990 and 15.6 percent in 1992. If we count the underemployed, it was 36 percent in 1992. Between November 1989 and November 1994, a whopping 57 percent of East Germans had participated at least once in measures organized by the state labor agency.[21] Almost every household had felt the cold breath of job insecurity and experienced

20 Ritter, *Preis*, 206.
21 Ibid., 118ff.

existential fears. Political pressure on the government grew and unification euphoria quickly ebbed away.

Statistics show that East German women were disproportionally affected by unemployment or underemployment. Whereas before unification most women actively participated in the labor market, the official unemployment rate in East Germany in 1994 was 10.9 percent for men, but 21.5 percent for women. Even more alarming was that in 1995, 76.7 percent of the long-term unemployed in East Germany were women.[22] The elder generation was most heavily affected; for example, the proportion of employed women in the age group 55–59 was 77.8 percent in 1989, but had decreased to 36.6 percent only two years later in 1991.[23]

Despite a unification boom in the West, the overall negative effect of unification on the labor market in East Germany remained. An intense debate has been waged as to whether this could have been avoided. The most popular proposal in this context was the creation of a special wage zone for East Germany.[24] It was not implemented, however, out of fear of a massive wave of migration into the high-wage zone. Eastern wages quickly rose to about 70 percent of the Western level. The remaining 30 percent differential was obviously too low to overcome the skepticism of potential investors who also feared a further wage increase. Thus, job creation, the most sustainable strategy to counter unemployment, fell far short of expectations.

It is interesting to note that there is a debate whether such large-scale migration from East to West would indeed have been so unbearable.[25] Economically, it would have been more feasible to expand existing, modern production facilities in the West, rather than duplicating them in the East. Germany had a historical precedence: after 1945, a total of 10 million Germans who were ousted from their homes in what today is Eastern Europe joined a West German population of about 50 million. In 1990 only about 5 out of 16 million East Germans would potentially have moved to join 64 million West Germans, and not necessarily on a permanent basis. However, allowing such large-scale migration was not even discussed; it seemed politically unthinkable.

This is one of those cases where, as I would argue, Korea can learn more from being pointed at the problem, and less from studying the German solution. Given the different conditions in Germany and Korea, different

22 "Long-term unemployed" is defined as without a job for more than one year.

23 Ritter, *Preis,* 117.

24 Klaus Huhn, *Raubzug Ost: Wie die Treuhand die DDR plünderte* (Berlin: Edition Ost, 2009).

25 Paqué, *Bilanz,* 20ff.

policies could indeed be possible. I suggest that it is at least worth discussing whether Korea should accept the possibility of a large-scale migration of North Korean labor into the South. The alternative would be to first sacrifice a large portion of North Korean industry due to overly high wages, and then to pay for that action by enormous transfers of unemployment benefits and other social welfare expenditures. Last but not least, given the geographic proximity to China and large deposits of minerals, investors might turn out to be less reluctant to create jobs in the North, thus alleviating the migration burden.

Privatization of State Property

Among the most hotly debated issues in economic policy in the course of German unification was the privatization of formerly state-owned East German enterprises. The "Treuhand,"[26] a holding company founded by the German state, became the owner of most of these enterprises with the task of quickly restructuring or privatizing them, hopefully at a profit. In the end, the Treuhand generated an enormous loss. The operation of the Treuhand and the result of its activities constitute a significant part of the costs of German unification.

In October 1990 the now-unified Germany became the owner of all GDR assets and had to "marketize" these quickly. A discussion took place around two competing concepts: the social model (restructuring) and the liberal model (privatization). Following the spirit of the Reagan/Thatcher era, the Treuhand chose the latter path. Voucher privatization was opposed,[27] and offers were made to the highest bidders, who often in fact were competitors from the West. In only a few cases, the Treuhand opted for a sale to former managers of the companies in question. Between 1990 and 1994, a total of 8,500 companies with (originally) 4 million employees were privatized. Many of these companies were split up, which resulted in a total of 14,000 enterprises. About 3,700 of these (26 percent) were liquidated. To stimulate rehabilitation, the state paid a total of DM 211 billion in investment subsidies.[28]

26 "Trust agency."

27 It has to be noted that the Soviet Union and other cases have shown the shortcomings of voucher privatization. For a brief discussion, see David Ellerman, "Voucher Privatization with Investment Funds: A Sure Way to Decapitalize Industry," in *Beyond Transition: The Newsletter about Reforming Economies* (Washington, DC: The World Bank,1998), http://www.worldbank.org/html/prddr/trans/novdec98/pgs10-13.htm, accessed 11.01.2011.

28 Paqué, *Bilanz*, 46–47.

About 60 percent of all employees of Treuhand enterprises (or 2.5 out of 4 million) lost their jobs within a very short period of time. Costs resulting from corruption, fraud, and misconduct amounted to DM 10 billion, according to an estimate by the Bundestag.[29] Most severely hit were former GDR companies from heavy and chemical industries. Few steelworks, chemical factories, and heavy-machine-building factories survived.

The Treuhand thus developed a very negative image, in particularly in East Germany. It was accused of unilaterally benefiting the West and destroying healthy East German companies for the sake of their Western competitors. Feelings of becoming colonized arose among East Germans, feelings that still, twenty years later, have implications for election behavior on the local and federal level.

The German federal state was shocked by the massive deficit that remained after the work of the Treuhand was completed. Rather than generating an estimated DM 600 billion of profit from selling the assets of what used to be the economically most prosperous socialist country, the German state incurred a loss of DM 240 billion after spending 300 billion and generating revenues of only DM 60 billion.[30]

The reasons for these wrong expectations were manifold and provide important lessons for Korea and its own estimates of the costs of a similar process. One key problem has already been mentioned: the debts that were carried over from pre-unification times. The currency union had overnight created real, massive debts that choked vulnerable East German companies, often lethally. This problem could have been solved easily by forgiving all (at that time meaningless) debts of state-owned enterprises before the currency union.

In addition, estimates of the actual value of East German assets were too optimistic. Patents and machinery were often not salable. The condition of real estate required massive investments, often including the rehabilitation of poisoned soil. Many industrial installations did not conform to labor protection or environmental laws. Thus, assets often turned out to be liabilities.

Despite the general disaster, there were a few success stories. These also point out which North Korean companies can realistically be expected to survive and actually contribute to making Korean unification economically successful, or at least less costly. In particular, the East German companies that were successful were the ones that produced products with a robust

29 Ibid., 67.
30 Ibid., 49.

local brand image. Their consumers were regional and their characteristics (actual or perceived) were locally specific enough so that they could not easily be copied or substituted.

Property and Capital

Among the basic requirements for a functioning market economy are well-defined and legally protected property rights. Without these, urgently needed investments such as modernization of real estate or machinery would not take place. This point is related to the questions of currency union and of privatization as they have already been covered above, but a few additional remarks are necessary regarding the conversion of existing property.

To begin with, the seemingly easier part: most industrial facilities were *Volkseigentum* ("the people's property"), i.e., owned by the state. This state ownership was transformed into private ownership via the Treuhand, as discussed above. A few privately or cooperatively owned businesses existed in the GDR, too. These were mostly small-scale operations such as bakeries and repair shops, many of them family owned and with roots before 1949. While they often had a hard time surviving under socialism, after unification they were among the first fully operational private enterprises in East Germany.

A more complicated question concerned ownership in agriculture and in real estate. In East Germany after 1945, as in most other socialist countries including North Korea, large-scale landowners had been expropriated, although definitions of "large" varied. The land was separated into smaller plots and distributed among local peasants by the new socialist rulers. However, such ownership of means of production collided with the ideological convictions of the Communist Party. The long-term goal was to turn farmers into agricultural workers. Expropriation of the just-created group of small-scale land owners took place through forced collectivization. By 1989, the GDR agricultural sector was dominated by large-scale cooperatives that operated more or less like state-owned enterprises. The situation in North Korea is similar in legal terms, although the nature of the terrain does not in all cases allow truly large production units.

The German government now faced a similarly existential choice in agriculture as it did in industry: privatization or restitution. But restitution to whom? Land had been expropriated twice: first in 1945 by the Soviet administration, and after 1949 through collectivization. In Germany, a political decision was made to regard the situation as of 1949 as legal. It was driven by strong pressure from Moscow, due to concerns about possible repercussions from similar cases, including the former German areas in what is now western Poland. The West Germans accepted because they knew that otherwise the whole question of German unification would be jeopardized.

In Korea, the situation is much more complicated. Three overlaying waves of expropriation have taken place, with less than perfectly documented property rights. The first one happened under the Japanese colonialists, who through their newly introduced cadastral survey mechanism expropriated many Korean landowners. The other two are more or less the same as in the German case: post-1945 land reform and forced collectivization after the Korean War.

Accordingly, Korea faces three options. It could restore the status quo before 1945, which will lead to massive legal and political problems as it would mean the restoration of ownership by Japanese colonialists and collaborators.

The second option is to follow the German example and treat property rights in place by September 1948 (founding of the DPRK) as legal. In case of restitution, farmers would have a chance to decide what to do: till the land on their own, or join collectives. The East German case indicates that forming voluntary collectives is not an unrealistic expectation, although we have to consider the different geographical conditions for agriculture in both countries. In East Germany, the old collectives are now very efficiently operated agricultural ventures that enjoy a much higher labor productivity than their Western counterparts. This is a unique success story, in particular if compared to industry. However, this came at a cost; the number of people working in East German agriculture decreased from about 500,000 in 1990 to less than 200,000 in 2008.[31]

The third option is to regard all land as state property, declare all pre-unification ownership as invalid, and sell the land off to the highest bidder along the lines of the Treuhand policy in East German industry.

In addition to industry, agriculture, and real estate, Korea will have to consider another form of property: savings. This has already been discussed in the context of currency conversion, so I should just add here that savings in socialist countries are usually quite high thanks to a lack of opportunities to spend money. But while savings were enormous in size and scope in the German case, the situation in North Korea as of 2011 is still very different. The majority of the population has little savings, in particular as the markets offer products at competitive prices that consume most of the available income. Inflation is enormous and, unlike in Germany, is to a certain degree

31 Ibid., 79.

tolerated. Measures like the currency "reform" of November/December 2009 in North Korea not only destroy trust and eliminate money's value storage function, but also devalue savings.[32]

The conversion of savings will therefore be of less concern for Korean unification. However, Korea will face another problem instead. Although East German households were on average much less affluent than West German households (in 1993, average household savings in the West was DM 53,800, compared to DM 15,300 in the East),[33] this gap will be much wider in the Korean case, implying greater inequality with all its consequences, and a much weaker domestic demand.

Business Promotion, Investment, and Social Overhead Capital

As I have pointed out above, the quick establishment of a functioning economy in North Korea will be a key task of Korean unification. Political stability and social welfare costs directly depend on the state of the economy in the Northern part. In the beginning, the aim will be a reduction of transfer-based unification costs; in the long run, stable growth and prosperity will have to be achieved. I have discussed a number of important institutional steps towards that goal, including the introduction of a hard currency and the establishment of property rights on the individual level as well as for industry and agriculture.

Now, I turn to the question of business and investment promotion. In Germany, there have been two ways towards these objectives: the improvement of the business environment through building a competitive infrastructure and an effective administration, and direct investment promotion through incentives such as subsidies and tax reductions.

The amount of money invested into the rehabilitation of the East German infrastructure was enormous. The connection of roads and railway lines disrupted by German division alone cost about DM 75 billion.[34] Other investment was made into the extension and expansion of highways, building up of telecommunication networks, development of industrial sites, education at all levels, administration, etc. Ecological rehabilitation of areas that suffered from pollution or mining was a very costly endeavor, too.

---

32 Rüdiger Frank, "Money in Socialist Economies: The Case of North Korea," *The Asia-Pacific Journal*, 8-2-10, February 22, 2010, http://japanfocus.org/-Ruediger-Frank/3307.

33 Ritter, *Preis*, 135.

34 Paqué, *Bilanz*, 89.

Business promotion included an investment subsidy in the East of 8–15 percent of the invested amount through the annual tax declaration, an allowance for depreciation in the range of 50 percent of costs, direct investment subsidies from the federal and local governments up to 35 percent in addition to the tax-deductible investment subsidies, and loans from the European Recovery Program (ERP). Cumulatively, this resulted in a subsidy of about 30–50 percent for investment in East Germany in the 1990s. Until 2008, the total amount spent on this purpose was in the range of EUR 400 billion.[35]

It is not surprising that the first and most immediately felt effects were observed in the construction industry. Growth in that sector amounted to 22 percent (in real terms) from 1991 to 1994. By the mid-1990s, 17 percent of all jobs in East Germany were in construction, whereas the number for West Germany was only 5.4 percent. However, as the construction boom ended, about 50 percent of all construction workers in East Germany lost their jobs between 1995 and 2006.[36]

I see two implications for Korea. First, money transfers into the rehabilitation of North Korea's infrastructure will not only be inevitable for the promotion of new businesses, they will also have a significant positive effect on the job market. Secondly, the latter will only be temporary; accordingly, it will be important to find alternative solutions to prepare in time for a drop in employment in the construction sector. We can also expect the development of a real estate bubble immediately after unification, as well as its burst a few years later. In the case of East Germany, the value drop in central city real estate was around 40 percent over the first decade after unification.

Welfare, Pensions, Social Policies and Transfers

Substantial transfers from the richer to the poorer part were necessary in Germany in various fields: unemployment benefits, health care, pensions. These transfers helped to maintain or increase domestic demand, and a certain portion flowed back to the state in the form of value added or income taxes. Nevertheless, the initial burden on the state household was enormous. Transfers (see below) form the core of the still-negative perception of unification by West Germans.

Health insurance was implemented quickly, but costs exploded and now are about 15 percent of German gross salaries. The total amount of unemployment benefits grew as millions of East Germans lost their jobs, a

35 Ibid., 93–94.
36 Ibid., 99ff.

situation that has led to growing state debt. None of this was surprising. I will not cover all the details here, but it is useful to look at one example that shows how unexpected many problems were. The question of pensions turned out to be a more complex matter than expected. One reason was that the degree to which senior citizens in the West and in the East depended on their monthly pensions was different. In the West, many of them owned houses, stocks, or held large savings. Their counterparts in the East very often had nothing but their pensions for survival in an environment in which prices quickly rose to Western levels. In 1993, only 27.7 percent of East German households owned real estate, while that number was 50.5 percent in the West.[37] Accordingly, the amount of monthly pension impacted the welfare of the elderly in East Germany much stronger than in the West.

For Korea we can expect a similar situation, although no data are available. Few elderly North Koreans will be able to survive based on what they had accrued during their lifetime of hard labor. Facing rising prices and changing demand structures, families will be less and less able to provide for their senior members. Accordingly, pensions for North Koreans will become an issue for the South Korean state.

This leads us to look at the various transfers that have been made since unification. For South Koreans, the most shocking number seems to be this: between 1991 and 2003 a total of EUR 1.4 trillion were transferred from West Germany to East Germany. If we consider the flow of taxes and social insurance premiums back to the federal state, the net transfer amount was about EUR 1 trillion. In the first four years after unification alone, the gross transfers amounted to DM 812 billion or EUR 415 billion—with a growing year-on-year trend.[38]

By far the major source of this huge amount was the federal government, i.e., the German taxpayer. The second-largest contributor was the state-run Labor Agency (*Bundesanstalt für Arbeit*), which administers the unemployment insurance premiums of all German employees. The "unification fund" (*Fonds Deutsche Einheit*) contributed the third-largest sum. This fund had been founded in 1990 with the goal of providing a financial basis for East German area municipalities, thus taking into account the administrative structure of Germany where the federal state and local states coexist.[39]

37 Ritter, *Preis*, 135.

38 Ibid., 127.

39 Such a system has existed in the West before unification, and it is in place until present time. The richer of the local states subsidize the less successful ones through an equalization fund (*Länderfinanzausgleich*).

The tax income from the East flowing back into the federal budget increased annually, from DM 31 billion in 1991 to DM 43 billion in 1995, but net transfers nevertheless kept growing. This demonstrates how crucial the rehabilitation of East Germany's economy was to reducing unification costs, as higher employment means more taxes and insurance premiums for pension and unemployment, and at the same time less spending on social benefits. The latter grew from DM 56 billion in 1991 to DM 79 billion in 1995, thus each year being more than twice as high as investments. The amount of subsidies more than doubled between 1991 and 1995 from DM 8 to 18 billion.[40]

For Korea, the chances are good that the amount of transfers will not necessarily be as high as it was in the case of Germany. A major reason is the (so far) significantly lower level of expectations in North Korea. East Germans had for decades been under the influence of Western media that, supported by the state in the context of the Cold War, had created an image of the West as the promised land, full of prosperity, security, and opportunity. The warnings of the GDR media against unemployment and the colder social climate in the West had routinely been discarded by most East German citizens as pure propaganda. Helmut Kohl since autumn 1989 had led his political campaign (first for unification, later for a CDU government[41]) under the explicit promise of "flourishing landscapes." Accordingly, after unification the government had to live up to these expectations.

Political Campaigns and Risky Promises

There is broad agreement in the literature on socialist transformation as well as on unification that the key to a quick cost reduction is the build-up of a viable domestic economy in a formerly socialist society. I have discussed a number of technical factors that play a vital role towards that end, such as a hard currency, the establishment of solid property rights, the modernization of social overhead capital, the promotion of local businesses, or the introduction of welfare policies. However, the German experience has shown that we should also look beyond these technicalities.

Economics is a behavioral science. From that perspective, the above-mentioned promises of "flourishing landscapes" had a number of fatal effects. Although driven mainly by the 1990 electoral campaign and based on unrealistic expectations of the East German economy's strength and a general lack of understanding of the complexities of the unification process, this

40 All numbers after: Deutsche Bundesbank, quoted in Ritter, *Preis,* 128.
41 Christlich-Demokratische Union, the major conservative party in Germany.

image became the yardstick by which the government's economic policy was and still is measured. This created enormous political pressure and led to a number of expensive subsidization programs and costly attempts at channeling investment into the East.

An important psychological factor for the modernization of East Germany's domestic economy was the acceptance of the new, market-based ideology by East Germans who had been socialized under a very different system. However, this turned out to be difficult. The impression that the market system made on most East Germans was closely connected to the collapse of their economy soon after unification. People were displaced and forced to become mobile in order to find work. Social networks, future plans, careers—many of them were destroyed within a few months. Many East Germans ignored that the actual reason for this was not the market economy as such, but the desolate state of their own socialist economy that was on the brink of collapse when unification happened. They identified the new system with economic hardship, insecurity, and a loss of social warmth.[42]

TABLE 11.1

Opinion survey among West and East Germans regarding German unification

Year	Opinion	West (%)	East (%)
1993	The importance of labor as part of life is very high	37	58
1993	Leisure time is more important than work	30	11
1993	Women between 18–63 who wanted to work	23	76
1990	Securing economic growth is a task for the state	52	80
1994	Social benefits should be increased	28	71
1990	Have a good opinion of the economic system of West Germany	—	77
1994	Have a good opinion of the economic system of West Germany	—	38
1994	Socialism is, in principle, a good idea	<40	78

Source: Ritter, *Preis,* 152ff.

Such nostalgia is visible in table 11.1, when we find that support for the market economy dropped from 77 percent to 38 percent within four years. Note also that labor had been given a much higher value and priority in the East, which includes female employment. The state is expected to take care

42 Paqué, *Bilanz,* 42.

of people's livelihood. Importantly, East Germans regard social security as an essential part of democracy.[43]

The Korean society is in many ways unlike that of Germany. Based on experience with defectors, we can expect, however, a certain nostalgia in the North; high expectations of support from the state; and a generally very high interest in labor as the defining characteristic of the individual's place in society.[44] This political demand will have to be met and will contribute to the costs of unification.

Current State and Outlook: How Far Has North Korea Come?

Taking the German case as a reference point, I have discussed what the Korean state and society have to expect, and how they can hedge in very general terms against an unforeseeable future. I avoided making specific policy recommendations as these would depend strongly on the actual state of development at the time of unification—which is so far unknown.

Aside from the need to mobilize the necessary resources, which will be the burden of South Korea, I have found that the success and costs of actual policy measures heavily depend on the status of the part of the country that has to be transformed into a market economy. I will therefore in this final section try to summarize what we know about the current status and development trends in North Korea, roughly following the analytical structure as used above.

Currency

The North Korean won is as valueless and useless as its equivalent in East Germany had been. However, three developments of the last decade have to be noted. The first is the monetization of the North Korean economy. Until at least the mid-1990s, North Korea was effectively demonetized. Money played almost no role at all. Having money provided no guaranteed access to anything in North Korea. This had a significant impact on the behavior of the individual, who knew that the only way of upward social mobility was through the state. The situation changed in the aftermath of the famine of 1995–1997, and was amplified by the July 2002 measures.[45] As

---

43 Ritter, *Preis*, 157.

44 Tongilbu (ROK Ministry of Unification), 북한이탈주민 현황 [Present situation of North Korean defectors], 2010, http://www.unikorea.go.kr/CmsWeb/viewPage.req?idx=PG0000000365.

45 See Frank, "Economic Reforms in North Korea."

of 2011, North Korea has become very similar to East Germany in terms of monetization, and might even go beyond.

The second development concerns the existence of alternative currencies. East Germany and North Korea both had a special currency for foreigners, called *Forumscheck* or *oehwawa pakkun ton* (money in exchange for foreign currencies), respectively. In fact, North Korea even had two of them—one for socialist foreigners, and one for capitalists. However, while the *Forumscheck* disappeared together with the GDR in 1989/1990, in 2002 North Korea abolished both types of its forex certificates and now has only one domestic currency. In addition, as in East Germany, hard currencies circulate semi-legally.

Thirdly, North Korea has done something that East Germany never dared—it officially allows inflation. Even though prices are adjusted only arbitrarily and not on a constant basis, this nevertheless presents great progress on the way towards a stable currency that is capable of expressing the true value of goods and services. Actual success notwithstanding, the North Korean state has shown its willingness to use economic levers, including monetary policy, to achieve its goals. Individuals and enterprises are getting used to the fact that there is inflation, and can develop strategies to cope with it.

Domestic Production

The desperate situation of North Korea's industry and agriculture are among the best-publicized issues about this country. North Korea's economy shows the same kind of inefficiency as East Germany. This is not surprising, as the systemic reasons are the same: a lack of competition, market exit, and responsibility. It is to be expected that many North Korean enterprises would not survive if they were suddenly exposed to market forces. There are two trends that tackle this issue. One is set by the state. In a move that shows surprising similarities to East Germany in the 1980s, Pyongyang seems to follow what we call a *"Wunderwaffe"* policy. Like Hitler, who hoped to turn around a lost war by developing new weapon systems, East Germany focused on specific economic sectors to revive a dead economy. This included microelectronics and computer numerical control (CNC) machines. North Korea, too, in 2010 increased its promotion of CNC machines and called for a revolution in electronics and computerization. Since the 1980s, it has also discovered the need to produce consumer goods to keep the population happy (such as "August 3 goods"), and in a programmatic publication promoted light industry.[46] Based on the experience of East Germany, there is reason to be pessimistic about the effectiveness of such measures.

However, North Korea also follows a second, much more promising strategy. Partly forced by the absence of any alternative, the DPRK has significantly intensified its economic cooperation with the People's Republic of China (PRC), which is essentially a capitalist economy. This cooperation goes far beyond mutual verbal assurances of friendship. Today's North Korean economy seems to depend heavily on imports from and exports to China.[47] Regardless of the actual size of this cooperation, which is difficult to quantify in its entirety, this represents an opportunity East Germany never had—to cooperate with a state that is (officially) socialist and friendly, but has an economy that is competitive and profit-oriented. If North Korea manages to transform its domestic economy in a way that enables it to cooperate with the Chinese, and there are signs that this process is ongoing, then it will be much better prepared for the harsh winds of the global market after unification.

Labor, Wages, and Workforce Mobility

There are reports from North Korea indicating that in some cases, state enterprises have not been able to pay their wages. We also know that those companies that do well, mostly because of cooperation with Chinese partners, pay higher wages to their employees. This has led to a growing awareness of job security as a potential problem, and to the emergence of a yet-underdeveloped job market. On the other hand, mobility in general is much more restricted in North Korea than it has been in Germany. It has to be assumed that despite a relatively high level of education, North Korea's workforce is not competitive and is ill-prepared for a market economy. The work unit fulfills an important political function for disciplining and

46 Joint New Year editorial (2011): 올해에 다시한번 경공업에 박차를 가하여 인민생활향상과 강성대국건설에서 결정적전환을 일으키자 [Bring about a decisive turn in the improvement of the people's standard of living and the building of a great, prosperous and powerful country by accelerating the development of light industry once again this year], Joint New Year editorial of *Rodong Sinmun, Chosŏn Inmingun*, and *Ch'ŏngnyŏn Chŏnwi*, http://www.kcna.co.jp/calendar/2011/01/01-01/2011-0101-008. html.

47 Jaewoo Choo, "Mirroring North Korea's Growing Economic Dependence on China: Political Ramifications," *Asian Survey* 48, no. 2 (March–April 2008): 343–72; Pomnyun Sunim, "*North Korea's Growing Dependence on China: Implications for the Future of Northeast Asia*," transcript of a talk on September 23, 2010, at the US-Korea Institute at SAIS, Washington.

controlling the population; accordingly, there is full employment with a substantial degree of hidden unemployment. The latter is also promoted by a lack of machinery and technology, which leads to a high demand for manual labor that will quickly disappear after unification. In short, if Korean unification were to happen tomorrow, unemployment would be an issue the population is by no means prepared for.

Privatization of State Property

We currently observe two opposing trends: North Korea's society is headed for decentralization, with individual activities growing and diversification and segregation in society becoming more and more visible. On the other hand, there is the state's policy that seems to aim for a re-centralization in an attempt to bring society and the economy back under its control. Signs of this are the recent upgrading of the Price Bureau to the status of a Commission, and the merging of all investment and joint venture activities under the control of the Committee of Investment and Joint Ventures in January 2011.

In 1998, the North Korean constitution was changed and came to include passages on the protection of private property and the enlargement of private plots—so-called kitchen gardens (article 24). In 2002, there were attempts to reform the structure of agricultural collectives. In Pyongyang, there seems to be an illegal housing market although legally, all real estate is owned by the government. So it is safe to state that a growing awareness of property is developing. However, in the context of an attempt at undoing most of the reforms, the state for a while tried to severely reduce private property. The de facto expropriation in the context of the currency reform in late 2009 is only one expression of such a policy. All industrial enterprises are state owned and agriculture is collectivized, although rumors about reforms have become more intense under Kim Jong-un. Even so-called private restaurants, often housed in service complexes called *sangjŏm* (shop), in Pyongyang and a few major cities are in fact collectively owned by various constituencies, including the military.[48] There is no system of documentation of property rights. This is still less than East Germany had in 1989, where some small-scale service industries were privately owned, although heavily restricted. We can therefore expect at least the same difficulties in the context of unification if it would happen any time soon.

48 Such as the 승리 (*sŭngni* [victory]) Group.

Property and Capital

The idea of private property rights is relatively new to North Koreans. With the emergence of a middle class as a consequence of the economic reforms, there has been a development toward private ownership of certain proportions, but much more needs to be done to reach a level similar to East Germany. The average North Korean has no significant savings or other property. This might change in the future, but currently, a conversion policy in the case of unification would not have to consider the effects on private savers as much as it had to in the case of Germany.

Business Promotion, Investment, Social Overhead Capital

Anyone who has travelled inside of North Korea can confirm what the experience with the Kaesŏng Industrial Zone has shown: the need for social overhead capital (SOC) investment in North Korea is high. This concerns almost anything—transportation, communication, and human resources. However, it has also been demonstrated that progress can be achieved. Nevertheless, the infrastructure of North Korea still lags behind East Germany significantly. In addition, new needs have emerged that were not an issue in 1990—such as broadband Internet access. A largely singular yet visible sign of improvement is the installation of a nationwide mobile phone network with the help of the Egyptian company ORASCOM, having attracted more than one million customers by 2012. The same company has also resumed work on the crumbling shell of the Ryugyŏng Hotel, deserted since the late-1980s, and turned it from a symbol of economic decay into a sign of hope for North Koreans.

Welfare, Pensions, Social Policies

Among the few strong points of state socialist systems is social egalitarianism. It usually includes free health care and a pension system. However, these are as costly as they are in other countries and hence usually either suffer from inferior quality or create costs that in the end contribute to the ruin of the state, as was the case in East Germany. In the north of Korea, the state started right after liberation in 1945 with the introduction of social policies. Despite their low level, they represented a major improvement over the past and were widely welcomed.[49] Now facing food shortages and a malfunctioning economy, North Korea is not capable of providing all necessary social

---

49 Charles K. Armstrong, *The North Korean Revolution, 1945–1950* (Ithaca and London: Cornell University Press, 2003).

services for free, although it regularly makes "social policies" (*sahoejŏk sich'aek*) a priority in programmatic announcements. We can thus assume that a few decades of socialist social policies have generated relatively high expectations, even if these have not been met adequately in the past years.

Regarding pensions, the amount of transfers will depend on the actual status and terms at the time of unification but in general, it can be assumed that transfers will have to be substantial. This is based on the relatively high urbanization rate of North Korea (around 60 percent),[50] which goes along with a decline in traditional, non-state systems of caring for the elderly such as the extended family. A key difference between the Korean and the German cases so far is the level of development of the welfare and social insurance system in South Korea.[51] Due to historical reasons, it is less encompassing and less costly if compared to West Germany around 1990. This has two opposing effects: on the one hand, the minimum level to be expanded to North Korea is relatively low. However, existing social security funds are potentially too small for an inclusion of 24 million new citizens. Given the lower level of reliance on the state in South Korea, doubts are also in place regarding a broad consensus on massive transfers to the North.

Transfers

We have seen that post-unification transfers from South to North will have to be massive. A way to gauge the related public sentiment is to look at the attitude towards pre-unification transfers, such as food aid and other forms of assistance. Here I note that in response to the notorious behavior of North Korea as a receiver, the South Korean public seems to be particularly critical. In correspondence with my observation that the focus of the South Korean government's learning from the German case was on the huge costs and their financing, in August 2010 the South Korean president revealed plans for a Unification Fund that will have a unification tax as its main source.[52] Given the high amount of needed transfers, the limited availability of domestic funds, and the low public approval, I would expect

50 Yonhap News Agency, "Two Koreas' Urbanization Gap Likely to Widen Further by 2015: Reports," January 2, 2011, http://english.yonhapnews.co.kr/northkorea/2011/01/02/65/0401000000AEN20110102000500320F.HTML.

51 See Ian Holliday, "Productivist Welfare Capitalism: Social Policy in East Asia," *Political Studies* 48 (2000): 706–23; and Soonman Kwon, "Healthcare Financing Reform and the New Single Payer System in the Republic of Korea: Social Solidarity or Efficiency?" *International Social Security Review* 56, no. 1 (2003): 75–94.

52 "Gov't Plans Reserve Fund for Reunification," *Chosun Ilbo,* August 16, 2010, http://english.chosun.com/site/data/html_dir/2010/08/16/2010081601038.html.

international financing to play a more important role for Korea's unification than it did in the German case.

Risky Promises

Expectations in North Korea regarding economic prosperity after unification are high,[53] and they are rising as materialism makes its inroads into the DPRK. DVDs of South Korean soap operas, and increasingly also the image of affluent Chinese neighbors import the image of a lifestyle to North Korea that is usually not very realistic. It cannot be excluded that in the future, the South Korean government will intensify propaganda toward the North emphasizing economic superiority, which will further raise expectations of a prosperous life after unification. Unlike East Germany, where unification was excluded as a political option, the North Korean government itself contributes to the creation of high expectations by propagating a bright future after unification. The strategy of depicting the South as being poor and backward was discontinued many years ago. The expression "this will get better after unification" is heard frequently in conversations with North Koreans. The German case provides only a vague estimate of the political ramifications if North Koreans wake up to a harsh reality.

In conclusion, I argue that the hypothesis as posed at the beginning of this chapter could be verified. Korea has indeed many things to learn from German unification, in particular related to the question of unification costs and their financing. However, the details will be very different, and in some fields, this gap is growing. In others, it seems too narrow. However, with a few exceptions, the issues that Korea will face are the same as those that emerged in Germany. The two Koreas' great advantage is time: they can find ways to deal with these issues now, before unification.

53 See Haksoon Paik, 북한 권력의 역사: 사상, 정체성, 구조 [The history of power in North Korea: ideas, identities, and structures] (Seoul: Hanul Academy, 2010).

12 North Korea and the Fall of the Soviet Union and the Soviet Satellite States

Andrei Lankov

What can we, students of North Korea, learn from the experience of the Soviet collapse? This is a natural question since North Korean society, while being quite different from the Soviet prototype in many important regards, once—in the late 1940s—emerged as a result of a Soviet experiment in social engineering, and to this day still has certain commonalities with the Soviet Union. Even though North Korea's social and political evolution is not necessarily similar to that of the USSR, at least in some cases the circumstances of the Soviet decline and collapse might help us to understand the likely outcome of the ongoing North Korean crisis.

So this chapter aims at producing a quick snapshot of Soviet society in the last decades of its history, and then at comparing this picture with present-day North Korean society. I will warn readers that the chapter is bound to be somewhat impressionistic: I have lived through the last years of the Soviet collapse and have been watching North Korea (occasionally from the inside) for some twenty-five years, so what I write is to a large extent based on my own observations.

Being a Russian historian of North Korea, I am frequently asked which period of Soviet history North Korea of today resembles. This question is actually far more difficult to answer than it might sound, and not so much because the observable trends are different between those two societies (in fact, these trends are remarkably similar). However, for somebody with Soviet experience, North Korea of 2013 presents a curiously confusing and eclectic picture.

The official ideology of North Korea still can be described as "Stalinism with (much pronounced) national characteristics." When one reads the editorials of *Rodong Shinmun* or looks at posters somewhere on the streets of Pyongyang, the emerging picture is reminiscent of Moscow in the late 1940s, the time when Stalin's black car still made a daily commute to and from the Kremlin. The official media still repeats the same worn-out clichés and breathes fire when "imperialists" and their "puppets" are mentioned. The usual late Stalinist fare of ossified Leninism and nationalism still reigns supreme in propaganda and official ideology.

However, the public mood is different. When one talks to the people in the same city of Pyongyang (including intellectuals and minor functionaries), the picture appears much more similar to the Soviet Union of the 1960s and 1970s, the era when dissenters were engaged in their night-long talks in the kitchens of Moscow. Open dissent seems to be very rare in present-day North Korea—at least, it is invisible to a foreign observer. The average person still follows the prescribed ideological routines. Nonetheless, few if any people take the state's official line at face value, even though many seem to buy at least some elements of the official ideology. Most North Koreans seem to suspect that something is wrong with the entire system or at least some important parts of it. The diminishing fear of authority is also quite palpable. Like Soviet citizens of the 1960s, North Koreans are not eager to discuss politics with foreigners (with the exception of a few trusted ones, but such trusted foreigners seldom share their experiences with outsiders). However, some hints of displeasure began to surface with remarkable frequency—it is sufficient to say that after the botched currency reform of 2009 a number of diplomats stationed in Pyongyang told the me that their North Korean contacts were openly critical of the reform and expressed their annoyance in remarkably sharp terms (like a North Korean military intelligence officer who said that "the [North Korean] government does not understand what it is doing with the economy").

And the economy is different from the Stalin era, too. A trip outside Pyongyang would remind one not of the Soviet days, but rather of Russia in the 1990s, in the early post-Soviet years when the state-run economy collapsed and everybody tried to make a living by selling anything that was salable and/or by starting a small business. The demise of the public distribution system (PDS) in North Korea, which for decades supplied food to the people, as well as the general economic collapse of the mid-1990s, produced the same results as in early post-Soviet Russia, that is, the growth of grassroots capitalism. Crowds of vendors, booming markets, rampant official corruption, proliferation of small businesses, frequently of an illegal nature—all these are features of Russia and other post-Soviet states of the post-1991 period (only large-scale organized crime seems to be absent from North Korea).

Therefore the Soviet experience is clearly of much use for a student of North Korea, but one has to be careful and keep in mind not only the similarities but the differences that exist between these two regimes.

The Soviet Collapse: The Dangerous Truth and How It Was Learned

Why did the Soviet Union collapse? In the final count, its fate was sealed by the gross and probably incurable inefficiencies of a centrally planned economy, which have been studied and re-studied so many times. The national question was another important contributing factor, even though its significance was aggravated by mounting economic difficulties. Another, arguably the least important but still significant factor was the general dissatisfaction with the undemocratic and restrictive nature of the political system.

Here I will not discuss the national minorities' question that was important, perhaps even decisive, in the case of the Soviet Union. I would agree with Astrid Tuminez, who suggests that "nationalism and ethnic pressures were facilitating and precipitating variables in the breakup of the Soviet Union, rather than the primary cause."[1] At the same time, I suspect that the nationality question would *eventually* undermine the Soviet federal state even if Moscow had somehow succeeded in reforming the Soviet economy. At any rate, North Korea is an ethnically homogenous state, so this issue is not relevant for our main topic. Rather we will concentrate on economic inefficiency and political restrictions instead.

From the 1960s the Soviet economy began to slow down, and by the 1970s it grew slower than the economies of the developed West. Interestingly, the official Soviet media of the time did not try to hide the statistical evidence for this growing gap in economic performance; yet newspapers did not draw much public attention to this and also reported the official data, which tended to present a rosier picture of the situation. However, the economy of diminishing returns and steadily growing shortages was not a political

1 Astrid Tuminez, "Nationalism, Ethnic Pressures, and the Breakup of the Soviet Union," *Journal of Cold War Studies* 5, no. 4 (2003): 82.

factor itself. It came to be seen as a major political problem only because the Soviet populace could and did compare their consumption levels with those of the developed West—and came to the conclusion that the West was well ahead.

It is important to remember that it was the countries of Western Europe and the United States who were seen as benchmarks in the late Soviet era. In the 1970s, the Soviet citizen lived better than an Iranian or a Bolivian, but this did not matter for Soviet public opinion. Soviet propaganda would never dare to compare the USSR with developing countries, since such a comparison would be seen as outrageous. Public opinion was firmly anchored in the idea of the Soviet Union's potential to be equal to the richest developed nations. It was taken for granted that the Soviet Union, with the right political and economic system, would be the equal of the most developed countries in the Western world (in the late Soviet days, the developed West came to be known, with a telling touch of Orientalist anachronism, as the "civilized world"). This was the reason why the Soviet public was upset by information about the much higher living standards enjoyed by the countries of the West.

It seems that North Korea similarly has countries that are taken almost by default as points of reference. Those countries are China and, to a far larger extent, South Korea, its twin state. As was the case with USSR-U.S. comparisons, no amount of economic success in relation with Third World countries will matter to the average North Korean if he or she becomes aware that North Korea is lagging behind the South. The South is *the* benchmark, so North Korea's continuous inability to approximate South Korea's living standards is bound to become a major political problem (of course, such an inability first must become known to the average North Korean). This will remain a destabilizing factor even if the North Korean government manages to launch truly spectacular economic growth (by emulating China, for example). The average North Korean will be unsatisfied with the government's economic performance as long as he is aware that the North remains much behind the South. The fact that the "benchmark society" speaks the same language is likely to further amplify the subversive impact that will be produced by the spread of information about South Korea's prosperity.

However, economic underperformance becomes a political factor only because it is known to the general public. I personally believe that the spread of information about the economic success of the developed West was the single-most important factor in the demise of the Soviet Union. The spread of this subversive information slowly undermined and eventually wiped out the popular belief in the superiority or, at least, potential, of the Leninist

state socialism. Its impact was strongest among the educated urban population, who had better access to the information from overseas and also had
the education and leisure time that made unofficial political discussions possible.[2] Nonetheless, it was felt in all other social groups, including mid-to-
high-level cadres.

For a while the economic woes of the Soviet Union could be explained
by unfavorable circumstances, like the disastrous consequences of Hitler's
invasion of 1941 or even the negative impact of the alleged prerevolution-
ary "backwardness" (the latter explanation was especially popular with the
Soviet official media). But these excuses had lost all their resonance by the
early 1970s, more so because the gap between the Soviet Union and the developed West began to widen. As late as 1980, the official Soviet media still
occasionally spoke of unemployed Americans queuing for a bowl of free
soup, but nobody believed those tales anymore. Everybody knew it: the West
was well ahead, and something had to be done about this.

How did the Soviet people learn about U.S. prosperity? To simplify things
a bit, there were two major channels that brought this dangerous information inside the country: first, official exchanges; second, systemic attempts
by the West to disseminate information in the Soviet Union ("psychological
warfare," if you like). Both channels were important but the former probably had significantly greater impact.

To an extent, the relative liberalism and permissiveness of the Soviet system contributed towards its demise. Unlike North Korea, the Soviet Union
tolerated a relatively wide range of personal, academic, and cultural exchanges. For example, the government allowed screenings of selected and
edited Western movies, some chosen works of contemporary Western fiction
were translated, and original Western books were on sale in major cities. Of
course all imported texts and shows were carefully screened to ensure that
they would not produce undesirable impressions amongst the Soviet people.
For example, Soviet censors always preferred those American movies that
depicted the class contradictions, social disasters, and the sorry plight of the

---

2 It is telling that in their study of Soviet immigrants to the United States in the
mid-1980s, Milar and Clayton found a remarkable correlation between the age and level
of dissatisfaction in regard to the Soviet system. While for those above 54 years of age the
index of subjective satisfaction with the system was above 2.7 (4 meant "very satisfied"
and 1 meant "very unsatisfied"), for those below 31 the mean index was merely 2.4. See
James R. Millar, ed., *Politics, Work, and Daily Life in the USSR: A Survey of Former Soviet Citizens* (Cambridge; New York: Cambridge University Press, 1987), 33. Had such a
study been possible in the USSR at that time, it would have produced very similar results.

working poor in the countries of developed capitalism (escapist fantasies and light comedies also had some chances to be accepted).

This policy worked—but only to a certain extent. Soviet viewers did not fail to notice that these American poor were not that poor by the Soviet standards of the time. When watching a movie about a labor strike the Soviet audience might have been sympathetic to the plight of exploited American workers, but they noticed that these "exploited workers" lived in houses that in the Soviet Union would be accessible only to a tiny minority, while their cars, too, were clearly superior even to the vehicles of mid-level party functionaries. Translated fiction (being text rather than image, and hence less powerful and also easier to manipulate for the censors) betrayed much less but it still constituted a useful avenue for the spread of "dangerous" knowledge.

Western popular culture, above all rock music, was extremely popular among the young in the Soviet cities of the 1970s. The authorities looked at this popularity with great suspicion and seldom allowed records of Western groups to be officially sold. However, with the spread of tape recorders, this ban became ineffective. Every Soviet teenager in the 1970s and 1980s listened to the Beatles, ABBA, and Led Zeppelin. They were trendy, they were cool, and they were far superior to the officially approved Soviet pop. In an attempt to dwarf their fame, the authorities supported the locally produced imitations, but these tended to be inferior in quality and did not enjoy much popularity. Instead, the youth produced non-conformist rock that was either ambivalent about or hostile to the official politics.

Interpersonal interactions were important as well. From the early 1970s Soviet citizens could go overseas as tourists if they wished to do so, had some money, worked for an influential company, and were approved for such trips by the authorities. The first few trips had to be done to "fraternal Socialist countries," but eventually people with the right connections could be cleared for trips to the countries of the "real" West. Apart from that, a large number of Soviet citizens travelled overseas as members of technical assistance missions, and as sailors and interpreters. Admittedly most of these advisers went to pro-Soviet regimes in the Third World, but while being there they had many opportunities to interact with the citizens of developed nations, or approach international media, so they could learn a lot about the real world.

These people with direct overseas exposure were still a small minority but they spent much time retelling stories of their experiences abroad. They might occasionally talk about homeless people in New York, but they were far more likely to tell stories of unimaginable consumer abundance, techno-logical sophistication, politeness, and efficiency.

These seem to be the reasons why promotion of personal exchanges might become a powerful tool to change North Korean society. It is often argued that these exchanges almost invariably involve money/expertise transfers and hence provide the Kim family regime with hard currency and other means to maintain the system. However, judging by the Soviet and East European experience, this is not necessarily the case: in the long run, the presence of foreigners might help to erode officially approved beliefs.

The presence of foreigners in the Soviet Union also was not a negligible factor in this equation. Those people were students, tourists, and foreign experts. Only a minority of them came from the developed world, and in many cases upwardly mobile Soviet individuals avoided excessive associa-tions with foreigners—such interaction could be harmful for their careers, albeit hardly for anything else. Nonetheless their dress, their consumer items, and the ease with which they could spend money—everything hinted they came from far more advanced societies.

For example, in the Leningrad of the 1970s, the city of my youth, on an average weekend everybody could see an impressive number of seriously drunk Finnish tourists who came to enjoy cheap Russian booze. Russians rarely engaged them in political conversations, but the presence of these people was important. Those drunk Finns clearly were not members of the privileged elite but their dress and their gadgets were luxurious by Soviet standards. Last but not least, the presence of a small but not insignificant amount of Western consumer goods in the domestic market also had politi-cal consequences. Those items and gadgets were remarkably advanced (and just looked so much better) if compared to Soviet analogues.

The import of Western consumption goods also played a major role in undermining the old propaganda myths. In the 1970s, faced with growing consumer shortages and also awash in petrodollars from the recently discov-ered Siberian oil fields, the Soviet government decided to drastically increase the import of consumer goods. Obviously it was hoped that the availability of such goods would increase the popularity of the regime. It did just that, but only in the short term. In the long run the presence of such consumer goods strengthened the equation of the West with technological sophistica-tion and daily comforts. The increase in imports made even more people aware of this superiority. This understanding did not necessarily transform loyal Soviet citizens into staunch proponents of the capitalist market econ-omy, but it contributed to the growing sense of skepticism about the Soviet system.

If we talk about deliberate efforts to disseminate information into the Soviet Union, one must pay special attention to foreign radio broadcasts. Indeed, with the technology available in the 1960s and 1970s, the broadcast was the only way to bypass the authorities and reach the Soviet audience. In spite of jamming, foreign broadcasts were hugely successful and enjoyed universal popularity, such that in the 1980s roughly one-quarter of urban households listened to foreign radio stations at least once a week. According to Massachusetts Institute of Technology studies of the period (which generally agree with my personal memories),

> the weekly reach of the combined Western broadcasters oscillated around 25%. VOA had the highest weekly reach, at around 15%, until it met direct competition from an un-jammed Radio Liberty in 1989. BBC was firmly anchored in the 5–10% range and Deutsche Welle hovered around 5% until 1986, when it began a slow but steady decline to around 2% in 1990.[3]

However, it is important to keep in mind that the average Soviet listener was quite skeptical about the political content of these broadcasts. With the exception of a few hard-line dissenters (contrary to what many Westerners want to believe, they never constituted a statistically significant group), most Soviet people understood perfectly well that they were the targets of an on-going psychological operation and therefore did their best to keep a critical mind when listening to Western radio stations. In those days I frequently heard it said that both foreign broadcasts and the Soviet media were biased and surely filled with lies but since the vector of these discourses was diametrically opposed, a reasonable and skeptical person could figure out the true picture by carefully comparing them.

This skepticism also might be the reason why more neutral, less politicized stations usually had more appeal to the average Soviet citizen, who at that time usually was skeptical about but not hostile to the idea of socialism and the official Soviet ideology in general. The hardcore anti-communist radio stations (like, say, Radio Liberty) had an audience, to be sure, but the BBC and Voice of America (VOA) tended to be seen as more trustworthy.

The efforts to disseminate printed material achieved only very limited success. Paper books are bulky, hence difficult to smuggle and hide. They are relatively expensive, too. Therefore in the Soviet Union of the 1970s one had to be a member of a network of opposition-minded intellectuals to have access to a more-or-less steady supply of such materials. Outside this milieu

3 Eugene Parta, *Discovering the Hidden Listener: An Empirical Assessment of Radio Liberty and Western Broadcasting to the USSR during the Cold War* (Stanford, CA: Hoover Institution, 2007), 8. By "weekly reach" Parta means "the percentage of the [Soviet] population reached in the course of an average week."

(perhaps somewhere between ten and ninety thousand active participants), the impact of the oft-discussed *Samizdat* and *Tamizdat* (illegally published and smuggled books) remained very low. The Russian of the 1970s would seldom come across such publications even if he or she lived in a large city, had a good education, and was moderately interested in politics.

It might have been different in those times had digital media existed— but it did not. The first videotapes began to appear in the mid-1980s, when the Soviet system was already crumbling.

All this seems to be applicable to North Korea as well, but we must keep in mind that unlike the Soviet Union, North Korea has outlawed the private ownership of tuneable radio sets—and this makes an important difference. In the last few years a large number of such sets have been smuggled into the country from China, so they are much easier to get. Nonetheless, listening to foreign radio is still usually perceived as a very dangerous pastime.

At the same time some new technologies that did not exist at the time of the Soviet collapse are now very much present in North Korea. For example, videotapes and DVDs are watched widely, with South Korean movies and television shows constituting a large part of the illegal but booming video market in North Korea. The penetration rate of DVD players is estimated to be 50–75 percent, so we can surmise that the average North Korean watches South Korean shows and movies even more frequently than the average Soviet citizen of the 1970s listened to foreign broadcasts. The difference is that South Korean television shows are not designed with a political goal in mind. They are pure entertainment, but the unintentional background elements of such entertainment may well be very powerful. North Koreans do not necessarily believe that television serials and movies depict the real life of the South. My interviews with defectors confirm that most of them, being conditioned to the gross exaggerations of their own media, assume that the South Korean movies also show a non-existent prosperity. However, there are things which cannot be specially made for the sake of movie-making—like, say, the high-rise buildings and highways that are clearly seen in the background. So, after being exposed to South Korean movies, most of these defectors came to realize that the South lives better than North, even though few of them understood how big the gap really is.

Another important factor is the spread of South Korean goods, which are smuggled via China and sometimes find their way to North Korean markets from the Kaesŏng industrial park area. Their quality is clearly superior to that of similar Chinese items, and this tells volumes to North Korean customers.

Last but not least, rumors of South Korean prosperity are widely cir-culating inside North Korea. In most cases, the source of these rumors are those North Koreans who in the last decade or so visited China—as smug-glers, illegal migrant workers, common law wives, or merchants (their total number seems to be quite large). Nearly all of them spent their Chinese sojourn in the borderland areas, where the South Korean presence is very large. The North Koreans are overwhelmed by what they see as "Chinese prosperity," so stories about the far greater richness of South Korea find fertile ground in their minds.

The Soviet Collapse: The Slow-Motion Death of Belief

So the internal ideological situation in North Korea is not dissimilar from that of the Soviet Union of the 1960s. People are increasingly skepti-cal about the statements they can find in official sources of information and they know there are serious problems with the system. Meanwhile, smug-gled Choco Pies and South Korean television shows indicate that the outside world and especially South Korea are doing remarkably well.

The recent popular revolutions in the Arab world encouraged hopes that similar revolutions might one day erupt in North Korea as well. In the long run it is possible and even very likely, but currently the situation seems to be different: in spite of the growing awareness of the outside world, we should not assume that many North Koreans have already become hostile to the Kim family regime. As the experience of the Soviet crisis and collapse has demonstrated, such hostility usually builds up quite slowly.

In the mid-1990s, when anti-communist feelings reached their height, more or less every educated urban Russian would probably have told you that in Brezhnev's times, in the 1960–70s, he or she had already been a closet anti-communist (now, when popular feelings have become far more nostalgic in regard to the Soviet past, one would not encounter such a uniformity—on the contrary, these days an average educated Russian is likely to say some-thing nice about the old Soviet system). Most people had no vested inter-ests in making such militant statements and clearly believed what they were saying. We should not be surprised about this. Human beings are remark-ably good at changing their opinions without noticing or admitting even to themselves that such change has taken place. In fact, in the Soviet Union of Brezhnev's era, a hardcore dissenter was a rare species indeed—though, ad-mittedly, a true believer in the party orthodoxy was probably an even more difficult creature to find. The vast majority of people were somewhere in between, neither enemies of the system nor its uncritical supporters, but increasingly annoyed by the political restrictions and increasingly aware of the yawning economic gap between the Soviet Union and the developed West.

A wonderful description of this mindset has been recently presented by Alexei Yurchak in his new study of late Soviet society, *Everything Was Forever, Until It Was No More.*[4] Yurchak concentrates on the place and times I know very well from my own experience—the Leningrad intellectual circles of the 1970s and early 1980s. So, the picture is impressively correct— and this is the picture of perfect alienation between the actual life of the people and the official rituals that were carried out without much protest, but also without any sincere belief in their value. People were quite ready to play according to the established rules, but they hardly took the rules seriously and lived their own lives, which had few references to the official demands and concerns. This seems to be the case of present-day North Korea: no significant dissent, but no enthusiasm for the system either.

By the early 1970s the spread of information about the outside world insured that nearly all young and middle-aged Russians had serious doubts about the system and agreed that some radical transformation would be necessary. Nonetheless, until the late 1980s most Soviet people wanted a reformed socialism, not a full switch to a capitalist market economy. The first generation of post-Stalin intellectuals, known as *shestidesiatniki* (literally "people of the sixties" or "60ers"), were increasingly aware about the consumerist advantages of capitalism as well as the greater freedom enjoyed by the citizens of the Western world. But they still believed in the socialist project and hoped that the future Soviet society would somehow combine the material comfort and individual freedom of the West with the "morally just" collectivist values and state-controlled economy of the Communist Bloc. Even the most radically minded of these people held these illusions until around the period 1975–80, and among the majority such expectations lasted for another decade. It is not incidental that even Andrei Sakharov, a leader of the radical dissenters, has expressed his belief in eventual "convergence," that is, the gradual fusion of Soviet-style socialism with Western-style capitalism.

To give a taste of how the early dissenters saw themselves in the 1960s, it makes sense to quote at length the "letter of twenty-five," a letter written by Soviet intellectuals to the Communist Party Central Committee that criticized the alleged plans of rehabilitating Stalin and restoring the late dictator

4 Alexei Yurchak, *Everything was Forever, Until it Was No More: the Last Soviet Generation* (Princeton: Princeton University Press, 2006).

into the official pantheon of Soviet heroes. This letter reads as surprisingly loyalist and, at first glance, could well be written by a more reasonable party apparatchik:

> Stalin bears responsibility not only for the numerous deaths of innocent people, for our lack of preparation for the [Second World] war, for the divergences from the Leninist norms of the party and the state life. Also, his crimes and wrongdoing distorted the idea of communism to such a degree that our people would never forgive him. . . .
>
> . . . The issue of Stalin's political rehabilitation is not only an issue for our domestic but also for our foreign policy. Any step towards his rehabilitation would undoubtedly lead to a new split within the world communist movement, now between us and communists in the West. . . . Nowadays, when we are threatened both by the activity of the American imperialists and the West Germans seeking revenge and by the leaders of the Communist Party of China, it would be absolutely unreasonable to create a pretext for a split, or even for new difficulties in our relations with the brotherly [communist] parties in the West.[5]

Against such a background one should not be surprised that many early dissenters' groups emphasized their loyalty toward the socialist ideal. Most of these opposition-minded people tended to believe that the early ideal of socialism associated with Lenin and the October Revolution was spoiled and distorted in Stalin's era. In an exchange typical of the mid-1960s, Bela Akhmadulina, a prominent poetess and one of the most influential 60ers, angrily reacted to a remark by a friend who said that "revolution is dead." This goddess of young Moscow liberals exploded, "Revolution is Not Dead! Revolution is Just Sick! We Must Cure It! We Must Help It!"[6]

Such an attitude was understandable. Of course, lifelong indoctrination played a role, since such words as "capitalism" and "market" had very unsavory connotations in the minds of the Soviet people. However, this political moderation relied on a powerful psychological and social mechanism as well. People are never eager to discard their own experiences and sacrifices (as well as those of their parents). The great suffering of the Soviet people in the previous decades was made in the name of socialism and it would thus be too painful to admit that all these sacrifices were in vain, that the supposed rationale behind the murderous policies was a lie or, at best, a gross mistake. So people naturally looked for some justification; they were much

---

5 Serguei Oushakine, "The Terrifying Mimicry of Samizdat," *Public Culture* 13, no. 2 (2001): 197.

6 This well-known exchange is described, among others, by Yevgenii Yevtushenko, another famous "60er" and one-time husband of Akhmadulina. See Yevgenii Yevtushenko, *Volchii passport* [A wolf's passport] (Moscow: Vagrius, 1998), 552.

attracted to the idea of an essentially noble ideal, one that became terribly distorted by unfavorable circumstances and bad people.

Until the late 1970s, very few people in Russia were willing to associate themselves with former opponents of communism. Since the 1960s, the White Army (that is, the forces of the armed anti-communist resistance during the 1917–22 Civil War) was often romanticized and glamorized, even, to an extent, in the official media, but the massive weight of internalized propaganda prevented the Soviet people from openly associating themselves with White Officers. The anti-communist fighters were pitied but only as stubborn fighters for a lost and basically wrong cause. It might somehow have been different in non-Russian areas where the Soviet regime could be construed as essentially a foreign occupation. But, in Russia proper it was psychologically difficult to reject the heritage of one's parents and grandparents and admit that their one-time opponents might have been right.

Of course, the efficiency of the political police also contributed towards stability. Even in the permissive Brezhnev era, the KGB exercised efficient control over society. It might not have been especially brutal, and the number of the political prisoners did not exceed a paltry few thousands (far less than most Westerners "intuitively" thought at the time—but still confirmed by the Amnesty International and human rights groups' estimates).[7] In the Brezhnev-era Soviet Union in order to be arrested one had to be seriously involved with anti-government activity. However, in spite of this relative mildness, the KGB had an ability to block virtually all career avenues for any Soviet citizen who would think of challenging the system, and it also had a large network of secret informers whose presence was much feared. Last but not least, the older generation still vividly remembered the arbitrary application of state terror during the Stalin years, and hence older Soviet people were deadly afraid to raise political topics. Younger generations were constantly reminded by their elders that nobody around them should be trusted when it came to talking politics, and these lessons did have some impact.

The switch to a more-or-less complete denial of the communist experiment began only in the years of *perestroika*—and not even in its first years, since for a while the idea of a (somehow) improved state socialism still dominated the minds of urban activists. Few people now remember the full official names of the various "People's Fronts," short-lived but powerful mass mobilization movements that for the first time in Soviet history gave institutional forms to opposition to Party rule and briefly constituted a backbone of the democratic opposition. These movements, active during 1988–90,

7 See Amnesty International reports for the relevant years.

were called the "People's Front in support of Democracy and Socialism." Only as late as 1989 did some daring publicists, often with backgrounds in economics (like Piiasheva and Popov), begin to express open doubts on the very efficacy of the Leninist state socialism project. Around the same time, other journalists and public figures began to criticize Lenin, hinting that the failed Soviet project was probably a logical development rather than distortion of the 1917 October revolution. Soon afterwards, this criticism produced a snowball effect, so during 1989–1991 all earlier illusions evaporated almost overnight; for a few years in the early 1990s, Russia became the world's most ardently anti-communist country (admittedly, around 1995–96 a backlash began to unfold).

This experience might also have some valuable lessons for anybody who thinks about North Korea's future. If North Korea is going to pass through its own revolution (by no means certain but a likely probability) one should not expect that even the most radical supporters of the opposition will immediately demand a complete break with North Korea's past. If anything, the sacrifices and tribulations of the North Korean people might have been even greater than those of the Soviet people, and it will be difficult even for a skeptical North Korean to admit that the soldiers of Syngman Rhee, those "running dogs of the bloodthirsty U.S. imperialism," once fought for what actually was proven to be the right cause while one's own grandfather, once a volunteer for the Northern armed forces and so the source of family pride, was deadly wrong from the very beginning. So one can expect that at least at the initial stages, the North Korean opposition will demand a return to the "good" and "distorted" past, probably associated with the Great Leader, Sun of the Nation, Kim Il-sung. This is even more likely in the case of North Korea because, judging by my North Korean refugee interlocutors, a majority of the common North Koreans see Kim Il-sung's era as a time of prosperity and stability, and retain a considerable measure of respect for the founding father of the North Korean state.

But one should also expect that the growing awareness of the outside world as well as a spread of knowledge about North Korea's actual history will undermine these expectations of "reformed *Juche*" quite rapidly. The changes might be greatly sped up in that the alternative is represented by a society whose members allegedly belong to the same nation as North Koreans themselves.

There is, though, one important difference between the Soviet Union and North Korea. In the Soviet Union, a large part of officialdom did not mind a radical change because they usually did not see reform (or even a revolution) as a direct threat to their own power and privilege. On the contrary, the former apparatchiks gained much from post-perestroika developments—at least as far as their incomes and standards of living are concerned. There were short periods around 1991–92 when it looked like former Communist apparatchiks would be banned from holding important positions and perhaps even persecuted in post-communist Russia (much in line with the East European policies of "lustration"). However, it was just a temporary aberration, and now post-communist Russia—as well as a majority of the Soviet successor states—is still largely run by people who began their career in the Communist Party or the KGB in the 1970s or 1980s.

At any rate, as some published documents (including diaries) and my own personal experience of interacting with Soviet-era officials testify, back in Brezhnev's era the political and administrative elite was by no means immune to the skepticism about the system. They had an even better understanding of the problems and shortcomings and most of them realized that some radical change was necessary, even though they did disagree on the desirable course of action.

It is remarkable that most leaders of early post-perestroika Russia emerged from the higher layers of the late Soviet bureaucracy. Mr. Putin is not exactly a darling of the West, so his KGB past is routinely mentioned in the media. However, one should not forget that the alleged "champion of democracy" and radical pro-market reformer Mr. Yeltsin once was a Party heavyweight, who ranked third or fourth in the party roster and who did not show any democratic inclinations until the late 1980s.

The same can be said about the leaders in the regions in post-Soviet Russia as well as the leaders of the newly independent states, former Soviet republics. In 2011, in two out of the fifteen Soviet successor states, the chief executives (now styled "presidents") were still the same people who were first secretaries of the local Communist Party branch at the time of the Soviet collapse, and in two others the current leader was first anointed as a successor by an aging former first secretary (in one case the top job was held by the son of the former Communist strongman). These days many of them are too old to still be politically active, but around 2000 a majority of the top politicians in Russia and other successor states were top functionaries who survived the collapse of the USSR by switching sides at the most opportune moment.

Even the people who are now perceived as hard-liners, like Grigory Romanov or Yegor Ligachev, wanted quite radical economic reforms back in the early 1980s.[8] They just happened to believe that these reforms would be

---

8 Michael Kort correctly described Ligachev, later seen as an embodiment of "reac-

made possible only by making the state more powerful and more authoritarian. But such solutions had little support among younger functionaries who were generally sympathetic to the views of the increasingly skeptical educated public. In other words, in the Soviet Union of the 1970s and 1980s one could observe the situation that was long ago described by Crane Brinton in his classic study of modern mass revolutionary movements. Brinton noticed that a ruling class itself increases the probability of a revolution when some members of the dominant elite become uncertain about the regime's legitimacy and suspect that the beliefs they took for granted are false, and that they should be sympathetic towards those who are challenging the existent order.[9] This was clearly the case in the USSR.[10]

This loss of belief in the system at the very highest levels was profoundly manifest during the pathetic failure of the 1991 August Coup. The victorious democrats were understandably reluctant to admit that their victory was so easy and swift exactly because their enemies were not willing to spill blood and resort to violence—in other words, to behave like the Soviet politicians of an earlier era would certainly have behaved under the circumstances. By that time even the supporters of the Soviet Union lacked the ideological zeal that would make the use of force justifiable—much in line with what Crane Brinton wrote about earlier revolutions. The 1991 coup leaders could easily have arrested or killed Yeltsin, Sobchak, and any number of key resistance leaders. As far as we now know, such a course of action was never seriously considered by the coup leaders. The coup leaders obviously hoped that a declaration of intent would suffice, and when it did not they surrendered to the overwhelmingly hostile public opinion. Of course it did help that these people understood that they were unlikely to be seriously punished for their deeds (actually, they got away with even lighter sentences than anyone expected at the time).

Unfortunately for us and, especially, for the North Koreans themselves, this will very probably not be the case in North Korea. Many North Korean bureaucrats seem to understand that in the long run the current economic and social model is unsustainable (in this regard they are no different from

tion" as "Yegor Ligachev, the efficient, reformist-minded Tomsk regional first secretary." Michael Kort, *The Soviet Colossus: History and Aftermath*, 4th edn., (Armonk, NY: M.E. Sharpe, 1996), 277.

9 Crane Brinton, *The Anatomy of Revolution* (New York: Prentice-Hall, 1952), 56–60.

10 For some evidence on how such doubts developed among the top functionaries, see Paul Hollander, *Political Will and Personal Belief: The Decline and Fall of Soviet Communism* (New Haven, CT: Yale University Press, 1999).

their Soviet colleagues of the 1970s). However, they also understand that any attempt to reform the system will be inherently risky to their position.

It is the existence of the rich and liberal South that makes a huge difference in the case of Korea. There was no booming capitalist Southern Russia that could absorb the failing Soviet Russia if a major crisis were to break out, thus destroying its statehood and sending its political functionaries to prison. In the case of North Korea, the situation is completely different. So, even those members of the elite who feel justifiable skepticism about the current system are still careful enough not to rock the boat. They prefer to remain silent or quietly look for ways to reform the economy without jeopardizing domestic political stability and the dominant positions of the current elite (alas, it is doubtful whether such ways exist). Eventually some of the bureaucrats will probably join the movement against the regime and perhaps even emerge as its leaders (at least, briefly), but we should expect that these people will wait until the very last moment.

North Korean leaders and, broadly speaking, its elite members, seem to believe in Franklin's famous maxim: "Gentlemen, we must all hang together or we shall most assuredly all hang separately." Unfortunately, this seems to be a correct estimate of their situation, and this is not good news for their citizens and their neighbors. This reluctance of the elite to support the opposition mindset might be among the major factors that inhibit the emergence of the North Korean opposition movement and greatly increase the life expectancy of the regime.

Conclusion

The Soviet experience might be of great use for every student of North Korea—as long as such student keeps in mind not only similarities, but also important differences between those two societies. On balance, North Korean society seems to have been following the trajectory of post-Stalin Soviet Union, even though in different areas the speed of changes is remarkably dissimilar.

North Korean society seems to be vulnerable to the spread of information from the outside world, and in the case of the Soviet Union, such information played a major, or even decisive role in undermining the system. Nonetheless, we should not be too optimistic: if the Soviet experience is a guide, it might take decades before this change in the worldview will produce meaningful political consequences. The Soviet experience testifies that the "psychological warfare" of the West did contribute to system disintegration, but the decisive role was played by the spontaneous spread of uncensored information, facilitated by interpersonal exchanges of all kinds.

One should not expect that a significant number of North Koreans are now in opposition to the system. It is equally unlikely that the average North Korean is a brainwashed robot of the Kim family. In all probability, they are neither dissenters not supporters, and most of them are likely to remain docile until the time of the final crisis.

Another important peculiarity is the existence of the rich and free South just across the border. This makes the North Korean regime more vulnerable than the Soviet regime once used to be—the economic success enjoyed by what once was an agricultural backwater is impressive enough. At the same time, the prospect of unification by absorption is terrifying for North Korean power holders, and this makes the partial defection of the elite less likely, thus increasing the cohesive power of the regime.

13 Risky Business: Chinese-Style Reform and the North Korean Regime

Andrew G. Walder

Could a Chinese-style (or Vietnamese-style) economic reform, combining economic liberalization with single-party dictatorship, prove to be a solution for the Democratic People's Republic of Korea's (DPRK, or North Korea) moribund economy? Could a resurgent economy stabilize the North Korean regime, as it has obviously done in China and Vietnam over the past three decades? Could a prospering market-based economy finally break the cycle of military confrontation and brinkmanship through which the DPRK has sought to extract economic subsidies from both its sponsors and its enemies?

There are good reasons for viewing Chinese-style reform as a highly attractive option for the North Korean regime. In conversations with colleagues in China, I have often seen them shake their head and wonder why North Korea clings to such a reactionary ideology, reminiscent of their own Maoist era, when the obvious example of post-Mao China shows the way forward. The facts are well known: China's economy has grown in real terms at a sustained annual rate of more than 9 percent a year since 1990. Vietnam's economy, which follows an almost identical path of reform, has grown at a sustained rate of 6 percent (see table 13.1).[1] These are by far

1 See David Dollar, "The Transformation of Vietnam's Economy: Sustaining Growth in the 21st Century," in *Market Reform in Vietnam*, ed. Jennie I. Litvack and

TABLE 13.1

Economic growth in surviving and former communist states, 1990–2008

Countries and regimes	GDP per capita (percent change)	Average annual growth (percent/year)
China	401.6	9.4
Vietnam	185.3	6.0
Laos	109.3	4.2
Poland	100.9	4.0
China-Vietnam-Laos average	232.2	6.5
All non-Soviet post-Communist regimes	54.4	2.5
All former Soviet republics	32.2	1.3
Countries experiencing civil war	17.5	0.49
Stable democratic regimes	54.7	2.5

Source: World Bank, World Economic Indicators

Notes: Countries experiencing civil war include Armenia, Azerbaijan, Croatia, Georgia, Moldova, Serbia, and Tajikistan; stable democratic regimes include the Czech Republic, Estonia, Hungary, Latvia, Lithuania, Poland, and Slovenia. GDP expressed in constant US$.

the best performing of the former state socialist economies, and they have done markedly better than all of the states that are no longer ruled by their Communist parties. The star among the post-Communist regimes is Poland, which has grown at 4 percent per year. Perhaps more important is the fact that the Communist parties of China and Vietnam (and Laos) have relied upon their economic successes to ride out the wave of regime change that swept the Communist world from 1989 to 1991.[2]

By "Chinese-style market reform" I mean a gradual but steady move away from central planning over a period of ten to twenty years. This would begin with the abandonment of collective agriculture and the legalization of small-scale private enterprise. It would also include the establishment of special economic zones for foreign investment. The economy would steadily open up to foreign investment and trade outside of the special zones to encompass virtually the entire country. In the course of this opening, state enterprises would obtain greater autonomy to conduct their business on a profit basis, and they would gradually lose state subsidies as obsolete state firms are consolidated and restructured. Within ten years the majority of enterprise assets would be under non-state ownership forms, and within

Dennis A. Rondinelli (Westport, Conn.: Quorum, 1999), 31–46.

2 Laos, which is tightly integrated with the Vietnamese economy and is essentially its political protectorate, has implemented similar market reforms. See Martin Stuart-Fox, *A Short History of Laos* (Cambridge: Cambridge University Press, 1997). Other than North Korea, the only other surviving Communist regime is Cuba.

twenty years private- and foreign-invested enterprise would dominate the economy.

By "Chinese-style reform" I do not mean limited and temporary concessions to private farming or a "second economy" that is designed to ride out crises or supplement the workings of a dominant, centrally planned sector. These measures were employed in China in the early 1960s to recover from the massive famine caused by the Great Leap Forward. They were also employed in Hungary beginning in the late 1960s, and helped for a period to improve the supply of food and light consumer goods. But in neither economy were these limited "reforms" able to achieve more than superficial and temporary improvements in the economic system.[3] In Hungary, they served only to undermine the coherence of the party-state system.[4]

So why not carry out a Chinese-style market reform? This is actually a two-part question. First, what would it take to convince the DPRK leadership to embark on a path of market reform? Second, what would the consequences of such a path be? The problem with a Chinese-style reform is not economic, but political. There is little doubt that the economic policies would work, and work very well. Geopolitical and domestic political considerations, however, make it unlikely that the new DPRK leadership will embark on a path of fundamental market reform. They would either have to be unrealistic about the political impact of market reform (which they do not at present appear to be), or resigned to the fact that their years of rule have come to an end. Even if the Kim family is eventually supplanted by a different set of Party leaders who subsequently choose a path of reform, it is unlikely that the regime could survive for long. Because the geopolitical circumstances of North Korea are so different from those of China and Vietnam at the time they embarked on reform, the political impact of market reform in the DPRK would likely be different, in all probability accelerating regime change.

---

3 See János Kornai, *The Socialist System: The Political Economy of Communism* (Princeton: Princeton University Press, 1992).

4 See Ákos Róna-Tas, "The Second Economy as a Subversive Force: The Erosion of Party Power in Hungary," in *The Waning of the Communist State*, ed. Andrew G. Walder (Berkeley: University of California Press, 1995), 61–84; and Andrew G. Walder, "The Quiet Revolution from Within: Economic Reform as a Source of Political Decline," in Walder, *Waning*, 1–24.

The Economic Calculus: Obvious Advantages

The economic advantages of Chinese-style reform are now obvious. In the 1980s, when China and Vietnam initiated market reforms that opened their economies to the outside world, it was not clear that such a strategy would work. And if the strategy worked economically, it was generally understood to involve grave political risks for a single-party dictatorship.[5] With almost thirty years of hindsight, one can now draw very different conclusions. The economic strategy is sound, and moreover a prosperous, open, market-oriented economy is compatible with regime survival, even regime strengthening. China and Vietnam have had two of the fastest-growing economies in the world for almost three decades. They survived the global collapse of Communism as two of five remaining Communist regimes, and (along with Laos) have experienced unprecedented prosperity, in sharp contrast with North Korea and Cuba, the remaining survivors, who have refused to reform, clung to power, and have been mired in stagnation. One could look at the recent historical record and conclude that a fundamental restructuring of the economy, and integration with the world economy, is the only plausible alternative to either regime collapse or permanent stagnation.

It is one of the ironies of recent world history that surviving Communist regimes have been more successful at market reform than the post-Communist regimes that have frequently tried to implement the kind of democratic political system usually thought to be uniquely compatible with a market economy. As a group, the gross domestic product (GDP) per capita of China, Vietnam, and Laos has more than tripled since 1990, enjoying an average annual growth rate of 6.5 percent (see table 12.1). The twelve post-Communist regimes that were not part of the Soviet Union have grown by an average of only 54 percent, an annual rate of 2.5 percent. The fifteen republics that were formerly part of the Soviet Union have had an even worse record. They have grown by an average of only 32 percent, a paltry annual rate of 1.3 percent. To be sure, these figures are biased downward by the impact of political crises and civil war in countries like Croatia, Serbia, Armenia, Azerbaijan, Georgia, and Tajikistan, which have barely registered any net economic growth (see table 12.1). But the nations that shifted quickly to stable multiparty rule have fallen far short of the surviving Communist regimes. These stable democracies have had annual growth rates that average

---

5 These arguments are outlined in Stephen M. Goldstein, "China in Transition: The Political Foundations of Incremental Reform," *China Quarterly* 144 (December 1995): 1105–31.

only 2.5 percent. There is, in short, undeniable evidence that market reform is highly compatible with a surviving Communist Party dictatorship.

Moreover, the collapse of Communist rule in the former Soviet Union and a dozen other former Communist regimes cannot be blamed on market reform. The transition to a market economy in these nations did not get fully underway until after the collapse of Communist Party rule. In fact, it was the unwillingness to contemplate serious reform, and the clinging to an obsolete model of a closed bureaucratic economy for far too long, that contributed to the overwhelming political crises and collapse of 1989–1991, and the continuing political struggles in many of the successor states.

This historical record was absent when China and Vietnam embarked on reform in the 1980s. It was a gamble then in ways it obviously is not now. North Korea, further, enjoys advantages that China and Vietnam did not enjoy at the outset. A North Korean reform would be encouraged and heavily subsidized by a much larger Chinese economy, and if suitable concessions were made on military and security issues, by South Korea and the international community as well. Neither China nor Vietnam had prosperous potential sponsors of this sort at the outset of their reforms. So the prospects of economic success for Chinese-style reform in North Korea would be, if anything, even greater.

The Political Calculus: Contrasts with China and Vietnam

The problems with this happy scenario are political. Let us first address the political calculus behind any decision to initiate market reform. To initiate market reform in North Korea would mean a repudiation of the ideology that has governed the regime for decades, essentially an admission that the model, and the leadership, has failed. Any leadership that initiates this kind of reversal needs political cover to do so—an explanation for why things had gotten so bad that does not create political blowback for the regime's leaders.

In China, this political cover was provided by the purge of Mao Zedong's radical followers as a conspiratorial "Gang of Four" and a repudiation of their ideological extremism as a deviation from the deceased Chairman's true aims. The new leadership of the Chinese Communist Party, which quickly lined up behind Deng Xiaoping, promised a new direction under a new political leadership.[6] In Vietnam, more plausible political cover was provided by the impact of decades of warfare against the South Vietnamese

---

6 See Richard Baum, *Burying Mao: Chinese Politics in the Age of Deng Xiaoping* (Princeton: Princeton University Press, 1994).

regime and the U.S. military. Moreover, only one decade after the end of the war, the South's economy had yet to be fully absorbed into the state socialist model, and the task of national unification and reconciliation was still underway. Le Duan, the hardline party leader who had initiated the war against the South after taking over from Ho Chi Minh in 1960, and who had overseen harsh purges in the South and the invasion of Cambodia after 1975, died in 1986, opening the possibility of rethinking the nation's course. When the decision to commit to market reform was made that same year, *perestroika* was fully underway under Gorbachev in the Soviet Union, and the flaws of bureaucratic socialism were widely discussed. These ideological trends were highly influential in Hanoi, and it was already clear that economic assistance from the USSR would be drastically curtailed.[7] Although China was an implacable enemy and supported insurgents fighting against Vietnam's occupation forces in Cambodia, China's market reforms were already in place for almost a decade, and China showed how to fashion ideological cover for a "socialist market economy."

It is hard to imagine how the current North Korean leadership could accomplish a similar U-turn. Several decades ago, Kenneth Jowitt referred to Romania under the Ceauşescus and North Korea under the Kims as "socialism in one family." The label now applies with even greater force to North Korea, essentially a hereditary monarchy grafted onto a communist party-state.[8] To initiate even gradually the policies necessary for reform to work—opening the economy to the outside world and letting market forces reign—would fly in the face of everything that the Kim dynasty has stood for. So long as the Kim family reigns, this would be unlikely. It is no coincidence that Romania's Ceauşescu (along with Erich Honecker of East Germany, about whom more below) was an implacable foe of Gorbachev and reform in the Communist world.[9] Ceauşescu carried this hostility to his

7 See Leslie Holmes, "Vietnam in a Comparative Communist and Postcommunist Perspective," in *Vietnam's New Order*, ed. Stephanie Balme and Mark Sidel (New York: Palgrave Macmillan, 2007), 11–27; Gareth Porter, *Vietnam: The Politics of Bureaucratic Socialism* (Ithaca, N.Y.: Cornell University Press, 1993); and David Wurfel, "*Doi Moi* in Comparative Perspective," in *Reinventing Vietnamese Socialism: Doi Moi in Comparative Perspective*, ed. William S. Turley and Mark Selden (Boulder, Colo.: Westview, 1993), 19–52.

8 See Daniel Chirot, *Modern Tyrants* (Princeton: Princeton University Press, 1994).

9 See Stephen Kotkin, *Armageddon Averted: The Soviet Collapse, 1970–2000* (New York: Oxford University Press, 2008); Stephen Kotkin and Jan T. Gross, *Uncivil Society: 1989 and the Implosion of the Communist Establishment* (New York: Modern Library, 2009); and Vladimir Tismaneanu, "Romanian Exceptionalism? Democracy, Ethnocracy, and Uncertain Pluralism in Romania," in *Politics, Power, and the Struggle for Democracy*

early grave. Without the installation of a new post-Kim leadership within the DPRK, a decision to implement Chinese-style market reform seems unlikely.

Political Consequences: Lessons from China's 1980s

What would be the political consequences of market reforms in the unlikely event of a voluntary decision by the DPRK leadership to initiate them? China's experience during the first decade of reform in the 1980s is instructive. The early stages of market reform, which require the creation of a growing sphere of economic activity outside of the control of the government and a greater openness to the outside world, are in retrospect the most politically risky period to a Communist regime that attempts them. China in the 1980s was a much more unstable place than it has been in the subsequent two decades, and this experience is easy to forget.

The opening wedge of market reform is the liberalization of petty trade and street markets. This typically leads to the open flourishing of activities formerly associated with the black market (which has existed in North Korea for a long time), and the accumulation of considerable wealth by low-status individuals formerly denigrated as virtual criminals. China's first generation of petty entrepreneurs, the "individual households" (*geti hu*), quickly accumulated money wealth that they used to purchase newly-available but still scarce luxury consumer goods, and to pay their way into service establishments formerly reserved for those with political rank and social status.

The income of this first generation of entrepreneurs quickly outstrips that of the blue-collar occupations, and even those in the favored professions and government and party posts. This creates transitional status conflicts that were felt with particular acuity in urban China in the early to mid-1980s.[10] Those in elite positions, lacking the money income of the entrepreneurs, use their positions to advantage to acquire the scarce consumer goods directly, or begin to think of ways to extract money incomes from their positions. Ordinary citizens who are neither members of the elite nor engaged in private trade resent the conspicuous new wealth of the private traders on the streets and the increasingly open abuse of politically privileged positions to accumulate wealth and acquire scarce consumer items.

---

in South-East Europe, ed. Karen Dawisha and Bruce Parrott (Cambridge: Cambridge University Press, 1997), 403–51.

10 See Andrew G. Walder, "Workers, Managers, and the State: The Reform Era and the Political Crisis of 1989," *China Quarterly* 127 (September 1991): 467–92.

The first stages of market reform also face a major economic hurdle with large political implications: the inflation that is inherent in the decontrol of prices. Socialist planned economies are "economies of shortage"—inputs for all manner of industrial operations, and especially consumer items, are in short supply, scarce, and often rationed. When it becomes possible to acquire scarce items on the market, pent-up demand ensures that the prices are many times higher than the artificially low, state-set prices that previously reigned. This creates consumer price inflation that leads to a widespread sense of falling living standards even when real incomes are rising. It also creates incentives, under a transitional "dual price system," for individuals with access to low-price items still allocated within the plan to engage in arbitrage and divert them to the market, reaping windfall incomes. This becomes an important source of income for relatively low-paid government employees and officials, who will otherwise miss out on the new income opportunities presented by the growing private economy. This, in turn, leads to a growing perception of widespread corruption by those within the system.[11]

These phenomena have a second-order implication: a growing sense among youth that the traditional path to success through political activism in patriotic youth organizations and party membership has little value, and to a sense among college students that the state jobs that await them upon graduation will earn them rewards that are much smaller than those reaped by the ill-educated, formerly marginal individuals who seized the first opportunities in private trade. In China during the 1980s, Communist Youth League membership and activism fell to crisis levels, and surveys of student attitudes showed alarming disdain for the party-sponsored paths toward elite status.[12]

Then there is the impact of the inevitable opening to the outside world, even in modest steps, an impact that is likely to be exaggerated in a country that has been so isolated for such a prolonged period as North Korea. Foreign consumer goods, which inevitably become prized household items, are themselves symbolic of the higher living standards abroad. The presence of foreign business people, and the establishment of hotels and restaurants to cater to them, is another reminder. Restricted at first, information about the outside world will inevitably begin to spread, and modern means of communication (initially photocopy machines and radios, later cell phones

11 See Walder, "Workers, Managers, and the State," and Andrew G. Walder, "Wage Reform and the Web of Factory Interests," *China Quarterly* 109 (March 1987): 22–41.

12 See Stanley Rosen, "Prosperity, Privatization, and China's Youth." *Problems of Communism* 34 (March–April 1985): 1–28.

and internet access) will eventually spread well beyond the regime's efforts to control them. Knowledge of how far China lagged behind Japan, Taiwan, and especially colonial Hong Kong led to a thorough reassessment of living standards and regime performance in China in the 1980s.[13] The gap between the catastrophic living conditions in North Korea today and the extraordinary wealth of the demonized enemy states of South Korea and Japan would likely have even greater consequences.

These early stages of market reform create new problems for a regime at the same time that they inevitably involve a steady loss of control over economic activity, routes to material success, and information and modes of indoctrination. On the eve of the 1980s urban China experienced a new wave of underground publications critical of the regime, the emergence of critical intellectuals who voiced independent opinions, and a population of university students who demonstrated initially for campus democracy and eventually for broader political democracy. The decade after 1978 was a tumultuous one in China, far more unstable than the China of today and the recent past. No sooner had the government suppressed the partially underground "democracy wall" campaign of 1978–79 than university students campaigned for independent candidates to county-level People's Congresses.[14] Youth in China's special economic zones shouted down party leaders who lectured them at forums designed to warn them against the corrupt values and lifestyles associated with capitalism.[15] Universities became hotbeds of independent thinking, with intellectual salons devoted to the study of liberal democratic thought, Western political history, and modernization theory. A nationwide wave of protests by university students began in Anhui Province in November 1986 and spread through a series of provincial cities before reaching Shanghai and Beijing at the beginning of 1987, at which point it led to the purge of Party General Secretary Hu Yaobang, a reshuffling of the national leadership, and a crackdown on critical establishment intellectuals.[16]

13 See Baum, *Burying Mao*.

14 See Kjeld Erik Brødsgaard, "The Democracy Movement in China, 1978-1979: Opposition Movements, Wall Poster Campaigns, and Underground Journals," *Asian Survey* 21, no. 7 (July 1981): 747–74; and Roger Garside, *Coming Alive: China After Mao* (New York: McGraw-Hill, 1982).

15 See Luo Xu, "The 'Shekou Storm': Changes in the Mentality of Chinese Youth Prior to Tiananmen," *China Quarterly* 142 (June 1995): 541–72.

16 See David Kelly, "The Chinese Student Movement of December 1986 and its Intellectual Antecedents," *Australian Journal of Chinese Affairs* 17 (January 1987): 127–42; and Baum, *Burying Mao*.

This provided only a temporary respite. The first serious effort to shift to market prices for most commodities led to a wave of inflation and panic buying in 1988, and widespread popular dissatisfaction with the regime's handling of the economy. The death of the deposed Party leader Hu Yaobang in April 1989 sparked student protests that led to a national wave of demonstrations that paralyzed the nation's capital for almost five weeks until the beginning of June. The *denouement* is well known—the declaration of martial law, a failure of troops to intimidate the protesters, even larger massive popular demonstrations against martial law, culminating in the brutal military crackdown of June 4. Beijing remained under martial law well into 1990, in part because the autumn of 1989 witnessed the unraveling of communism throughout Eastern Europe.[17]

Geopolitics: A Divided Nation

Through the brutal application of military force, China was able to weather the political storm it experienced at the end of the 1980s. That storm was the culmination of the characteristic features of the early stages of market reform and opening—the disruption of career paths formerly monopolized by the Party, the creation of an alternative status order, the temptation of corruption and arbitrage in a partially reformed price system, the threat and reality of inflation, and especially the Party's eroding ability to control information and sell its message. Vietnam experienced similar problems, with less dramatic consequences, but like China has been able to ride them out.

If similar reforms were implemented in North Korea, we should expect similar problems. They could be contained if the reforms were limited and the degree of openness kept very small, but such a reform would not have the necessary positive impact on the economy. This would not be a Chinese-style reform; it would be a partial reform of the type earlier tried with little lasting success in Hungary in the 1970s and 1980s. Any market reform and opening that went far enough to begin to solve North Korea's economic maladies would surely encounter the same political difficulties experienced in China. If anything, they would be even more severe.

North Korea has little prospect of surviving the political consequences of the first stages of market reform. Its geopolitical circumstances are fundamentally different from that of either China or Vietnam in the 1980s.

---

17 See Andrew G. Walder, "The Political Sociology of the Beijing Upheaval of 1989," *Problems of Communism* 38 (September–October 1989): 30–40; and Baum, *Burying Mao.*

North Korea is the impoverished smaller half of a single nation, with a larger and infinitely more prosperous and democratic rival in South Korea. In the mid-1980s the Hanoi regime had recently won a war of national unification; there was no rival Vietnamese state when it began its move to a more open market economy. The Chinese Nationalist regime still ruled on Taiwan as a single-party dictatorship in the 1980s and had exhausted its political legitimacy on the mainland in the late 1940s; its economic takeoff was still in its early stages. North Korea's problem is that South Korea is on the verge of becoming a high-income country, not simply a successful development model. According to publicly available World Bank data, South Korea's per capita GDP in 2008, whether in real terms or in terms of purchasing power parity, was already higher than Portugal and just below that of Spain, which would place it somewhat below the average for the European Union as a whole. And it has been a stable multiparty democracy for more than two decades.

North Korea's political dilemma is therefore an exaggerated version of the problem faced by the regime of Erich Honecker in East Germany at the end of the 1980s. If the regime shifts the basis for its legitimacy away from adherence to a rigid anti-capitalist and anti-imperialist ideology to a promise to improve living standards by engaging with the world economy, what possible reason is there for the existence of a separate regime? West Germany was a successful state that had already delivered the economic prosperity that the East had so obviously failed to provide. Promise greater freedoms under a more liberal form of rule? West Germany already had a functioning multiparty democracy.[18] Therefore the East German Communist Party was the most rigid and conservative of the East European satellite states, hewing to a rigid anti-capitalist ideology, resisting the wave of reform coming out of Gorbachev's USSR until the very end. And when it was clear that the USSR would no longer prop it up in the face of mounting street demonstrations, the party leadership simply capitulated, and the East was integrated peacefully, and quickly, into a united Germany.[19] North Korea's situation in this specific respect is even worse than that of East Germany under Honecker. To be sure, its geopolitical situation remains different in two key ways: it still has a powerful sponsor and protector in Beijing, and it has nuclear weapons. Nonetheless, Chinese-style market reform, given its inevitable political consequences, presents grave political risks.

18 See Kotkin and Gross, *Uncivil Society*.
19 See Kotkin, *Armageddon Averted*.

Conclusion: Market Reform as Risky Business

Chinese-style economic reform would provide solutions for North Korea's economy, but as it progressed beyond its initial stages it would entail political risks that could threaten the very foundations of the regime. It is therefore unlikely that a political leadership headed by the Kim family would choose to embark on a full course of Chinese-style reform, and it is also unlikely that a post-Kim reformist party leadership could long survive the inevitable political consequences. Any North Korean leadership willing to embark on this course, if realistic about its prospects, would need to accept the likelihood of the regime's eventual demise. A North Korean leadership that embarked on this course without an awareness of the likely political fallout would be in for a very bumpy ride.

For a Chinese-style reform to be compatible with the survival of a separate North Korean regime, there would need to be international guarantees for the continued sovereignty of the DPRK. China would need to provide increased aid, technical assistance, and investment in return for economic liberalization and opening. South Korea would need to pledge to refrain from involvement in the North's political affairs and would also need to pledge increased forms of assistance analogous to that offered by China. Both parties, and the international community, would need to stand aside if and when popular protest was met with brutal force, as in China in 1989. Whether such a solution could become acceptable to any DPRK leadership or to international parties, and whether the North's regime could still survive the likely political consequences of market reform and opening are far from clear. It is relatively clear, however, that Chinese-style market reform could be a viable option for the North only under vastly altered geopolitical circumstances

14 State Under Stress: Prospects for Transformation in North Korea

Daniel C. Sneider

In the early days of the Cold War, North Korea was widely viewed by Western analysts and scholars as a creature of the Soviet Union. Its system was modeled on that of its powerful neighbor. Even after the withdrawal of Soviet occupation forces in 1948, the emergent Democratic People's Republic of Korea (DPRK) seemed to function as a part of the post-war Soviet Empire. Its leadership, including the first head of state Kim Il-sung, was largely composed of Koreans who had been trained in the Soviet Union, backed by Soviet Koreans who were sent in with the occupation. The DPRK, an early American intelligence study argued, succeeded in both creating a "satellite government modeled after the USSR," but also in "preserving the fiction of an independent state."[1]

As the Cold War stretched on, and the deep split between the Soviet Union and the People's Republic of China (PRC) emerged into the open, a more textured understanding of North Korea was formed. The Pyongyang regime was more of an independent actor, creating space for itself by

---

1 Department of State, *North Korea: A Case Study in the Techniques of Takeover* (Washington, DC: U.S. Government Printing Office, January 1961), 2. The study was based on the work of an intelligence team sent into North Korea in 1950 during the brief period of American control and initially published as a classified report in May 1951.

maneuvering between, and playing off against each other, its two powerful communist patrons.

More profoundly, in recent years, some scholars have also challenged the definition of North Korea as a socialist state built on the Soviet model. That Cold War perception of North Korea fails to grasp the essentially indigenous nature of the "North Korean revolution," they argue. As Columbia University scholar Charles Armstrong puts it:

> North Korea simply cannot be seen as a typical post-World War II Soviet satellite along the lines of East Germany or Poland, where leaders with longstanding ties to the USSR and long periods of residence in the Soviet Union were implanted by the Soviet occupation forces, where the Soviet Army remained the authority of last resort for decades afterward, and where the withdrawal of Soviet support quickly led to these regimes' demise. The North Korean revolution may not have been entirely autonomous, but its indigenous elements allowed it to endure.[2]

Even Armstrong does not deny the influence of Marxist-Leninist state socialism in the Soviet Union and the PRC on the North Korean state. But the North Korean state should be seen, he and others argue, as an outgrowth of a longer history of Korean nationalism, defined more by its embrace of ethnic nationalism.[3] The North Korean promulgation of a state ideology of self-reliance, or *Juche*, is evidence of its distinct character, the argument goes. And the adoption of dynastic succession and family rule, followed since the death of Kim Il-sung in the mid-1990s, also sets North Korea apart from its socialist brothers, an expression of its "oriental," if not Korean, nature.

In the view of such scholars, this unique character accounts for the enduring nature of the North Korean state even as other socialist states fall by the wayside of history. Almost alone in the communist world, North Korea refused to go down the road of large-scale market reforms, fearful that it would lead, as in the Soviet Union, to the collapse of the communist state. The North Koreans have apparently been able to overcome the growing stresses on their society without bowing to pressures to adopt a Chinese-style system. North Korea "had outlived forecasts of its imminent demise that had been predicted since at least the late 1980s," notes Armstrong.[4]

---

2 Charles K. Armstrong, *The North Korean Revolution, 1945–1950* (Ithaca: Cornell University Press, 2003), 4.

3 Aside from Armstrong, this argument is made most forcefully by scholars such as Bruce Cummings and, in a somewhat different vein, by Brian Myers in *The Cleanest Race: How North Koreans See Themselves and Why it Matters* (Brooklyn, N.Y.: Melville House, 2010).

4 Armstrong, *North Korean Revolution*, 1.

Undoubtedly, the early Cold War depiction of North Korea as a Soviet satellite, fashioned by rote in the model of the Soviet Union, was overly simplistic. It understated the Korean cultural, social, and political dimensions of the state. And certainly predictions of the imminent demise of the North Korean state in the aftermath of the collapse of the Soviet Union and the famine of the mid-1990s proved to be wrong.

Critics of the Cold War view of North Korea tend, however, to understate the importance of the socialist system that was built, and remains intact, in North Korea. Consequently, they tend to see North Korea in isolation and miss the comparative analysis of its development with those of other socialist states. Rather than being distinct, North Korea suffers from many of the same systemic failures that all socialist systems have faced, whether in the Soviet Union, Eastern Europe, and even China.

The fact that the North Korean state has survived until now does not diminish the dysfunctional nature of that system evident over the last two decades. The North Korean state has used certain tools to survive—from its ability to mobilize Korean nationalism to the use of the instruments of repression—but those factors are not unique, nor necessarily stable. And North Korea has the peculiar capability, fed by its nuclear weapons program, to exploit the tensions on the Korean Peninsula in order to extract vital amounts of economic aid to compensate for its systemic failures.

But, as I will discuss below, those measures have their limits and the North Korean state has already had to make considerable concessions to the pressure for market reforms in order to ease tensions within the country. Looked at in a comparative context, the evidence suggests that the North Korean state can postpone certain effects of the crisis but it cannot ultimately remain intact without either transforming itself, as China and Vietnam have done, or collapsing, as happened to the states of the Soviet Empire.

This debate over the nature of the crisis facing the North Korean state and its ultimate resolution has profound policy implications. If policymakers assume that the North Korean state will survive for an extended period of time, it tends to lend weight to those who favor a form of engagement that accepts its status as a de facto nuclear weapons state. If, on the other hand, the North Korean state is seen as under severe stress and facing a systemic crisis, it might imply a different set of policies. For some it lends credence to a strategy of confrontation, in the belief that pressure, both economic and military, can trigger regime collapse—what some in the Bush administration called "regime change."

But it can also call for forms of engagement aimed strategically at encouraging reform and undermining the repressive authority of the state. In an important essay in *Foreign Affairs*, the Russian scholar Andrei Lankov proposed a long-term strategy of what he cleverly termed "subversive engagement," aimed at spurring the transformation of North Korea.[5] In some respects, that was the premise of the "Sunshine Policy" adopted by the progressive South Korean government of Kim Dae-jung in the late 1990s. While that policy did not yield the change that its supporters believed would occur, such transformation may ultimately offer the only real path out of the apparent dead-end stalemate of the current security situation on the Korean Peninsula.

The Nature Of Crisis in Socialist Systems and Their Reform

In order to understand North Korea, it is first important to discuss what defines socialist systems, why such systems invariably face crises and the nature of those crises, and the difficult process of reform.

I approach this subject in part through the lens of personal experience. During my earlier career as a journalist, I served as the Moscow Bureau Chief of the *Christian Science Monitor* from 1990 to 1994. I arrived in Moscow on May 23, 1990, and spent the next four years there, witnessing the crisis of Soviet communism, multiple attempts to reform that system, the collapse of the Soviet Union, and the emergence of a post-communist state in Russia and the former Soviet republics. I came to Moscow from Tokyo where I also covered, as a journalist, the political transformation of South Korea from an authoritarian state to a democracy. I have also, during my career, spent considerable time in Vietnam and China, trying to understand the reform process in both those socialist systems.

All these countries have their own history and culture that differentiate them. Yet the adoption of a socialist economic system also put them in a group of nations that was set apart from the rest of the world. "Despite all the individual attributes that distinguish each of these socialist countries from all the others, they resemble one another and exhibit important attributes in common," wrote the brilliant Hungarian economist Janos Kornai, considered the foremost authority on socialist economics.[6]

---

5 Andrei Lankov, "Changing North Korea: An Information Campaign Can Beat the Regime," *Foreign Affairs* 88, no. 6 (November/December 2009): 95–105.

6 János Kornai, *The Socialist System: The Political Economy of Communism* (Princeton, NJ: Princeton University Press, 1992), 5.

In his oft-cited textbook on this subject, Kornai defines socialist systems as both a structure of political control and an economic system. Following the paradigm of Stalin's Soviet Union or China under Mao, all such socialist systems have included one-party rule (distinguishing it from "socialist" forms in the West) and state control and command of the economy. Such systems go through three prototypical phases: an initial revolutionary-transitional system, characterized by the transition from capitalism to socialism; a classical system; and a reform system in which the classical system attempts to reform itself to survive.[7] While the Soviet Union went through an extended transition, the same process took place rapidly in Eastern Europe and North Korea in the few years after 1945 under the force of Soviet occupation.

All classical socialist systems share certain features, Kornai writes. While the party and bureaucracy exercise control, these are not monolithic systems—conflicts take place among groups and lobbies. Ideology and ideas can play a key role in trying to mobilize support for policies. But the state also relies on the considerable tools of repression at its disposal and the ability to impose its will into every sphere of life, even the private.

The classical socialist system is thus intrinsically totalitarian in nature.[8] Even where private ownership continues to exist, the state retains a preponderance of ownership of the means of economic production and distribution. "The indivisibility of power and the concomitant totalitarianism are incompatible with the autonomy that private ownership entails," says Kornai.[9]

During the initial period, socialist systems can deliver relatively rapid growth, characterized by their ability to maximize output and centrally allocate investment. As we saw in the Soviet Union—and also in North Korea up through the 1970s—such "forced" growth can even outpace market economies for a period of time. Socialist systems also deliver rising living standards and growth in consumption, but historically the consumption growth rate lags behind gross domestic product (GDP) growth as resources are funneled into capital investment to build heavy industry, often driven by the need to build up military and defense capability.

These periods of extensive growth eventually hit a wall. Without a market to allocate resources, state enterprises produce without regard to actual consumer demand. It is a system characterized by chronic shortage, low

---

7 Kornai, *Socialist System*, 19.
8 Ibid., 46.
9 Ibid., 362.

efficiency, waste, and growing technical backwardness.[10] After a while, the growth rate slows and without innovation that can provide gains in productivity, or intensive growth, the reliance on forced growth reaches clear limits. This poses several challenges, including the growth of public dissatisfaction.

The Soviet Union began to experience such a slowdown already by the 1960s. The increasing demands for resources from other socialist states added to the burden on the Soviet economy. Despite the control on the flow of information from the outside, the Soviet elite and even some of the public knew that as their economic difficulties grew, the capitalist system was thriving. This fed a sense of unease and a loss of confidence in the system.

In the mid-1960s the Soviet Union launched limited reforms—the so-called Kosygin reforms—to try to stimulate growth by allowing small experiments in the use of market mechanisms and decentralization of the bureaucracy along the lines of experiments in Yugoslavia. In Eastern Europe, this opening led to even bolder experiments in political and economic reform, most famously the Czech attempt to create "socialism with a human face." The Soviet leadership feared, probably correctly, that this would undermine the system itself. The military intervention into Czechoslovakia in 1968 effectively ended these reforms, including in Moscow.

Despite those fears, the Soviet Union probably would have been forced to carry out fundamental reforms to revive its lagging economy had it not been for the huge discoveries of oil and gas in western Siberia in the 1970s. The oil shock of 1973 was a windfall for the Soviet Union as prices in the world market skyrocketed and Western economies looked for alternative sources to the Middle East. "The Soviet leaders directed this wealth primarily to military expenditures," says economist Anders Åslund, one of the foremost experts on the Soviet economy. "Because of this apparent abundance of money, they did nothing to improve the economic system in the 1970s."[11]

The decline of oil and gas revenues in the early 1980s upset this equilibrium. The Soviet Union increasingly felt threatened by its inability to keep pace with technological innovation in the West, especially in the realm of electronics, which was revolutionizing warfare and weapons systems. "The grave problems in the economy, particularly the sluggishness of technical development and the inefficiency and blockages in production, become a threat to the military might of the socialist countries," Kornai observed.[12]

10 Ibid., on shortages, 252; on low efficiency and backwardness, 301.

11 Anders Åslund, *Russia's Capitalist Revolution: Why Market Reform Succeeded and Democracy Failed* (Washington, DC: Peterson Institute for International Economics, 2007), 17.

12 Kornai, *Socialist System*, 384.

The government of Mikhail Gorbachev, formed in 1986, launched a series of limited reforms—under the banner of *perestroika* or restructuring—aimed at loosening the controls of the command economy. Small-scale private enterprise, from private plot agriculture and handicrafts that could be sold at relatively free markets to "cooperative" ventures spun out of state enterprises, was legalized. Reform of the huge enterprises that controlled the economy was frustrated, however, by the resistance of the state bureaucracy. This prompted Gorbachev to push for limited democratization, under the slogan of *glasnost,* or openness, to combat his foes. But the partial and often halting—one step forward, two steps back—nature of the reforms only served to expose further the dysfunctionality of the system.

By the late 1980s, the Soviet system had entered a terminal crisis. In 1990 there were such severe shortages that emergency food aid was being shipped in from the West. Long lines formed for the most basic of commodities, from sugar and bread to vodka. Stores were almost empty of goods. Strikes began to break out. Private traders, including "shuttle traders" who went across the border to places like Poland and Turkey to acquire goods to sell back in Russia, filled the void of the failed state system. Even trading in currency became a lucrative venture for new banks formed as cooperative ventures. State enterprise managers used their new freedoms to sell their goods, mainly minerals and oil and gas, for huge profits in the world market, often keeping the profits out of state hands. The Soviet public, thanks to the freer flow of information, now understood that their sacrifices had left them impoverished relative to the affluence of the West.

The Soviet state struggled to regain control. On one hand, massive wage increases were offered to buy off an unhappy public, adding to the inflation fueled by private traders. In a desperate and ultimately failed attempt to control inflation, curb the growing use of dollars and other hard currencies, and pull in the reins on the emergent entrepreneurial class that operated the second or black economy, the Soviet Union instituted a surprise currency reform in 1991, forcing Russians to exchange "old" rubles for a new revalued ruble.

The forces trying to preserve the socialist system repeatedly undermined bolder attempts at reform. In August 1991 they attempted to seize power and crush the reformers. Their failure led to the collapse of the Soviet Union and Soviet communist rule by late 1991. In early 1992, under the leadership of Boris Yeltsin, the new Russia went into a totally different and radical direction, lifting controls on most prices and liberalizing foreign trade, bringing a rush of foreign goods into the previously empty stores, though accompanied by huge price increases. The Communist Party monopoly on power was swept away and Russia entered a new era.

The Chinese pursued a different path to the market, one that was more gradual and preserved the Communist Party's hold on power. Vietnam, following unification in 1975 by the communists, followed a similar model. Both were largely agrarian societies, however, in which the early stages of reform were focused on agriculture, freeing peasants from the collectivized farm system that was the backbone of the socialist system in those countries. That created both a pool of labor for low-wage manufacturing for export and a boom in agricultural production. That allowed the party to deliver early economic gains to the populace in the form of rapidly rising living standards.

North Korea's Systemic Crisis

The path of development in North Korea follows much more closely the Soviet experience than most analysts have understood.

Possibly as late as the mid-1970s, North Korea outpaced its capitalist rival in the South in terms of economic growth rates. Thanks to its inheritance from the era of Japanese colonialism—the north was the industrial and mining center of the country compared to the more agrarian south—and to the ability of the command economy to mobilize resources, the North achieved a more rapid recovery from the effects of the Korean War. But from the late 1960s, under the leadership of Park Chung-hee, the South pursued its own policy of rapid industrialization, fueled by foreign investment. By the end of the 1970s, the South had outstripped the North in every category of economic growth.

In the early 1980s, North Korea began to show the signs of slowdown of a classical socialist economy—shortages, inefficiency, decaying infrastructure, energy problems, and technical backwardness. The North Korea regime pointedly rejected the option of following China down the path of market reform. It sought to ease stagnation by soliciting foreign investment and loans but ended up defaulting on those loans in 1987.

The collapse of the Soviet Union in 1991 hit North Korea hard as well, ending subsidized trade with the Soviet Bloc and direct aid from Moscow. China followed suit, as it no longer felt the need to compete with the Russians for influence in Pyongyang and was absorbed with its own domestic needs. The North Koreans were suddenly left without the ability to extract capital by playing off Beijing against Moscow. In the 1990s, the nation's GDP shrank by half, according to the estimates of the Republic of

Korea's (ROK, or South Korea) Bank of Korea.[13] State-owned factories shut down for lack of inputs, leaving facilities that nominally existed but were functionally idle. Chronic food shortages, triggered by inefficient collective farming practices and shortages of fuel, fertilizers, and mechanization, led to widespread famine in 1996–1998, killing at least 600,000 and up to 1 million North Koreans by conservative estimates.[14]

North Korea's development arc cannot be attributed to anything other than its adoption of and participation in the socialist system. As a recent report from the International Institute for Strategic Studies puts it:

> North Korea's economic problems stem primarily from the inefficiencies of its socialist command economy, exacerbated by the fall of the Soviet empire. North Korea is by far the most controlled among the remaining socialist countries, with most means of production under state ownership. The economy is structured to bolster political leadership, with economic principles overruled by political considerations. These structural hurdles severely limit the potential for economic development.[15]

The North Korean leadership made sporadic forays into economic reform, similar but even more limited than those attempted by the Soviet Union in the 1980s. At every key turning point, the regime's fears of political instability—with the example of the Soviet Union and Eastern Europe firmly in their minds—trumped the prospects of economic prosperity. For North Korea the danger of opening up is even greater because of the existence of an alternative model of economy and society right at hand—South Korea. Any suggestion that the North Korean state no longer has the legitimacy granted by the superiority of its socialist system merely feeds the attractiveness of the South (Vietnam, it should be noted, did not go down the path of reform until *after* unification was achieved, and in part because the Communist leadership in the north failed in early attempts to socialize agriculture in the south).

Without the option of serious reform, Pyongyang has instead used its nuclear program and the threat of war to extract significant economic aid from South Korea, China, and even the United States, replacing in some part the aid lost after the collapse of the Soviet Union. This has been the backdrop of the repeated crises and negotiations over the North Korean

13 Mark Fitzpatrick, *North Korean Security Challenges: A Net Assessment* (London: International Institute for Strategic Studies, 2011), 17.

14 Stephan Haggard and Marcus Noland, *Witness to Transformation: Refugee Insights Into North Korea* (Washington, DC: Peterson Institute for International Economics, January 2011), 6.

15 Fitzpatrick, *North Korean Security Challenges*, 18.

nuclear program since 1992. Pyongyang has been remarkably successful in using this blackmail gambit to garner the capital it can no longer generate from within.

Early reforms were more a product of necessity than policy. The partial collapse of the state food rationing distribution system in the mid-1990s forced the state to look the other way when private plot agriculture and private markets stepped into the breach. This was formalized during an interlude of reform, beginning in the late 1990s, spurred in part by a thaw with South Korea and an accompanying flow of aid and investment into the North, including food and fertilizer supplies that allowed the North to make up for its production shortfall.

In July 2002 the government announced a package of reforms that while limited did allow incremental changes in collective agriculture, including access to private plots and more discretion for factory managers. As in the case of similar Soviet reforms, there was an attempt to bring wages up, in line with rising prices. But similarly, the 2002 reforms triggered massive inflation, well in excess of 100 percent a year for three years, as shortages could not be easily erased.[16] Private traders grew as well, along with a growing cross-border traffic into China. The traders brought back not only goods but smuggled DVDs of South Korean TV shows, cell phones, and other glimpses of the reality of how far North Koreans had fallen behind their cousins in the South.

Beginning in 2005, the North Korean state attempted to roll back the reforms and reassert the primacy of the socialist economy, limiting the role of the emergent private sector and trying to curb inflation. They reinstated the food rationing system, banned private trade in grain, and clamped down on private markets. These efforts fell short of their goal—even after the public distribution system was revived, it could only provide half of the caloric needs of the population and private markets proved difficult to stamp out.[17]

Still, the North Korean regime has persisted in anti-market campaigns in an effort to not only reassert the command economy but also to repress the growth of an entrepreneurial class and the flow of outside ideas that accompanied their trading. In 2009 the state revised laws on economic planning, reviving top-down planning. In November the government, following the Soviet example of 1990, announced a sudden currency reform aimed at confiscating the holdings of the private traders, controlling the use of hard currency, and reviving classical socialism. A senior official of the North Korean

16 Haggard and Noland, *Witness to Transformation*, 9.
17 Fitzpatrick, *North Korean Security Challenges*, 17.

central bank made it clear the currency reform was intended to curb the private sector. North Korea, he told an official newspaper, is "not moving toward a free market economy but will strengthen the principle and order of socialist economic management."[18] But the move created chaos, sparking reported incidents of protest and forcing the government to quickly ease some of the restrictions on how much currency could be exchanged (a similar pattern occurred in the Soviet Union following the currency reform of 1990).

New laws were promulgated, aimed at reducing economic activity outside of the state sector. "The hope of the government is that this loss of private economic activity will be offset by the return of labor into state-owned enterprise sector," wrote two prominent analysts. "Authorities are seeking to reduce the scope of decentralized, market-oriented activity and are thus restricting the ability of the economy to respond to market signals and instead force development to occur according to state dictates."[19]

Not coincidentally, these moves on the economy coincided with a reassertion of political controls, tied to the health problems of North Korean leader Kim Jong-il and the need to prepare the way for the succession of his young, and unproven, son, Kim Jong-un. The somewhat dormant communist party—the Korean Workers' Party (KWP)—has been reinvigorated, alongside the military, as the instrument of political rule. That structure has asserted itself as a form of collective leadership following the death of Kim Jong-il in mid-December 2011. As Kornai laid out in some detail, the socialist system is both a structure of political control and economic organization.

The North Korean regime has also tried to cope with its systemic failure by finding new sources of aid. It received a blow when the conservative Lee Myung-bak government came to power in South Korea at the end of 2008. The Lee government ended the massive subsidies to the food sector in the form of grain and fertilizer shipments, with resumption conditioned on progress on nuclear disarmament. And after disputes following the shooting of a South Korean tourist, it ended the Mount Kumgang tourism project that had funneled small but significant amounts of hard currency into the North. The industrial park in Kaesŏng in North Korea, where dozens of South Korean firms had set up assembly plants using cheap Northern labor (with the pay funneled mostly to the state) kept operating and inter-Korean trade slowed but still continued.

---

18 Cho Song-hyon, cited in Stephan Haggard and Marcus Noland, *The Winter of Their Discontent: Pyongyang Attacks the Market* (Policy Brief PB10-1, Peterson Institute for International Economics, Washington, DC, January 2010), 1.

19 Ibid., 9.

The North Koreans sought to compensate with greater flows of trade and investment from China. Trade dependence on China rose from 41.6 percent of North Korea's overall trade in 2007 to 57.1 percent ($3.47 billion) in 2010.[20] The flow of Chinese trade, investment, and aid has reportedly been increased even more rapidly in the immediate aftermath of Kim Jong-il's death, which appeared to have caught many by surprise. The Chinese leadership clearly made a decision to ease the succession and preserve stability in the North, though there are signs of Chinese attempts to put pressure on the new government in Pyongyang.

Prior to Kim Jong-il's death, the North Korean leadership also stepped up tensions with the South in an effort to pressure for resumption of aid and investment, a familiar tactic for Pyongyang. But statements issued since the succession make it clear that the North Koreans were hoping for a change in power in the South, back to the progressives, to lead to a resumption of the vitally needed economic assistance from Seoul.[21]

Despite these attempts, there is already evidence that the North Korean state is unable to stave off the crisis of the socialist system. The state sector is simply unable to fill the role that it used to perform. The government, in a rare admission, apologized in February 2010 for the manner in which the currency reform was carried out and dismissed the official in charge (according to some unconfirmed reports, the official was executed). In May 2010 the government lifted restrictions and bans on private retail trade and those markets are again operating, a de facto acknowledgement that the state can no longer manage food distribution.

The obvious question is why the North Korean state has not yielded to the pressure to adopt the Chinese path. The North Korean leadership has no lack of exposure to this model of reform. Kim Jong-il and his senior leadership made numerous visits to China where the Chinese Communist Party steered them through examples of reform, from special economic zones to high-tech firms. The Chinese preference for North Korea to take this path has been made abundantly clear and every small step that suggests such a

---

20 Scott Snyder, "North Korea's Deepening Economic Dependency on China," *The Atlantic*, September 28, 2011 (Council on Foreign Relations post), http://www.theatlantic.com/international/archive/2011/09/north-koreas-deepening-economic-ties-with-china/245724/.

21 See the "Open Questionnaire of the Policy Department of the National Defence Commission of the DPRK," issued on February 2, 2012, outlining conditions for resumption of dialogue with the South Korean government, making it clear that the North was not eager to resume dialogue with the conservative government of Lee Myung-Bak.

course, such as the creation of some enterprise zones near the border areas, is trumpeted by Beijing.

The political obstacles to this path remain the most daunting. The China model holds out the hope of moving to the market without surrendering party control. But with the South looming next door, the North Korean leadership remains terrified that opening their doors to this kind of marketization, with accompanying foreign investment and involvement, would lead to a complete loss of legitimacy in the enduring struggle between the two Koreas. The state is already engaged in a losing campaign to curb the spread of South Korean cultural influence, via smuggled and widely circulating videos and DVDs. The subversive power of a Korean alternative is a challenge even the Soviet Union didn't face. The difficulty of manufacturing legitimacy of leadership by the young and unproven grandson of North Korea's founder only serves to heighten the risks of opening and reform, at least for the immediate period ahead.

There are also, beyond this, economic and social obstacles to following that model of reform. Unlike China and Vietnam, North Korea does not have a large labor-intensive agricultural sector from which to initiate reform and to draw the benefits of low-wage labor for foreign investors. "In terms of the sectoral composition of output and employment, the North Korean economy more closely resembles Romania and parts of the former Soviet Union than it does the agriculture-led Asian reformers," conclude Haggard and Noland.[22]

North Korean farmers are much more dependent on industrial inputs than in China and Vietnam. Without chemical fertilizer and machinery, productivity in agriculture cannot grow much, even if reforms to free prices and allow private production were implemented fully. The industrial sector is even more resistant to reform—as is the state sector in China and Vietnam to some extent—and especially without the boost of the countryside. More importantly, the state is therefore unable to deliver the quick benefits of reform that enabled the Chinese and Vietnamese communist parties to claim new legitimacy.

The adoption of the Chinese model is still possible, especially now that leadership in Pyongyang has changed, but the room for such an option to succeed is already very small. It is far more likely that North Korea will persist in following a pattern of grudging toleration of the market under the

22 Stephan Haggard and Marcus Noland, *Famine in North Korea: Markets, Aid and Reform* (New York: Columbia University Press, 2007), 211.

pressure of necessity and an abortive pattern of half measures and retreats that characterized the reform period in the Soviet Union prior to its collapse.

Under such circumstances, can the North Korean state still survive? The answer is that the system cannot solve its underlying problem of systemic failure. There is a pattern of breakdown of classical socialism, as Kornai and others have argued, that is almost impossible to escape. But the North Korean state can certainly continue to prolong its slow death as it has in the past—by extracting aid, largely through the blackmail of nuclear and other threats to disrupt security in the region, and through the ruthless use of an apparatus of repression to suppress dissent. Though the 2012 elections returned the conservatives to power in the South, the North Koreans may still hope for a return to a significant flow of aid from Seoul.

The Policy Implications of Transformation in North Korea

The systemic crisis facing North Korea, and the obstacles to transformation that I have discussed above, necessarily define the context for dealing with the security problems posed by North Korea's ongoing nuclear weapons and ballistic missile programs. It also suggests both the goals of Pyongyang in pursing those programs and the limits of dealing with this threat through the existing diplomatic process, most prominently the Six-Party Talks launched in 2003.

The diplomatic process may still conjure up a miracle, especially if it is the accompaniment to a decision by the North Korean leadership to abandon fear and embrace full-scale market reform. But past history suggests that will not take place. For the North Koreans, at least to date, the nuclear and missile programs have much greater efficacy as instruments to extract economic aid and to secure the regime.

Moreover, there is also a compelling strategic and military logic for North Korea to possess nuclear weapons—having a demonstrated nuclear capacity provides regime security, deters a possible U.S. military attack, and compensates both militarily and politically for its weakness in the ongoing contest for leadership and legitimacy in the Korean Peninsula.

This logic was present before the Bush administration came to office but the events that followed, including the invasion of Iraq and now the fall of the Libyan regime, can only have solidified this position within the North Korean leadership. It is important, however, to understand that these are the actions of a weak state. The North Korean leadership is well aware of the failure of their economy and the undermining of their authority and legitimacy that accompanies the flow of consumer goods from China, along with South Korean films and television shows that have cracked open the tight control over the flow of information to their populace. The sudden illness of Kim Jong-il in 2008 and the succession crisis that was triggered by his brush with death seems to have both deepened the sense of weakness of the North Korean leadership and strengthened the hand of those who see nuclear weapons as necessary to ensure regime survival.

How then should the world respond to North Korea? The goal of policy should not be denuclearization per se but rather to assist the transformation of North Korea from a classical to a reformed socialist economy. That goal should be the case whether that transformation leads to a Soviet-style collapse of the North Korean state or to a successful adoption of the Chinese model. In either case, it would yield a North Korea that is open to the outside world, accelerate the process of economic and social change within North Korea, and likely lead to political change, and eventually to some form of reunification of the Korean Peninsula.

A transforming North Korea would no longer need nuclear weapons as an instrument of economic blackmail. Nor would it need them to retain legitimacy in the competition with the South. Hopefully it would see the greater value in giving up those weapons in exchange for a more rapid process of transformation. But even if that were not the case, full transformation that leads to unification will resolve the security issue.

In the short term, the response to the security threat for the United States and its allies should follow the lessons of the Cold War. There is little alternative than to adopt a long-term and consistent strategy of deterrence and containment. That strategy should be clearly articulated to the North Korean leadership, preferably at the highest level, and to our allies and partners in the Six-Party process. This should be done quietly, without bombast and not in an atmosphere of threat.

Deterrence and containment does not rule out engagement, aimed at aiding the process of change within North Korea—the strategy should be accompanied by a clear offer of an alternative path that the North Koreans can pick up at any time. That would be the now familiar exchange of verifiable denuclearization for full diplomatic recognition, a peace treaty to end the Korea War, and economic engagement.

A deterrence policy toward North Korea must deal with three principal threats to American national security—the danger of rising tensions on the Korean Peninsula; the undermining of regional security, including triggering a regional nuclear arms race; and the proliferation of weapons, nuclear materials, or key technological information to other states, particularly Iran, or to non-state actors.

First and foremost, the United States needs to make it clear to its allies in the ROK and Japan that it is prepared to come to their defense in the event of North Korean aggression. Without being provocative, the South Koreans must be reassured that the United States stands by its side in the case that North Korea decides to escalate tensions with the South. If necessary, we should take appropriate steps to bolster our conventional capability in and around the peninsula.

Second, the United States must be concerned about the perception amongst its allies that it is acquiescing to the North Korean desire to be treated as a nuclear weapons state. To do so would only encourage others to follow in its wake. And it would undermine extended deterrence for the ROK and Japan. For both these challenges, the United States needs to convey as unambiguously as possible that the use of a North Korean nuclear weapon, or a weapon derived from North Korean manufactured plutonium or highly enriched uranium, against ourselves or our treaty allies, will invite massive retaliation by the United States.

This deterrence strategy can be communicated as stated policy but it may also be effective to indicate indirectly that certain military assets, such as submarines equipped with nuclear-armed ballistic missiles, will be assigned this retaliatory mission. The United States should continue to jointly develop missile defense systems with Japan—and with the ROK if it desires it—even if they are of limited effectiveness.

The danger posed by proliferation of North Korean nuclear capability is the most difficult threat to manage. A broad United Nations Security Council resolution authorizing efforts to counter the proliferation danger is important to provide the international framework and legal authority for a range of actions, from restricting financial flows to the transfer of nuclear and missile equipment and materials. Slowing, if not halting, North Korea's cooperation with Iran is a priority. Interdiction of the supply of missile systems, either via air transport or sea, from North Korea to clients in the Middle East should be examined as an option. The movement of personnel, who could transfer knowledge to Iran, is harder to control, though North Korea air flights via third countries, such as Indonesia or Myanmar, could be targeted. This kind of counter-proliferation strategy cannot work effectively without the full cooperation of China, the main route for air traffic from North Korea to Iran.

As the Cold War demonstrated, containment is a long-term policy that aims at diminishing the specific national security threats posed by North Korea's nuclear program while encouraging a process of internal reform that will eventually lead to transformation. As Lankov proposes in *Foreign*

Affairs, academic, student, and even economic exchanges with North Korea can effectively subvert the regime through engagement. "Truth is subversive in regimes built on lies and isolation," Lankov writes, "So to crack Pyongyang's control over information and bring about pressure for change from within, truth and information should be introduced into North Korean society."[23]

Containment and deterrence does not rule out the resumption of diplomatic negotiations, either in the Six-Party or a bilateral framework, not only by the United States but also by South Korea and other parties. We have nothing to fear from negotiation provided the goals are clearly defined. But we also do not need to be in a hurry. Time is on our side, not on the side of a weak and crisis-ridden North Korean regime. We must demonstrate patience, consistency, and confidence that, as with the Cold War in Europe, the realities of systemic failure will eventually assert themselves.

23 Lankov, "Changing North Korea."

Index

Bank of Korea (BOK), 101n5, 107, 108,
  236, 293
banks
  and currency reform, 102, 127–28
  European, 221–22
  in GDR *vs.* DPRK, 234, 236
  PRC, 115, 183
  and reform, 101, 103, 220
  and Second Economic Committee, 109
  Swiss, 35, 216–17
  in USSR, 291
BBC (British Broadcasting Corporation),
  262
Belgium, 218
Bend It Like Beckham (film), 214
Birindelli and Associates, 222
Bowring, Philip, 3n3
Brazil, 102
Brinton, Crane, 270
British Council, 220
Bulgaria, 208, 210, 211
Bundesbank (West German central bank),
  236
Bureau 39, 84, 109, 111
bureaucracy
  in DPRK, 3, 10, 21, 271
  in GDR, 233
  in socialist systems, 289, 290
  in USSR, 269–70, 277, 278, 291
  See also Korean Workers' Party
Bush, George H.W., 172
Bush (George W.) administration, 17,
  47–48, 145, 155, 287
  and U.S.-DPRK relations, 176, 177, 189,
  298
Buzo, Adrian, 5n4

Cai Jian, 3n3
Cambodia, 278
Campus für Christus, 218
Cap Anamur, 218
capital, 99
  in GDR *vs.* DPRK, 235

and reunification, 241–43, 246, 252
capitalism
  in DPRK *vs.* USSR, 265
  and German *vs.* Korean reunification,
    233–35
  grassroots, 257
  vs. socialist systems, 290
Carlin, Robert, 110–11, 172
Carter, Jimmy, 42
Ceausescu, Nicolae, 123, 159, 278
cell phones, 131, 190, 252, 280, 294
Central Bank (DPRK), 102, 128
Central Committee of the Democratic
  Front for the Reunification of Korea,
  184
Cha, Victor, 3n3, 159
chaemyun (saving face), 12, 93
Cheonan (South Korean ship), sinking of,
  52, 102, 145, 146, 154
Children's Aid Direct, 218
China, People's Republic of (PRC)
  agriculture in, 39, 292, 297
  dissent in, 281–82
  vs. DPRK, 4, 5, 24, 149
  DPRK migrants to, 121, 130, 150, 158,
    264
  economic growth of, 25, 115, 197, 258,
    273–74
  economic reforms in, 5, 13, 16, 20, 21,
    23–24, 49, 100, 124, 137–38, 158,
    159, 170, 190–92, 195–97, 237, 258,
    273–84, 286, 287, 288, 292, 296, 297,
    299
  fears of expansionism of, 200–201
  firms from, 187, 199, 202
  Kim Jong-un on, 39
  and Korean War, 143
  military power in, 65–66
  as model, 5, 13, 20, 21, 23–24, 190–92,
    195–97, 237, 258, 273–84, 286, 287,
    292, 296, 297, 299
  objectives of, 197–99
  and proliferation, 300

and United States, 203
Iran, 174, 179, 300
Iraq War, 143, 298
Ireland, 218
Ireson, Randall, 18n8
Israel, 179
Italy, 212, 213, 215, 218, 220, 222

Jang Jong-nam, 57
Jang Kum-song, 49
Jang Song-kil, 49
Jang Song-wu, 48
Jang Sung-taek, 13, 47–49, 50, 55, 74
    and Kim Jong-un, 10, 36, 37, 51, 53, 54,
        56, 157, 158
    and succession, 8, 52–53
Japan
    abduction of citizens of, 164, 182, 190
    domestic politics in, 203
    vs. DPRK, 281
    economic slowdown in, 182
    Kim family members in, 46
    Kim Jong-un in, 39
    Korean residents in, 163–64, 180, 181–
        82, 183, 184
    media in, 50, 55, 87
    vs. PRC, 281
    and ROK, 155, 156, 160
    and U.S., 164, 179, 201, 300
    See also anti-Japanese guerrilla
        movement; colonialism, Japanese
Japan-DPRK relations, 2, 8, 16–18
    and aid, 135, 182
    and Chinese investment, 189–90, 194,
        200–201, 203
    and currency, 163, 180–83
    and DPRK worldview, 163–64
    economic, 100, 103, 164, 180–83, 185,
        203
    and Korean nationalism, 163, 166, 180,
        184–85
    and military exercises, 184
    and nuclear program, 182, 183

and potential DPRK collapse, 56
and PRC, 16–17
and reform, 25, 124
and sanctions, 105, 183
and trade, 102, 180, 181–82, 183
Jiwon (aiming high) idea, 64
Jo Myong-rok, 35, 66
Jordan, Michael, 38
Jowitt, Kenneth, 278
Juche (self-reliance) ideology, 4, 105, 120,
    172, 268, 286
    and Kim Jong-un, 50
    and public opinion, 83
    and ROK, 155
    and succession, 61, 62, 74, 75
Junichiro Koizumi, 182

Kaesŏng Industrial Zone, 115, 144, 145,
    221, 252, 263, 295–96
Kang Sok Ju, 178n29
Kanter, Arnold, 172
KGB, 267, 269
Khrushchev, Nikita, 41
Kim Byung-Yeon, 13n7
Kim Chun-guk, 211
Kim Dae-jung, 142, 144, 145, 155, 167,
    288
Kim Hakjoon, 9–10
Kim Hye-kyong, 31
Kim Hyung-jik, 64
Kim Il-sung
    and agriculture, 118
    in anti-Japanese independence
        movement, 41, 148, 149, 169
    birthplace of, 62, 64
    death of, 68, 69, 77, 149, 165, 286
    and Eastern Europe, 123, 209
    and economy, 14–15
    family life of, 30–31
    and famine, 91
    on human rights, 90
    in joint regime, 44, 45, 67
    and Kim Jong-il's family, 32, 37

in USSR, 290

Médecins du Monde, 218

Médecins sans Frontières (MSF), 218

media, DPRK, 151, 158, 222, 256, 262, 264

New Year's editorials in, 52, 72–73, 74, 75

media, foreign, 36, 214

access to, 86–87

ban on, 89, 263

Chinese, 188, 254

on DPRK, 1–2, 20, 147, 165, 175

Japanese, 34, 50, 55, 172n20

radio broadcasts, 262, 263

ROK, 89, 141, 254, 263, 264, 294, 299

Soviet, 256, 257, 259, 260, 262

Mexico, 102

Micaelo, Joao, 38

middle class, new, 128, 132

Middle East

Arab Spring in, 159, 160, 264

and oil, 290

and proliferation, 300

See also particular countries

migration, 82–86, 94

and Chinese investment, 198

to Europe, 19, 222

and famine, 91–92, 106, 121, 130, 150, 158

and markets, 85–86

to PRC, 121, 130, 135, 150, 158, 159–60, 264

and reunification, 238–39

to ROK, 82, 150, 154, 155, 222, 239, 263

See also defectors; refugees

military, DPRK

and currency reform, 132

and economy, 69, 70, 75, 101, 103–5

and external threats, 133

and famine, 122, 129

and food, 15, 16, 124

funding for, 137

and Kim Jong-il, 40

and Kim Jong-un, 39, 149

vs. KWP, 43, 51, 54, 67–74, 75

and nuclear weapons, 298

and private property, 251

and reform, 57, 133, 134

revolts in, 122, 130

separate economy of, 14, 109–11, 115

and succession, 44, 65–67, 295

military, in socialist systems, 289, 290–91

military-first (*songun*) policy, 4, 6, 7, 78

and Kim Jong-il, 67–71, 75

and Kim Jong-un, 9, 10, 51, 63, 64

and regime legitimacy, 149–53

and succession, 61–62

miners, 15, 120, 125–26, 132, 137

missile program, 3, 58, 298

and international relations, 145, 173, 177, 179, 183, 213, 224

and military-first, 70

vs. victimization narrative, 6, 169

Mongolia, 133, 134

Mount Kumgang tourism project, 295

music, 46–47, 64–65, 260

Myanmar (Burma), 25, 300

Myers, Brian R., 5n4, 8n6, 83, 166, 286n3

National Defense Commission (NDC), 35, 54–55, 70, 74

and Kim Jong-il, 29, 40, 51, 66, 68

and Kim Jong-un, 52, 63

nationalism

in GDR, 232

in USSR, 256, 257

nationalism, Korean

and character of regime, 4n4, 5

and Chinese investment, 193, 200

ethnic, 154, 156, 166, 168, 286

and Japan, 163, 166, 180, 184–85

and regime survival, 151–52, 287

and reunification, 169

and ROK, 154–56

and U.S.-DPRK relations, 172

Natsios, Andrew S., 13, 14, 15, 16, 17, 22

Index

Yeonpyeong Island, bombardment of, 52,
    141, 144, 146, 152, 154, 161, 224
Yi Han-young (Ri Il-nam), 31n1, 32, 33,
    34
Yongbyon nuclear complex, 145
Yoon Deok Ryong, 110
Youth Union, 80n11
Yugoslavia, 208, 210, 290
Yurchak, Alexei, 265

RECENT PUBLICATIONS OF THE
WALTER H. SHORENSTEIN ASIA-PACIFIC RESEARCH CENTER

BOOKS (distributed by the Brookings Institution Press)

Joon-Woo Park, Donald Keyser, and Gi-Wook Shin, eds. *Asia's Middle Powers? The Identity and Regional Policy of South Korea and Vietnam.* 2013.

Kenji E. Kushida and Phillip Y. Lipscy, eds. *Japan under the DPJ: The Politics of Transition and Governance.* 2013.

Jang-Jip Choi. *Democracy after Democratization: The Korean Experience.* 2012.

Byung-Kook Kim, Eun Mee Kim, and Jean C. Oi, eds. *Adapt, Fragment, Transform: Corporate Restructuring and System Reform in South Korea.* 2012.

John Everard. *Only Beautiful, Please: A British Diplomat in North Korea.* 2012.

Dong-won Lim. *Peacemaker: Twenty Years of Inter-Korean Relations and the North Korean Nuclear Issue.* 2012.

Byung Kwan Kim, Gi-Wook Shin, and David Straub, eds. *Beyond North Korea: Future Challenges to South Korea's Security.* 2011.

Jean C. Oi, ed. *Going Private in China: The Politics of Corporate Restructuring and System Reform.* 2011.

Karen Eggleston and Shripad Tuljapurkar, eds. *Aging Asia: The Economic and Social Implications of Rapid Demographic Change in China, Japan and South Korea.* 2010.

Rafiq Dossani, Daniel C. Sneider, and Vikram Sood, eds. *Does South Asia Exist? Prospects for Regional Integration.* 2010.

Jean C. Oi, Scott Rozelle, and Xueguang Zhou. *Growing Pains: Tensions and Opportunity in China's Transition.* 2010.

Karen Eggleston, ed. *Prescribing Cultures and Pharmaceutical Policy in the Asia-Pacific.* 2009.

Donald A. L. Macintyre, Daniel C. Sneider, and Gi-Wook Shin, eds. *First Drafts of Korea: The U.S. Media and Perceptions of the Last Cold War Frontier.* 2009.

Steven Reed, Kenneth Mori McElwain, and Kay Shimizu, eds. *Political Change in Japan: Electoral Behavior, Party Realignment, and the Koizumi Reforms.* 2009.

Donald K. Emmerson. *Hard Choices: Security, Democracy, and Regionalism in Southeast Asia.* 2008.

Henry S. Rowen, Marguerite Gong Hancock, and William F. Miller, eds. *Greater China's Quest for Innovation.* 2008.

Gi-Wook Shin and Daniel C. Sneider, eds. *Cross Currents: Regionalism and Nationalism in Northeast Asia.* 2007.

Philip W. Yun and Gi-Wook Shin, eds. *North Korea: 2005 and Beyond.* 2006.

STUDIES OF THE WALTER H. SHORENSTEIN ASIA-PACIFIC RESEARCH CENTER (published with Stanford University Press)

Gene Park. *Spending Without Taxation: FILP and the Politics of Public Finance in Japan.* Stanford, CA: Stanford University Press, 2011.

Erik Martinez Kuhonta. *The Institutional Imperative: The Politics of Equitable Development in Southeast Asia.* Stanford, CA: Stanford University Press, 2011.

Yongshun Cai. *Collective Resistance in China: Why Popular Protests Succeed or Fail.* Stanford, CA: Stanford University Press, 2010.

Gi-Wook Shin. *One Alliance, Two Lenses: U.S.-Korea Relations in a New Era.* Stanford, CA: Stanford University Press, 2010.

Jean Oi and Nara Dillon, eds. *At the Crossroads of Empires: Middlemen, Social Networks, and State-building in Republican Shanghai.* Stanford, CA: Stanford University Press, 2007.

Henry S. Rowen, Marguerite Gong Hancock, and William F. Miller, eds. *Making IT: The Rise of Asia in High Tech.* Stanford, CA: Stanford University Press, 2006.

Gi-Wook Shin. *Ethnic Nationalism in Korea: Genealogy, Politics, and Legacy.* Stanford, CA: Stanford University Press, 2006.

Andrew Walder, Joseph Esherick, and Paul Pickowicz, eds. *The Chinese Cultural Revolution as History.* Stanford, CA: Stanford University Press, 2006.

Rafiq Dossani and Henry S. Rowen, eds. *Prospects for Peace in South Asia.* Stanford, CA: Stanford University Press, 2005.

The authorized representative in the EU for product safety and compliance is:
Mare Nostrum Group
B.V Doelen 72
4831 GR Breda
The Netherlands

www.ingramcontent.com/pod-product-compliance
Lightning Source LLC
Chambersburg PA
CBHW020334270326
41926CB00007B/179